# VOGUE
BEAUTY
## AND
HEALTH
## ENCYCLOPEDIA

Library of Congress Cataloging-in-Publication Data
Probert, Christina.
    Vogue beauty and health encyclopedia.
    1. Beauty, Personal.    2. Women – Health and hygiene.
I. Title.
RA778.P9147    1987        613'.04244        87-549
ISBN 0-385-24224-7
First published in 1986 by Octopus Books Limited.
59 Grosvenor Street, London W1
Illustrations: © 1986 Octopus Books/Condé Nast
Text: © 1986 The Condé Nast Publications Limited
This 1987 edition published in the United States
of America by Doubleday & Company, Inc.,
245 Park Avenue, New York, New York.
ALL RIGHTS RESERVED
ISBN 0-385-24224-7
Printed in Hong Kong

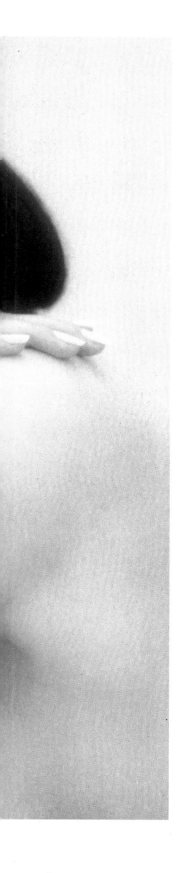

# VOGUE

## BEAUTY
## AND
## HEALTH
## ENCYCLOPEDIA

## CHRISTINA PROBERT

EDITORIAL CONSULTANT **FELICITY CLARK**

DOUBLEDAY & COMPANY, INC.
GARDEN CITY, NEW YORK

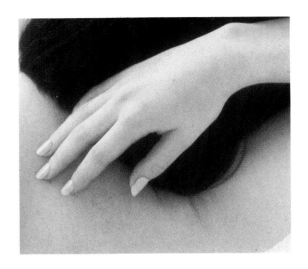

# AUTHOR'S ACKNOWLEDGEMENTS

An encyclopedia is almost by its very nature a team effort. This volume is no exception. It has been produced with the co-operation of a veritable battalion of highly qualified and talented people who have generously given the project their time and energy. I am indebted to all the consultants who answered queries and later commented on the resulting text, but especially to Dr Caroline Bradbeer, Dr Charles Darley and Tony Lycholat for their patience with and constructive comments on the great tracts of text which plopped regularly through their letterboxes over several months. Any errors which may remain in the text are entirely my own.

It has been a great pleasure to work with them, and with the Octopus team, too. Special thanks to Marilyn Inglis for all her work and the great spirit of camaraderie in which all our editorial negotiations were undertaken, to Lisa Tai for designing the book and completing the layouts in such a short space of time, to Penny Summers, Peter Butler and Isabel Moore. I am grateful for all the backing given to me at Condé Nast, especially that of Alex Kroll who has, as ever, been a great support, and to Deborah Hutton for her innovative book, *Vogue Complete Beauty*, which opened new vistas in the health and beauty field, and of course to Felicity Clark, the consultant editor.

Several very talented individuals made contributions to my text. Of them I would especially like to thank Georgina Butter who provided not only text but masses of moral support through every stage of the book's development, also Julia Sherbrooke and Maddy Youlten.

But above all I want to thank my assistant Lucy Anderson who was a tower of strength. She researched, co-ordinated, typed, sent packages hither and thither, sympathised with every problem, put up with me in the various moods one is subject to when writing a rather large book. Last, but by no means least, I dedicate this book to my father with much love.

A

# ABDOMEN

*See also: cosmetic surgery; diet; diets; exercise; exercises; faradic exercise; fitness; massage; weight-training*

The abdomen consists of the lower part of the trunk, from the diaphragm, just below the bustline, down to the groin. The term is usually used to include the pelvic cavity also. The abdomen is packed with muscles which, running horizontally, vertically and diagonally, help to give it its shape. This wall of muscle acts like a corset to hold the abdominal contents in place. Any exercise programme must give a wide range of movement in all directions, as well as dealing specifically with the hip, waist or midriff zones.

Exercise is not the only way to keep the abdomen in shape: weight is also an important factor. Measure your hips, at their widest, and your waist: if the difference between them is less than 23 cm (9 inches) you are probably overweight, and a combination of diet and exercise will be most effective. See **diet** for weight control plan suggestions.

Beauty therapists use spot reduction massage, either manually or with suction pads such as the G5 system for quick results. Faradic exercise also tones up muscles, but long-term improvement is only to be found through changes in eating and exercising habits. Spot reduction exercises, like those below, are easy and very effective.

■ See EXERCISES for Caution Box page 123 before starting exercise

■ See ABDOMEN for Core Exercise box page 6 before starting exercise

## CORE EXERCISES

Throughout the book are some exercises boxed in yellow and flagged in the margins. These are **core exercises**, providing comprehensive exercise for the part of the body in question, and are thus ideal to use as part of your warming-up routine for any sport or activity where this part of the body will be in focus.

Remember that it is important, however, to vary your exercise frequently so that joints and muscles get maximum range, type and strength of movement, and so that you do not get bored with the same old routine, too.

▶ **Exercise A**
**1** Lie flat, arms by your sides. Bend your knees, and ensure that feet are flat on the floor parallel to your legs and hip-width apart. Breathe in, then breathe out lifting head and shoulders off the floor and hold. Breathe in and return head and shoulders to the floor. Repeat 3 times.
**2** Now roll your head from side to side to loosen muscles and take a deep breath – then breathe out. Repeat the whole sequence 2 or 3 times ensuring that you build up the amount you lift your shoulders, and the time you hold this position.

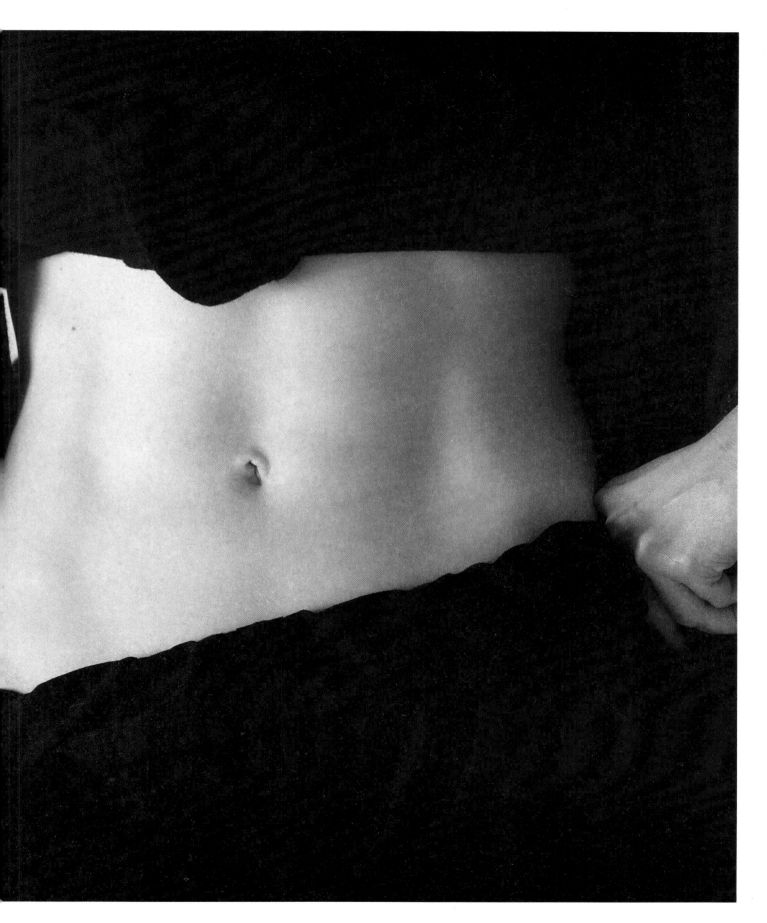

**◄ Exercise B**
1 Sit on the floor with knees bent, feet pointing straight forwards, flat on the floor. Raise arms to straight horizontal position.
2 Breathe in, then as you breathe out, lean slowly and steadily backwards pressing your lower back to the ground, then gradually lower upper back, shoulders and head in a curling down motion. Breathe in and come up again, steadily. Repeat 6 times, building up gradually to 18 times.

**◄ Exercise C**
1 Lie on your back with your knees bent, feet facing straight forwards, flat on the floor. Place one arm out to your side, and the other arm across your body diagonally so that one shoulder is just lifted off the floor.
2 Now breathe in, and as you breathe out, curl up gradually, turning your shoulders in the direction of your outstretched arms. Hold the topmost position momentarily, then slowly lower your body to the floor. Repeat on the other side, then repeat 5 times for each side. Build up gradually to 18 times for each side.

**► Exercise D**
1 Lie on your back with arms by your sides and knees pulled up to your chest.
2 Breathe in, then as you breathe out raise your hips and bottom up off the floor, bringing your knees up further towards your head without jerking. Hold for several seconds, then return steadily to original position. Repeat 6 times, establishing a smooth rhythm. Build up to 18 times.

# ACHES AND PAINS

*See also: acupressure and shiatzu; acupuncture; Alexander Technique; aromatherapy; autogenics; chiropractic; herbalism; osteopathy; saunas*

Pain is exhausting and debilitating, a sign of a physical or psychological problem, which should never be disregarded. Sensation can range from minor discomfort to searing pain that can be quite intolerable. The way in which people react to pain and the amount of pain different people can bear (known as your pain threshold) varies enormously: extroverts seem to be able to endure more pain than introverts. Even personal pain thresholds vary: if you are under stress or feeling depressed, for example, your pain threshold is lower.

Minor aches, such as those experienced after prolonged exercise, may well be alleviated by soaking yourself in a warm seaweed or herb bath, or by applying a poultice of seaweed powder mixed with hot water to the painful area: warmth is very beneficial in relieving aches. There are many commercial bath preparations, too, which help the muscles relax. Pain as a result of stress may also benefit from this treatment. Aspirin can alleviate some pain as it has an anti-inflammatory effect, but it should not be used for more than a few days without medical advice. Aches and pains which do not respond to relaxation, massage, warm baths and self analysis may need professional help. Consult your doctor, however, if you suffer severe pain as a result of exercise, sudden pain or persistent headaches. He or she will treat your pain variously according to its cause, and may possibly prescribe analgesics or anti-inflammatory drugs.

Traditionally various methods have been used to deal with pain. Today there is increasing interest in the following:

■ **Regional therapy** A treatment involving injecting a wide variety of traditional pain-killing substances directly into painful areas, the substance used depending on the type and location of pain. Regional therapy works quickly and, because it bypasses the digestive system, it avoids some of the side-effects of drugs and assimilation difficulties.

■ **Acupuncture** Either the traditional needle method or the modern application of tiny electrical currents to the customary needle zones can help. Acupuncture is believed to relieve pain by stimulating the body's own central nervous system to produce its natural pain-killers called endorphins and enkephalins (see separate entry) which lie in the spinal cord.

■ **Autogenics, autosuggestion, autohypnosis and meditation** By altering the subject's state of consciousness, all these techniques can be effective in reducing or removing pain.

■ **Aromatherapy** There are approximately 60 essential oils with local pain-killing properties, the most common being rosemary and sage. Choice depends very much on the person being treated, what suits both their skin and their problem (see **aromatherapy**). Ask your aromatherapist for advice.

- **Dietary alterations** Discomfort resulting from food allergy can very often be remedied by detailed investigation, then controlled diet. Dietary alteration to alleviate pain from other causes, unless directly medically indicated (such as in the case of diabetes) is considered controversial by doctors. Special diets for conditions such as arthritis abound, and some individuals have found them helpful.
- **Shiatzu/acupressure** These can be used to relieve pain, but trained practitioners should be consulted as there are some situations where they are best avoided, particularly if conventional pain relieving methods are being used. The treatment involves use of manual pressure along energy channels.
- **Osteopathy, chiropractic and the Alexander Technique** Manipulative therapies can remove or alleviate pain, either by acting on the specific source of a pain, or by correcting bad posture and low body performance. These are often used in conjunction with therapies that concentrate on the psyche.
- **Herbalism** The holistic approach is applied to problems like pain. This means that the whole being and situation are taken into consideration when prescribing herbal remedies.

# ACNE

*See also: anxiety; blackheads; cleansing; contraception; hormones; puberty; sebum; skin; tanning; whiteheads*

Acne is the name given to the condition which involves an inflammation of the sebaceous glands which are attached to the hair follicles. Sebum from the glands drains into the top part of the follicle, then on to the skin's surface. Important aspects in the development of acne are an increase in the production of sebum, blockage of the escape of sebum from the gland, and subsequent inflammation of the gland. Blockage produces blackheads (comedones) or whiteheads (closed comedones) depending at which level it occurs. A red spot (papule) or pustule develops if inflammation is present. The most vulnerable areas are the face, upper back and chest where the sebaceous glands are concentrated.

## CAUSES

Increased sebum production is to a great extent caused by androgens – male hormones present in lower levels in women than in men. At puberty there is a surge in androgens in both sexes, and this is why acne often occurs at this time of life. A slight imbalance of androgens can cause acne at other times, too.

In women, oestrogens, which suppress the production of sebum, are usually produced in balance with progesterones, which are more akin to androgens. The worsening of acne before the menstrual period is probably due to high progesterone levels. Women sufferers taking a contraceptive pill, which alters these balances, may find that it affects their acne. The oestrogen content in combined pills may alleviate acne. Some synthetic progesterones, however, in either combined or progestogen-only pills may act like male hormones and thus make the acne worse.

Anxiety can aggravate acne. It seems that stress may increase the production of some hormones which affect the sebaceous glands. Acne is not contagious, it does not imply a lack of cleanliness, nor is it spread from one area to another by the fingers.

## COPING WITH ACNE

1 Keep the affected area clean, but do not wash the skin more than twice a day (preferably just once at the end of the day if you are not wearing make-up): excessive washing may actually precipitate acne.

2 There is no reason not to wear make-up provided that you remove all traces of it at the end of each day. Choose a light cleanser, preferably a lotion, unperfumed if your skin is sensitive. Follow up with a mild toner (too much alcohol in a toner may cause irritation and drying), preferably lightly medicated (antiseptic).

3 Ointments, creams, lotions and gels may be of some help in mild cases of acne, but can cause irritation because their action is normally abrasive or peeling to prevent blockage of the sebaceous glands. Use sparingly, only on affected areas. The types which have been found to be most effective contain benzoyl peroxide, salicylic acid or retinoic acid (vitamin A). If your acne is severe, go to your doctor or a dermatologist; do not rely on commercially available acne 'cures'.

4 There is no very good evidence that diet affects acne. Some individuals, however, are adversely affected by some foods such as chocolate: experiment for yourself.

5 Natural ultraviolet light usually benefits acne sufferers: acne is usually better in summer. Sunray lamps may be helpful, but should be used carefully, with exposure time being built up gradually. The dangers of over-exposure to ultraviolet light should not be forgotten. The required effect is mild peeling, not burning: too much sunlight can be bad for the skin (see **tanning**).

6 Antibiotics suppress acne successfully without curing it completely. Tetracyclines are most widely used, often over several months, ranging from 8 weeks to 6 months or more, in small doses. (See **drugs and medicines** for possible side effects.) Their effectiveness suggests that bacteria may play a significant part in the development of acne. It is important to take these drugs on an empty stomach, half an hour be-

**Acidity**
*See pH*

fore meals, with water, for maximum absorption. Do not take during pregnancy.

7    Synthetic hormones, usually in the form of the contraceptive pill, can be used. The female hormone oestrogen in the combined pill can reduce sebum production. Anti-androgens are a new hormonal treatment which can be helpful in resistant acne. The anti-androgen, cyproterone acetate, is combined with oestrogen in a pill which is both an anti-acne and a contraceptive pill.

8    13-cis-retinoic acid (Roaccutane in the UK, Accutane in the USA), which is closely related to vitamin A, is a remarkable new treatment for acne. Because it is still under trial and is extremely expensive, it is reserved for the most severe cases. But a four-month course results in a cure in the majority of patients.

9    Dermabrasion and chemical peeling (see entries) can be used to help remove scarring as a result of severe acne which is no longer active. Dermabrasion is used in selected cases, chemical peeling particularly for pitted and 'ice-pick' scars. Rarely, severe scars can be excised, and collagen injections can be used to plump up depressions left after acne has gone.

# ACUPRESSURE AND SHIATZU

*See also: aches and pains; acupuncture; massage; reflexology*

The therapy of acupressure, sometimes known as G-Jo in its Western version, originated in China as a form of First Aid. Acupressure and shiatzu are very similar techniques. While acupressure is chiefly used for pain relief, the thinking behind shiatzu tends to lay more emphasis on therapy to prevent disease.

In acupressure, finger pressure is applied to particular areas of the body for a few seconds at a time. The areas worked on are similar to the pressure points used in acupuncture, each relating to different parts and functions of the body which lie along the energy channels and are chosen according to the specific pain being treated. By stimulating chi (*ki* in Japanese) energy in the body, pain such as that of toothache, back pain, neck tension, is alleviated. In shiatzu the emphasis is more on freeing the energy channels generally for overall health.

It is possible to teach yourself this therapy from books. It is advisable, however, to have at least one consultation with a trained practitioner who will examine your case history in detail and advise you, before launching out on your own. There are some contraindications to acupressure or shiatzu: it is not recommended for people with chronic illness except under expert supervision, nor should it be used in conjunction with any drugs or alcohol.

# ACUPUNCTURE

*See also: aches and pains; cosmetic acupuncture; dependencies; moxibustion; smoking*

The word is a combination of the Latin *acus* (needle) and *punctus* (a prick). Acupuncturists believe that the body cannot function satisfactorily unless what is called chi or *ki* energy flows freely: the ancient oriental therapy of acupuncture involves stimulating specified points on the body and clearing them of obstructions to increase the flow of energy and to alleviate a wide range of body ailments. These acupuncture points are joined up to form meridian lines through the body which transport energy from point to point. Fine gold, silver or copper needles are inserted into acupuncture points lying along one or more of these meridian lines. Sometimes low-frequency electric currents or heat (see **moxibustion**) are run through the needles, or electrical stimulation is used without needles. Usually needles are used alone.

### THE PROCEDURE

1    You will be asked to come for your first session not wearing any perfume. You may also be asked not to use any medication for several hours before the session and not to have a hot bath or drink strong coffee or alcohol: these might possibly interfere with both diagnosis and treatment.

2    A detailed case history will be taken.

3    The acupuncturist will conduct his own examination, beginning by feeling the pulse in the wrist, then each of the 12 pulses in the body. He will note all aspects of the body's state of health from breathing rate to sweat production in order to plan the most helpful treatment for the individual.

4    The needles will then be inserted. This is not painful, in fact sometimes no sensation is felt at all, as the needles are inserted just into the skin's surface. They will either be rotated, pumped or just left in place. The treatment will not take longer than an hour.

5    Normally more than a single treatment is required, perhaps up to 6 at about a week's interval each time, but the amount of treatment needed varies considerably according to the patient's situation.

### BENEFITS OF ACUPUNCTURE

Everyone responds differently to acupuncture treatment. Your response to treatment has nothing to do with your attitude to it; don't think that personal convictions about results will affect them – they won't.

■    Acupuncture can be used as an alternative to conventional anaesthetic for a wide variety of surgical operations: it is little used for this purpose in the West.

■    Acupuncture can be particularly helpful in cases such as that of low back pain where the

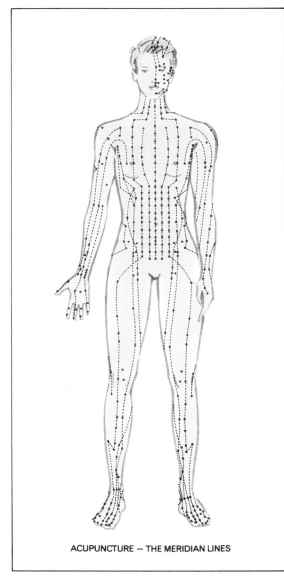

**ACUPUNCTURE — THE MERIDIAN LINES**

# ADDITIVES IN DIET

*See also: allergies and allergens; diet*

Additives are used in foods in order to increase their shelf life and improve their flavour and colour. Not all additives are artificial. The most common, for example, are water, salt and sugar, but recent research has shown that some artificial substances added to foods can be harmful to health and cause allergies. Additives have recently been accused of causing hyperactivity in young children as well as a wide variety of ailments ranging from gastric irritation to headaches and vomiting, but research to substantiate these accusations is still under way.

In both Europe and the United States, where additives are listed on food packaging they are listed in descending order by weight, so you can see at a glance which and relatively how much of each given additive is used. European Economic Community (EEC) regulations to ease movement of foods within the community introduced standardized 'E' numbers for the whole range of additives. By 1986 all additives, except flavourings, on European foods will be indicated on the packaging.

There are 9 main 'E' categories. Each is given a range of numbers.

- Permitted colours (E100-E180)
- Preservatives (E200-E290)
- Permitted anti-oxidants (E300-E321)
- Emulsifiers and stabilizers (E322 and 494)
- Sweeteners (E420-421)
- Solvents (E422)
- Mineral hydrocarbons (905-907)
- Modified starches (E1400-E1442)
- Miscellaneous additives (E170-927)

The standardized E system is not used in the United States, nor does every additive used always have to be listed on food packaging. Some food items, for example mayonnaise and ice-cream, have standardized food status. Standards of Identity established by the Food and Drug Administration state what additives and ingredients may be used for each item, but the item will not necessarily contain all the allowed substances. Some producers of standard items do, however, voluntarily list ingredients in the interests of the public.

Sulphites (sulfites) in the form of sulphur dioxide, sodium sulphite and potassium bisulphite are often used to treat fresh salads such as coleslaw and fruit salad as well as frozen potatoes, vegetables, dried fruits, wine and beer. People with atopic tendency – prone to asthma, hay fever and allergies – can be sensitive to sulphite and develop irritation of the skin or hives. On the positive side, BHT (Butylated Hydroxytoluene) has anti-oxidant properties like vitamins C and E. This additive is used in products such as breakfast cereals and potato flakes and some red wines. It is thought to provide some protection against the incidence of sun-related skin cancer (see **skin**) and protection against UV rays.

**Adrenaline**
See Hormones

conventional treatments, in this case bed rest, are very prolonged.
- Acupuncture can also be a preventative treatment. Ensuring that energy levels remain normal by regular acupuncture sessions can help to prevent disease.
- Acupuncture is now recognized even by practitioners of conventional medicine as helpful in cases of migraine and in other associated disorders of the nervous system.
- Acupuncture can be helpful in a wide range of physical and mental illnesses and diseases ranging from rheumatoid arthritis to depression, digestive disorders and toothache (see **aches and pains**).
- Acupuncture can be helpful in increasing and decreasing weight.
- Acupuncture can be helpful in curing dependencies on alcohol, drugs and smoking.
- Acupuncturists will not treat all cases; sexually transmitted diseases, for example, may not be treated by them.

A

■ See EXERCISES for Caution Box page 123 before starting exercise

# AEROBICS

*See also: dance; exercise; exercises; sports*

Translated literally, aerobic simply means 'with air'. Many people mistakenly associate aerobics just with the fashion for working out to music. Aerobic exercise, however, is really about taking oxygen from the air, transporting it to the working muscles and using it to liberate energy from foodstuffs and nutrients such as carbohydrates and fats. Fats can only be broken down to provide energy for muscle work in the presence of oxygen.

In order to get a 'training effect' for the body, an increase in efficiency of the systems involved – cardiovascular and respiratory – the exercise must be carried out at the appropriate intensity for the individual. This should be such that you become slightly breathless, and exercise must be continued for at least 10 minutes.

Any exercise can be classed as aerobic if it is of sufficient intensity, continuous, uses large muscle groups and is rhythmical in nature.

Almost everyone can take aerobic exercise: you can tailor your own regime according to your initial level of fitness. Everyone should go gently at first, exercising enough to get you slightly out of breath, but still able to carry on a conversation. Start with a few minutes, gradually increasing your time of exercise so that after 10-12 weeks you can exercise continuously for about 30-40 minutes, 3 times a week. The bonus is that not only do you become fitter and feel better, you begin to enjoy whatever exercise you choose.

The two most important things to remember are that you absolutely must warm up before launching

**WARMING UP**
Exercise makes certain demands of the body and for all systems of the body to cope with these demands safely, some time spent warming up the body is essential. Muscles and joints literally need warming up if they are to perform well, without danger of damage. Warming up gradually raises the body's temperature and slowly and steadily accelerates all its essential processes.

The specific type of warming up exercises you should do depends very much on what muscles and joints you will be using. Below are some basic warm-ups suitable for aerobics and helpful for most forms of exercise. You can also use the daily exercise plan (see **exercises**) as the basis for warm-ups too. Add extra exercises for the areas you will chiefly be using: choose from those in individual body area entries throughout the book. Start with those suggested as 'core' exercises (see **abdomen**), but add and swap exercises as you become more proficient.

For example, if you are going to bicycle for aerobic fitness you could use the aerobic warm-ups below, and add the core exercises given in the individual leg section for additional warm ups or as complementary exercises.

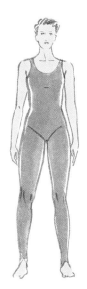

**◄ Exercise A**
This shoulder exercise helps loosen the muscles in the whole upper torso area.
**1** Stand tall with feet shoulder-width apart, arms hanging loosely by your sides, shoulders down. Bring shoulders forward.
**2** Now bring shoulders up as high as you can. Then move them as far back as you can and finally bring them down into the starting position. Repeat twice, gradually increasing to 6 times.

**▲ Exercise B**
This exercise mobilizes the neck.
**1** Stand tall with feet shoulder-width apart, arms loosely by your sides. Tilt your head forward, then raise it again, lengthening your neck as you return to the upright position. Repeat 4 times.
**2** Now tilt your head to your left, keeping shoulders down, bring it back to the centre and lengthen your neck. Repeat 4 times on each side.
**3** Then keeping head upright, turn so that you look over your shoulder, return to facing forwards and lengthen neck. Now turn so that you look over your right shoulder, return to facing forwards and lengthen neck. Repeat this section 4 times then repeat the whole routine twice, gradually increasing to 6 times.

into any vigorous exercise AND wind down slowly afterwards. Make use of the regimes shown opposite to guide you. Sustained exercise speeds up the heartbeat and metabolism: when you stop exercising keep moving slowly to allow yourself to recover and your body to return to normal. If you stop suddenly you may feel dizzy or faint.

### AEROBIC EXERCISE NOTES

- Most important of all is to plan your regime to include gentle starting and stopping exercises, vital for health and safety.
- Use your pulse rate as your personal barometer. Take your pulse rate when resting to establish your normal rate. Now take it when at the peak of your exercise regime and when resting again, to establish your starting pattern. Follow the pulse-taking instructions given on page 125 and ensure that you work within the range suggested for your level. Start slowly, aiming to increase each time by a few beats a minute. This slow growth is important: it ensures that you regain your normal rate within 5 or 10 minutes and thus avoid straining the heart unnecessarily. NOTE You cannot use this method if having drug treatment for hypertension (high blood pressure) as this controls pressure artificially.
- Wear comfortable clothes, perhaps a tracksuit or a leotard.
- Wear snug-fitting, cushioned, comfortable aerobics shoes for aerobics classes: they will support your ankles and act as shock-absorbers. (Always choose the right shoes for whatever sport you are doing.)
- If you feel uncomfortable without a bra, wear a supporting sports type. Those in a cotton/lycra mix are cool and provide maximum flexibility while helping prevent breasts from drooping as a result of action-stretched ligaments.
- Do not continue exercising if you are in any pain. Pain is NOT good for you. Work down slowly and rest. If you are still suffering consult a doctor or physiotherapist immediately. It is surprisingly easy to damage yourself while exercising, and ignoring injuries may render whatever fitness benefits you have gained worse than useless.

► Exercise C
1 Stand tall with feet shoulder-width apart, arms hanging loosely by your sides, with your body relaxed.
2 Allowing your back foot to turn (preventing strain on the knee), but not to leave the floor, twist very loosely around to your left, allowing your arms to swing around too, and bending your knees slightly as you move. Twist loosely back to the central position, straightening knees.
3 Repeat for the right side. The double movement should become one long, easy swing. Repeat 12 times building up to 20 times.

### WINDING DOWN

Allow your body to return to normal gently however fit you are. Your whole body needs to slow down, so repeat the basic exercises in your warming up routine to act as a bridge (see warming-up section in Daily Exercise Plan, p 125).

Do not get cold straight after exercise. Your muscles are very warm, so let them cool gradually to prevent sudden stiffness and tension. A stretching routine will have the most favourable and safe results if carried out now – and may also prevent stiffness. Do not take a cold shower immediately: have a warm bath or shower, and follow with a cold shower if you want to. If you are exercising at lunchtime, walking back to the office will give your mind and body time to return to their working modes.

◄ Exercise D
1 Stand facing forward with legs apart, bottom tucked under, and back long. Turn your right leg out from the hip making sure that your knee is aligned over your foot and pointing in the same direction.
2 Keep your left foot pressed into the floor and your left leg straight. You should feel a comfortable stretch in the inner thigh; if not place your feet wider apart. Repeat 5 more times, holding each position for 4 seconds, then reverse legs and repeat. Gradually increase the repeats for each leg to 18.

A

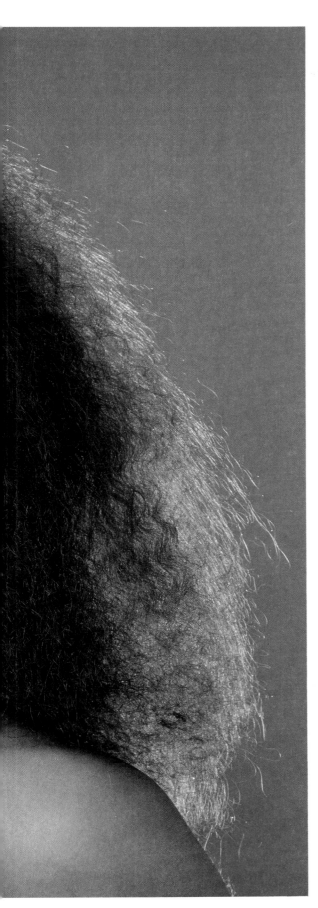

# AFFUSION

*See also: thalassotherapy*

A traditional water cure, affusion involves areas of the body being sprayed with a shower of cold water. The blood circulation is stimulated and the body is left feeling refreshed and lively. Affusion with cold water is not suitable for everyone, particularly not if you have heart problems. Consult your doctor if you are unsure, or use tepid water.

# AFRO HAIR

*See also: black skin; colouring hair; curling and straightening hair; cutting hair; hair*

Afro hair tends to be very curly, its texture varying from very soft yet elastic to coarse and brittle. If this type of hair is treated frequently with thioperms, sodium hydroxide or hot comb straightening to restructure it or remove curl (see **curling and straightening hair**), it will need more conditioning than other hair types to counteract this constant processing. It is important, also, to remember not to colour permanently for two weeks either side of processing (see **colouring hair**).

Plaiting, cornrowing and thread-binding (where thin sections of hair are wound round and round with brightly-coloured or hair-coloured threads) are very popular for Afro hair. Coloured beads can be incorporated along the plaits, or secured at the ends for a colourful effect. These look very attractive whether the hair is partially (see left) or completely braided, and the texture of the hair takes well to it.

# AFTER-SUN PREPARATIONS

*See also: aloe vera; moisturizing; tanning*

All the major sun product companies make after-sun preparations. Because the sun dries out the skin it is important to moisturize your skin after exposure. Adding moisture goes some way towards preventing peeling (it literally sticks dead skin cells together temporarily, making it more difficult for them to fall off); it helps preserve your tan (because if skin loses moisture more of the top layers peel off), and of course the skin needs moisturizing after all the swimming, salt water and washing that goes with sunbathing.

Many preparations can be used on the face as well as the body. Although most are based on oil-

and-water emulsions, the range runs from slightly stringent gels whose coolness is welcome after a hot day in the sun, but provide less moisture, to heavier glycerine- or lanolin-containing creams. All will moisturize, so choose one that is hypo-allergenic if you have sensitive skin, or whichever one smells and feels best to you: you can choose contents as exotic as coconut, avocado, aloe vera and cocoa butter. Do not use these products as sun protection; they do not contain sunscreens, and will not stop you burning.

NOTE Your hair will also need extra conditioning in the sun and on holiday, because sun and seawater dry it out (see **dehydration**).

The sun has a drying effect on the skin so wash off suntan creams, then moisturize well from head to toe. Remember aftersun preparations do not contain sunscreens.

# AGEING

*See also: anorexia; dance; exercise; exercises; fifties; fitness; forties; metabolic rate; minerals; relaxation; sixties plus; skin; teens; thirties; twenties; vitamins*

The ageing process is biologically determined: from conception to birth body cells multiply fast, but from birth onwards this process gets slower and slower. You can exacerbate the ageing process by smoking, drinking, eating too much or eating too little, not taking enough exercise, taking drugs, living under too much stress. But there are many ways, too, in which you can improve the quality of your life, and maintain your youthful self.

## EATING HABITS
Eating well throughout your life is essential to good health and may help prevent premature ageing. Unrefined carbohydrates, like bran, are a particularly important part of the diet as they help prevent heart and arterial as well as digestive tract problems, all of which are more likely to occur with age. Other recent research suggests that salt, sugar, cholesterol and saturated fats should all be kept to a minimum. Eat plenty of fresh fruit, vegetables, pulses and salads, keeping red meats to a minimum and including plenty of fish, chicken, nuts and other proteins with low saturated fat content.

While taking care over the quality of food you eat, be careful of quantity too. As you grow older, the amount of food you need decreases. Your metabolic rate decreases by 5 per cent for every decade after your 20th birthday, so do not imagine that you can continue to follow the same eating pattern for your whole life. See **diet** for requirements at each stage of life. Extremes of weight are ageing: obesity or anorexia nervosa strain the digestive system and age the whole body.

## EXERCISING
Regular exercise helps keep up muscle tone and general fitness, keeps your whole body healthy, and additionally can help ward off anxiety and depression and helps keep you youthful. Try swimming or cycling, always starting gradually and increasing the amount of time you spend on it. Take as much exercise as you can during the course of your working day, too; walk up stairs rather than taking the elevator; take an extra 10 minutes to walk from a bus stop rather than calling a taxi. Do a short series of exercises each morning (see **exercises**). Walking well prevents your age from showing; always walk with your shoulders relaxed but not hunched, bottom tucked in and head held high: this will help avert pains and tensions too.

## RELAXING
Stress is a major factor in the incidence of a number of diseases which in turn have an ageing effect on the whole body. And stress can be more directly ageing, too, giving a careworn look to the skin, preventing hair from having its natural shine and you from feeling energetic. Reduce stress in your life, and use a relaxation technique to help: yoga, meditation, self-hypnosis, just give yourself time alone to read a book, or to work in the garden. There is evidence that your state of mind can influence your body's health: combat adverse effects by keeping fit and relaxed.

## SMOKING AND DRINKING
Both smoking and drinking accelerate ageing. Smoking is a known cause of lung and other cancers. However, it kills more people through cardiovascular disease and bronchitis than through cancer. The action of smoking causes increased stress and facial lines, and the affinity of the carbon monoxide in cigarette smoke for the haemoglobin in the blood deprives skin of the nutrition it needs. Smoking makes blood platelets stickier, thus in-

creasing the likelihood of your suffering a thrombosis (blood clot). Excessive drinking can lead to a variety of liver diseases and early death, too. Light, social drinking may not necessarily be harmful, and a small amount of alcohol can aid digestion. Large amounts do, however, deplete the body's supply of vitamins C and B and dehydrate the skin.

### OVER-EXPOSURE TO SUN

As cell reproduction slows down, the skin's network of collagen and elastin gradually weakens, producing a slacker, wrinkle-prone surface. The top layer of skin (epidermis) becomes thinner, too, and the slower rate of cell renewal means that dead skin cells remain longer on the surface, making it look dull. The ageing processes are greatly exacerbated by excesses of climate and particularly by too much sun. Both UVA and UVB rays (see **tanning**) have a detrimental effect which accumulates over many years' sun exposure. Good, careful treatment and protection of your skin throughout your life (including daily use of sun-block on your face and hands in summer) will contribute a great deal to its continued youthful appearance, as will good vitamin supplies (see **vitamins**). Excessive smoking, drinking, eating, sunbathing in natural sunlight or on sunbeds, use of saunas and stress increase skin ageing: avoid these and ensure that you get plenty of exercise and sleep.

### ANTI-AGEING TREATMENTS

Most doctors are adamant that nothing can be done to delay the body's ageing process. There has recently been increased interest in this field by medical personnel, laymen and -women. The following are some of the treatments currently available.

- **Topical preparations** There are a plethora of 'anti-ageing' creams and lotions on the market. Products containing vitamins A and E are thought to be helpful, although opinion is divided; many doctors are sceptical concerning their usefulness. Those containing collagen and elastin proliferate, but doctors can find no evidence for the absorption of collagen or elastin through the skin. Products containing sun screens are important as they reduce the amount of sun reaching the skin to age it.
- **Cosmetic acupuncture** Facial acupuncture can tone and firm the skin and will also increase general well-being by balancing body energies. Several needles are used, followed by a facial massage. (See separate entry.)
- **Hormone replacement therapy (HRT)** Hormones can be administered orally, and may be helpful particularly during the menopause when supplies of progesterone and oestrogen diminish. (See separate entry.)
- **Cosmetic surgery** The drastic solution which does nothing to hold back the ageing process in the body, but rejuvenates its outward appearance by up to ten years. It is often successful, but can be uncomfortable and take time both to achieve and recover from. (See separate entry.)
- **Cell replacement/rejuvenation therapies** Much work has been done in this area.

Embryonic animal organs transplanted into humans have been found to stimulate production of new human cells. Ribonucleic acid (RNA), which was found to be the active component, can now be administered by injection. However, the efficacy of such treatment is considered highly contentious by most doctors.
- **Gerovital H3 therapy** This drug treatment of injections followed by tablets has been widely used since the 1950s and has been found helpful in treatment both of the symptoms of ageing and of depression. Its efficacy, however, is disputed by most doctors.
- **Glandular extract therapy** Extracts of glands have been found to be helpful in maintaining a youthful body. Extracts are either injected or taken in tablet form. Each type of gland extract supposedly benefits the matching gland, for example, pituitary extract will be attracted to the pituitary. However, the efficacy of such treatment is considered highly contentious by most doctors.
- **Lasers** Helium-neon lasers have been used unsuccessfully in attempts to produce non-surgical face lifts. Redness accompanied by swelling lasts 15 days: wrinkles return as soon as swelling subsides.
- **Vitamin therapy** Large doses of vitamins in the form of orthomolecular therapy (see entry) or megavitamin therapy are advocated by some therapists to delay the ageing process. Most doctors are sceptical of the value of such treatment and concerned at the possibility of overdoses of the fat-soluble vitamins A, D, E, F and K (see **vitamins**).

# AIDS

*See also: sexually transmitted diseases*

AIDS (acquired immunodeficiency syndrome) is caused by the virus HIV and is found in blood, semen and other body fluids. The majority of infected people are perfectly well, a few are unwell with fever, weight loss and enlargement of the lymph nodes. Only a minority develop fullblown AIDS, which occurs years after the virus is acquired. There is a loss of natural immunity and certain life-threatening infections and cancers develop. At present those mainly at risk of infection are male homosexuals and bisexuals, intravenous drug abusers, haemophiliacs, people from central Africa and sexual partners of the above, of either sex. Although the virus has been found in the saliva, there is no risk of infection passing with everyday contact, i.e. sharing food, sneezing or coughing. If you wish to be tested for the virus, do not go to a transfusion clinic, go to a special clinic or to your doctor; don't give blood, don't carry a donor card of any type and don't donate body fluids. Condoms give some protection during sexual intercourse.

**Age spots**
See Liver spots

# AIR

*See also: air ionizers; allergies; hay fever; pollution*

The air that we breathe in is by no means all oxygen. Oxygen is the gas which the body needs in order to function, but it only makes up about 21 per cent of the air we breathe. Nitrogen provides about 78 per cent, and the rest is a combination of 8 other gases.

There are a number of other substances in the air. Some of them are harmless, while others are not so innocent. There are dust particles, and in summer pollens (to which some people have allergic reactions), water vapour (the amount of which determines humidity levels), carbon monoxide from car exhausts, industrial waste such as lead and radio-active particles. Heavy industries are required by law to keep contamination in the atmosphere to 'acceptable levels'. Ominously, evidence is beginning to suggest that permanent, life-threatening damage may be suffered by those living in industrialized areas. And even in remote northern Scotland, a layer of polluted air can be seen very clearly on a sunny day.

Air particles carry a positive or negative electrical charge: clean, fresh air is normally negatively charged, while polluted, dust-carrying air is normally positively charged.

Air baths are often associated with mountain spas and clinics as cool air at high altitudes is relatively pollution-free and very bracing.

The benefits to be gained from air baths are temporary. The supply of good oxygen to the lungs increases body efficiency, and the air's stimulation of the skin and sweat glands accelerates the expulsion of impurity-containing sweat.

Treatment involves exposing the whole body to air, the temperature depending on the disease in each case: only very fit people should subject themselves to cold air. The exposure can be during activities, for fit people, or while lying on a bed, for convalescents. Saunas and Turkish baths are associated treatments.

# AIR IONIZERS

*See also: air; pollution*

Ionizers remove potentially damaging particles from the air and increase the number of beneficial ions. Positive ions carry dust, pollen, sulphates, and other undesirable substances from which negative ions are free. The machine works by attracting positively charged particles, filtering out all the substances clinging to them, and recharging them negatively.

Ionizers are particularly helpful to asthma, allergy and hay fever sufferers; negative ions are thought to heighten brain performance.

# ALCOHOL

*See also: alcoholism; dependencies; hangover*

Ethyl alcohol, $C_2H_5OH$, is the type which we drink. It can be distilled from various types of decaying vegetable matter. Long known for its pleasurable effects as a drink, alcohol depresses the action of the central nervous system, producing blurred reactions. Alcohol rubbed into skin dilates the blood vessels and produces a mildly counter-irritant effect.

### FOR AND AGAINST DRINKING ALCOHOL
**For**
- In small doses alcohol has a tonic effect, lifting tired spirits, relaxing tension.
- A glass of wine can heighten appetite and aid digestion, and thus is sometimes prescribed for convalescents.
- There is some evidence that small quantities of alcohol can help prevent coronary heart disease. In these quantities alcohol seems to increase the proportion of the protecting high-density lipoproteins (HDL) in the blood (see **cholesterol**).

**Against**
- Although there is little evidence that light drinking shortens life, heavy drinking does.
- Drinking alcohol can be addictive, producing a strong habit which is extremely hard to break (see **alcoholism**).
- Heavy drinking can exacerbate stress, increase cholesterol levels in the body.
- Heavy consumption of alcohol causes a variety of serious illnesses among which are:
  **chronic gastritis,** a severe stomach inflammation which renders digestion very difficult, producing weight loss.
  **cirrhosis of the liver,** an effect of heavy drinking which incurably damages liver cells.
  **peripheral neuritis,** causing damage to nervous system.
  **cardiomyopathy,** enlargement of the heart muscle, which can, ultimately, cause very serious damage to it.
  **severe brain damage** and even **dementia,** where mental processes are disordered.

### Sensible drinking
While not forgetting the dangers of drinking too much, small amounts are very enjoyable. In order to slow down alcohol absorption into the bloodstream, try to eat when you drink and dilute drinks whenever possible. Don't drink just because others are, but only when you really want to – and don't encourage others to drink; it can be far from kind or generous. Be aware of the amount you are drinking, watch yourself to check that you are not falling into a habit of drinking several glasses of wine every night after work and be vigilant for your friends too (see **alcoholism, dependencies**).

# ALCOHOLISM

*See also: dependencies*

Alcoholism – physical dependence on alcohol – is an extremely prevalent problem. The habit of heavy social drinking, i.e. more than eight glasses of wine or four pints of beer or four double measures of alcohol per day, can easily become a dependency. Heavy drinking will, in any case, deplete your energy and powers of concentration, increasing the likelihood of depression and illness (see **alcohol**). Dependency will not only decrease your quality of life, but will shorten it.

## TACKLING ALCOHOLISM

▓ Knowledge of how subtly alcoholism can insinuate itself into one's life helps prevent this happening. General awareness is important, outside help and prompting can prevent heavy drinking from becoming have-to drinking.

▓ One of the problems in alcoholism is that of accepting its existence, both for the alcoholic and for family and friends. Once this stage has been passed the problem becomes approachable and groups like Alcoholics Anonymous can be of tremendous help. Initially, those wishing to help will almost certainly be rebuffed. Acceptance will have to be worked through before any of the causes of the alcohol problem can be considered and discussed.

▓ A number of clinics specialise in treating alcoholism and have a good success rate. Overcoming the dependency is not easy, and requires the complete determination of the sufferer. Groups like AA (Alcoholics Anonymous) exist to help addicts, with Al-anon operating in parallel for family members. Both operate in the utmost confidentiality.

# ALEXANDER TECHNIQUE

*See also: body image; Feldenkrais; posture; Rolfing*

F. Matthias Alexander, who died in 1955, felt that modern-day man did not use his body to its best potential. He himself had suffered loss of voice as a result of holding his head wrongly. Stress-related muscle contractions and habitual bad posture, he thought, caused tension, compressed the spine and organs of the torso and produced joint and muscle pain – especially back pain – hypertension and even digestive pain and asthma.

He developed a system by which people could improve both their mental and physical states. It is based on a series of gentle exercises and movements, adjustable to personal conditions, rather than on rigid rules of 'correct' posture. The aim is gradually to remove harmful posture habits, the basis for which is stored in the unconscious memory. The Alexander Technique deals, therefore, with both the physical and mental aspects of posture.

The Basic Movement, illustrated below, is the foundation of the whole technique, incorporating the idea of lifting the head upward and away from the torso and stretching the body before beginning any other movement. It is not an exercise: the illustrations below are guidelines towards achieving a new way of moving, holding oneself, standing and sitting. Other movements follow on from this Basic Movement, which are taught in classes and well documented in books. If you are interested in the other movements of the Alexander Technique, it is a good idea to seek instruction from a qualified teacher.

1 Normal slumped sitting position.
2 While sitting lift the head upward and away from the body, while turning it from side to side.
3 Lift the head upward again and tip slowly forward and then back keeping the head up and away from the body.
4 Normal slumped standing position.
5 While standing lift and stretch the whole body upwards.

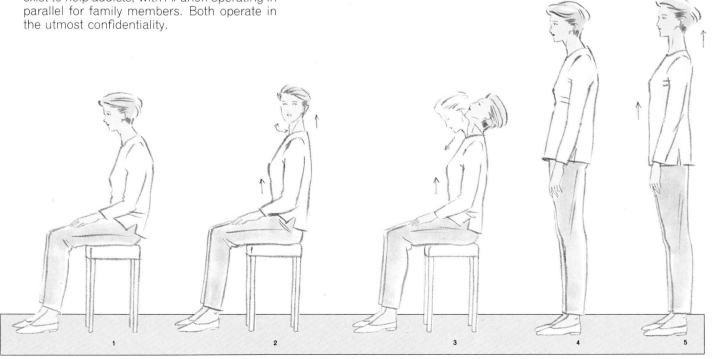

**Alunite crystal**
See Deodorant

**Ambergris**
See Scent

# ALLERGIES AND ALLERGENS

*See also: additives; hay fever; skin; tanning*

Allergens are substances which, though tolerated by most people, produce an adverse reaction (allergy) in hypersensitive (susceptible) individuals. On contact with an allergen, allergy sufferers produce abnormal antibodies which react chemically with the allergen to stimulate the release of histamine and serotonin. These cause inflammation and various other irritating symptoms of differing degrees.

There are many allergens and a number of allergic reactions. The increase in general pollution, food additives and crop spray levels may be important in the incidence of allergic reactions but solvents and additives to cosmetics are also indicated in allergies.

### ANGIOEDEMA AND URTICARIA

Acute swelling (angioedema) may occur as a sudden reaction to a drug or after eating certain foods such as shellfish. Recurrent itchy weals may also be more chronic (of long duration). This condition is called urticaria or hives, and may persist for months. Certain drugs including aspirin, dyes such as tartrazine and some preservatives may be responsible. Elimination diets are sometimes helpful in isolating the cause, but all too often none is found. Fortunately in most cases the condition resolves as suddenly and unexpectedly as it appeared. Treatment with antihistamines helps to reduce the symptoms.

### ASTHMA, HAY FEVER AND ECZEMA (ATOPY)

A tendency to these conditions, known as atopy, runs in some families and is present from birth. Asthma and hay fever may be aggravated by inhaled substances such as dust and pollens. Intradermal (just under the surface of the skin) prick tests of suspected allergens are sometimes helpful in establishing the cause. See also **hay fever**.

Infantile (atopic) eczema usually begins in the first year of life. The skin in eczema sufferers is abnormally sensitive to many irritants. Only occasionally is a true food allergy, such as a reaction to dairy produce, to blame, and this can be established by a strict elimination diet. Breastfeeding may lessen the chances of a child developing infantile eczema.

Cortisone creams are the main treatment given to eczema sufferers. Used with care and supervision they are safe and effective. Long-term use of potent preparations may cause skin thinning. However, 0.5 per cent and 1 per cent hydrocortisone is quite safe, and is likely to become available without prescription in the UK in the near future. 0.5 per cent hydrocortisone is already available without prescription in the US (see **dermatitis**).

### ALLERGIC CONTACT DERMATITIS

In contact dermatitis, substances such as metal, rubber, glue, lanolin, preservatives in creams, perfumes and many other chemicals may produce a reaction at the exposure site. This may occur suddenly, even though the sufferer has been exposed to the allergen for many years. The exact cause is established by patch tests: suspected chemicals are applied to the skin. If the reaction is positive, it shows itself after 48 hours as an area of eczema beneath a particular allergen. Once identified, the chemical or chemicals producing a positive reaction must be avoided.

# ALLOPATHY

*See also: herbalism; holism; homoeopathy; naturopathy*

Allopathy is the orthodox system of medicine whereby medication is used to produce opposite effects in the body to those produced by a disease or illness from which it may be suffering, in order to cure it. Conventional medicine today operates on this system, where objective tests form the basis of diagnosis. The opposite of allopathy is homoeopathy where emphasis is laid on building up the body's natural defence systems, and treating 'like with like'. There is increasing interest among allopathic doctors in the role of treatments for other systems, such as medical herbalism, also chiropractic and osteopathy. The British Medical Association (BMA) published an extensive report on complementary and alternative medicine in 1986.

# ALOPECIA

*See also: hair; trichologist*

The word 'alopecia' means baldness. It is used, however, to include all types of hair loss, whether general or patchy, from areas where it normally grows. There are several types of alopecia:
**Genetically induced alopecia** Extensive hereditary hair loss, rarer in women, though increasing and irreversible. The female hair loss pattern differs from the male.
**Traction alopecia** Resulting from over-brushing or styling. Hair will gradually regrow.
**Alopecia areata** This usually presents itself as one or more areas of patchy hair loss. Treatment is often unsuccessful but, fortunately, spontaneous regrowth occurs in most cases.
**Acute hair fall** At the time of a serious illness, operation, accident, severe stress or at the end of a pregnancy, the scalp hair may stop growing and enter a 'resting' phase. About 3 months later, new hair begins to grow and push out the old. This results in an acute hair fall which is short-lived as the new hairs soon appear.

# ALOE VERA

*See also: after-sun preparations; burns; tanning*

Aloe vera (*Aloe barbadensis* Miller) is a sub-tropical succulent of the lily family, known for centuries as a healing agent and as an aid to beauty. If the tip of an aloe vera leaf is snipped off, gel can be squeezed out. It is now commercially extracted.

The gel contains vitamins B1, B2 and B6, calcium, potassium, chlorine, enzymes and other as yet unidentified active ingredients. It has antibiotic, astringent, coagulating and sun-filtering properties. Helpful in promoting healing, it can be applied to burnt or blemished skin, and can even be used to assist healing in the mouth. Used internally, pure aloe vera seems to have anti-inflammatory effects, aiding digestion and alleviating bowel disorders. Its versatility means that it is included in hair, face, sun and bath products.

Rich in vitamins and minerals, aloe vera heals, moisturizes and protects. Massaged gently on to burnt or blemished skin it soothes and cools it quickly.

# AMENORRHOEA

*See also: anorexia nervosa; contraception; dysmenorrhoea; hysterectomy; menstruation; stress*

The word 'amenorrhoea' means absence of menstrual periods. There are two types of amenorrhoea: *primary amenorrhoea* when menstruation fails to start at puberty and *secondary amenorrhoea* when menstruation, having begun at puberty, ceases later, for example during pregnancy.

## CAUSES

Amenorrhoea has many causes. If your period is 2 weeks late, and you had sexual intercourse during the previous menstrual cycle, you should assume that you are pregnant and consult your doctor, regardless of whether precautions were taken. If you are 16 or over and have never had a period, or if you miss a period at any age, you should consult your doctor. Some of the most common causes of amenorrhoea are:

**Pregnancy** Periods cease during pregnancy and the full breast-feeding period (but see **contraception**: you may well be fertile while breast-feeding).

**Menopause** If you are over 40 and experiencing amenorrhoea, even spasmodically, you may be beginning the menopause (see separate entry). Hormonal problems, such as cystic ovaries, may be a cause, too.

**Stress, anxiety, change** Sudden change or problems, shocks, and flying with its disturbance of the body clock, can inhibit ovulation. If amenorrhoea persists, consult your doctor.

**Anorexia nervosa** Amenorrhoea is an early symptom of this illness.

**Overweight** This may produce amenorrhoea.

**Hysterectomy** Periods cease after this operation.

# ANAEMIA

*See also: diet; minerals; nails*

Anaemia is a shortage of the vital oxygen-carrying red haemoglobin in the blood. Symptoms are excessive tiredness, breathlessness after exertion and poor resistance to infection. There are several types of anaemia. Iron-deficiency anaemia is much the most common, due to dietary deficiencies, excessive loss of blood in menstruation or as a result of an accident. Spoon-shaped nails and lack of redness inside the lower eyelid are classic symptoms, but not necessarily signs that you are suffering from anaemia. Ensure that you eat iron-rich foods: liver, kidneys, beans, nuts and red meat to avoid this. Combine them with vitamin C which aids iron absorption (and not too much tea which inhibits it). If you think that you may have iron-deficiency anaemia, go to your doctor: iron supplements have to be calculated, especially when pregnant.

Other types of anaemia result from impaired production of haemoglobin, for example pernicious anaemia, or from the action of toxins or parasites in the body, for example malaria, and these need professional medical treatment.

---

A

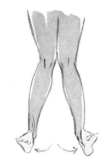

# ANKLES

*See also: exercises; feet; legs*

The average person walks more than 70,000 miles during their lifetime, so it is important to look after the foot and ankle joints and to keep them mobile, healthy and well-exercised. Exercises which increase the mobility of the ankles will also help to strengthen them, thus reducing the risk of damage, and improving the posture. Oedema (swelling due to fluid retention) can be a problem just before menstruation, during pregnancy, when taking the contraceptive pill (consult your doctor), or when flying (see **fluid retention**). Put your legs up whenever possible, preferably higher than your head, especially if you have been standing or sitting with your legs hanging down all day.

The ankle is a complex series of joints, where the largest of the 7 bones known as the tarsals joins the tibia and fibula, while the others provide flexible movement. The joint is one of the most vulnerable in the body.

■ See EXERCISES for Caution Box page 123 before starting exercise

▲ **Exercise A**
This exercise should be carried out while you are sitting straight and tall on a chair.
**1** With your knees together and your heels hip-width apart on the floor, bring your big toes up and in towards each other,
keeping them as high off the floor as possible.
**2** Now tilt and move both feet down and outwards from the ankle, pulling your little toes up and out off the floor as much as possible. Repeat 6 times working up to 24 times.

◄ **Exercise B**
This exercise is excellent for general relaxation, and for your back, too.
**1** Lying on your back on the floor, slide your knees up along the floor and then up to your chest and hold them there with your arms.
**2** Lift your head, point your toes and rock gently backward and forward for as long as feels comfortable. Breathe easily throughout.

▼ **Exercise C**
Rest one leg flat on the floor, hold the other against your chest (by the back of the thigh to leave the lower leg free) and rotate your foot 8 times clockwise and 8 times anticlockwise. Repeat with other foot. Increase number of repeats up to 28 for each foot, working alternately in groups of 7. Breathe easily throughout.

# ANOREXIA NERVOSA

*See also: appetite; bulimia; crash dieting; dependencies; diet; weight*

Anorexia nervosa (which means literally nervous loss of appetite) is a serious physical and mental illness which involves weight loss and determined control of appetite. It is sometimes known as the slimming disease because dieting is almost always its starting point. Its causes, however, go far deeper than fanatical slimming, and are the subject of current research. The disease affects approximately 1 per cent of girls of above average intelligence under 18 at academic institutions. Overall the incidence of anorexia is at the most 1:500 in females under 25 in developed countries where dieting is an option, not a necessity.

### ANOREXIA NERVOSA: MYTH AND REALITY
- Many anorexics suffer from amenorrhoea, low blood pressure, cold hands and feet, downy hair growth on the face, arms and back, and their weight drops to as little as 50 per cent of the average for their age. However, these symptoms can signal other problems, too, so consult your doctor for diagnosis.
- Is anorexia nervosa the result of pressure from fashion magazines that to be beautiful you must be thin? To some extent it is, since the desire to conform is part of the onset of the disease. More important is fear which makes women attempt to starve away their secondary sexual characteristics, thus releasing them from the need to succeed in the sexual field.

- Anorexia is not a disease you catch from too much dieting. It is a disease resulting from psychological problems which may have evolved over a long period. Because of this, attacking eating problems will not cure anorexia. And it is not a modern disease: its incidence is documented in the 17th century.
- Anorexia nervosa is not just a teenage problem. Although it is most common among pubescent teenagers who become as easily obsessed by dieting as by pop music, it is a disturbed mental and emotional state (as at the trauma of puberty or a death), not a hormonal one, which produces anorexia. So it can happen at any age.
- Anorexics often have distorted images of their own bodies. They often imagine themselves to be much fatter than they are, and have similarly distorted views of their own personalities.
- Most anorexics do not actually want to die although the incidence of death is high as a result of starvation and more importantly of prolonged damage to digestive organs, particularly the kidneys and pancreas. The incidence of suicide in longstanding anorexics is 5 per cent. They want to gain love and attention from parents and siblings, to change unhappy situations which may have been with them since childhood.

### COPING WITH ANOREXIA
Anorexia nervosa requires medical help. Traditional treatments such as force-feeding, withdrawal of privileges until the patient eats and puts on weight, rebuilding of dietary habits while in hospital and even psychotherapy and family therapy have not always been successful.

The main problems in anorexia which need treatment are the abnormal eating and living rituals, the sexual fears and above all the underlying sense of inadequacy and unlovability. The anorexic needs help, too, in coping with adult, independent life away from home. Coming to terms with the causes of the problem in the context of the whole family is crucial to a cure.

# ANTI-PERSPIRANTS

*See also: body odour; deodorants; sweat*

Anti-perspirants act on both types of sweat gland, particularly the apocrine glands in the armpits, to reduce sweating by up to 50 per cent. They contain mineral salts, particularly aluminium, zinc or manganese, which decrease sweat production within the gland. Odours come from sweat, itself odourless, reacting with bacteria on the skin. Frequent washing and wearing natural fibres next to the skin to aid sweat evaporation both help prevent odour. Some anti-perspirants are combined with deodorants (see separate entry) which contain antiseptic and destroy bacteria.

**Ante-natal care and problems**
See Pregnancy

# ANXIETY

*See also: meditation; migraine and headache; reflexology; relaxation; sports; stress; yoga*

Anxiety is a conscious expression of fears, the subject of which may well be stored in the unconscious. The subject matter can range from vague fears about losing a loved one to a specific, current problem at work, and anxiety can relate to past, present and future events.

### THE ANXIETY REACTION
In some cases the anxiety reaction can be constructive, for example when it concerns getting a job done to a time limit. The body reacts by secreting adrenaline which increases heart beat, blood pressure, breathing rate and muscle action: the job gets done quickly. When the problem causing anxiety is less specific the anxiety symptoms which appear are more difficult to cope with. They are of little help with the problem in hand, and in order to alleviate them the source of anxiety must be identified and then dealt with.

### PREVENTING ANXIETY
- Face problems head on as soon as you can; don't push them aside to be dealt with later.
- If you experience anxiety, make a list of potential problems in your life, however trivial. Bringing these into conscious memory will put you well on the way to solving them.
- Take plenty of exercise; swim, or go for a walk. Reorganize your office. Don't allow anxiety to affect your character, making you scratchy and doleful: you will regret the reaction and thus increase your anxiety.
- Since too much smoking, drinking and caffeine-containing drinks such as tea and hot chocolate can exacerbate or even induce anxiety symptoms, be moderate in their use.
- If your anxiety attacks persist, visit your doctor. He may prescribe tranquillizers or counselling: the former will suppress the symptoms while the latter will help reveal, and ultimately deal with, their cause.

# APPETITE

*See also: anorexia nervosa; appetite suppressants; bulimia; diet; exercise; hunger; relaxation*

Appetite, the desire to eat, is regulated by the hypothalamus gland in the forebrain, which also controls other functions like sleep and sexual activity. Appetite is subject to factors other than essential bodily needs. It can be lost just by looking at food, or after one mouthful. Hunger plays only a small part in the appetite's demands. The sensation of fullness takes 20 minutes to affect hunger, and appetite can continue well after this, especially in the case of those with bulimia nervosa. Conditioned eating habits, emotions and the amount of exercise being taken all affect the appetite. Anorexia nervosa can seriously impair its function, too. Appetite changes can also be experienced during pregnancy, sometimes incorporating unusual food cravings which cease after the birth.

### MAINTAINING A HEALTHY APPETITE
Appetite and hunger are linked (see **hunger**) and play an important role in keeping the body nourished.

#### Increasing appetite
1   Try to relax. Tension often suppresses appetite: try some new relaxation methods.
2   Make extra effort with presentation. Attractive food stimulates appetite.
3   Take more exercise: this stimulates hunger and thus appetite too.

#### Decreasing appetite
1   Eat more slowly, savouring the taste of each mouthful.
2   Stop eating periodically during a meal and ensure that you are not still eating when the hunger mechanism has stopped. The less you eat after hunger has gone, the sooner your appetite will adjust. (See also **appetite suppressants,** below.)

# APPETITE SUPPRESSANTS

*See also: appetite; crash dieting; diet*

Commercially available appetite suppressants are not helpful in reducing either appetite or weight in the long term. Most are fibre-based bulking agents which work by swelling up in the stomach to produce an artificial 'food fullness' feeling which the stomach soon accepts as normal. Sweet products raise blood sugar levels quickly, but the body soon adjusts and the benefit is lost; anaesthetic chewing gum dulls the taste buds and pleasure in the flavour of food, but soon wears off. The appetite will only be controlled in the long term by other means (see **appetite, eating habits**). Try increasing levels of the amino acid phenylalanine, however, which occurs in protein-rich foods such as cottage cheese, almonds, peanuts, pumpkin and sesame seeds and soy products. The body turns it into the hormone noradrenaline which helps suppress hunger, but not appetite. In severe cases of obesity your doctor may prescribe drugs to override appetite and hunger reactions at their source, in the hypothalamus (in the brain). But these drugs still do not alter your underlying appetite reaction: it is up to you to change that.

# APPLICATORS

*See also: brushes; eye make-up; foundation; mascara; pencils; sponges*

Although clean fingertips are the most natural and obvious make-up applicators, they contain natural oils and moisture which can cause make-up to dissolve more quickly. Brushes, sponge-tipped applicators for eye shadows, mascara wands, pencils, sticks and foundation spatulas are all available to apply, blend and define your various types of make-up. Unfortunately, they can trap dirt and bacteria, particularly the cream-based products, which may cause infection or irritation. Eyes are especially sensitive, so change sponges and cream applicators about every 6 months, and clean them frequently with warm water between uses. Mascara wands should be replaced regularly, and returned to their containers directly after use. Keep protective covers on lip brushes too. Avoid sharing applicators or make-up with friends. Not only can bacteria be carried from one skin to another, but you may well find that products not carefully chosen by you are unsuitable for your skin, especially if it is sensitive to cosmetics.

# A

■ See EXERCISES for Caution Box page 123 before starting exercise

## ARMS

*See also: cellulite; exercises; muscles*

The shape of the arms remains fairly constant throughout life except in cases of extreme weight loss or gain, where fat levels depart from their normal percentage and fat is laid down in or taken away from the arms. General exercise and even weight training will increase muscle tone and ability, not size. For most people muscle tone is the main change factor: lack of it will allow muscles to become slack and skin can take on a mottled appearance due to bad circulation. This can be rectified by following an exercise programme (see below). Avoid removing excessive or very dark arm hair if possible; bleaching is a better alternative (see **unwanted hair**). Tension is often reflected in the way you hold your shoulders, arms and hands, and this can give you severe muscular pain. When in this situation, concentrate on relaxing each muscle down from shoulder to fingers.

**◄ Exercise C**
**1** Stand tall, feet hip-width apart, back long and straight with shoulders down. Start with arms by your sides, upper arm close to the body, palms inwards.
**2** Lift one forearm right up and turn wrist so that palm is facing and right up against your shoulder, elbow still in original position. Straighten arm and repeat with other arm.
  Repeat 6 times for each arm, but gradually increase to 24 times. Once you have worked up to 24 repeats, use a 1 lb (0.4 kg) weight or a can of beans in each hand and begin from 6 repeats again.

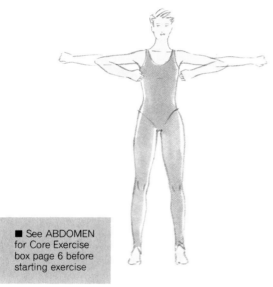

**◄ Exercise A**
**1** Stand tall with shoulders down, feet hip-width apart, long back and neck. With arms bent, raise upper arms until they are parallel with the floor, and tuck lower arms in underneath as tightly as possible. Form hands into loosely clenched fists, with outside of hand facing forward.
**2** Now, keeping fists loosely clenched, raise lower arms slowly in an arc parallel to the body (do not swing out forwards or backwards) until arms are straight and horizontal, then return steadily to starting position. Repeat 6 times building up to 18 times.

■ See ABDOMEN for Core Exercise box page 6 before starting exercise

**◄ Exercise B**
**1** Sit on a stool, with back long and straight, and shoulders level. Bend your arms and bring your clenched fists, palm inwards, up to your shoulders.
**2** Now press your arms down and back as far as you can behind you, turning them meanwhile so that palms are facing out and up. Keep a long back throughout. Bring arms back to shoulders and repeat 12 times, increasing gradually to 36 times.

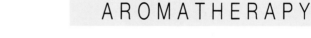

## AROMATHERAPY

*See also: facials; herbalism; herbs*

Aromatherapy is a form of complementary medicine. It was used by the Ancient Chinese and the Egyptians and there is mention of it in the Bible. Although it sometimes borders on herbalism, the two therapies have always been kept apart by their practitioners. Unlike herbalism, aromatherapy has no formal training institute. It involves using essential oils on the skin, in baths or even at times internally, to prevent and cure illness, and to produce a wide range of therapeutic effects.

  The therapy gets its name from the idea that benefit was contained mainly in the smell of the oil. The smell of essential oils alone has indeed been beneficial in cases of anxiety and depression, but more emphasis is laid on the effects of penetration of oil through the skin.

### ESSENTIAL OILS
Essential oils are the odiferous substances in plant roots, leaves and flowers, in barks and resin. Some plants contain several essential oils. The orange tree, for example, has neroli in the flowers, petitgrain in the leaves and orange oil in the fruit's rind. Oils are sometimes clear, others lightly coloured, ranging from pink to brown, green and yellow. The main constituents of essential oils are alcohols, aldehydes, acids, esters, acetones and terpenes. Avoid any essential oils which are not pure and have been treated in any way. Their action will be different from that of pure oils. In addition, there is a much increased chance of your suffering an allergic reaction to such an oil. All essential oils are easily damaged by light and should be kept in dark bottles.

### THE AROMATHERAPY PROCESS

1  Aromatherapists take a full case history before choosing oils appropriate to that patient.
2  A 'tally', perhaps a lock of hair, is placed in the centre of a dowsing disc surrounded by a group of oils chosen by the therapist. This is important: rules for using oils are not absolute, as effects vary from person to person.
3  Dowsing then determines the most suitable oil and method of treatment.
4  Treatment may take the form of inhalation, where a few drops of oil are put into a bowl of boiling water and the healing vapours are inhaled, but more generally of massage: the oil is diluted and massaged into the area indicated by the problem.
5  Some therapists prescribe internal use of essential oils, but there is much dispute concerning this, and this form of treatment should be regarded with caution.

### Aromatherapy and beauty

Aromatherapists believe that massage with essential oils and the use of hot compresses to aid absorption can be very beneficial to facial skin. The individual combination of oils used depends on the skin type (see **skin**) and on any skin problems which may be present.

### Aromatherapy and pain

There are over 60 oils which have local painkilling properties, most common of which are rosemary and sage, and others such as camphor and peppermint are widely used. Clove oil is commonly applied to the teeth and gums as a local painkiller for toothache. Eucalyptus is used for sore throats. Aromatherapists treat painful conditions such as rheumatism and arthritis. Choice of essential oil depends very much on the skin and problem of the individual. Consult your aromatherapist before treating any pain with essential oils.

## ESSENTIAL OILS USED IN AROMATHERAPY

| ESSENTIAL OILS | PROPERTIES | ESSENTIAL OILS | PROPERTIES |
|---|---|---|---|
| Basil | Light green fragrance, from the herb basil; aids concentration, clarifies thought and lifts spirits. | Lemon | From the rind of the fruit; refreshing and cooling, antiseptic properties. |
| Benzoin | Vanilla scent, in resin from trees found in Malaysia, Java, Borneo; aids respiration, used for skin pigmentation problems. | Lemongrass | Lemony aroma, from the grass grown in Brazil, the Far East and Africa; external antiseptic, decreases perspiration, relieves migraine, refreshing as bath oil. |
| Bergamot | Spicy lemon scent, from the peel of the citrus bergamot in the orange family; antiseptic, internally fights infection. *NOTE Do not use on skin which is to be exposed to ultra-violet light or sun, as it can cause uneven pigmentation.* | Marjoram | Herbal aroma, extracted from the common herb; comforting and calming, alleviates insomnia and migraine. |
| Cedarwood | Violet/woody fragrance, from the cedarwood tree found in Northern Africa; antiseptic, aids urinary system, good for hair and skin. | Myrrh | Camphor-like smell, from gum resin originating in the Middle East; traditionally used for embalming and religious ceremonies, has antiseptic and anti-inflammatory properties. |
| Chamomile | Warm aromatic odour, from the herb's flowers; many properties including soothing inflammation, aiding healing, acting as tonic, digestive and sedative. | Neroli | From the flowers of the orange tree, particularly the bigaradia or bitter orange; hypnotic, tranquillizing effects, induces sleep, alleviates depression. |
| Clary sage | Nutty/floral scent, from the French clary sage herb; aids menstrual problems, warming, gives sense of euphoria. | Orange | From the rind of the common fruit; uplifting and refreshing. |
| Clove | Grows around the Indian Ocean, familiar aromatic, spicy scent; local anaesthetic, antiseptic. | Patchouli | Mysterious, persistent oriental aroma, from branches of the plant native to Malaysia and the Seychelles; reduces inflammation, antiseptic, alleviates skin problems, stimulating and seductive. |
| Cypress | Fresh and woody, long-lasting smell, from the eastern Mediterranean cypress tree; aids circulatory problems and is relaxing. | Peppermint | From a subspecies of the mint plant native to the Mediterranean; invigorating and refreshing, aids digestion and helps prevent seasickness. |
| Eucalyptus | Aromatic, medicinal smell, from the leaves of the eucalyptus tree native to Australia; antiseptic, good for respiratory problems, promotes healing. | Pine | Fresh country aroma with balsam notes, from resin but better from needles of Northern European and Asian trees; antiseptic, aids respiration, refreshing. |
| Frankincense | Spicy, dry, woody aroma, from the gum resin of a tree in the genus *Boswellia* which grows in Oman; antiseptic with elevating and soothing effect on emotions. | Rose | Familiar throughout the world, native in the East; tonic, aphrodisiac, alleviates skin problems, aids circulation and respiration. |
| Galbanum | Hot, pungent smell, from a species of fennel which grows in Iran; promotes healing, reduces inflammation. | Rosemary | Strong resin aroma, originates on Mediterranean shores; antiseptic and stimulating, diuretic. |
| Geranium | Green, floral scent, from the geranium, usually a fragrant pelargonium type, originally found in North Africa and in Reunion; invigorating used in the bath; anti-inflammatory. | Rosewood | Rosy, spicy, refreshing scent, from rosewood trees native to Brazil; uplifting and enlivening used as bath oil. |
| Juniper | Green, woody scent, from the berries of the evergreen juniper tree; traditionally burned to ward off plague, it reduces tension, is diuretic and cleansing. | Sandalwood | Light, musky scent, native to India; traditionally burnt to produce aroma, calming, relaxing, health-giving, enhances sexual awareness. |
| Lavender | Flowery, clinging scent, the plant comes from the Canary Isles, Iran and the Mediterranean coast; soothing, relaxing, promotes healing of burns. | Tangerine | Light, fresh aroma with energizing qualities. Excellent skin-care properties. |
| | | Ylang Ylang | Exotic scent, from blossom of trees native to the Far East; traditionally a love potion, antiseptic, tonic, improves hair condition. |

# ARTIFICIAL LASHES

*See also: eye make-up*

Artificial lashes are available in various lengths, thicknesses and colours, and some are even spangled for a party effect. Ensure that they are not so long and thick that they unbalance the eye's shape, and that the glue is carefully applied – too much can cause irritation to the eyelid, too little can cause artificial lashes to drop off.

### METHODS
Eyelashes can be applied in single strips, in sections or individually.

For a full strip, first measure up the lashes. They should not go beyond the outer corner of the eye. Snip them to the correct length with scissors. If your natural lashes are blonde, put on mascara first. Apply glue evenly along the bottom of the strip with an orange stick. Leave for a few seconds until the glue gets tacky. Stretch the eyelid slightly with your fingers so that the lashes can come as close as possible to your natural lash line. Stick on the centre, then each side, making sure that the shortest lashes are innermost for natural effect and comfort. Use eyeliner to conceal the line where lashes and skin meet, unless you are using false lashes with the eyeliner already applied.

Strips of lashes can be cut from a length and applied in the same way. Placed in the centre of the eye they give a widening effect; on the outer edge, they give an illusion of length.

To remove, support the temple with the fingertips of one hand and gently pull the lashes starting at the outer edge.

Individual lashes are best applied permanently by beauty salons as the process is time-consuming and fiddly. To do it yourself, each lash has to be cut from a strip, attached on top of every natural lash and pushed as far in between as possible. Start from the inner corner of the eye and stroke a little glue down each natural lash with an orange stick. Press on each false lash with tweezers and hold to set. Brush and separate the lashes with a lash brush-and-comb or clean mascara wand. Use an oil-based eye make-up remover to remove. False lashes can be cleaned with surgical spirit.

# ARTIFICIAL NAILS

*See also: nails*

Artificial nails are available singly or in complete sets and are useful for concealing bitten, split or crumbling nails, as well as for lengthening short nails. Most beauty salons also offer nail rebuilding treatment, which is a more resilient and effective alternative to putting on artificial nails yourself.

Care is taken to match the shape of the nails to the hands, and the process is fairly lengthy (about 2 hours). All methods need regular, professional follow-up treatment (every 2 weeks); as the existing nail grows out it lifts up, and the gaps between the real and false nail need filling in. Also tips may need to be reglued, or removed altogether.

### METHODS
1   False plastic tips can be glued on to existing damaged nails and the surfaces of the tip pared down to conceal the join.
2   Tips can be dipped in acrylic powder. First the surface of the nail is roughened so that the false tip will stick on easily. The tip is filed until the join no longer shows, painted with a thin layer of glue, then dipped in acrylic powder, filed and buffed.
3   Tips can be painted with an acrylic chemical. The nail surface is roughened before the chemical is painted on. When this hardens, the nail is suitably shaped.
4   Nails can be silk-wrapped. This is a good method for preventing long nails from breaking. A thin layer of silk is glued on to the whole nail, then smoothed to take away the edges and filed into shape.
5   Nails can be sculpted. An oval paper form is put underneath each nail before a chemical substance with a transparent base and white tip is painted on to the nail and allowed to set. The nail is then 'sculpted' to the correct shape and

**Ascorbic acid**
See Vitamin C

**Aspirin**
See Drugs and
medicines

**Astringents**
See Toning

**Athlete's foot**
See Ringworm

length, and when hard, the paper form is removed and the nail buffed until shiny. No varnish is required, and the false nail will grow out with the normal one in roughly two weeks. Sculpted nails are thicker and potentially more damaging to the real nail beneath than the tip method.

6  'Lite' nails are a new method in which the real nails are roughened, then smoothed over, and shaped with a crystal gel. This is held under an ultraviolet lamp for 3-4 minutes to harden. No varnish is required, as the gel makes the nails naturally shiny. They only need buffing. The nails will not dissolve, but can only be removed by filing. Replacements are necessary every 3-4 weeks.

### WARNINGS
- Always go to a good manicurist or a salon specializing in nail rebuilding. If you use a do-it-yourself kit the nails generally look unnatural, and the glue is not always effective.
- If you start to react against chemicals, the false nails must be removed at once – professionally.
- Machine filing can remove the surface of your nail and cause weakening, so should be avoided.
- Do not have a manicure the same day as false nails are applied.
- Always have tips removed by the salon.

# ASPIRATION

*See also: abdomen; chin; cosmetic surgery; elastin and elastone; thighs*

Fat aspiration is a relatively new development in the body sculpture field. Although up to 2 kg (4½ lb) of fat can be removed, it is *not* an alternative to dieting. Fat is removed from areas where the number and distribution of fat cells mean that no amount of slimming or exercise will shift them. In removing the fat cells, or lipocytes, the fat-forming potential of the area goes: cell numbers and distribution are thought to be fixed during the first year of life when eating habits and patterns are established. Common areas for aspiration are the buttocks, thighs, abdomen and chin.

### THE PROCESS
Aspiration is carried out under general anaesthetic. Although it does not rate as full cosmetic surgery, it should only be carried out by a competent, qualified surgeon. Great care has to be taken over the amount of fat removed in order to retain the body's natural contours and to ensure that thigh matches thigh, and so on. An incision approximately 4-6 mm long is made. A tube is inserted, and the fat cells (lipocytes) literally sucked out. The tube itself is used to break fatty tissue from its fibrous connections. The incision is covered with a dressing for 10

days, after which there are twice-weekly massages for 6 weeks to stimulate the circulation and disperse oedema (swelling due to fluid retention). Twelve weeks after the operation, bruising and swelling will have disappeared, leaving just a tiny scar.

### PROBLEMS WITH ASPIRATION
- Aspiration is most successful on people under 40: skin elasticity, which decreases with age (see **elastin and elastone**), is an important factor in overall success.
- Incompetent aspiration can leave odd bumps and ridges beneath the skin which will not disappear, or sagging folds of skin which will need surgical removal.

# AURICULOTHERAPY

*See also: aches and pains; acupuncture; dependencies; moxibustion; reflexology*

Auriculotherapy is a branch of acupuncture in which treatment is concentrated on the ear. Some acupuncturists turn to this therapy when whole-body acupuncture has not produced results, although the therapy is also practised independently. There are over 120 acupuncture points on the ear, which are believed to relate to the organs and parts of the whole body. Here, tenderness in ear areas may correspond to the part of the body causing trouble. Finer needles are used for this therapy than for body acupuncture. Auriculotherapy can be used to treat a variety of problems. In the treatment of drug dependencies more permanent stimulation of a point is sometimes achieved with the use of 2mm deep press pins. One or more can be used in an acupuncture point in the ear and are normally left there for 1-2 weeks.

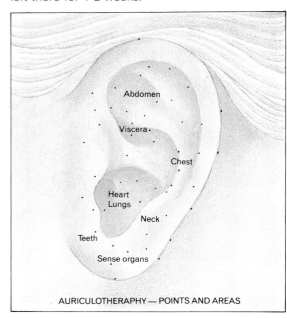

AURICULOTHERAPY — POINTS AND AREAS

# AUTOGENICS

*See also: anxiety; autosuggestion; dependencies; hormones; relaxation; stress*

Autogenic means literally 'self-produced'. The training was evolved by Johannes Shultz, a Berlin neurologist, and further developed by Wolfgang Luthe in Montreal. Autogenic training aims at teaching pupils to turn off anxiety and stress reactions, and to set the processes of relaxation and rest in motion (see **stress**).

Very often the cause of the stress 'fight or flight' reaction (see **hormones**) is in the unconscious mind and therefore difficult to understand and treat. Autogenics enables pupils to achieve a state of 'passive concentration' through exercises in body awareness and physical relaxation. In this state the symptoms can be alleviated. The technique can be learnt by anyone: it does not involve difficult positions, and can be carried out anywhere, in bed, in the bath, sitting or lying down. Many physical problems which are psychosomatic in origin respond well to autogenics: skin ailments, speech disorders, obesity, depression, insomnia and anxiety, for example. It can also be helpful with some dependencies, hypertension and menstrual problems.

### LEARNING AUTOGENICS
It is necessary to take a preliminary course of lessons. You will be screened for mental and physical suitability, and may need help with learning concentration. A few people suffer abreactions like pain, sudden bursts of laughter or tears which are best coped with by qualified trainers. Avoid 'teach-yourself' tapes, too, for the same reasons. The six basic exercises revolve around learning to listen to your body, becoming aware of, and feeling sensations such as warmth and heaviness.

# AUTOSUGGESTION

*See also: anxiety; autogenics; stress*

Autosuggestion was devised by Emile Coué in the late 19th century. He believed that the key to maintaining good health lay in emphasizing the role of the imagination rather than the will. In educating the imagination, he found that the rapid repetition of mantras to reach deeper than the conscious mind, was helpful in producing a mind clear of all thoughts and worries. His famous incantation 'Every day, in every way, I am getting better and better' has been much misunderstood. It is not intended to help people will themselves better, but to induce deep concentration, stimulating the imagination to believe that the body and mind can improve.

The technique is widely used and can easily be learnt once the underlying principle is understood.

# AVOCADO PEAR

*See also: after-sun preparations; diets; facials*

The avocado pear is so rich that it was once known as midshipman's butter, or butter pear. It contains no cholesterol, up to 50 per cent oil, 11 vitamins and 14 minerals. A 200 g (7 oz) avocado yields approximately 330 Calories. The most nourishing of all fruits, it is often incorporated in diet plans. Its high vitamin content makes it popular for face creams: locally applied vitamins A and E may both be implicated in maintaining skin elasticity. Because avocado oil can penetrate the skin so well it is used in after-sun, skin and hair-conditioning products.

# AWARENESS

*See also: breasts; breast examination; contraception; dependencies; diet; fitness; health and health checks; stress; weight*

Awareness of your physical, mental and emotional state is a major contribution to maintaining good health. Being aware gives you the opportunity to cope with any problems immediately. Check the following regularly (details on these subjects are given in the individual entries):
- **Breast examination** You should do this every month.
- **Smear ('pap') test** You should have these at regular intervals.
- **Contraception** The method you use needs reviewing from time to time, and you need to be examined, too.
- **General health and dental checks** Remember to have these at the necessary intervals, and particularly if you feel especially tired or have unusual symptoms.
- **Stress and anxiety levels** It is important to keep these at an acceptable level. Awareness itself can help reduce them, and various techniques can help with control.
- **Dependencies on drugs, alcohol and cigarettes** Remain aware of the dangers for you and others; take action where necessary.
- **Weight and diet** Check these regularly and adjust your eating habits accordingly.
- **Fitness** Whatever your age you should keep your body operating healthily and at its best.
- **Self-image** A whole variety of problems, including depression, can diminish your self-esteem. Take action to prevent depression from damaging your self-esteem.
- **Hair and skin condition** If these are bad it may well mean that you are under too much stress, over-tired, unwell or that your diet is inadequate. Both problem and symptom need treating to restore a healthy condition.

B

# BACKS

*See also: aches and pains; beds; exercises; posture; pregnancy; sports; stress*

Down the centre of the back runs the spine, which is composed of 7 cervical, 12 thoracic, 5 lumbar, 5 fused sacral and 4 fused coccygeal (fused groups are treated as one bone), totalling 26 vertebrae separated by shock-absorbing cushions of cartilage commonly known as discs. The spine is attached to the pelvis at the lower end and the skull at the other. The spinal cord runs along a narrow channel in the spine. Nerves branch off from it in pairs, connecting it to the rest of the body.

### BACK CARE
Four out of five people will suffer severe back pain at some time in their lives. By following these guidelines they may help you avoid the onset of back trouble.

**DO** look after your back by developing good posture: keep weight evenly distributed to prevent distortion in the spine's shape.

**DON'T** bend over using just your spine and back muscles. Bending awkwardly can damage the spine and the muscles surrounding it. Always bend the knees and hips rather than just the spine when bending down, and especially when lifting up heavy items and children. This puts the emphasis on the pelvic girdle, the largest and strongest bone in the body, which takes the strain in partnership with the spine when it is straight, and therefore at its strongest, and also enables you to use the very large and very strong muscles of the buttocks, hips and thighs.

**DO** measure kitchen units and work tables before buying them and check that they are the correct height for your back whether standing or sitting.

Incorrect — Correct

Incorrect — Correct

**DO** take time to choose the right bed: the ideal bed should be firm and supportive, but not hard, so that pressure on the spine is evenly distributed (see **beds**).

**DON'T** delay in consulting your doctor if back pain is persistent. He may be able to identify a specific cause and alleviate it.

**DO** choose a straight-backed chair if you spend a lot of time at a desk, or place a folded towel or small cushion in the small of your back to support your spine. Look out for new 'posture' seating.

**DO** exercise your abdominal muscles (see **abdomen**) regularly so that they give extra support to the back. Keep shoulders back, down and relaxed to relieve tension at the neck.

■ See ABDOMEN for Core Exercise box page 6 before starting exercise

■ See EXERCISES for Caution Box page 123 before starting exercise

**◄ Exercise A**
This exercise is particularly good for providing upper back stretch and for relaxation, too.
1 Stand tall, head raised and feet hip-width apart. Raise arms straight out in front of you until parallel with the floor. Reach forwards with each hand individually 6 times, then with hands together 6 times.
2 Now interlace fingers, turning palms away from you and push away with hands, simultaneously tucking in buttocks. Repeat 6 times. Gradually increase repeats of the whole exercise to 3 or 4 times.

**◄ Exercise B**
1 Stand with your feet slightly wider apart than shoulder-width, hands loosely on hips. Breathe in, then without moving forwards or backwards, breathe out and bend as far as you can to one side.
2 Without moving your pelvis return to the central position, breathe in and then breathe out as you repeat on the other side. Repeat 12 times on each side.

B

▶ **Exercise C**
You need the assistance of a partner and a broomstick or pole for this exercise.
**1** Kneel on the floor (on a mat or towel to protect knees) with your knees hip-width apart, and your partner standing behind you, feet either side of your knees.
**2** Hold broomstick behind your head with arms wide, reaching up as high as you can. Now ask your partner to hold the stick in the centre. Breathe in, then breathe out gradually, pulling broomstick down to touch the back of your neck, while partner resists. The whole movement should last approximately 10 seconds. Repeat 4 times, building up to 12.

▼ **Exercise D**
**1** Sit on the floor with feet together (preferably sideways on to a mirror so that you can judge your improvement). Use a small towel or teatowel: pass it round your feet, holding an end with each hand.
**2** Lengthen your spine as you breathe in, bend forwards breathing out, work your hands down the towel and keeping your back straight bend from the hips. Repeat. You should be able to go further each time if you are exercising regularly.

▼ **Exercise E**
This is good for beginners, since the lower back is supported and protected. It helps increase your ability to lengthen your back which is important for posture and everyday life as well as for most other exercises.
**1** Find a convenient surface at about hip height (a barre in an exercise studio, a chair back or table top at home), bend your knees and bend forward from the hips to rest your folded arms on the surface. Walk backwards until your trunk is parallel with the floor.
**2** Now gradually straighten knees, keeping back long as you do so. Repeat bending and straightening 6 times, building up gradually to 24 times.

▲ **Exercise F**
**1** Position yourself as for Exercise E, Step 2.
**2** Do several pelvic tilts (tilting your pubic bone up towards your ribcage, then back), breathing out as you tilt.
**3** Now breathe in, breathe out and tilt pelvis, contracting your tummy muscles and allowing your back to round. Repeat 6 times. Gradually build up repeats of the pelvic tilt and muscle contractions to 3 or 4 times.

**▲ Exercise G**
This exercise aids relaxation and is not dangerous for people with lower back problems if taken very gently. Do not strain or force yourself.
**1** Lie on your back on the floor with arms stretched out at right angles to your body, palms flat on the floor, legs bent up to your chest.
**2** With knees together, keeping your shoulders flat on the floor, put legs to one side of your body, your head to the other. Now repeat on other side. Gradually build up repeats from 6 to 24 or more. You will find that legs move further down on each side after a while: to improve this still further do hip and waist exercises too (see **buttocks**, **abdomen**).

**▼ Exercise H**
This exercise is for when you are in good condition, have worked through the other exercises in this section, and are supple at hip, shoulders and in the legs.
**1** Warm up with other exercises above. Stand tall with your feet shoulder-width apart. Hinge forward from the hips until your flat back is held parallel to the floor. Legs should be straight or just slightly bent at the knee. Breathe in. As you breathe out bring your arms through your legs, bend knees, round back at the same time.
**2** Gradually straighten from this curl, leaving your head till last, being careful not to put undue strain on any area. Repeat 6 times, building to 24.

**Bad breath**
See Halitosis

**Badminton**
See Sports

A cooling gel made from natural ingredients such as lemon, orange or cucumber gently applied with a cotton bud refreshes and revitalises tired eyes, relieves under-eye circles and helps reduce puffiness.

# BAGS UNDER EYES

*See also: camouflage; cosmetic surgery; sleep*

Bags under the eyes are caused either by an inherited condition called blepherochalasis which is not reversible or by gradual loss of flexibility due to ageing. Delay the latter with good vitamin supplies and local surface treatments (see **skin** and **diet**). Puffy lower eyelids can be caused by illness, stress and lack of sleep and are reversible: soothe by covering them with dampened cotton wool pads, slices of cucumber, or chamomile tea bags dipped in cool water and lying down for 10-15 minutes.

### REMEDIES
Once bags have formed they can only be camouflaged (see separate entry) or surgically removed (see **cosmetic surgery**). Moisturizing the area softens the hard lines of eyelid bags and wrinkles.

# BALANCE

*See also: ears*

Keeping your physical balance depends on your eyes and your ears. Most important is the inner ear, where semi-circular canals are arranged at right angles to one another and filled with fluid. When the body moves, the fluid in these canals is set in motion, sending impulses to the brain by way of tiny hair cells. The brain then stimulates the appropriate muscles in the body to make necessary postural adjustments. Vigorous movement, spinning or rocking can confuse these messages, causing giddiness and nausea.

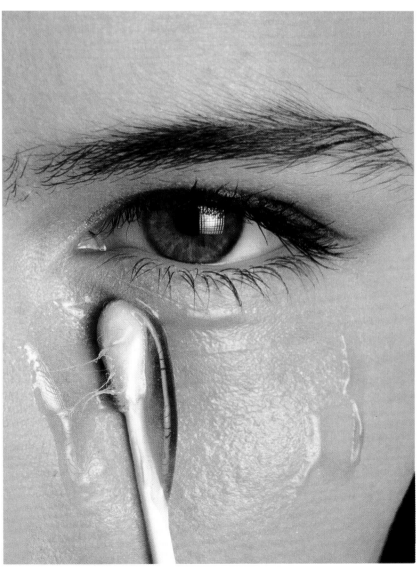

**Balanced diet**
See Diet

**Baldness**
See Alopecia

**Basal cell carcinoma**
See Skin

**Base**
See Make-up

# BATHING AND BATHS

*See also: aromatherapy; body moisturizers; brushes; herbs; hot tubs; hydrotherapy; loofah; mud treatments; pumice; relaxation; saunas; sponges; steam treatments*

Bathing is a very ancient form of recreation, as well as a means of cleansing. The Romans perfected the art of social bathing, a tradition which continues today in countries as varied as Japan and Tunisia.

In recent centuries bathing has generally become a private occupation affording the opportunity to relax, with the bathroom being one of the focal points in the home.

The word 'bathing' has a whole range of connotations. Since it can mean not only cleansing, but also soothing burnt skin, relaxing, pure enjoyment or exercising, there are numerous types of bath ranging from the footbath to the plunge-bath, and numerous ways of bathing:

## Warm baths

- Warm baths cleanse the skin, and moisturize it too: pores open in the heat and take in water. Apply body moisturizer after the bath (see **body moisturizers**) to leave a film of oil on the skin and prevent moisture loss.
- Warmth helps relieve aches and pains and prevent stiffness after exercising: it relaxes muscles, dissipates tension around the neck and back, eases arthritic joints and alleviates tension headaches.
- Warm, not hot is best. Over-hot baths (over 38°C/100°F) put unnecessary strain on the heart as it works to dilate blood vessels in order to cool the body. If you have low blood pressure you may find that over-hot baths make you black out for a second when you get out. Hot baths are weakening, too, and can dry the skin out by washing away too much of the natural sebum which helps hold in moisture.
- A warm bath relaxes you both mentally and physically ready for sleep, and provides the opportunity for time alone which everyone needs each day.
- Warm baths are the most generally popular and the basis of most special-treatment baths (see special baths list).

## Cool baths (98.4°F/37°C or below)

- Cool baths gently wake both you and your muscles up ready for the day.
- Cool baths revitalize the body after work in preparation for the evening, especially when infused with herbs.

## Cold baths

- Cold baths are only advisable for people in good health: like very hot baths, they can strain the heart.
- Cold water provides a sudden shock to the whole system. This type of bath is most successful when used as a cold plunge after a warm shower.
- Cold baths cool down sunburn, preventing it from penetrating still deeper layers of the skin.
- Cold baths temporarily alleviate skin irritation caused, for example, by insect bites, nettle rash and minor allergies.

## SPECIAL BATHS

There are innumerable ancient and modern recipes for baths, some of which are:

- **Herbal baths** These fulfil a variety of functions from stimulation to relaxation. Choose your bath herb or mixture of herbs according to their properties (see **herbs**). You can either steep 2 oz in 600 ml (1 pint) of boiling water for 20 to 30 minutes, then strain the liquid into your bath, or alternatively tie them into a piece of muslin and hang this from the hot tap. You can re-use the bag 3 or 4 times. Cover it with fine silk or cotton print if you want to make it look more attractive.
- **Aromatherapy baths** The addition of 3 to 7 drops of an essential oil to the bath can be healing, relaxing or stimulating and will not make your bath oily. See **aromatherapy** for properties of the oils.
- **Scented oil baths** Few of these oils will disperse into the water, but will float on the surface and cling to your skin as you emerge. A more practical solution is to have a non-oily aromatic bath (see herbal and aromatherapy baths above), followed by an application of body oil or other moisturizer. If you do put oil in your bath be very careful not to slip as you hop out of the tub.
- **Cider or wine vinegar bath** Add a cup of one of these to the bath to relieve dry, itchy skin.
- **Oatmeal or bran baths** Tie a cup of one of these in a square of muslin as for herb baths, above. Both have a cleansing, soothing and whitening effect on the skin.
- **Salt bath** Like seawater, salt baths invigorate. In addition, salt baths help alleviate thrush and other vaginal yeast infections.
- **Milk bath** A cup of powdered skimmed milk in the bath helps nourish and smooth the skin. Cleopatra used ass's milk.
- **Sitz bath** Wrap your upper half in a towel or bathrobe, run enough warm or cool water into the bath to reach your navel and sit in the bath for 10 minutes. Alternatively, have a large bowl of cold water and sit in this and the warm bath alternately, starting with the warm bath. Sitz baths stimulate the circulation, and work equally well to aid sleep at night, taking blood away from the brain, and for waking up in the morning, by stimulating the leg muscles ready for action.

A body rub before a bath or shower is invigorating and also helps to exfoliate (see separate entry) the body skin. Rub sea salt or commercial exfoliating cream into the skin, using circular movements, excluding the face and neck. Rinse off well with cold water for maximum stimulation.

# BEAUTY

Over the centuries the ideal of beauty has been subject to the fluctuations of fashion as much as to individual perceptions.

There have been times when beauty was thought to be found in a perfectly proportioned face or a body whose statistics were voluptuous rather than angular, periods when faces were ornately made-up, or left ethereally pale, when freckles were scorned, or hair adorned. Women were painted, powdered and patched, ducklings striving to be swans. Today, beauty is not merely a by-product of cosmetic artifice, it lies deeper than the skin, emanating from an inner awareness and acceptance of your own innate qualities and values. Concentrating on how to maximize your good points and diminish your faults is more constructive than envying spaghetti-thin models or cover-girls' complexions. Just as you are what you eat, you look as beautiful as you feel. A balanced diet and regular exercise ensure optimum health. Looking after your skin, caring for your hair and using suitable cosmetics are all vital components in good looks too. It is your individual combination of these, not each component part, that makes for beauty – a beauty which is within everyone's grasp.

# B

**Bending**
See Backs

# BEAUTY SALONS AND HEALTH CLUBS

*See also: artificial lashes; artificial nails; facials; faradic exercise; manicure; massage; pedicure; unwanted hair*

Whether you squeeze an hour's facial into a hectic working schedule, or spend a day being smoothed and soothed, time spent in a beauty salon is a luxury every woman deserves. Certain treatments such as Cathiodermie and electrolysis must always be left to experts. Some salons will advise on diet as well as skin care and make-up, others offer beauty 'packages' in which several treatments are available for a set price. Tension can be relieved by a relaxing body massage or by a session in a steam cabinet or bath. Fat can be attacked by vacuum suction massage, muscles stimulated by faradic exercise. Hands and feet always benefit from cosmetic treatment, but foot infections should be referred to a chiropodist. Unwanted hair is effectively removed, broken veins and problem skins treated, and often eyebrows and lashes can be tinted. Salons often have solarium courses to prepare skins for the sun or you can visit a specialist tanning establishment (see **tanning**).

# BEDS

*See also: backs; insomnia; posture; sleep*

A good bed is absolutely essential to good health and good sleep. A bed should provide firm, comfortable support. If it is too soft or too hard your muscles and joints will be strained and unsupported. The price of beds may seem expensive until you remember that you spend approximately a third of each day in bed.

When buying a bed bear in mind the following guidelines for you and your partner.
- You can only evaluate a bed by lying on it, rather than perching on the edge. Take off your shoes and lie full out on your back. In the small of the back there should be no space between you and the bed. If there is, the bed is too hard. If, however, the mattress fills all your body hollows it is too soft. Try lying on your side and front, too: you must be comfortable in every sleeping position.
- You need to allow 15 cm (6 inches) between your feet and the bottom of the bed.
- Heavy people need firmer beds.
- Beds last approximately 10 years.

Bed types vary from futons – Japanese bedding rolls traditionally made from cotton layers – which are very firm, to foam and sprung mattresses of varying firmness. Buying the very best bed you can afford is wise.

# BEESWAX

*See also: buffing; cosmetics; unwanted hair*

Melted beeswax mixed with olive oil and rosewater was the basis of one of the first cleansing creams. Today, because of its softening properties and ability to emulsify when combined with other ingredients, it is included in many creams and lotions.

Hot beeswax is also used to remove unwanted hairs from the body, particularly in delicate areas such as under the arms and the bikini line.

# BEVERLY HILLS DIET

*See also: diet; slimming; weight*

This diet was developed by Judy Mazel in California. Fruit-based, it aims to 'burn, feed and wash' the body. The theory is that the fruits wash out the system and burn up fats and proteins, while the segregation of protein and carbohydrate other than fruit is designed to help the body digest and use the nutrients contained in them at the same time. Mineral supplements are incorporated. Week 1 is a reducing and cleansing diet based on fruits such as pineapple, papaya and watermelon, week 2 is fruit combined with other carbohydrates, and week 3 fruit combined with proteins. The thesis lacks medical credibility, but the diet is very popular.

# BINGEING

*See also: anorexia nervosa; bulimia; slimming*

Bingeing can often be a sign that something is very wrong in your life, either emotionally, at work or in your family. By no means everyone who binges is suffering from bulimia nervosa (see entry) where bingeing has become a regular part of an eating pattern. If you find yourself bingeing halfway through an effective diet ask yourself whether you still really want and need to lose weight: if you do, change to a more attractive plan or seek dietary advice; if not, give it up. If you are not dieting, try to analyze what is worrying you; take action to sort out the problems. Check your diet, too, to ensure that you are getting enough essential food elements, vitamins and minerals (see **diet**). Shortage of carbohydrate can cause a drop in your blood sugar level, and thus a 'bingeing' fit as you suddenly feel very hungry and need to raise it. If your bingeing still continues, see your doctor.

# BIOFEEDBACK

*See also: anxiety; blood pressure; relaxation; stress*

Biofeedback is the process of giving yourself or being given information about normally unconscious bodily processes, such as your body temperature or your heart rate. The word has come to be used for the process of attaching various gadgets to the body to measure its changes, and for the resulting training which enables patients to control aspects of their autonomous nervous system by psychological rather than physiological means. This involves the patient being attached to a biofeedback machine which emits sound, printouts, colour or needle readings. The equipment may be of several types: the electrocardiograph machine (ECG), which records the electrical activity of the heart, can be used for this purpose, although the machines are usually much simpler.

Biofeedback training helps control blood pressure, heartbeat, breathing rate and other functions, making it useful in alleviating conditions like hypertension (high blood pressure). It is beginning to be used by doctors in association with other forms of treatment.

# BIORHYTHMS

*See also: circadian rhythms*

The theory of biorhythms was evolved by Dr Wilhelm Fliess and later developed by Professor Herman Swoboda. The role of biorhythms is not as yet fully understood, however, nor is their existence recognized by the medical profession. The theory is based on 3 cycles: physical, emotional and intellectual, which run throughout everyone's life and govern behaviour. The cycles, which come into operation at birth, are of different lengths, and thus fall in a different relationship to each other each month. The physical cycle is 23 days long, the sensitivity cycle 28 days long, and the intellectual cycle 33 days long. You can have biorhythm charts drawn up for you, or work out your own from books on the subject: remember that charts are not horoscopes, they simply act as a guide to your likely physical, emotional and intellectual state on each day of the month.

The sample chart below indicates how to read your own chart. The numbers at the top are the days of the month. Zero marks the caution line: days on which a cycle passes through the line are likely to be your most vulnerable. You may be clumsy or bad-tempered, particularly when more than one pass through together. Where cycles are below the line, their attributes are in a negative phase, when above the line, their attributes are particularly important and positive.

# BLACKHEADS

*See also: acne; contraception; exfoliation; skin*

A blackhead or comedone is a blocked sebaceous gland in the skin, most often found on the face, but are sometimes found in other areas of pore concentration, such as the upper back or chest. The black colour is not dirt, but oxidated sebum and/or dead skin cells which have become trapped in pores. Inflamed blackheads are one of the symptoms of acne (see separate entry).

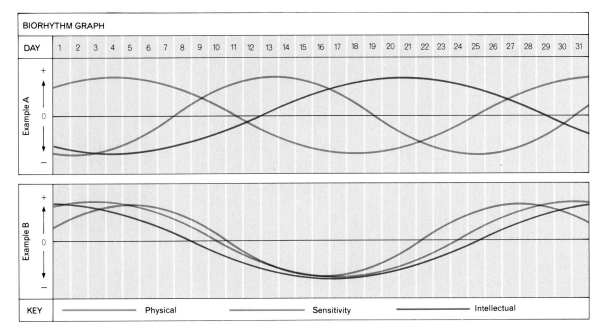

**BIORHYTHM GRAPH**

| DAY | 1 | 2 | 3 | 4 | 5 | 6 | 7 | 8 | 9 | 10 | 11 | 12 | 13 | 14 | 15 | 16 | 17 | 18 | 19 | 20 | 21 | 22 | 23 | 24 | 25 | 26 | 27 | 28 | 29 | 30 | 31 |

KEY — Physical — Sensitivity — Intellectual

B

**Blitz diets**
See Crash diets

**Bleaching**
See Unwanted hair

**Blemishes**
See Camouflage

## CAUSES

- Over-production of sebum by sebaceous glands stimulated by the male hormones or androgens: the sebum hardens and blocks normal secretion.
- Blockage of the normal secretion of the sebaceous glands can also be caused by the accumulation of dead skin cells.

## TREATMENT

- Leave blackheads alone: touching or squeezing will exacerbate the condition and may cause inflammation.
- Keep the skin clean: wash twice a day with medicated soap to help prevent infection. Do not over-wash as this may make it worse.
- Remove dead skin cells regularly (see **exfoliation**).
- Severe cases may require antibiotic treatment over a long period to reduce sebum and bacterial activity in the skin (see **acne**, point 6).

## BLACK SKIN

*See also: camouflage; exfoliation; make-up; skin*

There are many different shades of dark skin ranging from pale olive to blue-black, with varying undertones of reds and yellows. Black skin is thicker, tougher and contains more of the pigment melanin than white skin. It stays smooth and wrinkle-free for longer. Sweat glands are more numerous, and sebaceous glands are larger which may account for its oily appearance and tendency to enlarged pores. In cold weather black skin can become very dry and flaky, looking dull and grey, so regular exfoliation is important. Skin tones are often uneven – darker round the forehead and mouth, lighter on the cheeks and lower lip. Pigmentation problems, especially vitiligo (see entry), are more likely, but can be remedied by camouflage make-up. If you have black skin you should avoid medicated soaps and products containing irritants such as resorcinol (some commercial acne products, for example) which can cause mottling. Otherwise cleanse, tone and moisturize using products according to your skin type. Chemical peeling, dermabrasion and cosmetic surgery are not recommended for black skins since injury causes scars to become raised, and either turn lighter or more deeply pigmented than the surrounding skin.

Special foundations are available, as those made for white skins can appear greyish on black complexions – avoid heavy, greasy types and use a fade-out cream first to even out skin tones. As the skin has natural shine, cosmetics should be matt rather than shimmery or frosted. Use colours with strong pigmentations, not pastels – the lighter the skin tone, the truer colours appear. On darker skins, colours appear more muted. Lips are full but can be made to look smaller, if you wish, by pencilling an outline of

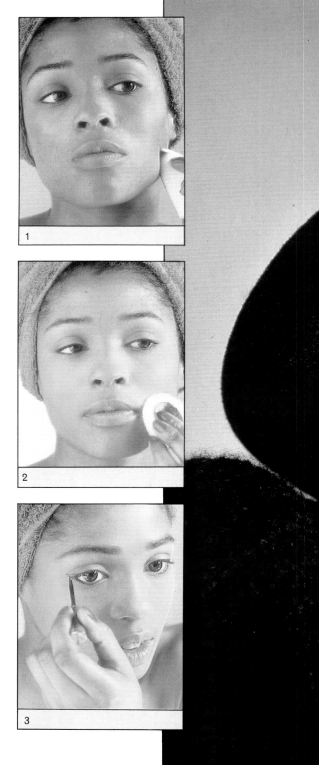

**1** Blend base with a damp sponge under eyes first, then across cheeks, around nose, mouth and neck, evening out skin tone.
**2** Press loose, translucent, waterproof powder all over face and neck for a matt finish which absorbs moisture, lasts all day without need of renewal, and helps prevent shine.
**3** Outline the contour of the eye with black liquid eyeliner working outwards to the corner of the eye to create an almond shaped effect.

**4** Brush matt, pewter eyeshadow along the eyelid, working on the outer corners first. You could use dark kohl inside the lower eyelid rims.
**5** Stroke spicy cinnamon blusher below brow and across cheeks to add warmth.

**6** Mascara top lashes first, starting in the outer corner, brushing up. Start lower lashes on inner corner, brushing down.
**7** Outline lips with a fine lipstick brush then fill in. Dust face with translucent powder to set.

# B

colour darker than your lipstick just inside the lips (see also **lips, lip colour**). Paint with burgundies, plums, deep browns or rich russets. Shape eyes with electric blue or lapis around the eye contour. Burgundies, russets, fuschias, oranges and golds are effective eye colours. Eyelashes tend to be short, so choose a mascara with a small wand to lengthen them. Plum-gold blushers enhance dark skin, and tinted face powders should be chosen as light shades make the skin look grey.

## BLONDES

*See also: cleansing; colouring hair; hair; make-up; moisturizing; toning*

Blonde colouring varies so much that it is difficult to establish rules for skin-care, hair-care and make-up. However, there are two main types of blonde. *The Nordic blonde* is very fair with a pink and white complexion which has a tendency to become dry and flaky, pale eyes, eyebrows and lashes. To keep dry, delicate skin at its best, cleansing morning and night should be light, using mild soap and water or light cleansing cream, followed by alcohol-free toner (see **cleansing** and **toning**).

Skin must be kept well moisturized, too, with additional moisturizer in extreme cold or sun (incorporating sunblock) as it will chap and burn easily. A rich, oil-based moisturizer should be used for the day: a green-tinted moisturizer under foundation helps counteract red blotchiness (see **moisturizing**). If the skin becomes very dry and flaky a stimulating face mask can be used to encourage the glands to produce more sebum (see **masks**).

Due to the sensitive, easily irritated skins of Nordic blondes, strong astringent creams and shampoos should be avoided.

*The Mediterranean blonde* has more of an affinity with the darker brunette; darker skin with more natural protection as it produces more sebum, darker eyes, eyebrows and lashes. These blondes tend to have oilier skins than Nordic blondes as their sebaceous glands are more active. Check your skin type carefully. Thorough cleansing is important, using a cleanser containing grains helps to clean pores thoroughly. Regular exfoliation is important, too. Use an alcohol-based (if your skin is not sensitive) or alcohol-free toner and moisturize frequently with a light, water-based product.

Blonde hair tends to be fine and become greasy easily: wash daily if you want to, using a mild shampoo designed for frequent use. Chamomile brings out your blondest highlights.

Well planned make-up applied to the right areas will bring shape to the face and emphasize eyes and lips. Choose make-up colours with care to guard against looking overly made-up. Heavy, dark colours tend to drown you out if you are very blonde, but pastels can be insipid. Don't be afraid to experiment to achieve a look which you like and will suit

you best. The general rule for blondes is to apply cosmetics lightly and evenly, being careful to blend one colour into the next. Warm colours work well with a darker blonde complexion: soft browns and peaches, and strong pales – such as blue and pink can create a dramatic effect on a pale complexion.

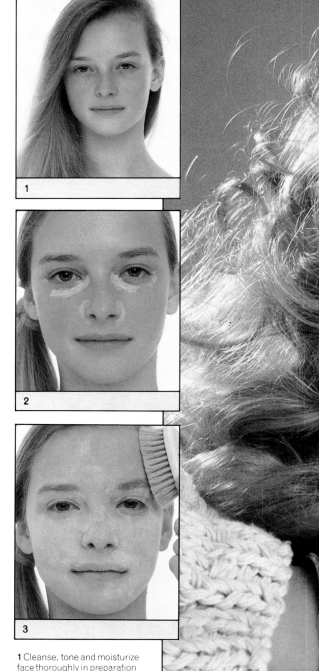

**1** Cleanse, tone and moisturize face thoroughly in preparation for make-up.
**2** Apply flesh-toned concealer beneath eyes and around nose and blend in.
**3** Dust powder all over face for a natural, matt look. Brush off excess with a soft brush.
**4** Blend peach eyeshadow below brow and across lids. Apply grey eyeliner, then soft brown shadow shaded up the lid and navy powder shadow smudged over edges of upper and lower lids. Add a touch of grey shadow in outer corners.

If hair has been coloured blonde the skin may be darker than that usually common to blondes and suitable for heavier make-up using darker, brighter colours. Follow the guidelines for Mediterranean blondes. Ensure that eyebrows do not clash with dyed hair, and, if they stand out too darkly you may want to colour them too – have them professionally coloured, or use a commercially available product with care. Lashes can be pale: have them tinted too, brown rather than black, for a more natural look than mascara. Moisturized foundation is an excellent skin protection, especially in cold weather.

5 Apply glossy black mascara, combing through upper and lower lashes when they are dry for a more natural look.

6 Now apply soft peach powder blush out from the cheek to the temples, to give a natural glow.

7 With a lip brush apply rose pink lipstick to lower lip then upper – blot with a tissue for a matt look.

Add a touch of gloss to centre of lower lip to add a little shine for night-time glamour.

# BLOOD PRESSURE

*See also: aerobics; biofeedback; diet; exercise*

Blood pressure is the force of blood against the walls of the major arteries, normally measured at the arm's brachial artery where pressure most nearly corresponds to that of blood leaving the heart. A dual reading is taken to record pressure for both the contracting and resting heart. Pressure varies with age: a normal young adult pressure is about 120/80.

Hypotension is abnormally low pressure which can accompany some illnesses, but is a bonus in general healthy life. Hypertension, abnormally high pressure, increases the risk of heart disease, strokes and kidney disease. Generally speaking the incidence of hypertension is higher in men than women. Among men blood pressure tends to increase progressively from the early twenties, while with women the rise is more marked after the menopause. In younger women, it can remain symptomless until exacerbated by, for example, pregnancy or strenuous exercise (hypertension puts extra pressure on the heart and exercise increases this still further). In cases of sustained hypertension your doctor will prescribe drugs such as beta blockers, often in association with diuretics. These control pressure and its effects artificially, and if taking such drugs you should not rely on the pulse-rate method of controlling exercise (see **exercises**). New 'danger factors' are constantly being discovered: below are some of the better-established guidelines for hypertension.

### AVOIDING HYPERTENSION
- Have your blood pressure checked regularly; say every 3 years before you reach 35, then annually. This is easily done by your doctor. Additional readings should be taken before you start taking the contraceptive pill and every time you renew your prescription, when pregnant and each time you renew your hypertension drug prescription. Note that the combined contraceptive pill has the effect of raising blood pressure as well as increasing the likelihood of thrombosis (clotting). Women between the ages of 35 and 40, when blood pressure increases naturally, should move on to another contraceptive method. Annual readings, whatever your age, are advisable if you have diabetes, or if your parents had high blood pressure. If both parents suffered from high blood pressure their children have about a 50:50 chance of developing it later in life.
- Smokers are among those most at risk of developing hypertension, and any smoker diagnosed as having high blood pressure will have been strongly advised by their doctor to try and give up smoking, or at least cut down significantly.
- A diet high in polyunsaturates and low in saturated fats is widely thought to help reduce the risks of developing hypertension. This involves cutting down on animal fats, particularly fatty cuts of meat and full fat milk and cheeses, and eating more fish, lean meats, skimmed milk and so on.
- Reduce your salt intake: salt is thought to be a major food hazard in hypertension, particularly in severe cases. Avoid high-salt foods such as crisps and anchovies, reduce the amount of salt added in cooking and break the habit of adding it to cooked food. Reduce sugar, too. Recent research indicates that combined with a high salt intake sugar may also have a detrimental effect.
- Keep fit: regular exercise strengthens the heart, lowers blood pressure, counteracts stress – another danger factor in hypertension.
- Don't let yourself get overweight; this exacerbates and can even cause hypertension.
- Eat plenty of fruits, vegetables and grains. Get plenty of calcium, too, preferably from low-fat foods like cottage cheese. Reduce your caffeine intake.
- Include garlic (or tastefree capsules) in your diet: it thins the blood and aids circulation.
- Biofeedback (see separate entry) has been found to help reduce blood pressure: patients follow readings on biofeedback machines which document their progress in controlling the autonomous nervous system. Some other therapies such as meditation, autosuggestion, autogenics and self-hypnosis have been found helpful, too. Do not try these as an alternative to drugs prescribed by your doctor.

# BLOTCHY SKIN

*See also: blushing; circulation; massage*

Extreme nervousness, apprehension, embarassment or even excitement can cause blushing which manifests itself as outbreaks of red, blotchy skin on the face, neck or chest. These areas may also feel very warm to the touch. Such attacks should not last long and will certainly disappear overnight. If, however, they are more prolonged, they may be the sign of an allergy, of bad circulation, or of an infection such as German Measles etc. If the blotchiness is sore or itchy, or is accompanied by feeling unwell, see your doctor.

Alcohol, which dilates the blood vessels, and smoking, which constricts them, can also cause blotchiness. Using abrasive treatments on the face during exfoliation can irritate sensitive skins, while the effects of the sun combined with taking antibiotics or wearing certain cosmetics or scents causes blotchy areas on photosensitive skins.

Skin which is prone to red blotchy patches can be toned down by regular moisturizing which alleviates dryness, and by the use of a green-tinted pre-foundation cream which helps to camouflage redness and blushing and unequal skin tone.

# BLUSHER

*See also: cheeks; colour choice; cosmetics; gels; make-up; rouge*

Blusher warms and enlivens the skin, helping to accentuate cheekbones and contoured areas. It should tone with your foundation and lip colours, and must be applied lightly – colour can always be intensified – and in the right place (see below). Blusher need not be restricted to the cheeks. For an all-over glow, whisk lightly over forehead, temples and browbone – and add a touch to the chin. Use cream blusher on the lips for complete co-ordination with your cheek colour. Always blend carefully to avoid hard wedges of colour.

### CHOOSING A BLUSHER

- Cream and liquid blushers are good for young, dry skins as they give added lubrication. Blend in with the fingertips after applying foundation, but before powder. Applied with the fingertip, they can be used as a lip colour. Cream blushers in stick form tend to drag and are less easy to blend in to dry skins.
- Powder blushers are similar in composition to pressed face powder, and should be applied after powdering the face, using a large soft brush to spread colour evenly. In hot and humid climates, powder blushers have the most staying power.
- Gels are water-based products and give a transparent, natural glow which looks good on highly coloured, freckled or bronzed complexions. They should be used over moisturizer or foundation and without powder. Gels can cause dryness on sensitive skins, so try out carefully before buying.
- One of the oldest forms of blusher is rouge, a solid cream (see **rouge**).
- Always test blusher on your cheekbones before buying to see whether you like the colour and finish and to check that it blends into the skin smoothly. The skin on the back of the hand is quite different in colour and texture and is not an accurate guide.
- Colour should blend away evenly and gradually without leaving grease or glitter and without setting into a hard-looking streak. Check by looking in a mirror from the front and side of the face.
- For fair skins choose rosy, pink shades with a hint of blue; oriental, yellowish skins look good with peachy blushers, while dark skins suit brick or wine shades. Remember that the deeper the colour, the more subtlety is needed in blending in the edges to avoid a harsh, unattractive streak of colour.
- Don't ever rely on just one shade of blusher. Choose two shades so that you can mix them to match or tone with your lip colour.
- Blusher lasts longest and has the best colour intensity if you apply cream blusher on top of

The natural glow of gel blusher enlivens most complexions, and can be used over foundation, or on moisturized skin. Blend the colour following cheekbone contours.

Applied over the face powder blushers should be blended in with a gentle circular motion. They create a soft matt finish and help to reduce shine.

foundation. Set with a light dusting of powder applied with a large brush.
- For sensitive, allergy-prone skin choose a hypo-allergenic blusher.
- For a dramatic evening make-up which will dazzle under more subdued lighting, intensify your appearance by choosing a blusher several shades brighter than your daytime choice, and compliment it with a brighter lip colour.

### APPLYING BLUSHER

Use a large soft brush for powder blushers, or fingertips for gels and liquids. Apply a small amount of colour high on the cheekbones, below the eyeball. Blend outward, away from the nose, but not too near the hairline. Finish with a light layer of translucent powder, unless you have used a gel.

**Body massage**
See Massage

**Body wave**
See Curling and
straightening hair

**Body alignment**
See Posture

# BLUSHING

*See also: blotchy skin*

Blushing is emotionally triggered, by shame, embarrassment, anger, sexual arousal, even happiness. Generally only the face is affected, although sometimes the blush may extend to cover the neck and upper chest. Very fair-skinned people are particularly prone to blushing. If it worries you, try to avoid situations and subjects which make you blush and tell your friends that you really hate blushing and prevent them from using your problem as a source of amusement for themselves. If you feel as if you are about to blush, relax: fear of the blush makes it become intenser and last longer.

Far from being a disfigurement, blushing has traditionally been regarded as a sign of life, beauty and youth as in Gray's *Elegy Written in a Country Churchyard*: "Full many a flower is born to blush unseen, And waste its sweetness on the desert air."

# BODY IMAGE

*See also: anorexia; bingeing; body type; self-image; weight*

Your body image, held in the association areas of the brain, influences the amount you eat, the way you dress, the amount you exercise, even your sexuality. Your view of yourself may be far removed from reality: anorexics, for example, often imagine themselves to be obese when in fact they are painfully thin. Fashion now tends to emphasize tall, slender, healthy looks. Almost everyone can achieve fitness, but no one can change his or her body type (see separate entry). Increasing the amount of exercise you take, starting a new sport or dance class can help keep you in trim and provide enjoyment. Exercises for individual problem areas can help. Shape them up (see **arms, legs**, etc.) too.

In order to have confidence in yourself you need to adjust your body image to reality. Most women need to change their eating habits in their mid teens when puberty has taken place and the major growth spurt is over. Failure to do this can start a chain of dieting, perhaps combined with bingeing, which can culminate in bulimia or anorexia nervosa. Be aware of the dangers: concentrate on eating healthily (see **diet, eating habits**), check your weight and if it really is a problem consult your doctor or dietician for advice. If it is not a problem, try to stop thinking about it. Most important, work on your overall self-image. Be proud of yourself as a whole person. Wear clothes in shapes and colours you find exciting. Your body image may be at a particular low after illness or surgery. Try to accept your physical limitations.

# BODY MOISTURIZERS

*See also: aloe vera; honey; hypo-allergenic products; lanolin; massage; moisturizing; skin*

Some of your natural body oil, sebum, is removed every time you wash with soap and water. Exposure to sun, wind and wintry weather conditions reduces the water content in the upper layers of the skin, too. Body moisturizers help redress both types of moisture imbalance and slow the skin's visible ageing by providing a protective, waterproof layer: they combine with sebum on the skin's surface. The frequency with which you should use body moisturizers varies according to your skin type, how frequently you wash and how much exposure your body skin has had. They should be applied more generously when the skin is exposed to extremes of climate: when sailing, skiing, in hot sun, and in very cold, windy or humid weather, or just whenever skin feels dry or taut. See **moisturizing** for advice on dealing with face and neck skin.

### CHOOSING YOUR BODY MOISTURIZER
There is a very wide variety of body moisturizers on the market:
- **Milks** Lightest of all, these are usually water-based and are particularly suitable for people with oily skins, whose sebum supplies are good.
- **Greaseless lotions** Light too, again chiefly for oily skins, and suitable for frequent bathers. The lotion dries very fast and is quick to apply.
- **Mousses (aerated foams)** Lying somewhere between milk and cream in weight, more often water than oil-based, these are fun and easy to apply, and light enough for any skin type.
- **Creams** Richest of all, these are usually oil-based, often containing an aromatic oil like hazelnut or almond. They are particularly suitable for dry or frequently exposed skins.
- **Oils** Used for moisturizing oily skins and for massage or olfactory benefits on all skins.

There are no hard and fast rules about choosing body moisturizers, but the above notes will guide you towards the best for your skin type.

Specialized products include: hypo-allergenic and perfume-free products for sensitive skins; honey and beeswax products for dry skins; chemical-free aloe vera products for all skin types and Japanese silk- and seaweed-based moisturizers which are believed to make the skin extra-soft. Most scent companies produce body moisturizers, so you can have one which matches your favourite fragrance.

If you are going on holiday, choose an unperfumed facial moisturizer which you can use for face and body – never use scented body moisturizers on the face (see also **after-sun preparations**).

NOTE Many body moisturizers contain lanolin to which some people are allergic. Choose with great

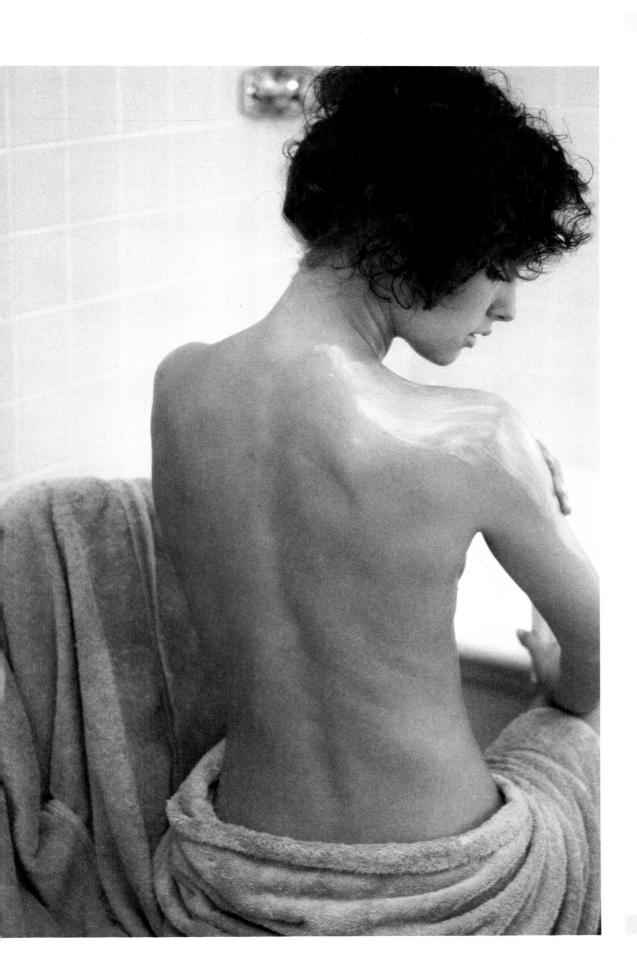

B

**Body sculpture/ contouring**
See Cosmetic surgery

**Boils**
See Diet; Stress; Vitamins

care. If you don't buy hypo-allergenic products and ingredients are not listed on the pack, ask the sales staff what they contain.

### USING YOUR MOISTURIZER

1   Moisturizers are most efficiently absorbed by warm, slightly damp skin. So first relax in a warm, not hot, bath: over-hot water has a drying effect on the skin.
2   Pat yourself thoroughly dry with a towel.
3   Apply body moisturizer while you are still warm, as your pores will be open and therefore absorb more. Spread the body moisturizer on to the palms of your hands and massage in well: this will help increase circulation as well as nourish the skin. Pay particular attention to the thighs, arms, feet, elbows, and any very dry areas.

### USING BODY OIL

Oils should be rubbed gently into warm skin to get the maximum benefit from the oil. Choose an essential oil or massage oil for additional benefits. Avoid using oil on your skin if you have to get dressed immediately afterwards: they are more slowly absorbed and may mark clothing.

## BODY ODOUR

*See also: anti-perspirants; deodorants; feet; halitosis; mouthwashes; personal hygiene; sweat*

Body odour is caused by the evaporation of bacteria-laden moisture molecules from the skin's surface. Sweat itself has no intrinsic smell (see separate entry), but picks up both the natural, individual smell of the skin as well as the smell of bacteria on the skin's surface.

### AVOIDING ODOUR

- Odour-laden sweat is easily trapped in hairy areas, so these need to be kept particularly clean. It can also be trapped by clothes, as it disperses with evaporation. Wear natural fibres, which allow moisture to escape, next to the skin wherever possible.
- Keep clean, have a bath or shower every day, but avoid too many deodorant soaps: they destroy helpful bacteria as well as odorous ones.
- Anti-perspirants reduce actual sweating (see separate entry). Deodorants (see separate entry) reduce bacterial activity and therefore odour.
- Anti-perspirants often contain zinc or manganese which impede sweating in the gland. Ensure that you eat plenty of foods containing these minerals (see separate entry) as they work from the inside, too.
- Smelly feet can be problematic. Keep scrupulously clean. Choose natural fibres, which allow moisture to escape, for socks and tights wherever possible. Change them every day and

wash them frequently. Deodorant sprays work just like underarm types. Medicated insoles and deodorant-impregnated socks can also be helpful.
- If your body odour presents a serious problem, consult your doctor. It may be a symptom of dietary problems or medical problems.

## BODY TYPE

*See also: weight*

Everyone falls into a body type category: ectomorph, mesomorph or endomorph and, while there is a degree of overlapping between types, one is usually predominant. Losses or gains in weight cannot change type: a fat endomorph is just that – not a mesomorph.

**Ectomorph** Small-framed with long limbs and a lean, angular outline. Shoulders, hips and joints are narrow. There is little muscle or body fat and few curves.

**Mesomorph** Compact, medium to large frames, with broad shoulders and well-developed pelvic girdle. Muscles are often well developed, particularly at calf and forearm.

**Endomorph** Heavy-framed and generally shorter-limbed than the other two types, with a lower centre of gravity, wider hips and a higher proportion of body fat to muscle.

## BRAN

*See also: diet; fibre*

Unrefined bran, the outer layers of wheat grain, is a very important constituent of the diet. It provides vitamins B and minerals, but more important is its fibrous nature which helps prevent digestive tract problems such as constipation, diverticulitis (inflamed pouches in the lower bowel) and haemorrhoids, by keeping the tract's muscles healthy and speeding the progress of food through the body. Bran is also implicated in the prevention of heart disease: it reduces absorption of cholesterol into the system.

Don't rely solely on processed bran breakfast cereals: sprinkle a tablespoonful of unprocessed bran each day on food, it is particularly palatable on cereal, soup and in yogurt. Don't rely solely on bran for fibre, either, or your absorption of calcium, iron and zinc may be impaired by the phytate it contains. Eat plenty of pulses (see entry for details of types), wheat, oats and high-fibre fruits and vegetables: cook potatoes in their skins whether baked or boiled and eat skin as well as flesh since it is an excellent source of fibre.

# BRAS

*See also: breasts; exercise; mastectomy*

Although the breast has muscle beneath it, it is its ligaments which give it shape. These ligaments do not have the resilience of muscle and need support to avoid sagging: only the smallest-breasted can afford to go braless, especially when exercising.

### YOUR BRA SIZE

■ Work out your body size by measuring your ribcage and adding 12.5 cm (5 inches). This measurement is rounded up to the nearest even number – 32, 34, etc. – as most bras are adjustable to approximately 2.5 cm (1 inch). To find your cup size subtract your body size from your overall chest measurement. If there is 2.5 cm (1 inch) difference your cup size is A, 5 cm (2 inches) difference B, 7.5 cm (3 inches) difference C, 10 cm (4 inches) difference D. If in doubt, ask advice in your underwear/lingerie department or shop.

### CHOOSING A BRA

■ If your bra does not fit properly it will give you little support. If possible, try it on before buying: failing this, check before purchasing that you can change it if it does not fit.
■ If there are bulges over the bra top it is too small or the straps too tight.
■ If there are bulges beneath the bra it is too small.
■ If the bra rides up your back it is not providing enough support for the weight of the breasts: choose a style with a deeper band around the body as this provides greater support.

### SPECIAL BRA REQUIREMENTS

**Small breasts** Need no underwiring and are well suited to all-stretch cotton and Lycra, or fine lace styles with narrow back and shoulder straps. Choose a style with light padding if you want to enlarge your shape.

**Medium breasts** Choose a style with a deeper back, and preferably with light underwiring.

**Large breasts** Choose a style with underwiring, preferably with support right around the ribcage beneath the breasts.

**During pregnancy and when breastfeeding** Breasts enlarge and increase in weight at this time. You will need bras in a larger size, designed to give good support: remeasure yourself, as described above. While feeding, wear either a front-fastening style, or one with removable front sections.

**After mastectomy** If you are wearing a prosthesis, choose a more highly cut support bra in your normal size so that the top of the prosthesis is hidden. After breast reconstruction you should be able to wear your original bra size.

**For sport** Look for both support and yet plenty of flexibility to avoid any discomfort and damaging strain on ligaments.

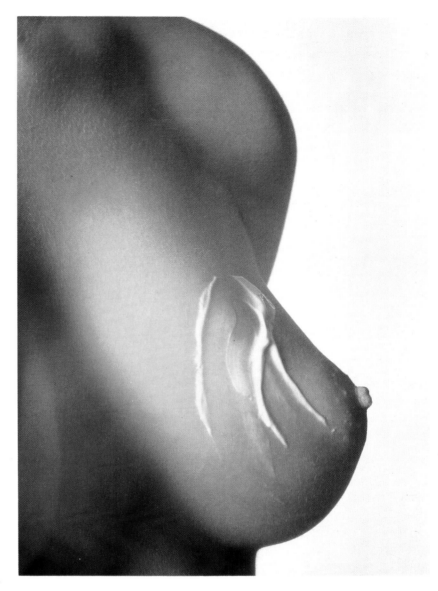

# BREASTS

*See also: bras; breast examination; exercises*

The breasts, which develop at puberty, extend from the second to the sixth rib on either side of the breast bone and are composed of milk glands encased in a surround of fatty tissue, supported by suspensory ligaments, called the ligaments of Ashley Cooper, which give breasts their line, support and lift them too.

While the size of the breasts remains fairly constant, they can be affected by dieting, the contraceptive pill and the phases of the menstrual cycle, becoming fuller and slightly tender just before the start of a period. They also increase in size during pregnancy and breastfeeding.

The biggest enemy of firm breasts is gravity and lack of support (see **bras**). Excess skin and tissue can be removed from large, cumbersome or very

drooping breasts by cosmetic surgery (see separate entry), while small breasts can be increased by implants. In a few cases mastectomies can also be followed by reconstructive implants.

### BREASTFEEDING

During pregnancy the breasts swell in preparation for breastfeeding. For babies, the overall benefits of breastfeeding, even for a short period, are undisputed; the advantages for mothers include a faster weight loss due to energy requirements of milk production. Feeding stimulates tightening of the lower abdomen muscles and stimulates the production of oxytocin, a pituitary hormone which helps the uterus to contract. Long-term effects on breasts vary, and damage is minimized by a good support bra worn all the time, even in bed. There is a tendency for breasts to become smaller and less firm after breastfeeding. Excessive weight gain in pregnancy (or at any time) will make this worse. Help avoid stretch marks by eating a good diet in pregnancy (see **diet**) which will help prevent excessive weight gain, and avoiding engorgement when feeding. Take advice from your health visitor or doctor about feeding and expressing and act promptly when breasts begin to feel full. Effects are more pronounced with successive babies and the longer breastfeeding is maintained. Given the right help, most women who choose to can establish breastfeeding, and with adequate nutrition and rest, do so for as long as they wish to make the commitment. Occasional feeds can be expressed by pump and fed by bottle to the baby. Unprescribed medication, immoderate alcohol intake and smoking are inadvisable while breastfeeding.
NOTE Breastfeeding is not a contraceptive.

### EXERCISE

Because the breasts are not composed of muscle, exercise does little to preserve shape and tone. Nevertheless it is important to keep the major underlying muscle, the pectoralis, toned to provide a firm base for the breasts.

■ See EXERCISES for Caution Box page 123 before starting exercise

◄ Exercise A
1 Stand tall with shoulders down and feet shoulder-width apart. Make sure that you keep your spine straight, not arched, throughout. With arms straight, make a scissor action at waist level, as illustrated.
2 Now make the scissor action at chest level, then at head level. Work several of each with an easy swinging action. Increase the number of scissor actions gradually to a total of about 60, which means about 20 at each level. The action should be a controlled swing, not an abandoned fling.

■ See ABDOMEN for Core Exercise box page 6 before starting exercise

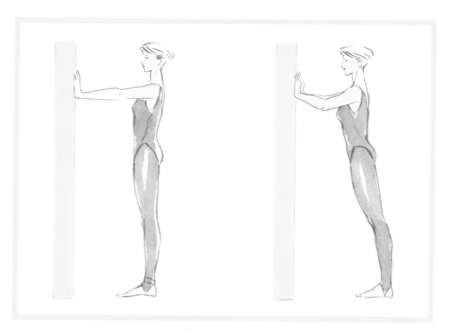

◄ Exercise B
1 Stand with long back, head raised and shoulders down, at arm's length from the wall. Hands should be at shoulder height, held straight.
2 Keep body straight (don't sag), breathe in and lean body as close as possible to the wall. Now breathe out and push back to your original standing position. Repeat 10 times at first, building up to 30.
   Once you are proficient at this exercise, move on to more advanced versions where gravity makes the movement harder. First use a (stable) table edge, then the floor. When working on the floor, begin with your lower legs flat on the floor, then move on to the traditional, straight-body version. Remember to start with between 6 and 10 repeats of each, building up again later.

# BREAST EXAMINATION

*See also: breasts; health and health checks*

All women should examine their breasts every month, ideally just after the menstrual period has ceased. By doing this you will become familiar with their shape and structure and be able to pick up any significant changes at the earliest possible moment. It is important to realize that breasts are naturally a little lumpy and granular to the touch.

## SELF-EXAMINATION
1  Stand naked in front of a large mirror, concentrating on exactly how your breasts look. Then place your hands on top of your head and, turning slowly to the left and right, look for any dimpling, puckering or swelling.
2  Put your hands on your hips and press firmly to stretch the pectoral muscles and look for any dimpling. Keeping your hands on your hips, lean forward so that your breasts fall straight downwards. Look for any tautness in the skin tissue.
3  Lie on the floor or bed with a folded towel or pillow beneath your left shoulder. Let your left arm lie beside your body. Examine your left breast with the flat surface of the first three fingers of your right hand; this technique is known as palpation. Press the breast tissue firmly but gently towards the chest wall, starting just above the nipple, rotating your fingers in small concentric circles. Make sure that you feel every part of the breast, beneath as well as above.
4  Place your left arm above your head and repeat the above examination, paying particular attention to the upper part of the breast as it extends into the armpit.
5  Repeat steps 3 and 4 on your right breast, using your left hand.

## WARNING SIGNS
▪ A lump that suddenly appears: anything suspicious should be checked immediately by your doctor. At least 90 per cent of lumps are benign tumours, scar tissue, blocked milk ducts, cysts (most common in early adulthood) or fibroadenomas (benign fibrous tissue lumps most common between the ages of 25 and 35). In fact, even less than one in 10 lumps found are malignant. Manual examination alone cannot determine the nature of the lump.
**Treatment** The lump will either be mammogram x-rayed, and may also be aspirated (fluid syringed out of it) or an open biopsy will be performed on it (minor surgery to remove a sample of lump tissue). The fluid or tissue will be tested. Treatment for non-malignant lumps varies. Some disappear of their own accord. Some are best removed to avoid the very remote chance of it masking a new lump. No

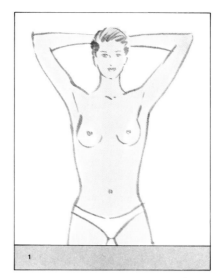
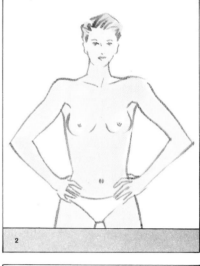
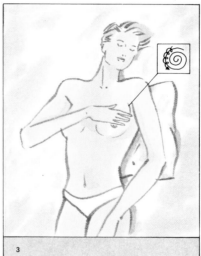
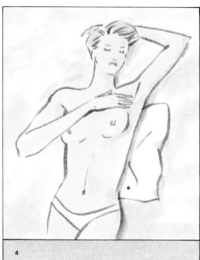

extensive area of flesh should need removing, so scarring will be minimal and the shape of the breast should not be affected. Cysts are often treated purely by aspiration, or with hormone or vitamin E or B6 treatment to reduce the size of the cyst. If the lump does prove to be malignant, swift action can prevent both losing too much breast tissue and possible spread of the malignancy.
▪ Thickening, dimpling or puckering of the skin which could indicate the presence of a lump, or any inversion of the nipple which is unusual.
▪ A bloody or brown discharge from the nipple. Where discharge occurs from both nipples it is much less likely to be due to cancer. Consult your doctor if the nipple is sore or ulcerated.
▪ Sore or inflamed lymph glands in the armpit or around the breast which do not subside within three weeks.

## BREAST CANCER SCREENING
You should ask your doctor or gynaecologist for an annual manual examination: he or she may find something you have missed.
    If your doctor feels you are a high-risk candidate

for breast cancer he or she may recommend an annual breast X-ray mammogram, which can detect tumours and pick up between a quarter and a third of all breast cancers before they become large enough to be felt. However, not all cancers show on these special X-rays so a combined examination is best.

**Broken veins**
See Thread veins

**Brown spots**
See Liver spots

■ See EXERCISES for Caution Box page 123 before starting exercise

# BREATHING

*See also: exercise; pregnancy; relaxation*

The art of breathing properly is vital to the correct functioning of the heart, good health and successful exercising. The way in which you breathe is a reflection of your emotional state as well as your physical condition: when angry, your breathing becomes shallow and rapid; when excited, you take longer out-breaths and breathe in more quickly; when depressed, you continue to take air in and tend to delay letting it out again. By reappraising how to use your lungs, ribs and interconnecting muscles, you can reap the benefits of improved posture, increase fitness and achieve relaxation and peace of mind in a matter of moments.

## BREATHING TECHNIQUES
One of the quickest ways to relax properly is through various breathing techniques. Yoga places particular importance on correct breathing as an effective way of banishing stress and tension. While the yogic practice of deep breathing is best learnt from a qualified teacher, the establishment of steady rhythmic breathing is easily achieved.

If you feel particularly upset or agitated, try breathing in over a count of 12 (preferably by an open window), holding for 12, and releasing the air with an audible 'haah': this will instantly calm you.

## BREATHING EXERCISES
Breathing properly is essential to good health, and breathing correctly during exercises increases their beneficial quality, too. The vital thing to remember about breathing during exercise is that generally the out-breath is the all-important one for the most active part of the exercise: you should breathe out on the effort. When you first start exercising, your breathing may well be erratic and you may find that you hold your breath for the duration of the exercise, leading to dizziness and nausea. Gradually, however, breathing in before movement, breathing out during it, will become second nature. And you will find that with many exercises there is no safe alternative: in abdominal exercises, for example, the torso plumped up by an in-breath would not be able to curl up and curling up with an in-breath is also hazardous since the increase in pressure acting upon the abdominal contents may lead to pelvic floor injuries and/or hernias. Generally, you should breathe in as the front of the body expands, breathe out as it contracts.

◄ **Exercise A**
**1** Stand very tall keeping your back long and straight. Put one hand on your upper chest, one on your abdomen. Take a deep breath and watch which hand moves out first. If it is the top one, you are not breathing really deeply and making use of the whole ribcage area for expansion. Concentrate on really deep breaths, and you will find that the abdomen begins to move out more as you practise.
**2** Now put your hands on your back just above the waistline, breathe in and feel how your ribcage expands at the back too. Do this exercise whenever you feel tense, or before you embark on an active exercise routine.

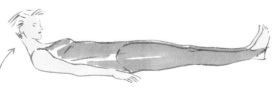

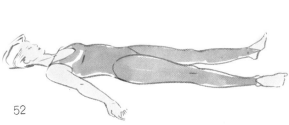

◄ **Exercise B**
**1** Lie flat on your back on the floor, with feet together and body straight. Lift your toes and without lifting legs off the floor, lift your head and check that you are lying in a straight line.
**2** Now lie back, part legs slightly and allow legs and feet to roll comfortably outwards from the hip joints. Shut your eyes and breathe deeply and easily. Notice how your breathing becomes more even and shallower as you relax and your lack of movement means that the body needs less oxygen.

# BRIDAL BEAUTY

*See also: beauty; colour choice – cosmetics; hair; hairstyles; make-up*

Your beauty plans, like all your other wedding preparations, must be organized well in advance of the great day: but before you decide on a dramatic transformation, remember that your fiancé loves you the way you are, and that he certainly doesn't want to see a complete stranger heading towards him down the aisle!

## HAIR
Do not have a last minute perm or drastic haircut; if you want a change, do it well in advance to avoid disappointment. If not, keep your hair trimmed regularly and condition it well so that it is shining and healthy. If you are having your hair, head-dress or veil arranged by your hairdresser on the day, make sure they have several practice sessions beforehand, and that you are happy with the results.

## SKIN

Several visits to a beauty salon for deep-cleansing treatments can be most beneficial, but go well in advance as impurities are drawn out of the skin which can lead to spots for a few days immediately after the treatment. If your skin is not at its best, your make-up will not look as good as it could, so get plenty of sleep, drink plenty of water and fruit juices and make sure it is well moisturized.

## MAKE-UP

A good base is very important. Avoid a heavy foundation that will clog and 'crack' during the day, instead of looking flawless and natural. Depending on your skin, try out a light, moisturized foundation before the day. If you have freckles or skin in glowing health, try a tinted moisturizer for a very natural look. When planning eye, cheek and lip colours bear in mind your natural colouring and the colours of dresses and flowers.

## GUIDELINES FOR THE DAY

1   Cover any blemishes and shadows under the eyes with a cover-up cream, preferably a shade lighter than your foundation.
2   Use a wedge-shaped sponge to blend foundation thoroughly on your face and into the neck to avoid unsightly 'tide marks'.
3   Any blemishes that still show can be hidden by dabbing on cover-up cream with a fine brush.
4   To set the base, pat on loose powder (translucent is most natural) and brush away excess.

For ideas on suitable eye, lip and cheek colours, look in new magazines and take advice at beauty counters. Do plenty of trial runs to make sure you are not only happy with the results, but also well practised. Remember that a white or cream wedding dress can be draining to the complexion, so give your make-up a healthy glow of colour while avoiding looking over made-up.

# BROWN FAT

*See also: metabolic rate; weight*

Brown fat accounts for about 2 per cent of adult body fat and is stored mainly around the kidneys and between the shoulder blades. It is a more metabolically active form of adipose tissues than white fat and its main function seems to be to create heat by breaking down *triglycerides* into fatty acids and *glycerol* – the normal fat breakdown process for storage and use – then rebuilding them again. It also increases the metabolic rate by 5-10 per cent after meals. Brown fat helps keep babies warm: unlike adults, they do not shiver to create extra heat. Experiments on rats show that high brown fat levels help prevent obesity, but it is not yet known whether this applies equally to humans, nor how humans can increase their supply, nor why human brown fat levels vary.

# BRUISING

*See also: herbs; witch hazel*

Bruises are produced when a blow to the body crushes or breaks the blood vessels under the skin and blood seeps into the surrounding tissue. The area appears red at first and then bluish-black, turning greenish-yellow as the escaped blood is broken down and re-absorbed by the body. Once a bruise has appeared, little can be done to speed up its disappearance but the prompt application of ice packs or cold swabs may lessen severity. A compress of comfrey, a cooling witch hazel massage and the essential oils of camphor and hyssop may also help minimize bruising symptoms. A bad sprain can appear just as a very swollen and painful bruise; see your doctor if this occurs.

# BRUNETTES

*See also: Afro hair; blondes; cleansing; eye make-up; greying; hair; make-up; moisturizing; redheads; skin; toning*

Hair colouring varies among brunettes from very light brown to deep copper (see also **redheads**), with skin tones varying from fair (sometimes with freckles and moles) to olive.

For brunettes with a pale complexion which tends to become dry it is important to use an oil-based moisturizer which will supplement the sebum naturally produced in the skin. Those with oilier skin caused by more active sebaceous glands need more abrasive cleansers, such as those containing grains, to keep pores unblocked and avoid blackheads and spots. Cleansing must be thorough and regular. Avoid oil-based products and use a light, water-based moisturizer. Brunettes with pale skin may have dry hair which looks dull and lifeless, caused by loss of water at cellular level. It will be more prone to breaking and splitting, due to lack of elasticity. Ensure that you are drinking enough fluids – preferably water and fruit juices or herbal teas – to keep your hair (and skin) in good, well moisturized condition. Condition before and after washing. Avoid harsh shampoos, and restrict brushing and combing to a minimum. Henna shampoos and waxes will improve condition, making hair softer and supplementing the natural hair oils. Try rinsing your hair before the final rinse with beer or stout to add extra lustre to dark hair. A chamomile infusion will also emphasize pale lights in light brown hair.

When choosing make-up study your skin colour as well as your hair colour. Pale complexions can look over made-up if heavy cosmetics are worn. However, brunettes can generally wear heavier, more sultry colours than those with paler hair. Pale-skinned brunettes should choose warm but pale tones such as dusky violets, browns, peaches, pinky greys. If your skin is sallow, avoid yellowish tones and use a mauve-tinted moisturizer or foundation. Brunettes should be particularly conscious of the contrast in skin tone between the face and neck as there can be a difference, particularly obvious during the summer months when necklines are lower, or when wearing a ball gown. Deal with this by extending foundation over neck and shoulders – depending on what you are wearing – or simply by powdering further down than you would normally. Thick, dark eyelashes can look dramatic on all brunettes; if your lashes are short use a lash-building mascara and precede this by curling your lashes for extra emphasis (see **eye make-up**). Rich, jewel colours can look very effective with a dark complexion, and plums and golds also enhance dark skin. On darker complexions, wear tinted face powder as translucent types can make the skin look grey. Pale-skinned brunettes should wear moisturized foundation, particularly in cold weather, as it provides extra protection against dehydration and chapping.

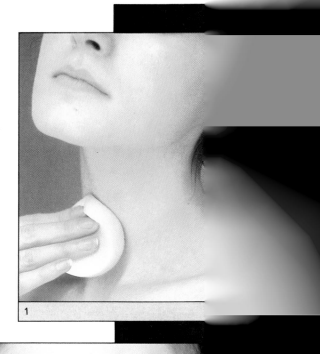

**1** Pat ivory liquid foundation lightly on to the face and neck with a damp cosmetic sponge to give a smooth, even surface.
**2** Paint concealer cream under eyes with a brush to cover shadows, then blend gently into base with fingertips. Repeat around nose, corners of mouth and over any blemishes.
**3** Apply loose translucent powder with a large wad of cotton wool all over face and neck to fix foundation and give an opaque look. Brush on over and around ears.
**4** With a large soft brush, dust warm rosy powder blusher lightly on to cheeks for a natural healthy glow.
**5** With soft blue/grey eye pencil work up lid to crease near lashes. Then work from outer corners with taupe shadow, working inwards, blending softly.
**6** Brush glossy black mascara down on to tips, then brush upper lashes upwards, lower lashes down.
**7** Apply fuchsia lipstick with a fine, thin brush starting in the centre of each lip and working out to the edges. Finished look is sophisticated, yet simple and adaptable for day or evening.

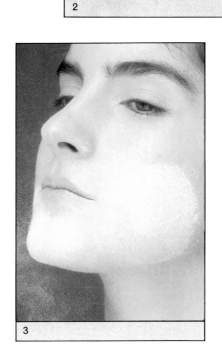

5

6

7

# B

# BRUSHES

*See also: applicators; blushers; eye make-up; gums; hair; make-up; teeth*

### MAKE-UP BRUSHES

A good selection of brushes in different shapes and sizes will help to blend make-up colours accurately or create clear, neat outlines. Each particular task requires a different shaped brush. For example, eyebrow brushes have a slanted edge, eyeliner brushes are very pointed and narrow to draw fine lines, while blusher brushes have thick, dense bristles to distribute colour over a wide area with a soft outline. Artists' brushes are suitable (as long as they do not moult), but real hair brushes are preferable to nylon ones. Whichever sort you use, all brushes should be kept clean (eye brushes in particular can trap bacteria and cause infection), and replaced at least once a year.

### HAIR BRUSHES

Choose hair brushes according to your hair texture. Fine hair should have a soft brush, while thick-bristled brushes, or a bristle and nylon mix, are best for thick hair. A brush with widely spaced, natural bristles is the least likely to cause hair damage, but if you buy a nylon brush, ensure that the bristle ends are rounded. Brushes with rubber cushions help prevent hair from being tugged by bristles. Flat brushes are for straightforward brushing and un-tangling, while circular brushes act like a roller, shaping and curling the hair when used with a hair dryer. Again, choose brushes with widely spaced bristles to allow hot air to circulate during drying which will prevent hair being scorched.

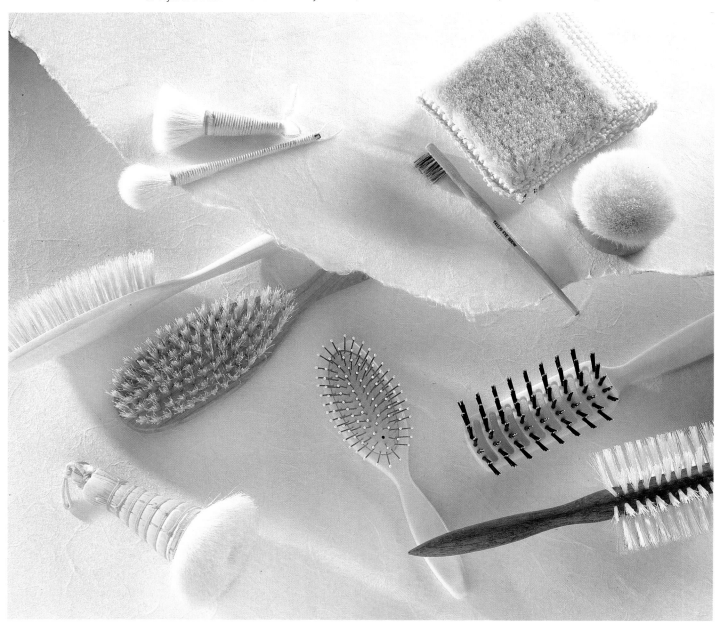

### Keeping brushes clean

Avoid brushing dirt and grease back into your hair by washing brushes regularly in tepid, soapy water. Do not soak rubber-cushioned brushes as the bristles tend to loosen, or wooden framed brushes which will rot. If the brush is very dirty, try dipping it in a weak solution of ammonia and water. Rinse well in clean water and shape when wet. Dry on a rolled towel with the bristles face down. Never dry over direct heat.

### BODY BRUSHES

A long-handled body brush is useful for scrubbing the back, both for cleaning and mild exfoliation, while smaller body brushes can be used for hands and feet. Both should have firm, natural bristles.

trolled than anorexics or anorexic/bulimics. Because they find keeping to a diet or regular eating pattern hard, they interrupt their diet with periods of stuffing and then vomiting in order to maintain a steady weight. Most bulimics are very secretive and hide their problem even from close friends. When bulimia occurs with anorexia it is still more dangerous: the body is constantly subjected to dietary extremes and put under dangerous strain.

### COPING WITH BULIMIA

The vicious circle of bulimia is hard to break and requires medical help and counselling. As with anorexia nervosa, its underlying causes must be examined and worked through before the eating problem itself can be tackled.

**Bulking agents**
See Appetite suppressants

# BUFFING

*See also: cleansing; exfoliation; manicure; nails; skin*

### NAILS

Buffing is an excellent nail treatment, either as a substitute for polish or to stimulate blood circulation before polishing. Use a buffing cream in a tinted or neutral colour, or beeswax, and with a nail buffer or soft cloth, buff nails in one direction until shiny (about 1 minute). Do not use cream if buffing before applying polish.

### FACE AND BODY

Buffing the face gently with a special buffing sponge or pad and a cleanser (cream, liquid or soap) is a means of removing or exfoliating the skin's dead surface cells to give the complexion a fresher, softer appearance.

# BULIMIA NERVOSA OR BULIMAREXIA

*See also: anorexia nervosa; body image; slimming*

Bulimia (or bulimarexia) means gorging, or insatiable over-eating. Bulimics eat amounts of food ranging from large to enormous over a short period of time and then induce vomiting or take large doses of laxatives or slimming pills in an attempt to counteract their overeating. This condition can be fatal, and may in any case cause liver and kidney damage and severe tooth decay due to stomach acids vomited up. Bulimia can occur in phases with anorexia nervosa, or alone, and commonly occurs after anorexia itself has been treated and appears to have been overcome.

Generally speaking, bulimics are less self-con-

# BUNIONS

*See also: calluses; chiropodists; feet*

Bunions – enlarged toe joints – appear at the base of the big toes, gradually occupying more space leading to crowding and deformity of the other toes as well as the big toe. The enlarged joints become increasingly inflamed and painful and, in severe cases, surgery may be necessary to rectify the problem. Feet more inclined to bunions may be inherited. If you do suffer from bunions, be sure that shoes fit well and that toes move freely inside them; avoid tight-fitting tights and socks and wear lint or foam pads for protection.

# BURNS

*See also: scars; tanning*

Burns, which are caused by direct contact with heat or corrosive chemicals, and scalds, which are caused by hot liquids or steam, can be extremely serious and painful if not attended to immediately. Medical assistance is necessary for all but the smallest of injuries.

### BURN TYPES

Burns and scalds are classified in order of severity: first-degree burns (which damage only the most superficial layers of the epidermis) are the least serious and can usually be treated at home. Third-degree burns, which are very severe indeed (they cause damage deep down into the dermis and even beyond), will necessitate the calling of an ambulance and hospital treatment. The danger lies not only in the burn itself, but the accompanying loss of fluid from the skin and the risk of subsequent infection. Shock is also a serious side effect. The risk to small children and babies is particularly serious

**B**

since burns tend to affect a larger overall proportion of their body skin, thus increasing the danger and shock. Prompt treatment is essential.

### ACTION

**Burns** If clothes or hair are on fire, smother the flames with a heavy piece of clothing or a blanket. Then cover the patient with a blanket to prevent loss of body heat due to shock. Do not attempt to remove clothing as it may have stuck to the wound. Call an ambulance.

With less extensive burns, immerse the limb or affected skin in cold water for AT LEAST 10 minutes, keep it there until the wound has cooled to prevent heat from penetrating deeper into the tissue. If the burn is not serious, apply a sterilized dressing. Avoid sticking plaster, grease, cream and cotton wool, all of which may stick to the wound and exacerbate the problem.

If the burn looks serious, cover loosely with a clean handkerchief or strip of laundered sheet and seek advice from your doctor or hospital immediately. Again, prompt action is necessary.

**Scalds** Remove any affected clothing to prevent further burning and wash away any remaining chemicals under running water (in the bath, if necessary). Continue to cool the wound as above and seek help from the doctor or hospital if necessary particularly if the patient is seriously scalded.

All burns should be allowed to heal by themselves. Never be tempted to speed up the process by bursting blisters: this can lead to serious infection and to scarring. Where burns and scalds leave severe scarring, skin grafts may be done, sometimes in several stages, once the area is fully healed. Where scarring is superficial, dermabrasion may help, but not if basal skin cells have been damaged as new skin growth will also be irregular (see **scars**).

# BUTTOCKS

*See also: back; exercises*

The buttocks are an extension of the back, made up of 3 pairs of large muscles, the *Gluteus maximus*, *medius* and *minimus*, and fatty tissue. It is important to keep the buttocks firm and strong to prevent unsightly bulges below and at the side of the hips, and at the sides of the thighs. Fortunately the buttock muscles are particularly responsive to exercise and the results of a good exercise plan can often be seen quite quickly. Some of the best buttock exercises are those involving locomotion: brisk walking, jogging, stair-climbing. Keep buttocks smooth with plenty of moisturizer or body lotion massaged in after every bath or shower. Exfoliate regularly.

▲ **Exercise B**
1 Lie on your back with knees bent, feet parallel, flat on the floor directly under knees and hip-width apart. Your arms should lie flat on the floor at your side.
2 Putting weight on your shoulders and upper back, not your neck, raise your bottom to a comfortable height (not too high or you may over-arch your spine) and clench buttocks. Hold for several seconds, then return bottom to the floor. Repeat 6 times, building up to 24 times.

▼ **Exercise C**
1 Kneel on all fours on the floor with thighs hip-width apart, knees right under hips, hands shoulder-width apart and facing forwards.
2 Press your right leg out straight and back without arching your back or tilting your hips away from parallel. Now turn leg outwards from the hip and hold for several seconds. Return to kneeling position, then repeat with other leg. Repeat 6 times for each leg, building up gradually to 24 times for each leg.

■ See EXERCISES for Caution Box page 123 before starting exercise

■ See ABDOMEN for Core Exercise box page 6 before starting exercise

▶ **Exercise A**

1 Stand tall with good posture, head held high without the chin jutting out or head being thrown back.
2 Put your weight on your left leg and turn your right hip out (turn the whole leg at the hip, not the knee or ankle). Bring the whole right leg back without bending at the knee as far as you can without forcing the movement, or overarching your back. This will not be a big movement. Repeat with other leg. Begin with 6 for each leg, building up to 24 times each leg.

B

# C

**Calamine**
See Tanning

**Calciferol**
See Vitamin D

**Calcium**
See Minerals

# CAFFEINE

*See also: allergies; dependencies; depression*

Caffeine is an alkaloid, addictive drug which acts as a stimulant to the nervous system. Its presence in the body releases the hormone noradrenaline (norephinephrine) which in turn produces a swift release of stored sugar from the liver and insulin from the pancreas. Fatigue is lessened, mental activity speeded up and a 'buzz', which can last for several hours is experienced. Caffeine addiction can, however, lead to increased fatigue, anxiety and bad co-ordination, as the pancreas releases insulin more readily and plentifully, and so far more insulin than glucose is in the system.

In addition to acting as a diuretic (see **fluid retention**), caffeine has pain-killing properties; it is a constituent in some analgesics, cold remedies, slimming drugs, cola and chocolate as well as tea and coffee. A 250 ml (8 fl oz) cup of tea contains 25-100 mg; a cup of coffee contains 40-150 mg (weak instant coffee has least); even decaffeinated coffee contains approximately 2-8 mg per cup (weak instant decaffeinated has least).

Research, however, is now showing that caffeine is detrimental to health in many ways.
- It is a common allergen, causing migraine, headaches, irritability, anxiety and fatigue.
- It constricts blood vessels, exacerbating cholesterol- and fat-induced furring and producing headaches.
- It can cause nervousness and restlessness, sleeplessness and loss of skin texture.
- It can interfere with digestion and the absorption of vitamins and minerals, particularly B1, B5, calcium, iron, zinc and potassium.
- It crosses the placenta during pregnancy and is thought to be implicated in cases where newborn babies are small and suffering poor muscle tone, in spontaneous abortions, still and premature births. It also reaches babies in breast milk.
- Caffeine is implicated in high blood pressure.
- Withdrawal from very high doses of caffeine should take place over three or four days to avoid very considerable psychological effects (see **dependencies**).

# CALLUSES

*See also: body moisturizers; chiropodist; feet; hands; moisturizing; skin*

Calluses, which are hard patches of skin, generally occur on the palms of the hands, the toes and the soles of the feet. People who have dry skin are far more likely to suffer from these. They are caused by friction. You can help to prevent or alleviate them by liberal applications of moisturizer and body lotion each day, especially after a bath or shower when moisturizing is most beneficial. Try rubbing calluses gently with a pumice stone, using soap and water. Pat dry, and apply moisturizer. If this is not successful, calluses can be treated by your chiropodist. Always wear comfortable shoes that do not pinch or rub, and keep feet in good condition.

# CALORIE COUNTING

*See also: diet; fasting; fattening diets; slimming*

The Calorie is the measure most often used to denote the energy value of foods. One calorie is the amount of heat required to raise the temperature of 1 gram of water by 1°C. Food energy is measured in units of 1,000 of these: a Calorie with a capital C, also known as a kilocalorie. Further complication is added by the fact that joules are now sometimes used: 4.2 kilojoules = 1 kilocalorie or 1 Calorie. Calorie requirements per day, in order to maintain a given weight, vary from 2,200 for a sedentary adult female to 3,500 for a growing adolescent and 1,200 for a young child of 4 or 5 (see **diet** for more details).

Calorie counting has traditionally been used as a simple way of regulating diets. Calorie-wise, gaining or losing 0.5 kg (1 lb) of fat requires altering regular intake over a period of time by 3,500 Calories. Slimming diets often recommend, thus, eating 1,000-1,200 Calories a day to lose just under 1 kg (approximately 2 lb) in a week. The mathematics work, whatever the food the Calories are contained in, but increasing importance is now laid on the food itself. And other factors play a part in the speed of loss or gain, such as your basal metabolic rate, how much exercise you take and how fast you are metabolizing calories and how steadily Calorie intake is adjusted. Eating well for health – and required weight – along with a good exercise programme have taken over from manic Calorie counting (see **diet, slimming**).

# CAMOUFLAGE

*See also: blusher; chloasma; eye make-up; liver spots; port wine stains; scars*

Most of us need to disguise some blemish or discoloration in our complexions. Concealers, which are basically foundations with a high pigment content, are specially made to camouflage dark shadows, blemishes and broken veins. They come in cream and lotion form and should be applied before foundation to even out skin tones before another colour is absorbed. Either pat concealer lightly into the skin with your fingertips until the correct intensity of colour is reached, or brush on gently. The correct use of blusher (see separate entry) detracts from facial imperfections, while clumsily applied blushers and concealers make the face look blotchy.

### CAMOUFLAGE ZONES

Blemishes can be covered using a concealer stick in a colour to match your skin tone (medicated products are available), smoothing it on with the fingertips, or by stroking on a cream concealer with a fine brush – this helps cover a bump. Powder the area and set with a damp cotton wool pad. Then, with a slightly damp sponge, apply a sheer or water-based foundation rather than an oily, heavy type which can slip off spots.

**Under-eye shadows** should be concealed with a specially formulated under-eye cream as the skin here is thin and sensitive. Alternatively, use a concealer stick slightly paler than your skin tone (not too light or it will highlight the area), to stipple on colour very gently. Blend in well. You can also try patting on two thin layers of foundation, letting it dry before the second application.

**Red veins or blotchy skin** can be concealed by applying a light layer of green-tinted or warm beige foundation before your usual foundation.

**Freckles and brown liver spots** (see **liver spots**) can be treated with a fadeout cream containing hydroquinone which helps as well to decrease the build up of melanin.

**Cancer**
See Breast examination; Contraception; Skin

**Cap**
See Contraception

**Cathiodermie (T.M.)**
See Facials

1 Ensure that the surface of the stain is completely clean otherwise the concealer cream will slip off. Blot to remove any trace of moisture.
2 Start from outside edge of mark, using your finger tips. Dab cream on very gently, using light rolling movements and taking particular care not to drag the skin.
3 Be extra careful around the delicate eye area, stroke rather than roll concealer cream on around the eye.
4 Fix concealer cream with a generous application of colourless powder, lightly dab away excess with a small soft sponge.
5 Allow concealer to set for 10-15 minutes before applying base with a cool, damp sponge in the normal way. Port wine stains are very sensitive and can become red and blotchy, so try to use a hypo-allergenic make-up base.

**Cellulose**
See Fibre

**Chamomile**
See Herbs

**Chemo-surgery**
See Chemical
peeling

■ **Wrinkles or lines** can be minimized with concealer dotted along their length and blended in. Allow to dry before applying foundation.

### CORRECTIVE CAMOUFLAGE
A number of facial disfigurements, including scars, broken capillaries, birthmarks or pigmentation disorders such as chloasma (melasma) or vitiligo – see separate entries – can be disguised very successfully with camouflage make-up. A less dramatic yet effective alternative to cosmetic surgery, the success of this specially formulated make-up relies on deft and subtle application. The British Red Cross trains specially selected volunteers to instruct and advise on the use of camouflage techniques. A referral from your doctor is necessary, but for further information in the UK contact The National Administrator, Beauty Care and Cosmetic Camouflage Service, The British Red Cross Society, 9 Grosvenor Crescent, London SW1. Alternatively, consult your dermatologist.

### MATERIALS AND METHODS
The creams used are opaque and waterproof, designed to stay on the skin for longer than normal make-up. They also contain filters to protect the skin from UV rays which can worsen some of these skin conditions. Most of the creams are available on prescription. The creams will not adhere if the skin is greasy, and are harder to apply if allowed to become dry. Scars are more difficult to conceal than flat marks as unevenness is caught by the light. A brush applies cream more effectively than fingertips. For large areas of pigmentation problems, stippling on colour with a sponge produces a more natural look. If necessary, a layer of covering cream is used to shade white patches before a cream matching your skin tone is worked in using light patting and rolling movements. A blend of 3 colours may be required for a perfect skin tone match. This is set with a translucent or neutral co-ordinating powder, blotted then allowed to settle before applying make-up as normal.

# CARBOHYDRATE

*See also: diet; fibre*

With fat and protein, carbohydrate is one of the 3 main constituents of food. The carbohydrate group contains carbon, hydrogen and oxygen. Substances in the group include sugars, starch, dextrin, glycogen and cellulose. Carbohydrates provide energy for all the cells in the body; they are broken down into glucose and carried to their destination along the bloodstream. Surplus glucose can be stored as glycogen in the liver and muscles, then reconverted into glucose. Once the liver's storage limit is reached, excess is converted into fat and stored in the adipose tissue: this can later be converted into useful energy, but not into glycogen.

# CELLULITE

*See also: aspiration; fat; fluid retention*

Cellulite has been the subject of much dispute in recent years. Many doctors consider cellulite to be just another term for fat. What is described as cellulite is a kind of fat whose trademark is a dimpled effect on the body's surface, called *peau d'orange* by the French, who coined the word *cellulite* too. It is an almost entirely female problem, linked up with the hormone cycle and thus with fluid retention. Cellulite accumulates on thighs, buttocks, hips, even knees and ankles.

### CAUSES
There is still no general consensus of opinion as to how cellulite forms and why it settles where it does. Theories range from lack of exercise (although not all cellulite sufferers lack exercise) to bad dietary habits, which cause a high level of waste products to be 'dumped' as cellulite. The distribution of cellulite seems to parallel that of white fat in females, although, unlike white fat, it is not metabolized when food intake is reduced.

### CURES
There are none. A wide variety of treatments are available, but none has a satisfactory record of success. Various types of massage, faradic exercise, thalassotherapy and mud treatments increase local circulation which may help redistribute particularly lumpy areas of cellulite. Reducing salt and processed food intake is a healthy move which will decrease fluid and toxin excesses in the body, problems which are both associated with cellulite. One drastic remedy is aspiration (see separate entry) which should only be undertaken in severe cases.

# CHEEKS

*See also: blusher; make-up*

The large area of facial skin which forms the cheeks is a reflection of your health as well as a palette for make-up. Although cosmetic surgery can structure the shape of your cheeks by means of silicone implants, your face can be transformed by blushing the cheekbones with glowing colour, or by using highlight shaders to emphasize or minimize your natural features. Cheeks respond to weather and atmosphere, so should be kept well moisturized at all times, especially during exposure to the sun and if swimming in salt water. Dry, chapped and wrinkled skin can be caused by wind and extreme cold, when a richer moisturizing cream should be applied. Red, broken veins on the cheeks can be concealed effectively by a concealer or camouflage make-up (see also **thread veins**).

# CHEMICAL PEELING

*See also: acne; ageing; black skin; cosmetic surgery; dermabrasion; freckles; grey hair; lines; skin; wrinkles*

Chemical peeling or chemo-surgery aims to improve the skin's texture and eliminate surface defects by using a caustic solution to burn off the outer layer of the skin and reveal the new, unblemished layers beneath. The treatment is most successful in softening and minimizing facial lines and wrinkles. While freckles, pigmentation marks and some blemishes can be effectively removed, raised lines or scars often become more noticeable compared with the fresh layer of skin, although flat scars should be improved. The caustic solution is applied to a specific area, or over the entire face (this will induce a burning feeling), and the area may be covered with tape for 48 hours. The skin forms a dry crust in approximately one day after removing the tapes, which may be kept soft by ointments so that it can peel away to show the new underlying skin tissue. The current trend for a more natural, though more superficial, peel, is not to apply tapes. Until the epidermis grows (about 5-7 days), the skin will be very inflamed and often painful and swollen. It is advisable not to wear make-up for at least 17 days or expose the skin to the sun for about 6 months – the melanin-producing cells in the epidermis will be reduced by the chemicals, so the skin may form an uneven tan. If the skin has uneven pigmentation, a second peel can be performed on the blotchy areas about 3-4 months after the initial treatment. Dark or coloured skins run a greater risk of forming blotches, and the process is not recommended if you have black skin. The treatment causes scars to become raised and turn either lighter or more deeply pigmented than surrounding skin. Chemical peeling should only be performed by a doctor, and should not be performed for at least 3 months after a face lift, after which time some cosmetic surgeons recommend it to minimize operation scars.

# CHILBLAINS

*See also: circulation; ears; feet; hands; herbs*

Chilblains are generally believed to be caused by a combination of poor circulation and cold weather, though the reason why some people suffer from them, while others remain unaffected, is uncertain. Painful, itchy, inflamed swellings appear on the extremities of the body: the tips of the fingers, the toes, ears and nose, which can all become infected if scratched.

To help prevent chilblains keep the extremities warm, don't wear tight-fitting gloves and shoes which may constrict your circulation, and avoid sudden changes of temperature – warm up your extremities gradually after exposure to cold. Vasodilator drugs, which increase circulation, thus alleviating itching and reducing swelling, may rarely be prescribed by your doctor. If you are using these creams it is important to wash your hands thoroughly after application. Applications of lanolin, provided you are not sensitive to this, or boracic ointment may help alleviate discomfort.

# CHIN

*See also: camouflage; cosmetic surgery; make-up; massage*

The shape of the chin is determined by your bone structure. Cosmetic surgery can give prominence to a receding chin by means of an implant which is inserted through an incision either inside the mouth across the lower gum, or underneath the chin. The process can be carried out under local anaesthetic. More common and less drastic, is the use of make-up to minimize faults. Shorten the chin by using a darker-toned foundation to shade the tip, or use a small spot of blusher there. With age, the skin below the chin and neck begins to sag, so minimize a double chin by shading along the jawline with a darker-toned foundation blended under the chin. A touch of white highlighter in the centre of a dimple will help to even out the skin. Massaging the neck and chin with upward strokes tones the muscles and stimulates blood supply.

Not only the emphasis of your make-up, your cheeks reflect the way you feel. Keep well moisturized in all weather.

**Chlorine**
See Minerals

**Choline**
See Vitamins

**Chromium**
See Minerals

# CHIROPRACTIC

*See also: back; osteopathy; posture*

Chiropractic, founded in 1895 by Dr David Palmer of Iowa, is recognized as a branch of complementary medicine in the US, but not in the UK. Chiropractors undergo a four-year training, culminating in a professional qualification: few chiropractors are qualified as doctors of medicine. It is a manipulative art whose aim is to correct joint and spinal column disorders which interfere with their normal operation and with that of the spinal cord and nervous system. After the correction of such disorders, chiropractors believe that the body's 'innate intelligence' completes the healing process. Chiropractors never use drugs (they treat causes, not symptoms) or surgery, but make extensive use of X-rays and medical tests. Although the work of osteopaths is often seen as similar, osteopaths rarely use X-rays, and manipulate by using leverage far more than thrust (see below).

### THE PROCEDURE
1  In order to examine the problem in the widest possible light, chiropractors take a full case history, particularly where patients are not referred by doctors. Then follows a physical examination after which various tests on urine and blood may be required. X-rays are taken and consulted.
2  More detailed analysis of the local problem is then undertaken. Movement, muscle and tissue health in the affected area are assessed.
3  After explaining the problem to the patient, treatment takes place. The patient is encouraged to relax as much as possible, so that the thrust exerted on the joint by the chiropractor will cause the least possible pain.

### BENEFITS OF CHIROPRACTIC
Chiropractors specialize in all back problems: slipped discs, low back pain, sciatica and lumbago. They also deal with muscular, nerve and bone pain/numbness – for example resulting from arthritis – in arms, shoulders, legs, hips, chest and head.

# CHIROPODIST

*See also: bunions; calluses; corns; feet; ingrowing nails; pedicure; ringworm; warts*

Chiropodists study every aspect of the foot, its structure, care and diseases. Their work in dealing with foot problems can have wider implications: back problems, for example, can arise from bad posture due to painful feet. Skin problems of the feet, such as corns, are usually dealt with by a chiropodist rather than a dermatologist. In the UK

this means a State Registered Chiropodist, the only chiropodists recognized as competent by the government Health Office. In the US podiatrists deal with superficial foot problems, chiropodists with the whole range. Common problems dealt with are athlete's foot (ringworm), bunions, calluses, corns, ingrowing nails, warts and verrucas. Patients may be referred by a doctor, but usually consult a chiropodist directly.

# CHLOASMA

*See also: liver spots*

Chloasma (melasma) are brown patches on the skin caused by localized increase in melanin pigmentation. These occur most commonly on the upper lip, forehead, temples, on the nipples and genital area, and in the armpits. They are most common during pregnancy and can also occur in women who are taking the combined contraceptive pill. Sunlight deepens the colour: wear a sunblocking cream or stick preparation and avoid sunbathing. If you are on the Pill and have chloasma (melasma), consider altering your contraceptive method. Bleaching preparations are generally unsatisfactory and may irritate the skin.

# CHOLESTEROL

*See also: blood pressure; carbohydrates; diet; fats; heart; sugar*

Cholesterol, which is a fat-like substance normally found in the blood and all body tissues, is an essential compound of all cells. It plays a vital role in the formation of cell membranes, hormones, nerve fibre coverings, bile salts and vitamin D; it helps digest carbohydrates and lubricates the arteries. Despite the massive current interest in food cholesterol contents, only up to one-half of the cholesterol in the bloodstream is ingested in food; all the rest is synthesized by the body.

The dangers of high cholesterol levels in blood are now well documented. Cholesterol plays a role in the thickening of the walls of the arteries that doctors call atherosclerosis (commonly called hardening of the arteries). This thickening, which is in part due to deposition of cholesterol, narrows the artery, deprives the tissue it supplies of oxygen and nutrients and puts additional strain on the cardiovascular system. If this happens in a coronary artery a heart attack may be the end result.

Cholesterol is carried around the body by particles formed in the liver. The particle particularly to blame in heart and arterial problems is low-density lipoprotein, or LDL. Some cholesterol is carried around the body by high-density lipoproteins or HDLs, in themselves harmless or, some believe, actually protective. HDLs carry about 20 per cent of body cholesterol. They also contain high levels of lecithin which can break up cholesterol ready for its vital function and help prevent clogging of blood vessels. LDLs carry 65 per cent of cholesterol in the body, some of which is from dietary sources, some synthesized. The remaining 15 per cent of cholesterol in the body is carried by very low-density lipoproteins, VLDLs.

Diet is one of the important regulators of LDL levels. We all know now that eating large amounts of saturated fats (like animal fats and hard margarines) raises LDL levels. Unsaturated fats have the opposite effect, and this is true of polyunsaturated fats like sunflower oil, and also of monounsaturated fats of which olive oil is a good example.

The desirable level of cholesterol in blood plasma is probably up to about 200mg per 100ml, though many people have levels moderately above this value. Sensible eating habits greatly increase the chance of maintaining desirable levels (see **diet**). For people with excess of blood cholesterol (250-300mg/100ml or more), medical guidance should be sought. A precise diet will be prescribed, and for very high levels most doctors will consider prescribing one of the anti-cholesterol drugs. Foods high in cholesterol are eggs, brain, kidneys and shellfish. Other foods, especially saturated fats such as animal fats, induce raised LDL cholesterol levels.

There is now quite substantial evidence that regular aerobic exercise increases the HDL levels in the body and lowers LDL. Of course, it is extremely important that anyone with existing cholesterol or cardiovascular problems should take medical advice before embarking on a carefully monitored exercise programme. Pre-menopausal women have in the past had some hormonal protection against the detrimental effects of cholesterol, but womens' changing lifestyles, and excesses of alcohol and smoking are reducing this protection; after the menopause, sensible diet is essential.

# CIRCADIAN RHYTHM

*See also: awareness; biorhythms*

The Circadian rhythm is the body's 24-hour biological clock. It is an automatic, endogenous (built-in) rhythm stored in the hypothalamus in the brain. However, it needs signals to reinforce itself intermittently: light and dark and clock time provide these signals.

The Circadian rhythm can adjust quite readily to minor time, light and dark changes, such as those experienced in small amounts of long haul travel. Persistent changes of this nature, however, can upset the Circadian rhythm so radically that they

sometimes induce severe mental and physical disorders (see also **Jetlag**).

It is the Circadian rhythm which plays the largest part in determining whether you are a 'morning' or 'evening' person, when you are most productive, most awake. Whichever type you are, this is part of your own Circadian rhythm and is unchangeable.

One of the important roles that Circadian rhythms play is that of organizing the body's functions and renewal programmes. During the night, for example, when the rhythm decrees that the body should be less overtly active, it takes the opportunity to speed up digestive and cell renewal processes.

Recent research has shown that some drugs are more effective at certain stages of the cycle. Hormone treatment, for example, has been found more effective if administered at the time of the cycle during which the hormones are naturally produced in the body. Research indicates, too, that cancer treatments, such as chemotherapy, are more effective at some points in the Circadian cycle than at others.

# CIRCULATION

*See also: cellulite; chilblains; exercise; massage*

The circulation of blood, pumped by the heart around the body, is essential for the transport of vital elements, including oxygen, to all cells in the body, and for the removal of waste products. Blood vessels leading from the heart are called arteries; those leading back to the heart are known as veins. The importance of correct exercise in relation to the circulation cannot be underestimated: steady, regular exercise (see **aerobics**) will increase the capacity of the heart to pump blood through the system, strengthening it and increasing its output by as much as 20 per cent. Massage, too, aids local circulation in areas being treated, even water massage when swimming. Poor circulation produces problems like cold extremities in winter, chilblains and a pallid complexion. Take plenty of exercise and keep warm.

# CLAY

*See also: beauty salons; facials; mud; skin*

Clay is a natural, highly absorbent earth substance whose healing properties have long been recognized. These properties can draw out and help remove toxic waste products from the skin's surface (i.e. dirt and excess oils), or from the body's digestive system. Applied externally as a face mask, clay can be used to cleanse impurities from the skin, or it can be applied as a compress or poultice to heal

**Clarifying lotions**
See Toning

wounds as well as to soothe sores and inflammations. The clays used for cleansing the system internally are very fine, and are diluted with water before being taken orally. It is said that green clay taken in this way can absorb and drain impurities from the blood and lymphatic systems and help bowel disorders. Certainly kaolin, a fine white clay, is used as an ingredient to treat digestive disorders such as diarrhoea and vomiting.

### CLAY FACIAL TREATMENTS

The clays most commonly used for face masks are described below.

- **Kaolin** This is particularly beneficial for treating spots since its effects are to increase the blood circulation and bring impurities to the skin's surface. Also kaolin is grease-resistant, can absorb sweat and has a soothing and cooling effect on the skin.
- **Fuller's Earth** Greasy skins are well suited to this clay which has strong absorbent qualities, and a very stimulating effect on the skin.
- **Bentonite** This is another clay ingredient which is sometimes used to soothe and heal sores or wounds.

To increase the action of the mask, clays are combined with oils or solutions chosen according to the skin's condition. Witch hazel is used for greasy skins, rosewater for dry or sensitive skins, water for normal skins. Almond oil is used for mature skins or dryish, young skins in need of conditioning.

### CLAY BODY TREATMENTS

- **Green clay combined with plant extracts** and essential oils can be rubbed over the body to remove dead skin cells. This leaves the skin soft, smooth and white and is a mild form of exfoliation suitable for sensitive skins if applied gently with long, sweeping movements.
- **A course of green clay** applications can help treat spots on the back, drawing out impurities and eventually drying out the spots.
- **Green clay mixed with water** can be used as a paste or poultice to treat a particular area of the body. The clay is applied warm or cold, depending on the complaint. Inflammations, sprains or stiff joints are some of the conditions which can respond to the treatment, which is widely used in health farms, beauty salons and spas.

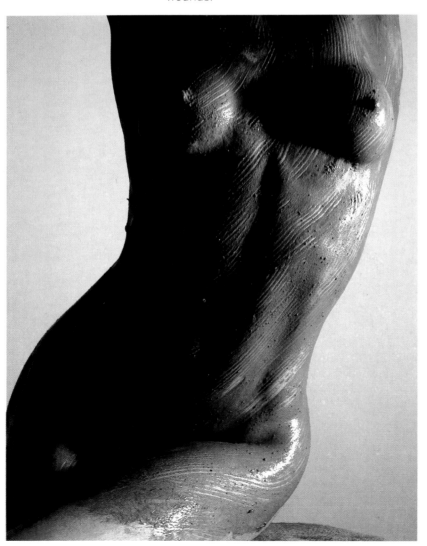

# CLEANSING

*See also: acne; creams; eye make-up; hypo-allergenic products; make-up; moisturizing; mousses; pH; skin; toning*

Skin must be cleansed morning and night to remove the make-up, dirt, oils and pollutants that become embedded in its surface. Using soap and water, or a cleanser followed by a toner, are equally effective cleansing methods whether used separately or in conjunction with one another. Choose your cleansing method to suit the condition of your skin, which can change according to environment and climate, but remember that excessive cleansing can cause sensitive skin to become dry and flaky. If you have sensitive, allergy-prone skin make sure that lotions and creams are free from possible allergens such as lanolin and perfume (well known irritants) before you buy them. You will, however, need to test them for yourself. If you have black skin, avoid products containing resorcinol (used in some commercially produced medicated cleansers and toners and some commercial acne preparations) as they may cause skin mottling.

### SOAP AND WATER

This combination is most satisfactory for normal to oily skins as washing removes the excess oils which cause greasiness. It is essential to retain some of the skin's natural moisturizers, so do not wash your face more than twice daily (once if the skin is sensitive, dry or acne-prone). Washing with a normal alkaline soap temporarily disturbs the skin's natural acidity, so use a pH balanced soap/liquid or cleansing bar. These products are also less drying. Soap will not remove non-water-soluble, oil-based make-up, so use a cream cleanser for this before washing with complexion soap. Medicated soaps are not advisable: they remove surface grease, but can be harsh, very drying, can mottle black skin and ultimately be ineffective in combating acne. Deodorant soaps which may contain harsh chemicals should never be used on the face.

### Washing Your Face

Always wash your hands before lathering soap or glycerine into the skin. Wet skin briefly with warm water before rinsing thoroughly with cold. Pat dry and moisturize. Skin can feel tight and dry if it is over-washed or poorly rinsed. Washing in hard water causes a drying scum of minerals to form on the skin, clogging the pores. Try using a water softener if you live in a hard water area, or switch to a cream cleanser.

### CLEANSERS

- **Liquid cleansers** The creamier liquids are suitable for normal skins whereas milky, water-soluble lotions are better for young greasy skins. They can be wiped away with damp cotton wool, or rinsed off with warm water.
- **Cream cleansers** Are best for dry, delicate or mature skins. They have a richer consistency and contain emulsifiers which dissolve dirt particles.
- **Gel or oil cleansers** Are available for most skin types. They should be massaged in with the fingertips and rinsed off with water.
- **Cleansing pads** Are made of lint soaked in cleansing lotion. Although handy when travelling, they can be harsh, very drying and are not advised for long-term use.

### Cleansing your face

Apply a light layer of appropriate cleanser to the face and lips and leave for a few moments to allow make-up to dissolve. Combination skins will need two products – one for the greasy area and another for the dry parts. Using a damp cotton wool pad (tissues contain resin and are too drying for sensitive skins), work upwards from the neck firmly sweeping away all traces of make-up and dirt. Finish when the cotton wool is clean. Apply toner to remove last traces then moisturize (see entries). Removing eye make-up needs special care (see **eye make-up**) because the skin around the eye area is particularly delicate.

# CLIMATE

*See also: chilblains; hair; hands; lips; skin; tanning*

Climatic changes and extremes of temperature can have a detrimental effect on hair and skin. Prolonged exposure to sunlight may cause skin cancers as well as premature skin ageing and moisture loss, particularly in those individuals who tend to

burn (see **skin**). Both wind and extreme cold cause chapping and dryness. Following preventive guidelines will keep hair and skin in best condition and avoid unnecessary damage and premature ageing of the skin.

### PROTECTION GUIDELINES

- In extreme heat, cold or wind, wear plenty of moisturizer. Use extra handcream in cold or windy weather and wear gloves to prevent chapping. Do not be tempted to wear less moisturizer in humid weather; skin readily loses water in these conditions.
- Use a lip protection stick: choose one with a sunscreen for sunny weather and skiing.
- Always wear goggles on sunbeds, and sunglasses when skiing to protect eyes from glare.
- Always wear a moisturizer or foundation which contains a sunscreen in sunny weather, even if you are not spending all day in the sun. Top this up with suncare preparations if you are sunbathing, starting with a high sun protection factor (SPF) (see **tanning**). Be particularly careful when skiing: reflections from the snow double the sun's burning effect (and sand and concrete also reflect ultraviolet rays). If you tend to burn in the sun, avoid excessive sunbathing and use high protection sun barrier creams (high SPF) to prevent burning. It may be advisable to wear sunblock (for example in a moisturizer or foundation) all the time in summer.
- Hair dries out in extreme climates: use plenty of conditioner on the ends of your hair each time you wash it. Use plenty of conditioner on *dry*

C

**Cobalamin**
See Vitamins

**Cobalt**
See Minerals

**Coil**
See Contraception

Reflection from the snow doubles the sun's damaging power: wear high-protection sun products or sunblock. Glasses/goggles are essential to avoid glare.

hair before going into the sun. This will protect hair when swimming and sunbathing and help with tangle-free combing after a day on the beach. If sunbathing, consider using a special sun protection product for the hair. If you are swimming a lot, use a mild shampoo designed for frequent washing and apply a good conditioner to your hair afterwards.

# COLDS

*See also: minerals; vitamins*

Colds, with their symptoms of wheezing, sneezing, coughing, runny noses and sore throats, are all too familiar. Causing all the discomfort are virus infections which produce inflammation of the mucous membranes, affecting the nose, throat and bronchial tubes. They are passed on by coughs and sneezes, taking one or two days to produce symptoms. You are more likely to catch a cold if you are under stress, whether the stress is pleasurable (such as planning a wedding) or not. Colds are not generally serious, except to those susceptible to chest complaints and occasionally to small babies.

### COLD PREVENTION
■ Research is constantly being undertaken into the prevention and cure of colds, particularly by the Common Cold Research Centre in Britain. As yet no drugs generally accepted as being capable of counteracting cold viruses have been discovered, although first results in trials of drug WIN 51711 at the Sterling-Winthrop Institute in New York look promising. Should the drug be found to be successful, it would not be available for several years.

■ There is no generally accepted scientific proof that megadoses of vitamin C prevent or cure colds, although trials in Massachussetts using vitamin C with bioflavonoids (vitamin C-complex rather than just vitamin C, which was found to be useless in Common Cold Centre trials) have found that taking up to 4g of C-complex spread over a day may stop a cold if treatment is begun when first symptoms appear.

■ Good general diet is helpful: if you are eating well and getting the necessary vitamin, mineral, protein, carbohydrate and fat intake, your resistance to germs will be as high as possible.

### COLD TREATMENTS
■ Stay at home to prevent passing on your cold.
■ Take the opportunity to rest.
■ 'Feeding a cold' is not a good idea. Give your body a chance to recover: eat lightly, including fruit juices, vegetables, meat and fish in your diet. Try taking C-complex (see above) with vitamins A and B: very important in fighting infection. Zinc is thought to be helpful, too.
■ Drink lots of fluids, such as fruit juice or water, to keep body fluid levels up and to help flush out germs.
■ Relieve congestion by hot inhalations rather than decongestant drugs. These drugs not only have a rebound effect (you get better for a few days, then worse again), but prolonged use can also damage the nose's self-clearing mechanisms. Try a chamomile infusion, using 25g (1oz) chamomile to each 600ml (1 pint) of boiling water. Sit at a table with a china bowl (or similar non-tip type) containing the infusion in front of you. Drape a towel over your head and breathe in the steam from the infusion for between 15 minutes and half an hour. Mullein or poplar are alternatives: poplar is balsamic and contained in many old-fashioned inhalation preparations.
■ Choose an appropriate cough medicine: an expectorant to shift mucous from the lungs, a linctus to soothe a nagging cough. Pastilles may help a sore throat: if unsure, consult your pharmacist.

# COLD SORES

*See also: sexually transmitted diseases*

Cold sores have nothing to do with colds. They are caused by a virus, Herpes Simplex I, which although it is closely related to Herpes Simplex 2 (the genital herpes virus) is not necessarily sexually transmitted. The virus affects the mouth, lips, nostrils and vagina, causing inflammation and blisters, but it is possible to contract the virus without showing any symptoms. Since it remains in the body even when not active, cold sores can recur.

There is no cure for cold sores, but applications of active yoghurt can be helpful. Increase the amino acid *lysine* (in cottage cheese, peanuts, tuna), vitamin C-complex and E in the diet: these will help fight the virus. Take care when brushing your teeth not to aggravate active blisters and do not touch them or you will make them worse.

# COLLAGEN

*See also: ageing; elastin and elastone; skin; stretch marks; tanning; wrinkles*

The protein collagen is the main element in fibrous connective tissue which occurs in bones, tendons, cartilage, ligaments and skin. In the skin it plays a vital role in providing strength, working alongside elastin, which gives skin its flexibility. The ability of collagen to regain its shape after being stretched is impaired with age, thus wrinkles begin to form. Later, elastin (see separate entry) and collagen form an inelastic, criss-crossed web called elastone.

### KEEPING COLLAGEN FLEXIBLE
- Avoid sunbathing: UV rays (see **tanning**) have a wide range of ageing effects on skin. In the case of collagen it speeds up the hardening process and the development of elastone, and increases the likelihood of wrinkles.
- Reduce your smoking or stop completely. Habitual contraction of the muscles of the face causes the collagen layer, which is far less flexible, to harden into wrinkles.
- Vitamin C and zinc help form connective tissue: include plenty in your diet.

## Treatments
- Collagen implants do not provide miraculous reversals of the evidence of age. They involve individual depressions, lines or wrinkles being injected along their length with a collagen solution (taken from cattle). The implant has the effect of plumping up the skin injected, so minor lines will disappear, but there is no reduction in slack skin, although skin texture changes. The process is relatively painless (the areas will be red for 24-48 hours) but it is very expensive and has to be repeated about every 2 years.
- Research continues into the benefits of RNA and SOD supplements for collagen and skin benefits. RNA (ribonucleic acid) helps form new cells in the body, SOD (superoxide dismutase) is an enzyme which fights free radicals which destroy cells, including collagen cells. Although some specialists are convinced of the anti-ageing benefits of these dietary supplements, their efficacy is not generally accepted.
- Creams and lotions containing collagen are available, but there is no medical evidence for the absorption of collagen through the skin.

# COLOURING HAIR

*See also: hair; henna; herbs; highlighting*

Colouring your hair can be very exciting, giving a lift to your spirits as well as to your general appearance. It is, however, quite a major step with a few adverse factors which you should be aware of before making a decision about the method to use. Consider the following before deciding:
1 Some people are contact-allergic to certain chemical colourants: it is advisable to do a patch test on your skin if you are thinking of using permanent or semi-permanent colour. Dab some colourant on your inner forearm and cover it with a plaster or bandaid. If, after 24 hours, there is any redness or swelling at all, DO NOT USE THE PRODUCT.
2 *Never* colour your hair permanently just before perming it, or until several weeks have elapsed after a perm. If you have naturally Afro hair which you usually have straightened, or wear an Afro style that needs regular curling, you will have to schedule your colouring and curling/straightening schedules carefully to allow necessary time to elapse between treatments. Furthermore, you may find that permanent colour, in addition to frequent processing, makes your hair too brittle. Consider either highlighting (see separate entry) or colouring the tips, or using semi-permanent colour. Semi-permanent colour will take very well straight after a perm when hair is particularly porous, and adds shine to it. *Never* tint hair which has already been treated with a metallic colourant product (and this includes metallic henna compounds). This can result in hair breakage or loss, or strange, permanent colours. If you are using a new colourant, or have had other hair processing recently, do a test in advance on a small strand of hair, as well as your patch test, and consult your hair colourist.
3 Permanent colourants contain paraphenylenediamine compounds which have in recent years been thought to be carcinogenic (cancer-causing). The controversy continues, but such claims have not yet been substantiated. However, since lightening your colour tends to enhance skin tones, and lighter colourants contain less paraphenylenediamine, stick to lightening your colour tones wherever possible. Traditionally, grey hairs have been covered up by dyeing back to the old, darker colour. Never do this: the colour is too harsh; hair colour fades with age, so it is advisable to dye back one shade lighter. Try having highlights or lowlights in several colours for a softer, safer, colour. Avoid reds which look brash on grey (see **greying, highlighting**).
4 As a result of the possible dangers mentioned above, do not use permanent colourants on your hair while pregnant. Chemicals can cross the placenta to the baby.

**Colonics**
See Fasting

**Colourants in food**
See Additives

**Colour therapy**
See Relaxation

## USING HAIR COLOURANTS
### Chemical colourants

It is advisable to have semi-permanent or permanent hair colour professionally applied. The colourist will do patch tests for you and advise on which colours will suit you best. He or she will apply the colour properly and give advice on aftercare and regrowth times. If you do decide to go it alone, choose a product from a reputable firm and bear in mind that the hair colour shown will not be identical to that achieved on your hair: results depend on how porous your hair is (and package printing distorts colours anyway). Make sure that you read the instructions at least twice and then follow them precisely: leaving colour on for too long can damage your hair and will affect final colour. Weather conditions make a huge difference, too. Colour which needs an hour to 'take' in cold, wintry conditions might only need 5 or 10 minutes on a very hot, humid summer's day: another reason for having colour applied professionally. Be very careful to keep dyes out of your eyes, and wear rubber gloves to protect your hands. Use permanent and semi-permanent dyes on your head hair only. Never use them to dye eyelashes, eyebrows or hair anywhere else on the body. Most important of all is to do a patch test in advance, see steps 1 and 2 on the previous page if you are in any doubt.

## Bleaching

Never bleach your hair. You can achieve similarly light results with permanent dyes. Bleaches are twice as damaging: hydrogen peroxide penetrates the hair, as dyes do, but ammonia then strips out all colour. Because of this fierce action, it is advisable to choose colourants, rather than just bleaches for most of your highlights (see separate entry), too.

## Natural vegetable colourants

**Henna** is one of the strongest natural dyes. It should be used with care for colouring as results vary according to natural hair colour, whether the hair has been processed previously, the type of henna used and how long it is left on (see **choosing colour** below). The most popular type of henna for hair is pure red.

To colour hair, mix neutral and red henna to a paste with hot water: approximately one cup of henna to half a cup of water. Replace water with a medium to strong chamomile infusion (depending on the depth of colour required), or hot red wine or lemon juice (replace half cup of water with equal parts water and wine or water and lemon) for redder colour, hot black coffee (add 2 tablespoons of powdered, not granular, instant coffee to hot water) for deeper colour, sage infusion (as for chamomile infusion above) for warmer colour.

Always wear rubber gloves. Apply paste to the hair (leaving the roots clear) and comb through thoroughly. Then apply paste to the roots, which take the colour more quickly due to the heat of the scalp. Wrap hair in cling film or foil and leave for 15 minutes. Test hair: you may decide to leave henna on longer, but do not leave longer than this if you have not used it before. Shampoo out and rinse until water is clear of colour as well as soap.

**Rhubarb root, sage, chamomile flowers, saffron root or flowers, marigold flowers, cloves, privet leaves, tea leaves, bark and walnuts** can all be used to colour hair. To use plant roots, simmer 50 g (2 oz) to each 600 ml (1 pint) of water for about 1 hour, and leave to infuse. For other herbs and flowers, make an infusion with 50-75 g (2-3 oz) of the herb to each 600 ml (1 pint) of water. Leave to infuse for 30 minutes. All should be strained before using as a final rinse, washing it through hair several times.

## CHOOSING COLOUR

### Permanent colour change

**Chemical dyes** work by penetrating the cuticle of the hair shaft, replacing natural pigmentation with chemical dye. Hydrogen peroxide is often used as the penetrating and colour-stripping agent, paraphenylenediamine dyes for colour (see above). These products work equally well on any hair colour, but tend to be unsuitable for Afro hair because of the frequency with which this type of hair is straightened or has curls chemically reshaped. You may find that your hair becomes dry, brittle and breaks easily. Try highlighting Afro hair instead (see **highlighting**): to lighten very dark hair more than four shades a bleaching process is used. The hair cuticle is opened and natural pigment stripped out.

A combination of this stripping and adding colour gives a 'naturally' lightened colour. Alternatively, colour tips, or use the less harsh semi-permanent dyes (see below). Take advice from your colourist, but generally a change through a few tones is more successful than a radical one: the colour will more readily match your skin and eyes.

The results are permanent, but roots need retouching within 4-6 weeks depending on the depth of colour change.

**Natural dyes** work by coating the hair, so they cause no damage to the hair's structure, unlike chemical dyes. Mixtures of those mentioned below can be good: you can experiment with all but henna and rhubarb as several applications are needed for deep, permanent colour. Colour changes are as follows:

- **Henna** works best on brown to black hair, giving colour from chestnut to strong red. Do not use on grey or fair hair: the result can be a shocking carroty colour.
- **Chamomile** is most often used on fair hair for its lightening and brightening properties. If mixed to a paste with kaolin powder (from pharmacies), it can be used to give highlights to mid-brown hair.
- **Marigold flowers** give a reddish yellow colour to fair hair, a yellowy tinge to white hair.
- **Saffron flowers and roots** produce a yellow tint on fair or blonde hair. Several applications are needed for permanence.
- **Walnut and barks.** Darken hair and work well on greying hair. Several applications are needed for permanence.
- **Rhubarb root** lightens any hair colour.
- **Sage** gives a browny tinge to grey hair. A deeper colour can be achieved if the sage infusion is mixed with tea.

Hair coloured with henna or rhubarb needs root retouching after 4-6 weeks if a deep colour has been achieved. If only a light colour change has taken place you may be able to wait 8 weeks. With other vegetable colours, rinse hair regularly in the infusion so roots will always be coloured.

### Semi-permanent colour change

**Chemical dyes** work by penetrating only through the outer transparent cuticle, not into the cortex of the hair. Chemicals used are often sulphur derivatives with colour molecules. They add a glint to hair and deepen tones already present, particularly bringing out chestnut and reddish tones; for this reason they are not recommended for fair hair. Less harsh than permanent colours, they are ideal for Afro hair.

These dyes last between 4 and 6 shampoos. Their tendency to fade gradually is accelerated by shampooing, so there is little time for regrowth to show.

### Temporary rinses

**Chemical dyes** work by coating the hair with colour. Because the dyes have slightly acidic base coats they cling to hair, which is more alkaline (see **pH**). Effects are very subtle indeed, often almost imperceptible, and are best suited to paler, even greying

hair. The acidic coating tends to make hair lose its shine. They last for one shampoo.

**Vegetable dyes,** such as barks, walnuts, sage and tea, work as chemical dyes do, by coating the hair with colour. Use only one or two rinses for strongest colour. They last through one or two shampoos.

### Temporary colour coating: sprays, brushes, sticks and crayons

Hair colourants in aerosol form work by spraying colour molecules finely on the hair. They are most effective on light hair, although the ones with a bright or metallic finish can be used successfully on dark hair. These sprays tend to grip on the particularly porous natural or chemically processed blonde hair and can be hard to remove. Brushes, crayons and sticks contain synthetic wax and stick firmly to hair, especially processed hair. Brushes are easy to handle, enabling you to highlight small sections of hair, and are as easy to apply as mascara. Check for allergy, particularly if metallic substances are included in a spray. They last until brushed out or washed out.

# COLOUR CHOICE COSMETICS

*See also: blusher; cosmetics; eye make-up; foundation; face powder; lip colours; make-up; mascara; rouge; skin*

There has never been a more exciting or varied range of colours available in cosmetics than there is today. Just a glimpse of a department store cosmetic section is enough to give you an idea of the thousands of make-up options available, not only in colour, but in type and texture, too. Here, and in the various make-up sections throughout the book, there are guidelines to help you in making your selection.

The spectrum of cosmetic colours is panoramic, from startling to smoky, peacock to pastel. Although your skin tone, eye and hair colours are a basic guide to what colours will suit you best (see separate entries on **Afro, blondes, brunettes,** etc), your way of life, choice of clothing and personality can make exceptions to any rule. You can use your face as a base to paint on colour artistically, so that features and co-ordination need not be considered, or go for monochrome matching, with blusher, lip and eyes toning perfectly. Colours can look dull on some complexions, clear on others. Interchange and adapt them to develop your own sense of co-ordination, making sure that they work together for a look that suits you. Acid in the skin tends to make foundation darken and turn slightly orange. It can also change your lipstick colour quite radically, the alteration depending on the individual. Test these carefully before buying. Eyeshadow colours do not usually change. Artificial light drains colour, so choose shades that look good in all lights. At night,

intensify your chosen colours, try using shaders and shiny highlighters on eyes and cheeks instead of matt colours.

**Red lighting** makes make-up colours look roughly twice as dark: greys appear black-brown, blues look blacker.

**Blue lighting** makes colours darker.

**Yellow lighting** makes colours look sallow and less intense, even insipid.

**Candlelight** mutes and softens colour. In general, use dark colours to make faults recede, light colours to highlight good features.

### COLOUR CODES FOR CLOTHES

You may like to base your make-up colour choice on your clothes. Pick out the most prominent colour in your outfit and match or co-ordinate your eye shadow. Green needs the warmth of yellows, apricots and coppers. White clothes reflect onto the face, but keep foundation skin-toned, and eyes shaded with neutral greys and browns: these look much more subtle than bright blues or greens. If red is the most predominant colour, eye colours should tend to be neutral, with your lipstick toned to match the red. With black clothes, use a bold colour on either eyes or lips, not both, or the effect will be overstated.

### YOUR AGE, YOUR STYLE

Youth is the time for experimenting and being daring with make-up. Young skins can take colder, sharper colours, such as shocking purples and vivid greens, and startling combinations of colour. Maximize or minimize colour used according to your features, your imagination and your budget. A kohl eyeliner pencil – now available in a wide range of colours – used in different ways can produce an entire eye make-up look, while blushers can double as eye shadow too. For parties try using iridescent colours, highlighting with glitter and colouring or tingeing lips with gold (see **make-up** for illustration of an evening look).

Adapt your make-up with the seasons. Have a natural look in summer, avoiding harsh colours and enhancing your tan with bronzes, bricks or cinnamons, swapping your foundation for a tinted moisturizer with UV filter. Use pearlized eye shadows. In winter, when the skin is paler, be adventurous with rich, burnished colours or jewel shades.

As you grow older, the eye area is the first to age, so tone down colours and use soft pinks, browns or greys rather than bright colours which make the eyes look dull and cold. Use matt, never frosted or shiny colours (they emphasize crêpey skin and wrinkles) and brown or navy (harder than brown) mascara as black is too harsh. Lips should be well-defined with bright, clear colours. Too-pale shades make lips look dry, but glossy colours look very good. Apply colours lightly since heavy application is harsh and ageing. The skin becomes gradually drier and can change tone, so adjust the shade of your foundation accordingly. Avoid blushers tinged with brown or mauve, which deaden the skin's natural tones – warm peaches and soft pinks, well-blended, are much more flattering.

**Combing**
See Hair

**Compulsive eating**
See Bingeing

**Concealers**
See Camouflage

**Condom**
See Contraception

**Copper**
See Minerals

**Conjunctivitis**
See Eyes

**Constipation**
See Diet

## COMBS

*See also: hair – washing, brushing and combing*

Combs are the most ancient of all beauty tools, used in ancient Egypt and Greece. Although combing hair should generally be kept to a minimum to reduce breakage and damage, combs do have important roles to play. Afro combs are good for very curly hair and for removing tangles after washing straighter hair. Combs are also useful for ensuring that conditioner reaches the ends of your hair: massage conditioner in well and comb through *gently*. Miniature combs can be used for decoration in the hair and for holding hair back from the face.

## CONCENTRATION

*See also: anxiety; biorhythms; circadian rhythms; sleep; stress; vitamins*

Learning to concentrate is one of the harder lessons of childhood, but something we all need to do. As life progresses, it becomes evident that concentration is a key to success in most spheres, and that to achieve it, you need to be able to concentrate on your aims and your immediate tasks. The ability to concentrate is a boon in dangerous or tense situations, and therefore one of the body's stress reactions is to increase it. It can also help you to improve your meditation skill (see entry) and vice versa.

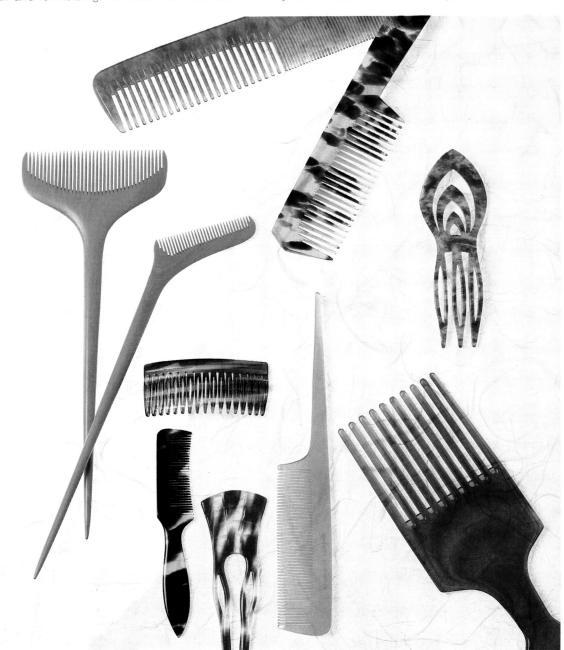

We all feel, at some time or other, that our concentration could be improved. This is why such advertisements in newspapers as 'Do you find it hard to concentrate? Write away for our miraculous aids to concentration' are so common. But there are no miraculous shortcuts. Although a degree of ability to concentrate is inbuilt, everyone has to work at improving these skills according to the needs of their lifestyle and their ambitions.

IMPROVING CONCENTRATION
- **Remove all negative factors** If you are a tidy person, ensure that your workplace is organized so that you won't keep mentally tidying it. Ensure that all the tools you may need are at hand. If you need peace for your work take the telephone off the hook if you can, or ask someone to answer it for you and to leave you undisturbed for a length of time. Most people find silence helpful, but if you prefer to have music in the background, have a radio to hand or set up a music system (but remember the dangers of persistent loud noise – see entry). Make yourself comfortable and warm: discomfort or cold will distract you and lower your productivity.
- **Don't 'overface' yourself** No-one can concentrate at a really useful level for too long. Set yourself a realistic target, say 30 minutes, and build on it.
- **Remove other problems from your mind** If you can deal with them before concentrating on your main objective of the day, so much the better. Failing this, write them down with a note of how and when you will deal with them. Then put the list somewhere safe, but out of your field of vision.
- **Reduce unnecessary stress** Although stress can improve concentration, such as when driving in the dark, or before exams, continued high levels blur the mind and its reactions.
- **Exercise regularly** Keeping your body fit is essential for general health. Alternating periods of exercise and concentration will improve the quality of both.
- **Eat well** Good nutrition is essential for every aspect of life. Vitamin B12, found in liver, kidneys, pork and dairy products, aids concentration (if you are vegetarian you may need to take B12 supplements anyway). Lysine, in proteins like beans, dairy products, fish and meat is another important nutrient, and one which you need more of as you get older.
- **Find your best concentration time** and if possible organize your life so that you can work then. Observe yourself for several days, note when you feel most energetic, least lively, study your Circadian rhythms and even your biorhythms. Everyone has a high-achievement time of day which can be capitalized on.
- **Get plenty of sleep** Observe your waking/sleeping patterns and ensure that you are getting enough sleep. Lack of sleep can be stress-inducing, while prolonged sleep deprivation lowers immunity to germs and decreases energy needed for concentration and achievement.

# CONTACT LENSES

*See also: eyes; glasses; optician*

The wearing of contact lenses has increased enormously since the development of the first soft lens 30 years ago, and there are few people who cannot tolerate one sort or another. Not only are they aesthetically appealing, contact lenses also give a better field of vision than glasses (where 15-20 per cent is lost). It is important to consult a good practitioner.

BEING EXAMINED AND FITTED
Your eyes will be examined in detail, measured and tested. The type of lens most suitable for your eyes will be prescribed. Once the prescription is made up, the optician will teach you how to insert and remove lenses, and will give advice on care and cleaning. He or she will also work out a programme for wearing them, detailing for how long you should wear your lenses at first, and how frequently. It is essential that you do not exceed the recommended times, or you could damage your eyes badly. Instructions will vary according to the type of lens chosen and your individual needs.

Some initial discomfort is to be expected; such things as smoky, windy or dusty atmospheres can cause problems. Insure your contact lenses against loss, and be sure to go for regular check-ups and eye tests, just as you would for glasses.
NOTES Although there are particular advantages for different types of lens, be guided by your optician in choosing lenses, as one particular type may well be indicated either by the shape of your eyeballs, your sight or other factors. Generally speaking, contact lenses are unsuitable for you if:
- You are found by your optician to have unusually sensitive eyes.
- Even after advice and assistance from your optician, you are squeamish about putting your fingers in your eyes (although this can usually be overcome).
- You suffer from dry eye syndrome.
- Your eyeballs are an unsuitable shape (this is unusual).

SPECIAL BENEFITS
Cosmetically, lenses are tremendous confidence-boosters and remove the necessity for heavy, cumbersome spectacles, although you should always have a pair of 'back-up' spectacles in case of eye infection, etc. Some types of lens are particularly useful for some sports (hard lenses tend to be unsuitable, however). In some cases where rigid lenses are worn, the progress of, for example, myopia (short sightedness) may be slowed down.

AGE SUITABILITY
Lenses are suitable for all age groups (provided that you can handle lenses correctly or have a relative who will help you), but are mostly prescribed to people between their mid-teens and middle to late sixties, who should have few problems with them.

C

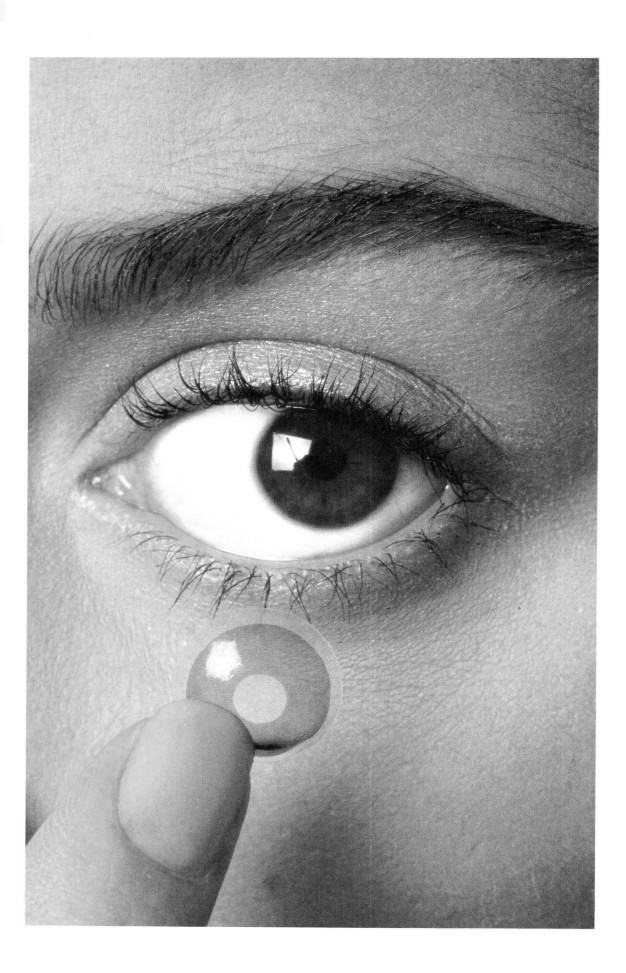

## POSSIBLE PROBLEMS

Lenses take time to get used to. The introduction of a 'foreign body' to the eye is likely to produce slight discomfort for only 10 minutes in the case of soft lenses, but 2-3 weeks in the case of hard lenses. When the cornea has adjusted to the lenses there should be no further problem. It is very important to have regular check-ups – only your optician can ascertain whether or not there *are* problems. Dust can collect beneath the lens and irritate the eye, especially in the case of rigid lenses, as can build-up of protein and calcium from tears: regular cleaning helps prevent this. Protein build-up problems can occur with soft and to some extent with gas permeable lenses, but are less likely with PMMA.

## CARE AND MAINTENANCE

It is important to keep the lenses scrupulously clean, although the process requires a little time and patience. Wash your hands thoroughly before applying lenses, as dirt on the hands can be transmitted to the lens and make the eye water. Other possible irritants include cleaning and storing solutions and smoky environments. If irritation does occur, consult your optician who will establish its cause and possibly recommend alternative solutions. Soft lenses usually last between 6 months (especially if you smoke, and live in a dirty urban environment) and 18 months/2 years, and need extra cleaning to remove tear and protein deposits. If handled poorly, they will last for even less than 6 months. Hard lenses may last much longer – 10-12 years – and are easier to clean. They may need regular polishing and, should the eye change, may not fit properly after a certain length of time: regular check-ups are essential.

# CONTRACEPTION

*See also: awareness; breasts; health*

Contraception is the prevention of conception. There are various methods of ensuring that sexual intercourse will not result in pregnancy. Some work mechanically, others chemically or hormonally, but the general idea is to interrupt one or other of the stages of reproduction, so that either the man's sperm never comes into contact with the woman's ovum (egg) and so cannot fertilize it, or the fertilized egg is unable to implant in the uterus (womb). The search for the perfect contraceptive has been going on for a long time: the Egyptians of around 1850 BC used a paste made of crocodile dung which was inserted into the vagina, while in ancient China women were advised to swallow 24 live tadpoles in the early spring to ensure 5 pregnancy-free years. Breastfeeding, coitus interruptus (withdrawal) and douching are still practised, though now recognized as unreliable. Reliable methods are easily available to everyone in the UK and the US, either from general practitioners, Family Planning Clinics, or over the pharmacist's counter.

## THE PILL

The oral contraceptive pill is the most reliable, reversible method of birth control available. There are two main types of pill. The combined pill is the most widely used and the most effective. It contains two hormones, oestrogen and progestogen. The mini-pill contains progestogen only which suits some women better; for example, those who are breast-

## CONTACT LENSES CHART

| TYPE OF LENSES | DESCRIPTION |
| --- | --- |
| Hard – scleral/haptic | The original contact lens, not worn very widely today – they are only usually prescribed by hospital consultants following eye injury. Coloured versions are also available to conceal scarring (see tinted/coloured lenses below). |
| Hard | Made of polymethylmethacrylate, more commonly known as PMMA. |
| Hard – gas permeable | A rigid lens made in a different material from PMMA: they allow more oxygen to penetrate the cornea which reduces 'crying'. Should you want to take off your lenses you can wear glasses without a period of adjustment. They are, however, as uncomfortable as PMMA when first inserted. |
| Soft | Made from a variety of different materials, they contain a high percentage of fluid, making them comfortable to wear. |
| Soft – extended wear | Similar to soft above, but specially designed so that they can be slept in and worn continuously for far longer periods than other types. However, it is unwise to wear these lenses for more than a week without removal: follow your optician's advice. Use also varies, so check carefully. |
| Soft – tinted | The newest type are soft lenses (hard are available but unusual). The tinted type are transparent; coloured ones are opaque, concealing the natural colour of the eye with an overlay to give a new colour. Coloured lenses give maximum flexibility for colour change. These can be very useful for people who have suffered damage to the eye through burns or scarring, although a hard lens is more often used for this purpose. |

feeding or who are older and should avoid oestrogen (see below).

### How it works
The combined pill works by preventing ovulation. Normally a woman's ovaries release an egg 12-16 days before the next period. If the egg is fertilized, the embryo produces a hormone which works on the egg follicles, making sure that they continue producing oestrogen and progesterone which are needed for the lining of the womb, to provide nourishment for the foetus. If the levels of these hormones remain high, this is a signal to the pituitary gland that pregnancy has been achieved and there is no need to stimulate the ovaries to produce any further eggs. The hormones in the combined pill mimic the stable hormonal state of the beginning of pregnancy and so dupe the body into stopping the release of eggs, without which pregnancy cannot occur.

The progestogen-only pill does not always prevent ovulation (only in about 40 per cent of cycles). It does, however, cause the mucus at the entrance to the cervix to become thicker and thus difficult for sperm to penetrate and enter the womb. This is its main contraceptive action.

### Taking the pill
**The combined pill** is taken once a day for 21, 22 or 28 days of the cycle, depending on the type. A 21- or 22-day type allows a break of 7 or 6 days between the end of one pack and the beginning of another, during which time there will be some bleeding. This is caused by the withdrawal of the hormones and is not a true menstrual period. On the 28-day pill there may be some bleeding during the last 7 days of pill-taking. This is because the last 7 tablets in these everyday pills are placebo, sugar, tablets (some women prefer to take a pill all the time to aid memory). There are also phasic pills, presented in packs containing 2 or 3 different-coloured pills indicating different combinations and levels of hormones. *It is important to take them in the right order* as they are designed to copy the natural hormonal changes that take place in the menstrual cycle.

If you forget to take a pill, take it as soon as possible and continue with the rest of the pack as normal. If you are more than 12 hours late in taking the forgotten pill, you will need extra contraceptive protection for the next 14 days, even if this means continuing the precautions over the pill-free week or into the next packet. Get your partner to use a sheath or, if you already have a diaphragm, use this with spermicide.

**The progestogen-only pill** must be taken at the same time each day, ideally about 4 hours before the time you would usually have intercourse (it is still effective if you want to have intercourse after this time). If the pill is taken more than 3 hours late, additional precautions as described above will be necessary for the next 2 days.

### Effectiveness
Certain drugs can interfere with the action of the pill, reducing its effectiveness. If you are prescribed any medicines, check with your doctor whether you need to take extra precautions. Vomiting or diarrhoea may mean that the pill is not absorbed by the body, so again you should take extra precautions from the first day of your illness until 14 days after the end of it (2 days in the case of women taking the progestogen-only pill).

The combined pill is considered almost 100 per cent effective, while the progestogen-only pill is about 98 per cent effective; both figures apply when the pill is being taken exactly as directed.

### Advantages, disadvantages and developments
Both types of pill have many advantages. They are easy to use and do not interfere with intercourse. The combined pill often has a beneficial effect on the menstrual cycle, making periods regular, lighter and less painful. It can protect against some benign (non-cancerous) breast disease and certain types of cyst on the ovary. It also has a protective effect against ovarian cancer and cancer of the womb, some pelvic infections and possibly rheumatoid arthritis. The progestogen-only pill has a varying effect on the menstrual cycle. Some women find it makes their periods less regular and lighter, other women have no periods at all and others have repeated breakthrough bleeding throughout the cycle.

There are many possible disadvantages associated with the combined pill. Most women do not experience them, but some women are unsuited to

| METHOD | EFFECTIVENESS RATE |
| --- | --- |
| **The combined pill** Oral contraceptive; Triphasic pills; Biphasic pills; Everyday/ED pill | Over 99% effective, if taken properly |
| **Mini-pill** Progestogen-only pill | 98% effective, if taken properly |
| **Injectable contraceptives** Depo-Provera; Noristerat; The jab | Over 99% effective |
| **Intrauterine device** IUD; IUCD; Coil | 96-99% effective |
| **Diaphragm or cap + spermicide** | 85-97% effective, with careful use |
| **Sponge** | 75-91% effective, with careful use |
| **Condom** Sheath; Protective; Rubber; Johnny | 85-98% effective, with careful use |
| **Natural methods** Safe period; Rhythm method | 85-93% effective, with careful use (symptothermal method) |
| **Female sterilization** | Occasional failures occur: 1 in 300 |
| **Male sterilization** Vasectomy | Occasional failures occur: 1 in 1,000 |

the pill among which are smokers over 35 and all women over 45. The chance of thrombosis (blood clotting) in a vein or artery is increased, particularly in older women who are overweight or who smoke. Blood pressure can also rise and therefore should be checked by your doctor regularly. Studies carried out in 1983 suggested that the pill might increase the risk of breast or cervical cancer in some women. Further studies are taking place. A few women find that taking the pill makes them feel depressed. The progestogen-only pill has few side-effects, apart from bleeding irregularities, mentioned above. Acne sufferers should ask their gynaecologist or dermatologist for advice on pill types: some progestogens exacerbate acne, others help allieviate it. There may also be some minor side-effects when you first start the pill, such as slight weight gain, nausea or breast tenderness. These are signs that your body is adjusting to the new hormones. Things should settle down within a few months.

Much work has been done to develop the pill since it was first introduced almost 30 years ago. The major changes have been to reduce the hormones contained in the pill to the lowest levels possible. Scientists now think that the optimum levels have been reached if they are not to reduce effectiveness or increase breakthrough bleeding. Research into a contraceptive pill for men is continuing, but there are many problems involved, and it seems unlikely that it will become a practical reality until the next century.

## INJECTABLES
### How they work
Injectable contraceptives work hormonally, in a similar way to the mini-pill. Progestogen is injected into the muscle of the buttock or arm every 2 or 3 months (depending on the type used) and is released gradually into the body.

### Effectiveness
Both Depo-Provera and Noristerat (the injectables most widely used in Britain) are over 99 per cent effective. Noristerat is not yet available in the USA.

### Advantages and disadvantages
The main advantage is that one dose gives contraceptive protection for up to 12 weeks in the case of Depo-Provera, 8 weeks for Noristerat, without the need for any further action on the part of the user. Like the pill, it does not interfere with lovemaking. The main disadvantage with injectables is that they are not readily reversible. If they cause any side-effects there is nothing you can do about them, except to wait for the drug to wear off, which will take 2 or 3 months or even slightly longer. The menstrual cycle usually becomes irregular and this effect can last for up to a year, even after the injection has worn off. Fertility may also be delayed for up to a year. Injectables are not yet approved for contraceptive use in the US, but they are available. In Britian Depo-Provera is approved for long term use only, for women who cannot use any other method, and Noristerat is approved for short-term use. They have to be prescribed by a doctor and are

considered only as a last resort method, when nothing else is suitable.

### New developments
Research is being carried out into a combined injection (containing oestrogen as well as progestogen). Monthly, instead of three-monthly, injections are also under trial, which may overcome the problem of irregular bleeding.

## THE IUD
### How it works
The IUD, coil or IUCD as it is more properly known, is an intrauterine contraceptive device first developed at the beginning of this century. Early IUD's in gold, silver and silk proved unsatisfactory. There are now several different types. One, the Lippes loop, is made entirely of plastic, the others are made of plastic wound with thin copper wire.

It is not known exactly how they work. The main theory is that they change the lining of the womb so that a fertilized egg is prevented from being embedded and growing there. This means that the IUD works by interfering with the reproductive process after conception, but before implantation.

### Fitting the IUD
The IUD has to be inserted by a specially trained doctor. It is threaded into an applicator, itself a narrow tube, which is carefully inserted through the opening in the cervix. Inside the tube, the IUD flattens out, but as the applicator is removed, the IUD will spring into its original shape and settle into position. It is easiest to fit during a period – and this has the added advantage of ensuring that the woman is not pregnant. The muscle of the womb will be stretched slightly and will contract in reaction to the foreign body, thus causing some discomfort for a few hours after fitting. IUDs made with copper are replaced every 2-5 years, but the plastic Lippes loop can be left in longer. Regular checks by a doctor are important, but you can check the IUD has not been expelled, as sometimes happens, by feeling for the thin plastic threads which pass through the cervical opening into the vagina. You should do this once a month after each period.

### Effectiveness
The IUD is 96-99 per cent effective, and works from the moment it is put in.

### Advantages and disadvantages
The IUD does not interfere with intercourse. Once in, the user does not have to think about it. It lasts for several years. It has no hormonal effect on the body. It is readily reversible. Some women experience heavier periods when using an IUD, especially for the first few months. There may be bleeding between periods too. Contractions of the womb may expel the IUD: if this is going to happen, it will usually do so within the first 3 months. The IUD may increase the chance of a pelvic infection – in particular pelvic inflammatory disease – especially if you are under 30 and have several sexual partners. Untreated, this may lead to sterility which is why

many doctors discourage women who have not had a child from using an IUD, though many such women do use one successfully. If you are not sure which IUD you have in place, consult your gynaecologist or Family Planning Clinic as there is one type, the Dalkon Shield, which should be removed.

### New developments
New developments in the IUD which are currently on trial include devices which release hormones or drugs which act locally to minimize blood loss or protect against pelvic inflammatory disease.

### THE DIAPHRAGM AND CAP
#### How they work
Diaphragms and caps are barrier methods which work by preventing sperm from entering the womb. Diaphragms are dome-shaped devices made of thin rubber kept in shape by a rubber-encased metal rim. They have been in use since the latter half of the late 19th century. Caps are smaller and made of rubber only. Both are used by placing them over the cervix and should be used in conjunction with a spermicidal cream, jelly, or foam.

#### Using a diaphragm or cap
Diaphragms and caps have to be used every time sexual intercourse takes place. A thin layer of spermicide is spread around the rim and on each side of the dome, and the diaphragm is then inserted into the vagina so that it covers the cervix. It can be put in any time before making love, but if intercourse occurs more than 3 hours after insertion or more than once, more spermicide should be used. The diaphragm should be left in place for at least 6 hours after intercourse.

Diaphragms should be fitted by a doctor or a specially trained nurse as there are several different sizes available. Every 6 months or after childbirth, losing or gaining more than 3 kg (7 lb) in weight, an abortion or a miscarriage, you should be refitted.

The diaphragm should be checked carefully and regularly to ensure it has no tears or holes. Washing it in plain warm water after use and drying thoroughly, then storing it in a cool, dry place, should lengthen its life and prevent the rubber from perishing.

#### Effectiveness
Both the diaphragm and the cap are 85-97 per cent effective with careful use.

#### Advantages and disadvantages
The main advantages are that they are used only when needed and have no harmful effect on the body. Use need not interrupt lovemaking as they can be inserted several hours beforehand. They may also offer some protection against cancer of the cervix. Women who dislike touching their genital area, or who dislike the premeditation required, will not feel happy with this method. Some women find that spermicidal creams interfere with oral sex, others find that the diaphragm aggravates cystitis, and a few are allergic to the spermicide or even to the rubber of the diaphragm itself. A type of cap

known as the 'honey cap', which is a standard diaphragm coated with honey with which spermicide is not used, has not been shown in trials to give a satisfactory level of protection. If prevention of pregnancy is important, you would be wise not to use this honey cap method alone.

### New developments
Scares about the pill have led to renewed interest in barrier methods and much research is going on into them. One new device now available, though not widely, is the contraceptive sponge (see below).

### THE CONDOM
#### How it works
The condom is a sheath of thin rubber which is worn over the man's erect penis to contain ejaculated sperm, thus preventing them from entering the woman's vagina. Earlier forms, made of skin or animal gut, were popular in the 17th century, though primarily as a protection against venereal disease rather than to prevent pregnancy.

#### Using the condom
Modern varieties are usually lubricated, which makes them easier to put on and to insert into the vagina. The condom is rolled onto the erect penis before intercourse, with the closed end pinched between the fingers to make sure that there is no air in it. After ejaculation the penis should be withdrawn carefully from the vagina, holding the condom in place. A condom should not be reused, a new one must be used each time.

#### Effectiveness
Condoms are 85-98 per cent effective with careful use. In Britain, the Family Planning Association recommends that condoms carrying the British Standards Institution Kitemark should be used.

#### Advantages and disadvantages
Condoms are particularly useful for casual sex. They have no medical side-effects (except the possibility of an allergy to the rubber) and may protect against sexually transmitted disease in the man and the woman, and possibly also cancer of the cervix in the woman. They are easy to obtain – free from Family Planning Clinics in the UK, or bought over the counter at pharmacies, barber's shops or from vending machines.

Some men find that using a condom dulls sensation and some women also feel the difference. The condom can slip off and care must be taken that no sperm are spilt near the vaginal area when removing condoms. The main disadvantage is that lovemaking has to be interrupted to put on the condom and many people, especially the sexually inexperienced, find this embarrassing, though others overcome the problem by treating it as a part of foreplay.

### THE SPONGE
#### How it works
The sponge is a barrier method made of soft polyurethane foam containing a spermicide, which is circular in shape and covers the cervix. It can be

inserted into the vagina any time up to 24 hours before intercourse takes place and must remain in for 6 hours afterwards.

### Effectiveness
Statistics vary from 75 to 91 per cent effective with careful use.

### Advantages and disadvantages
Once inserted, the sponge remains effective for 24 hours, however often intercourse occurs during that period. No added spermicide is needed. Unlike the diaphragm, special fitting is not required as one size fits all women. There is no need for careful cleaning, drying and storage as the sponge is simply thrown away after use.

The sponge is not generally available on the NHS in Britain. It cannot be obtained from General Practitioners and only from some Family Planning Clinics. Although it can be bought over the counter from pharmacists in the UK and US, professional instruction in its use is recommended.

The sponge should not be worn during a period and should not be left in for more than 30 hours. Some women may be allergic to the spermicide.

### NATURAL FAMILY PLANNING
### How it works
Some couples prefer to use one, or a combination of, the safe period methods. These involve working out when the fertile phase of the cycle is and avoiding intercourse during that time (or using a barrier method).

All the methods involve a sound understanding of a woman's body and require a good deal of motivation and self-discipline, but women who are interested in and knowledgeable about their cycle, and dislike interfering with the body's natural rhythm, may prefer using them.

### Using natural family planning
1 The most basic is the calendar or rhythm method. To use this, you need to know that a woman normally ovulates 14 days before her period is due and that sperm can live for up to 5 days inside the womb. A strict record of the menstrual cycle has to be kept for 6 consecutive months before using the method. The first unsafe day is worked out by subtracting 18 from the shortest cycle in the record. The last unsafe day is worked out by subtracting 10 from the longest cycle in the record. Intercourse is unsafe between the first and last unsafe days. This method is not reliable or recommended on its own, particularly if cycles are very irregular.

2 The temperature method is based on the fact that body temperature rises just after ovulation. First you need to know your basal body temperature, which you find by taking your temperature every day as soon as you wake up (a special thermometer showing small changes is available). Once you have recorded a higher temperature for 3 days running you should be safe until the beginning of your next period. In a 28-day cycle this means that there are about 11 safe days. The method does not, therefore, give many safe days and may be unreliable since your temperature may rise if you are ill or go down if you take drugs such as aspirin.

3 The mucus method or Billings method is based on the changes in quality and quantity of cervical mucus which occur over the menstrual cycle.

About 4 days before ovulation the mucus becomes clear, copious and stretchy, like egg white. Intercourse should be avoided (or a diaphragm or condom used) from the first 'wet day' until the fourth 'dry day' which occurs after ovulation.

### Effectiveness
Accurate effectiveness figures for these methods are difficult to obtain. Combining the mucus method with the temperature method (together

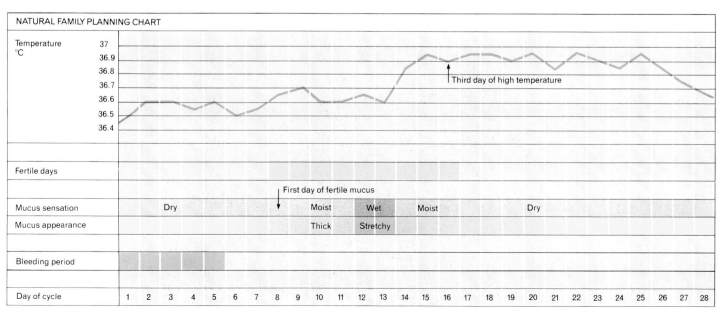

NATURAL FAMILY PLANNING CHART

known as the symptothermal method) and including the recognition of other ovulatory signs such as slight pains in the back or lower abdomen, headaches or breast discomfort, has given results as good as 85-93 per cent effective. This method takes time to learn, though, and needs expert instruction and considerable motivation.

### Advantages and disadvantages
The main advantage of these methods is that they do not interfere with the woman's body in any way. A full knowledge of the menstrual cycle and the ability to recognize ovulation may also become an asset once a pregnancy is desired.

The main disadvantages are the unreliability and the constant commitment required, as well as the necessity of abstinence, sometimes for quite considerable lengths of time.

### New developments
New developments, designed to pinpoint the exact time of ovulation more accurately, include a 'bionic thermometer', possibly in the form of an alarm clock or pendant worn on a necklace, dipsticks to test hormone levels in urine or saliva, and a mechanical device to measure mucus consistency.

### POST-COITAL CONTRACEPTION
This is an emergency measure, designed to be used if a contraceptive has failed or a risk is known to have been taken. Quick action is needed. There are two methods currently available: high doses of a particular contraceptive pill or the fitting of an IUD. The 'morning after' pill must be started within 3 days of unprotected sex and may cause severe nausea. The IUD must be fitted within 5 days and can then be left in if wanted. Both methods are over 98 per cent effective.

### STERILIZATION
Male or female sterilization is only a good method for those who are sure they have completed their families or who never want children.

### The operation
**Female sterilization** involves an operation to block the Fallopian tubes so that eggs cannot travel down to meet the sperm. It can be performed in a hospital or clinic under general or local anaesthetic. There are two main methods. Mini-laparotomy or tubal ligation involves a small cut being made just below the bikini line through which the Fallopian tubes are reached. The tubes are blocked by tying and removal of a small section or by sealing (diathermy). Laparoscopy is more common: the tubes are reached through one or two tiny cuts just below the navel, and a tiny telescope-like instrument (laparoscope) is then inserted so that the surgeon can see clearly. The tubes are then blocked with rings or clips. A few women may have heavier periods.

**Male sterilization or vasectomy** involves blocking or cutting the tubes (vas deferens) which carry the sperm from the testicles. The operation is usually done under local anaesthetic. Sperm may be left in the tube leading to the penis so contraceptive precautions should be used for 3 months, after which tests are done to confirm that there are no sperm left. There is likely to be some discomfort due to bruising for a while, but sex drive, orgasm and ejaculation are not affected.

### Effectiveness
Failures are about 1 in 300 for female sterilization, 1 in 1,000 for male sterilization.

# CORNS

*See also: calluses; chiropodist; feet*

Corns are inverted cone-shaped pads of hard, dead skin layers which press down on the inner layers of the skin. They can be very painful indeed. They occur on or between the toes, or even under the foot, and are caused by ill-fitting shoes, probably shoes that are too tight. To prevent them, wear comfortable, properly fitted shoes and visit your chiropodist (State Registered in the UK) regularly.

### TREATMENT
Soak your feet regularly in a bowl of bath-hot water to soften the corns. Dry feet and apply unmedicated, ring-shaped pads (available at pharmacies) to alleviate pressure. NEVER attempt to pare away hard skin yourself: you will only cause more damage and risk infection and sepsis. Your chiropodist will be able to deal with them.

# COSMETIC ACUPUNCTURE

*See also: acupuncture; ageing*

Cosmetic acupuncture cannot provide a facelift, but it can help tighten up facial muscles and stimulate good circulation in facial skin, thus increasing skin cell renewal and improving moisture retention, texture and colour. Facial acupuncture works on the same principles as any other type: energy channels are freed and the areas being treated stimulated to heal themselves, although the emphasis of this treatment is on surface effects on the skin.

### THE PROCESS
Needles are inserted into acupuncture points on the face (chosen according to individual needs) and sometimes also on the body. Alternatively, the points may be stimulated electronically, but in either case the treatment is quite short, including a concluding moisturizing facial massage. Several treatments are normally needed, with follow-ups.

# COSMETIC DENTISTRY

*See also: dental procedures; orthodontist; teeth*

Cosmetic dentistry is work carried out to improve the appearance of teeth. Any work carried out in the mouth for the sake of the health of teeth and gums should improve or at least maintain the attractiveness of the mouth. Natural-looking, tooth-coloured filling material has been developed for back and front teeth but nearly all fillings eventually wear and discolour. Frequent replacement weakens the tooth, making more drastic repairs such as crowning necessary. Other teeth may be lost completely, through neglect, accident or ill-health, and may need total replacement. Or teeth may simply look ugly, even though they are healthy. In all these cases, cosmetic dentistry can help.

## Crowns
A crown is a 'cap' made to look like a tooth, fitted onto the stump of the real tooth which has been prepared to receive it. Once crowned, a tooth will always need a crown. Crowns can be used to improve the appearance of teeth which are discoloured by dead nerves or acidic foods, broken by an accident or repeated fillings, misshapen or badly aligned. A single tooth or a group of teeth can usually be crowned. Porcelain crowns give the best appearance and recently new materials have increased the strength of these, permitting back teeth to be crowned. When there is going to be a lot of impact on the crown from opposing teeth, however, the porcelain may be fused onto a gold or metal alloy substructure. In either case colour can be matched to natural teeth.

If fitted well, crowns are fairly permanent and age well. Cosmetically, crowns work very well. Occasionally they will become uncemented, but re-cementing is quick and breakages are uncommon.

Crowns are only suitable where oral hygiene is good. They need to be well constructed and a perfect fit to minimize irritation to the gums. As an alternative to a crown, tooth-coloured resin can be painted onto a tooth and built up in layers. The natural tooth is treated with a weak acid to allow the resin to bond to it. This either sets chemically or is hardened using a special light gun. Acid-etched facings are a good 'long-term temporary' solution when full crown construction work is inappropriate, for example in young people whose jaws are still forming, or in adults to demonstrate the possible effect of a crown. They are much cheaper and quicker than crowns although they may discolour or chip in a few months.

## Bridges
Bridges are similar to crowns, and are used to replace missing teeth. Usually there must be teeth on either side of the space and these are crowned with porcelain on a gold or metal alloy substructure and a dummy tooth is fixed in between to fill the gap. There are various types which when carefully designed and perfectly fitted on good natural teeth will last many years. They need careful cleaning.

Bridges are particularly useful for filling in missing front teeth. The false tooth remains in position permanently and is not removed for cleaning as would be the case if a denture were used. Bridgework involves crowns, so the same problems may also apply. If the work is not done carefully, the false tooth may look unnatural or the bridge may not fit well, leading to early loss of the teeth supporting it.

## Partial dentures
Dentures are restorative and cosmetic. They are a set of false teeth, made of plastic or porcelain, joined together on a plastic or metal base, used when fixed bridgework is impossible because a great number of teeth are missing or remaining ones too weak to support the bridge. Dentures are removable, being attached to the natural teeth by clasps or other special attachments, and just sitting on the gum. The construction of a good, well-fitting partial denture is a lengthy procedure and may require many visits to the dentist to check the plate's accuracy before the final fitting. It may take some time to get used to dentures. A strict cleaning regime is necessary, using a soft toothbrush or special denture brush and a good denture paste.

Partial dentures are usually cheaper than bridgework, and normally require no tooth preparation. There is little chance of infection (easily treated if it occurs) if the dentures are properly cleaned.

Denture-wearers may have some initial difficulty articulating certain words, experiencing slurred speech and excess salivation. These problems should disappear once the wearer becomes accustomed to the denture.

## Full dentures
When all the teeth in one or both jaws are missing, the necessary dentures are known as 'full' or 'complete'. The advantages and disadvantages are the same as for partial dentures. The best denture is a poor substitute for natural teeth, but false teeth are aesthetically and practically better than no teeth.

## Implants
Implants are of two types. The subperiosteal implant is a metal framework which is buried beneath the gums and sits on the jawbone with vertical rods sticking up through the gums on which crowns or dentures are fixed. The endosseus implant is usually made up of individual blades embedded *in* the jawbone with studs coming through the gum to take the crown or denture. Both types require surgery.

They may be useful if it is impossible to wear conventional dentures, or greater stability is needed. Endosseus implants may be useful as one end of a bridge, the other end being a natural tooth.

Implants should not be used unless proven treatments have failed. They rarely last for more than 5 years. The health of the jawbone may be undermined by infection as the implant forms a direct route between the mouth, and its bacteria, and the bone.

# COSMETIC SURGERY

*See also: aspiration; chemical peeling; collagen – implants; cosmetic acupuncture; dermabrasion; lasers; mastectomy; skin*

Plastic surgery has two branches: Cosmetic surgery and Reconstructive surgery. Whereas in Reconstructive surgery the purpose is to reconstruct damaged or deformed parts of the body resulting from accident, burns or congenital defect, in cosmetic surgery operations are undergone to improve appearance. Sometimes both purposes come into effect.

The reasons why people undergo cosmetic surgery are wide-ranging, from the desire to make the face look younger, to reduction of over-large breasts or an over-large nose which have caused prolonged unhappiness. Whatever the purpose it is essential to remember that any surgery involves an operation under anaesthetic, stitches, some scarring, discomfort and a period of convalescence.

## IS COSMETIC SURGERY FOR YOU?
There is much to consider before embarking on this sort of surgery. It is a very major step in your life. Ask yourself these questions:
1   What change are you expecting in yourself? If a changed lifestyle is what you are really looking for, then you probably need to take up a new interest – learn a new skill, take a university course or change jobs. Cosmetic surgery will leave you bitterly disappointed, and is not for you. If you are expecting to gain new confid-

## GUIDE TO COSMETIC SURGERY

| REGION AND CONDITION | OPERATION PROCESS AND LENGTH |
|---|---|
| **Brow, upper face and eyebrows**<br>to remove sagging skin and signs of ageing | a) Deep creases: incision made 2-3 cm (¾-1 inch) into hair from hairline, reaching from above ear round across top of head to above other ear. Skin is lifted up and from the sides. Operation time: approximately 1 hour<br>b) Smaller creases: incisions made above brows which are then lifted. Operation time: approximately 1 hour |
| **Mid-face lift**<br>to lift and restructure middle and upper face, with some effect on brow, but none on eyes, upper lip, chin or neck | a) Younger lift or one where no restructuring is required: incisions made in folds in front of ears, may extend up into hair. Skin tightened, thus sometimes referred to as a 'tuck'. Operation time: 2-3 hours, sometimes done under local anaesthetic in conjunction with drowsiness-inducing drugs, as out-patient<br>b) Older lift or where restructuring is necessary: similar positions for longer incisions so that muscles can be tightened or adjusted to give new contours, cheek implants inserted as well as skin being tightened. Operation takes 3-4 hours, sometimes done under local anaesthetic with drowsiness-inducing drugs, but not as out-patient |
| **Neck and chin (segmental meloplasty)**<br>to remove sagging, crêpey, excess skin on neck, tighten up jawline or rebuild chin shape | a) To improve natural chin silhouette and tighten neck skin: incisions made down behind ears and round side of neck into hair. Muscle bed tightened, excess tissue at jaw removed, skin lifted to leave 'natural' creases<br>b) To alter chin shape, sometimes undertaken to balance new nose shape, or on its own. Tiny incision made under chin, or in lower gum inside the mouth to enable plastic implant to be slipped in. Skin stretches to accomodate new shape. May be done as out-patient under local anaesthetic |
| **Eyelids (blepheroplasty)**<br>to remove bags under eyes, puffiness from upper eyelid, to deal with exaggerated problem of this type called blepherochalasis where, due to excess skin, lateral vision may be impaired, and sometimes to resculpture eye area | a) Straightforward blepheroplasty: incisions made just below lashes on lower lid, in fold of eyelid extending to the corner of the eye for the upper lid. Excess fatty tissue which is causing puffiness removed; skin also removed in older patients as it will not contract. Operation time: approximately 1½ hours, and simple cases may be carried out under local anaesthetic as an out-patient<br>b) As above, but muscles can be tightened, or section of muscle can be removed above eye to give deeper socket, some of bone above eye removed to enlarge eye area, muscles at side of eye flattened to improve crow's feet. Operation time: varies according to amount of work, approximately 2 hours. |
| **Nose (rhinoplasty)**<br>to reduce, reshape, or increase nose size for medical reasons, such as breathing problems, or for cosmetic reasons | a) Can be carried out through the mouth or by making cut beneath lower eyelashes. Silicone implants inserted. Operation time: 1-2 hours, mostly under local anaesthetic.<br>b) All work done from inside nose: some bone and cartilage may be cut away, remodelled, or bone/plastic implants grafted on to existing bone. Operation time: 1-2 hours under general or local anaesthetic as an in- or out-patient; one of the most skilful operations. |

ence, however, you are likely to succeed in doing this. It takes determination to get through the cosmetic surgery procedure, just as it does to gain confidence. If you are expecting youth to return, you will be disappointed: you may end up looking 10 years younger, but you may also just look healthier.

2 Can you be certain that it is not a purely emotional problem which is prompting you to try surgery? Discussion with your doctor will help to clarify this and he will be able to refer you for specialist help in this area if necessary. Be honest with yourself, because if the problem is emotional, it will still be there after surgery. Be very sure that you want to have the operation for yourself, too, not for anyone else. You are the person who has to go through with it, not your partner, and you have to live with the results for the rest of your life.

3 Are your expectations for the results of your surgery realistic? Cosmetic surgery does not give you a new face, but it can make your face look 10 years younger and alter individual features. Your surgeon will tell you what results you can reasonably expect, although even he cannot give you an exact picture: your appearance afterwards will depend on healing speed and quality, skin elasticity and texture. The results of face-lift surgery vary but, generally speaking, you can expect your results to last as follows: 10 years if in the fourth decade; 7 years if in the fifth; 5 years in the sixth.

4 Are you happy with yourself generally? Your results are likely to be more successful if you are. Evidence shows that people who are happy and have concrete reasons for wanting this type of surgery adjust best to the changes and are most satisfied.

| RECUPERATION AND VISIBLE EVIDENCE | COMMENTS | MINUS FACTOR |
|---|---|---|
| a) Hospital stay: maximum 1 night; stitches removed after approximately 1 week. Sensation of tightness, numbness and some soreness for first few weeks. No visible evidence except for men if they subsequently suffer from receding hairline<br>b) Hospital stay: one night; stitches removed after approximately 1 week. Bruising and swelling take about 2 weeks to disappear, numbness approximately 12 weeks. Tiny but visible scars which can be hidden with make-up, see camouflage | May be carried out on their own, or as part of general face lift programme. Over-tightening of skin can produce permanently surprised expression, but well done, operation can give youthful look and last 5-10 years. Some surgeons recommend chemical peeling or dermabrasion several months later | Specific complications, which rarely occur, are given in comments column, for each operation. There are, however, several possible general complications in cosmetic surgery of which you should be aware. A small percentage of patients suffer haematomas, black marks in the skin where blood collects beneath it, minor nerve injuries which produce abnormal sensation or lack of sensation, and side-effects from general anaesthesia. If you are in good health and have never had a particular problem with general anaesthetics, you would be unlikely to experience any of these. Choosing the very best surgeon helps prevent the possibility of any side-effects: you and your operative and medical history will be very well known to him or her so that all possible precautions can be taken |
| a) Hospital stay: 1 night or as out-patient; stitches removed after approximately 7 days. There will be bruising, numbness, redness, soreness and swelling which will all disappear within a few weeks. Scars should be discreet, but visible<br>b) Hospital stay: 1 night; stitches removed after approximately 15 days. Alterations to facial muscles will feel strange and exercise will be required after healing, other symptoms as for a) above. Scars should be discreet, but will be visible | One of the most popular cosmetic surgery operations. The first type can be repeated or followed by b). Results should last for up to 10 years. Some surgeons recommend chemical peeling or dermabrasion several months later | |
| a) Hospital stay: 1 day; stitches removed after 7-10 days. Stiffness will be minimal, some bruising, swelling and numbness is probable. Scars are partially hidden in hair and a scar hugs the front of the ear<br>b) Hospital stay: 1 night or out-patient procedure; stitches removed after approximately 10 days. If inserted from mouth, soreness and swelling will be experienced; little discomfort if inserted from below. Firm chin bandage necessary, light diet of soft food | a) Popular operation for older patients, but can be done while young where double chin is marked, and repeated if necessary. Lasts approximately 10 years if young, less if older. Chin implants b) carry slight danger of rejection, infection and slippage, but results are otherwise permanent | |
| Stitches removed after only 3 days as eye area heals quickly and well: scars should be almost invisible. Bruising and swelling will be extensive at first so wear dark glasses. Feeling of tightness and slight numbness over eyes may continue for several weeks. No make-up should be worn for at least 5 days.<br>a) Hospital stay: 1 night or out-patient procedure<br>b) Hospital stay: 1 night, depending on amount of restructuring; whole eye area must be treated with special care for several weeks until muscles have healed | Often carried out on young people where medically indicated or, if patient has inherited bagginess, for cosmetic reasons. If for the latter reason results will be permanent, but ageing may produce new bags and the operation can be repeated to remove these. One of the most effective operations to improve the youthful appearance of the face, it may delay more extensive work for several years. Some surgeons recommend chemical peeling or dermabrasion several months later | |
| a) Hospital stay 1 night, or done as day patient. Stitches removed after 7 days. Extensive swelling in area and inside mouth if this method used. Otherwise bruised eyes which cannot be concealed with dark glasses owing to swelling in cheeks<br>b) Hospital stay: approximately 1 night. No scarring at all, all surgery inside nose. Plaster on nose for approximately 1 week. Discomfort is akin to having a clogged-up nose with extensive bruising and swelling. Breathing only through mouth for 1 week | Nose surgery should not be carried out on anyone who has not finished growing, approximately 15 for girls, 16 for boys, although nose shapes do continue to change later in life. Infection and nosebleeds are possible side-effects | |

5 Are you overweight? If you are, you are not a suitable candidate for cosmetic surgery until you have lost weight. Results are poorer in fat people. Lose weight slowly, in such a way that the weight will stay off (see **diet**), before considering the operation. Losing a great deal of weight after cosmetic surgery is not a good idea, either: ageing skin cannot adjust to huge weight changes, and lines and sagging will probably return.

6 Can you cope with one or more complex, often painful, operations and the time which it will take to make a complete recovery? Bruising invariably follows cosmetic surgery; stitches may have to come out in sections; the discom-

fort can be severe to start with, and the whole undertaking requires the complete commitment and foreknowledge of the patient. Consult the chart below for details.

7 Can you afford the operation? All cosmetic surgery is expensive: only some operations, in special circumstances, can be carried out under the NHS in Britain, or under medical insurance schemes in Britain or elsewhere. Examples of this are almost all operations which are necessary as a result of accidental injury, and operations where the area operated on has caused a physical or serious psychological problem to the patient. Otherwise you will have to pay for the operation and hospital

## GUIDE TO COSMETIC SURGERY

| REGION AND CONDITION | OPERATION PROCESS AND LENGTH |
|---|---|
| **'The facelift' (rhytidectomy)** to lift the whole face, and sometimes neck as well, removing sagging skin and wrinkles | The facelift involves removing excess skin on the face and sometimes on the neck. May be carried out under local anaesthetic if only face, general if neck. Operation time: approximately 2-3 hours. |
| **Abdomen (abdominal lipectomy)** to remove excess tissue, fat and skin from the abdomen, tighten muscles. Usually done after very large weight loss, more rarely after pregnancy | This is a lengthy procedure, not undertaken just to remove stretch-marked skin. Muscle and tissue are undermined as far up as the ribcage and pulled down. The navel is repositioned, skin stitched in long curving line from hip to hip. Up to 6.8 kg (15 lb) of skin and fat may be removed |
| **Breast reduction** to reduce breast size where this has caused severe problems, both physical and psychological | Incision made around nipple, then down and to both sides in T shape, or made sideways from nipple and then upwards. Operation time: approximately 2 hours for each breast. The operation removes breast tissue, fat and skin |
| **Breast augmentation** for cosmetic reasons, or for reconstruction necessary as a result of mastectomy | a) Cosmetic augmentation: incision is made either in fold beneath breast, in armpit or around nipple. Operation time: ½ hour for each breast, carried out either under general or local anaesthetic, in some cases as an out-patient. The implant, placed either just behind breast tissue or behind pectoral muscle, may be of silicone gel or be inflatable, to be filled with saline after being inserted. Newest type is double lumen, with an outer membrane around an inner core of silicone gel. The prosthesis least likely to harden (see comments) is one which has an outer layer of polyurethane and an inner layer of silicone gel b) Post-mastectomy augmentation: if mastectomy has been subcutaneous the process will be largely similar to that described above. If pectoral muscle, lymph glands and whole breast have been removed, the augmentation will be preceded by skin grafting or the use of skin flaps taken from, for example, the back, which contain blood vessels (depending on the individual situation), and creation of a new nipple and may be a lengthy process involving several operations |
| **Breast lifting** to lift drooping (ptotic) breasts, sometimes done in combination with augmentation | Incisions are as for breast reduction, but only skin is removed: nipples are moved upwards while still attached to tissue beneath. If increased size is required rather than return of previous contour, implant can be used, see above. Operating time will be similar to breast reduction |
| **Ear 'pinning back' (otoplasty)** to remove excess cartilage or create a fold in cartilage to stop ears sticking out: patients as young as 4 may have otoplasty | Operating time: 2 hours. The excess cartilage behind ear, which holds it out, is removed and the skin tightened |

time, and be prepared to take several weeks away from work in some cases. Most operations can now be done under local anaesthetic as an out-patient, which reduces the cost of the whole procedure (see chart).

## GOING AHEAD WITH COSMETIC SURGERY

The most important step after analyzing why you want surgery and whether surgery really will bring improvement to your problem, is to discuss the whole thing with your family doctor or another doctor whom you trust. Knowing your background, he will be able to give you a subjective assessment of the operation's benefits for you, and will also take an objective view (and consider the whole spectrum of help which you could receive). He will advise you and also be able to recommend a good surgeon, which is very important. DO NOT just go to whoever seems fashionable nor rely on the list of face-lift centres in advertising pages: follow reliable recommendation only.

## THE CONSULTATION

The surgeon will want to ask you all the questions which you have already asked yourself. He will also consult your medical history and ask you about your past experiences of surgery. He will discuss the various options with you and, if you both decide that an operation is the right thing, he will explain its process and after-effects to you in detail.

| RECUPERATION AND VISIBLE EVIDENCE | COMMENTS | MINUS FACTOR |
|---|---|---|
| Scars extend around temples, hugging the ear, skirting the lobe, then going round back of ear into hairline. Hospital stay: 1 night or as out-patient | The facelift is still a very popular operation with many age groups, although other operations on facial zones which involve structural work are becoming increasingly common | Specific complications, which rarely occur, are given in comments column, for each operation. There are, however, several possible general complications in cosmetic surgery of which you should be aware. A small percentage of patients suffer haematomas, black marks in the skin where blood collects beneath it, minor nerve injuries which produce abnormal sensation or lack of sensation, and side-effects from general anaesthesia. If you are in good health and have never had a particular problem with general anaesthetics, you would be unlikely to experience any of these. Choosing the very best surgeon helps prevent the possibility of any side-effects: you and your operative and medical history will be very well known to him or her so that all possible precautions can be taken |
| Hospital stay: approximately 6 nights, followed by a week in bed at home and several weeks of gentle recovery. Stitches removed after 10-15 days. Soreness will be extensive, post-operative treatment will involve rest alternating with exercise and physiotherapy. Central area of scar may be hidden by pubic hair, scars over hips will be visible | This operation should only be carried out on people who have achieved their best weight and intend to keep to it. Weight gain or pregnancy are likely to reverse the effects of the operation. Scars may become raised (hypertrophic) or inflamed. Effect of surgery on nerve-endings will cause numbness which will continue for some months. Some slight alteration in sensation around the scars is almost inevitable | |
| Hospital stay: approximately 2 nights, followed by 3-4 weeks of gentle life at home with no lifting or strenuous exercise of any sort. Stitches removed after 10-15 days. Scars are not hidden in folds, except beneath or at side of breast and will be evident, though fading after a year or so | Scars may become distended and raised (hypertrophic) due to tension and strain. Breastfeeding ability should not be impaired if the operation is correctly performed. Future pregnancies or weight gain/loss can undo some of the benefits of the operation. Loss of sensitivity in the nipple occurs, which usually lasts approximately 3 months, but can be permanent | |
| a) Hospital stay: approximately 1 night, or can be done as out-patient under local anaesthetic. Stitches removed after approximately 7-10 days. Gentle living necessary for at least 3 weeks, no strenuous activity for at least 6. Scar under arm is not generally visible; scar under breast not readily visible<br>b) As a), if subcutaneous mastectomy has necessitated operation, but it is slightly more difficult to produce absolutely lifelike results. After more radical mastectomy, scars will vary according to amount of grafting and work done. Hypertrophic scars are a possibility | a) Breast should feel supple and move normally and breastfeeding will not be impaired. Likelihood of cancer is not increased, nor is possibility of early detection impaired. Common complication is hardening of implant: patients are advised to massage breasts daily for at least 3 months to mobilize the implant and prevent scar tissue forming: manual compression of the breast by the surgeon can, however, rectify 90 per cent of cases with this problem. Rarely, implants have to be removed or repositioned.<br>b) As a), but perfect results more difficult to achieve and possibility of repositioning more likely. Implant should feel quite natural, however, imitating the original breast in weight and movement | |
| Hospital stay: approximately 1 night, followed by 3-4 weeks of gentle living. Stitches removed after approximately 10 days. Scars will be evident but will fade gradually over a year | Operation should not be carried out until after having children as further pregnancies can recreate the problem. Raised, enlarged scars are again a possibility as for other breast operations | |
| Hospital stay: 1 night. This can be done as an out-patient as the operation is normally carried out under local anaesthetic. Bandage round head to hold back ears must be worn for a week. Scars behind ears invisible. Stitches removed after 7-10 days. Some pain for several days which can be dealt with by painkillers | Operation produces permanent results | |

# COSMETICS

*See also: allergies; colour choice; eye make-up; hypo-allergenic products; lanolin; make-up*

Unlike Diane de Poitiers, a famous 16th-century beauty, few women can claim that they use only rainwater on their skin. Throughout history, cosmetics have been used to enhance looks and preserve complexions. The earliest cosmetics were made from vegetable dyes, colour pigments were formulated from natural ores, and leaves and flowers pounded to make pastes and powders. Although many of today's cosmetics are derived from plants and herbs, many are laboratory-processed. Now vitamins, hormones and proteins are incorporated into products claiming to regenerate the skin. Opinion is divided over their effectiveness. Skin can undoubtedly absorb some substances, especially essential oils, but there is no evidence to suggest

that what does penetrate the epidermis can perpetrate any radical change in the actual skin cells despite claims to the contrary.

Most moisturizing creams, however, will improve the texture and quality of the skin's surface and help retain its water content. This, together with a good skin-care routine, protection against the sun and eating a balanced diet will help to make the best of your complexion and help prevent all the signs of premature ageing.

Choosing cosmetics is largely a question of trial and error. Manufacturer's claims and individual results are often two very different things. Analyze your skin type before buying skin-care products – purchasing a rich, heavy moisturizer is pointless if you have an oily complexion. Remember that skin alters with age, often becoming drier, more sensitive and lighter in colour. To follow a good skin-care routine, you will need cleansing, moisturizing and toning products as well as specially formulated creams for the eye and neck areas. Since sunlight is a major cause of prematurely aged skin, choose products which include a sunscreen filter (see **tanning**). Higher-priced brands are not necessarily better for the skin, although their texture often makes them easier to apply.

Always read labels to discover the ingredients before buying: some common allergens like lanolin which is always marked on packaging in the UK and US (often found in superfatted or moisturizing products) and perfumes are best avoided by those with sensitive skins. Hypoallergenic products (see entry) have the simplest formulations, but like 'clinically tested' products, cannot be guaranteed not to provoke a reaction in some people. Most cosmetics contain preservatives to prevent contamination by bacteria and the air, although they are not always needed in toners/astringents: they often contain alcohol which itself has a similar, though not entirely prohibitive, effect.

Although synthetic chemicals make effective cosmetic ingredients, many people prefer to use herb- or plant-based products which release their properties when combined with water or alcohol. Commonly used ingredients in cosmetics are chamomile and calendula (marigold) for cleansing, nettles and fennel to clear skin impurities and comfrey (from which the chemical allantoin is derived) to promote healing and softening of the skin. Sage and yarrow are often used in preparations for greasy skins. Perhaps surprisingly, their natural ingredients can also cause adverse reaction (azulene, an active ingredient found in chamomile for example) especially as the products often do not contain preservatives. Remember that these products cannot be kept as long as those containing preservatives.

Whether you choose synthetic- or natural-based cosmetics, always evaluate the product carefully according to your individual requirements before buying. Experimenting at a later stage can be an expensive business.

#### KEEPING COSMETICS

Once opened, most commercial cosmetics will last for a long time if kept water- and airtight and away from heat. Store in a cool place, and replace tops of jars and mascara wands after use to prevent damage from bacteria and oxygen. Cream-based products are more prone to contamination than alcohol or powder-based products, so applicators must be changed regularly or fingertips kept scrupulously clean. Any product that begins to harden, discolour or flake should be replaced. Home-made cosmetics have a short life as they usually do not contain preservatives. Make them in small quantities and keep refrigerated.

Try to avoid sharing cosmetics or using communal make-up testers in shops.

## CRAMP

*See also: minerals*

Cramp occurs when muscles contract abnormally, cutting off the blood supply, and can be very painful. The most common cause is an imbalance of body salts, particularly calcium (although salt is the traditional scapegoat), which explains why runners and dancers suffer badly: they sweat profusely and excrete extra salts through the skin. Pregnant women suffer badly for different reasons: the baby's need for calcium takes precedence over their own, and thus increased doses in the diet (see **minerals**) or supplements are needed. Calcium is difficult to absorb and up to 80 per cent of intake is excreted. Since soft tissues and blood have only 1 per cent of calcium in the body, the balance is finely tuned. Other cramp causes are stress, tension and anxiety (see separate entries). When cramp is experienced, the only immediate solution is to stretch out the contracted muscle: in the case of legs, pull the foot back firmly, for example.

For menstrual cramps see **dysmenorrhoea**.

## CRASH DIETING

*See also: bingeing; body type; bulimia nervosa; diet; fasting; slimming; weight*

Crash dieting is the type that you might be tempted to resort to on Wednesday when you are going to a party on Saturday and discover that your best dress no longer fits. Crash diets tend to concentrate on very small amounts of two or three foods and restricted fluid intake. If you cut out enough Calories and fluid you will certainly lose weight quickly up to a limit, but very little of this can be attributed to fat loss, rather to glycogen (blood sugar) and water loss, and to lean tissue (muscle) loss. Not only can it be dangerous, it is neither a good policy nor a healthy way to run your body for a variety of reasons.

**Coueism**
See Autosuggestion

**C**

### AGAINST CRASH DIETING

- Because fluids are essential for good body functioning, any diet (unless medically prescribed) which restricts water and other non-harmful fluids which are not loaded with Calories should be avoided. One of the many vital functions of fluid is to flush out waste matter through the kidneys, and fluid is a major constituent of all body cells.

- Very little of the weight lost during crash dieting is fat, the substance which needs reduction in overweight people. The body assumes it is under siege from famine, not fad, and operates as follows: first goes up to 1-2 kg (2-4 lb) of extra glycogen stored in the body, taking with it 3 times its weight in water, then lean tissue such as muscle is metabolized for extra energy. This may cause further reduction in the metabolic rate, which has already dropped after 4 days or so to make the best use of incoming Calories, to preserve energy. A crash diet of a week is thus useless in terms of fat reduction. Weight will return very quickly when old eating habits revive: the temporary low in metabolism will ensure that.

- Crash dieting may cause a range of feelings such as lethargy, lack of energy, depression and moodiness as well as hunger. Your body is suffering from famine.

- Dietary needs are not met. Essential vitamins and minerals as well as most of the proteins, fats and carbohydrates are absent. Even for a week, this is unhealthy and will swiftly affect your hair and skin (and your skin will look pinched from fluid loss) if not produce more serious symptoms.

- It is thought that repeated crash dieting may alter the body's composition unfavourably; increasing the ratio of fat to muscle, as more and more muscle is metabolized when the body is under diet pressure. However there is no medical evidence of this as yet.

- Repeated crash dieting could make weight loss harder overall as your body becomes accustomed to a lower metabolic rate than normal. To maintain a good metabolic rate, the body needs a healthy diet (or healthy reducing diet) and plenty of exercise which keeps the rate up (see **metabolic rate**).

- One of the most frightening aspects of crash dieting (suggested by anecdotal evidence rather than medical trials) is that it can permanently damage the hunger-appetite link (see **hunger** and **appetite**). Habitual dieters tend not to be stimulated by hunger when they eat, so they have no inner guide to when or how much they should eat: they are always hungry because the body is losing vital energy which is not being replaced. Lack of this trigger can lead to phasic starving and bingeing, and can even produce bulimia nervosa under certain conditions (see **bulimia**).

- Crash diets are not needed to 'cleanse' or 'rest' the stomach or intestines: the digestive system is built for work and does not need 'cleaning'.

# CREAMS

*See also: cleansing; lanolin; moisturizing; tanning*

Creams are combinations of oil and water which protect and lubricate the skin. They sometimes contain common allergens such as lanolin and scent which can cause severe skin reactions: if you are allergic to these substances, always check the list of ingredients on packs. Choose products according to the functions you need them to fulfil then (1) according to your skin type (2) then check for sensitivity and only (3) by smell – and if you wear creams during the day, check that their fragrance does not clash with others you are wearing. Other added ingredients such as vitamins, hormones or proteins like collagen or elastin cannot, in fact, repair damage to the skin, rejuvenate or restore its elasticity. But they do soften, smooth, and help to retain the skin's moisture content, plumping up the surface and minimizing lines and wrinkles. Some creams incorporate natural substances extracted from herbs, flowers and vegetables. Vitamins are most effectively supplied to the skin through a balanced diet but vitamins A and E, both necessary for a healthy skin, have healing and protective qualities which may possibly be effective when applied to the skin. Creams vary in composition and weight depending on which area of the body they are to be used for. Richer creams should be used as the skin becomes drier with age, or in extreme heat or cold. Those containing emollients help retard moisture loss. Those with humectants attract moisture to the skin in damp or normal climates: in dry climates water is attracted out of the skin, so don't wear in this situation. Always use a moisturizing cream on your face (see **moisturizing**) and care for body skin, too (see **body moisturizers**). The following are creams for specific areas which may be used in addition to your normal moisturizing creams or lotions.

**Night creams** These are moisturizing creams which are thick oil-in-water products designed to seal in moisture. They are especially good for dry and older skins.

**Neck and throat creams** (nourishing creams, enriched creams, night creams) As skin tends to be dry here, special creams are oilier and thicker, and should be massaged in with upward movements, at night or after the bath, when muscles are most relaxed.

**Eye creams** The eye area is very sensitive, so creams are basically lightweight moisturizers, omitting the dyes thought unsuitable for eyes. Oil- and water-based products are better for use under make-up, but at night, when added lubrication is needed, a heavier water-in-oil emulsion can be used. Pat on very lightly to avoid stretching the skin.

**Hand creams** For daytime there are light moisturizing creams, or water-resistant barrier creams which give protection against wear and tear, and cold weather. Rich, emollient creams are suitable for night.

C

# CURLING AND STRAIGHTENING HAIR

*See also: Afro hair; cutting hair; hair – washing, drying, conditioning; hairdresser; hair styles; highlighting*

Curling or straightening your hair is an easy and enjoyable way of giving yourself a new look: you can 'alter' your face shape and revitalize your overall appearance in one fell swoop. There are lots of temporary processes which you can afford to experiment with, but approach permanent alterations in the hair's shape with much more caution. Effects last for months, until hair grows out and is cut off. Take care when you want to 'perm' and colour permanently: the perm should precede the colour by at least 2 weeks, and in the case of frequently processed Afro hair, you will have to work out your schedule carefully.

Remember that not all the curly or straightened looks you like in magazines will suit you (see **hair styles**). Ask your hairdresser's advice and try out the style you intend to have after 'perming' using one of the temporary methods below. Check that you can cope with caring for the new style. Ask about aftercare and the tools which you will need in order to reproduce the style: if the perm needs setting each time it is washed, practise using rollers so that you feel confident with your results.

Most temporary processes can be carried out successfully at home, although your hairdresser will produce a more professional result. Permanent processes should only be carried out by a professional. Curlers need perfect positioning, but more importantly, the chemicals used to loosen hair bonds for curling or straightening will destroy the hair completely if left on for too long, and can cause damage if they get into your eyes or onto sensitive skins: scalps with any cuts or abrasions should not be permed, and it is advisable to patch test perming and neutralizing solution on the inside of the elbow for 48 hours to check that there is no allergy. Don't proceed until you've made this test.

## CURLING AND STRAIGHTENING HAIR CHART

| TREATMENT | PROCESS |
|---|---|
| **PERMANENT CHANGE** | |
| Permanent wave | 'Perms' vary enormously in name, a little in strength and very little in function. Hair is cut, washed to remove any unwanted chemicals on hair, and rolled on to special perm rollers, their size determined by the curl required. Some hairdressers use a protein protectant on hair before rolling on to perm rollers. Foam or liquid perming solution is then applied. The chemicals, often derivatives of ammonium thioglycollate, open the sulphur bonds in the hair to make it flexible and unstable. The timing of this process is crucial, determined by the chemical used, the condition, type and texture of hair. Neutralizer is then applied so that hair bonds can reform in their new shape. The hair is rinsed and some hairdressers apply conditioner. Depending on the style required and strength of perm used, hair is shaped and dried by one of the methods in the temporary change section |
| Thio-perm | Similar in operation to regular perm, but aims to restructure existing tighter curl. Positioning of perm rollers thus takes natural curl into account to ensure that results will look very natural, but softer |
| Sodium hydroxide treatment | Chemical used works similarly to more usual permanent wave in breaking down bonds in hair, but is chosen because it is particularly good for relaxing and straightening out curl. Instead of being set, hair is treated with the chemical and combed out to stretch hairs, before being neutralized |
| **TEMPORARY CHANGE** | |
| Rollers/curlers | Hair is washed and conditioned; cut if required. Hair is divided into sections, then each section into small pieces for each roller. Each piece is held firmly at right angles to the head. The end is held to the curler as it is rolled up. The ends must be rolled very smoothly around the roller to avoid a frizzy result. Positioning of curlers depends on style required, but top section rollers normally face away from the brow, as do side sections, back sections face downwards. Setting gel or lotion may be applied to each section of hair before rolling. Hair in rollers can be left to dry naturally, dried with a hand dryer, heat lamp or under a hood |

|  | 1 | 2 | 3 | 4 |

On medium-length or long hair: wrap foil around end of each hair section (to keep ends neat) without twisting. Roll into head and fold both ends to middle to secure. Leave at least an hour, preferably overnight. Just run fingers through hair after removing shapers – don't brush or use a wide-toothed comb.

|  | 1 | 2 | 3 | 4 |

On long hair: twist each section of hair until firm, secure end between two halves of folded shaper. Spiral along to the roots, then fold again to fasten. Leave for at least 1-2 hours, preferably overnight. Remove shapers, untwist hair and run fingers through: do not brush or comb.

| SUITABLE HAIR TYPES | EFFECT | COMMENTS |
|---|---|---|
| Most hair which has not previously been similarly treated. Less successful on fine, silky hair, most successful on strong hair in good condition | Permanent curl varying from very tight frizz to loose, soft curls. Even after perming, curl can be varied by drying differently: finger-drying, for example, will produce a tighter, wilder curl than setting on large rollers | This type of permanent wave should not be used on hair which has already been permed. The hair becomes very weak and dry, and sometimes drained of its natural colour. Permanent waving should be carried out at least 2 weeks before permanent colouring to avoid damage and discoloration. Perms last for between 3-5 months. This process should not be used on your hair if you are over four months pregnant. The effect on the foetus is unpredictable |
| Specially designed for Afro hair, good for other very curly, preferably coarse hair | Permanent restructured curl, giving more of halo effect to Afro hair instead of tight curl, making it loose and pliable and easier to comb and style. Increases volume of all curly hair | Special products are available to condition hair after this treatment. It can be repeated every 2½-3 months after split and dry ends have been trimmed off. Conditioning is particularly essential for regularly processed hair. Colour/perm delay as for perming above. This process should not be used on your hair if you are over four months pregnant. The effect on the foetus is unpredictable |
| Any curly hair, most commonly used on Afro hair. Best results on strong hair: stretching weakens hair anyway, so stronger hair stands up best to process | Very curly Afro hair becomes much straighter, with only tiny bends in the elongated hair. It can be made to fall in smooth rolls and curls with good styling. Loose natural curls can be completely straightened out by this process | Hair needs firm styling after washing to prevent possible frizziness down the length of the hair. Do not leave hair to dry naturally: blow-dry, use rollers, heated rollers or tongs for best effect. If this is carried out, regrowth area will not need reprocessing for 10-12 months. This process should not be used on your hair if you are over four months pregnant. The effect on the foetus is unpredictable |
| Most hair, whether chemically processed or not | Depends on roller size (larger roller = larger, looser, curl), on hair and on hair treatment after removal of rollers. The effect is tighter on natural or processed curl which is only mildly brushed out; softer on otherwise straight hair. Positioning of curlers is important, too. If rollers are badly put in, i.e. not close to root and at right angles, curl will be only on end of hair, giving a very flat silhouette to head. On chemically straightened hair gives firm, smooth curl | Do not overdry hair in curlers: hair can be damaged, as can very exposed scalp. Over-use of curlers can cause split ends and dryness: keep hair ends well conditioned. Curl can last to next wash if not subjected to damp or humidity |

## CURLING AND STRAIGHTENING HAIR CHART

| TREATMENT | PROCESS |
|---|---|
| **TEMPORARY CHANGE** | |
| Heated rollers | Heated rollers are only for use on very slightly damp or dry hair. They can be used after shampooing and drying or between washes. After heating them up, they are applied as for non-heated styles, although often only one or two sections of hair are curled at once. Hair gel or lotion can be used |
| Heated tongs | Curling tongs are only for use on very slightly damp or dry hair. Like heated rollers, they can be used after shampooing and rough-drying, or between washes for extra curl. Hair to be curled is divided into sections and each small piece then worked on. The end of the hair is held firmly to the tongs by their spring clip, the remainder of the strand wound around the tongs and held briefly in place (follow manufacturer's instructions). Unwind hair and repeat with next strand. Always let hair cool totally before brushing out or curl will drop out. Tongs will need reheating after each group of 3 or 4 curls have been made |
| Foam-rubber-covered wire shapers | Use only on dry hair; most effective when used on newly washed and dried hair. Results take time to achieve even when hair is dry, and it is best to leave shapers in place overnight. Divide hair into sections. Pin up upper part of each section and begin with the lower part. Make a bend in the centre of each shaper if this has not already been done for you and only wind hair around one half. To protect hair, and prevent frizz, use a small piece of aluminium foil on the end of each section. Start winding the first piece of hair round the shaper near its centre, covering the ends of the hair with the next wind. Work up to the end, fold up shaper and fasten securely. Work up each section and begin the next as above |
| Cornrowing or plaiting | Cornrowing is a very tight form of plaiting (braiding) carried out on very small sections of hair. It is normally worked on Afro hair though it can be successful on long, non-Afro hair. Usually, hair is incorporated into plaits all the way down the head: the process requires a great deal of skill. Hair can be wet or dry. For straightforward plaiting, if hair is later to be worn unplaited, best effects will be achieved with wet hair. Loose or tight plaits must be carefully done to ensure that every hair is included: work in sections as for other methods above. You can incorporate beads into these. Avoid fastening with rubber bands which damage hair: wind lengths of sewing cotton (not polyester) around each plait. Use smooth hair clips for plaits |
| Heated brush | Using a heated brush is a cross between blow-drying and using curling tongs. For best results hair should be damp. Read the roller section, above, and follow the sections and curl directions given. Treat the brush like a roller, holding it in position for a minute (or as directed by the manufacturer) for each curl |
| Blow-drying with brush | One of the most widely used and simple methods of making hair straighter or curlier. Most successful on damp hair which has been towel-dried, or rough-dried with a hairdryer. There are a number of different techniques, and it is advisable to watch your hairdresser carefully when your hair is being dried after a new cut, and to ask for advice. Otherwise work around head to make curls as for rollers, above |
| Scrunch-drying | A relatively new and simple technique. First towel-dry your hair, or bend forwards and blow hair upwards from tips with hairdryer until it feels almost dry. Now rub a small amount of gel between your hands and run hands/fingers through one side and front, back of hair; repeat with other side. Turn dryer to very low, scrunch up a small section of hair in your hand and hold dryer quite close. Release scrunched section and pick up the next. Work across desired area or entire head in this way. |
| Natural or finger-drying | As simple as it sounds. Towel out excess water and leave hair to dry in the air or under a heat lamp. It is not a good idea to wander around outside with damp hair: heat loss through the head will be increased. Finger-drying uses the heat of fingers run through the hair to dry it, and will give the hair more body than natural drying |
| Hot comb straightening or Thermal styling | Hair is washed and thoroughly conditioned. Each section of hair is then firmly combed through with an electrically heated comb to straighten it. It is time-consuming and therefore an expensive process, as each section must be slowly and thoroughly dried for best effect |
| Sewn-on or bonded plaits or braids | If you have Afro hair and want long, straight, braided hair, this is one way to avoid chemical straightening. Long or short, thick or thin plaits can be sewn into your hair. This process is very expensive, but long-lasting, even almost permanent as plaits can now be 'bonded' to your own hair. In practice, however, some of the bonds do eventually break, and joins become unsightly as natural hair grows out. The bonding process can take as much as 6-10 hours. Plaits can equally well be attached to non-Afro hair |

| SUITABLE HAIR TYPES | EFFECT | COMMENTS |
|---|---|---|
| Best on hair with some natural bend or curl, or on permed hair. Very straight hair will not hold this curl for more than an hour or two. Gives chemically straightened hair soft curls | Similar to rollers, above, but overall less drastic and softer effect. The finer and straighter the basic hair, the less effective the curl. Brush minimally after curling for strongest results | Be careful not to get heated rollers wet; store them carefully. Over-use can damage hair, see above. Curl does not last well, usually just for a day |
| Harsh process, particularly for dry hair, but will work on any type | Bubbly curl if carefully executed on short, layered hair. On longer hair tends to curl ends only, as heat cannot penetrate whole roll of hair around wand. Firm curl on hair whose shape has been chemically processed. Comb out each curl gently | Practise using unheated tongs at first: you can burn your face or scalp badly with inexpert use. Best for occasional use as they damage hair ends, causing splitting more than any other temporary methods |
| Best on shoulder-length to long hair, coarser hair takes shape better | Initially long curly ringlets dropping to waves on most hair types. Fine, straight hair often produces regular waves/kinks down its length even initially | These need patience and practice, but can be used anywhere as no heat is required. Store in a dry place to prevent metal rusting. Wave does not last very well on straight hair, just 1 or 2 days, but may last longer on hair with natural bend |
| Difficult to achieve good results on hair shorter than shoulder-length. Hair with bend or curl is easier to plait and forms better cornrows, but any hair type is suitable for plaiting | Neat waves down length of hair | Cornrows can stay in hair for several weeks. Wash head very gently by dipping in basinful of water with a squirt of shampoo well dispersed in it. Gently shower out every trace of shampoo solution; failure to do this will attract dirt more quickly to hair and may also cause irritation. Ideally, dry hair under heat lamp, or use hand dryer or hood on low setting. Plaited effect in hair will drop out after about a day, less on very fine, straight hair |
| Any type except tight curls or Afro hair | Mildly wavy, smooth effect | Do not use gel unless brush attachment can be removed from electrical section, for washing. Curl will not last between washes, suitable for one evening |
| Any type except tight curls or natural Afro hair. Best results on coarse hair, and on hair with natural or processed curl | Very curly on permed or naturally curly hair. Mildly curly with enough body to stand out well from the head even on straight hair, if gel is used. Over-brushing will reduce effect | Buy brushes of several sizes for different effects. Curl usually lasts well |
| Any type | Messy, natural curl on most hair types, but best on short- to medium-length curl. Don't brush or comb, just run fingers through | Looks especially effective on highlighted hair, giving it still more dark/light contrast. If hair loses bounce, spray lightly with water (but DO NOT use a plant sprayer which may have had harmful chemicals in it – buy one just for your hair) and re-scrunch ends |
| Any type | As natural as name implies, finger-drying gives extra body, but not curl unless hair has natural/processed curl already in it. Don't brush or comb, just run fingers through to lift hair periodically | Spray hair very lightly with water and run fingers through to rejuvenate style |
| Afro or other very curly hair | Straightened, but with tiny bends visible in Afro hair | Almost as harsh on hair as chemical processing: remember to condition hair well |
| Any type | | Think carefully before undertaking this expensive and time-consuming process. Washing hair is VERY difficult as hair becomes massively heavy even when dry: you will have to be content with very infrequent washing. Bonding is done very near the scalp, so if you change your mind even as long as 2 months after bonding your own hair will be very short |

C

**Curling tongs**
See Curling and
straightening hair

**Cuticle removers**
See Cuticles

**Cyanobalamin**
See Vitamin B12

## CUTICLES

*See also: hair; hands; manicure; moisturizing; nails; pedicure; sebum*

### NAIL CUTICLES
The cuticle is the outer layer of skin surrounding the nail, securing it to its base. It needs to be kept soft and separate from the nail (see **nails; manicure**), so push back gently with an orange stick wrapped in cotton wool. Keep well moisturized with cuticle cream, massaging cream in with small circular movements with the thumb to stimulate circulation (see **moisturizing**). Avoid cutting or clipping the cuticle which can cause the nail and skin to separate, encouraging the influx of chemicals and dirt which may cause infection.

### HAIR CUTICLES
This is the transparent, outer layer of cells that protects each hair. The cuticle is oiled and smoothed by secretions of sebum which causes the cuticle to reflect light and so gives the hair a healthy shine. If the cuticle cells are disrupted (by illness or chemical processing for colouring or curling), hair may become dull and lacklustre. As the cuticle is very resilient, it will not be affected by ordinary day-to-day frequent shampooing or essential brushing and combing.

## CUTS

*See also: scars*

Most minor cuts heal quickly and do not require medical help unless bleeding is profuse or the cut becomes inflamed or exudes pus. In a healthy person, the initial flow of blood will carry away some of the dirt before a clot forms to seal the cut, but an anti-tetanus injection may be required if dirt has entered the cut (check with your doctor if in doubt).

### HOW TO COPE WITH CUTS
1   Make sure your hands are clean before touching the cut.
2   Remove any small loose pieces of glass, grit or dirt from the cut and surrounding area.
3   Wash cut under running water and cleanse with cotton wool soaked in diluted antiseptic if available, otherwise use mild soap and water. Wipe away from the cut.
4   Control bleeding by pressing firmly with your hand, or elevating the injured area.
5   Dry the wound carefully. Apply a sterile, non-adhesive dressing, and keep the cut covered changing the dressing if necessary, until a scab has formed.

## CUTTING HAIR

*See also: colouring hair; curling and straightening hair; hair; hairdresser; hair styles; highlighting*

The effects of a new haircut are going to last for some while, because hair only grows at a rate of about 14 mm (½ inch) a month, so think carefully before launching into any major change. Avoid being lured into salons by offers of free haircuts: the choice of style will be the hairdressing student's, not yours, and you may hate the finished results.

### DECIDING ON YOUR HAIRCUT
■   Haircut ideas are easy to come by: in hairdressing and fashion magazines, in the street, on television, even on your friends' heads.
■   Try out the effect a particular new style will have by pinning hair back to make the new shape, pinning back/mocking up a fringe etc.: you must feel sure that the style suits you.
■   Remember that very short styles will need more frequent cutting: growth will show very quickly. Unlayered styles need least frequent attention.
■   Study your natural hairline at neck and forehead: if attractive, display them with short or swept-back cuts, if not, disguise them. Also consider how your hair grows – straight, in a natural kink, back or forwards.
■   Styles with short layers can take up to a year to grow out: avoid them if you like change.

- Check on how difficult drying and styling will be, and consider whether you can cope.
- Find a really good hairdresser for your new style. Whatever the latest fashion, it is better to follow reliable recommendation, better still to build up a relationship with a hairdresser who understands you, your hair and the needs of your lifestyle.

### MAINTAINING YOUR HAIRCUT
Your hairdresser will advise you on conditioning, drying, and the tools you will need in order to cope with the new style and how soon it will need trimming – normally 6-8 weeks later (4-6 if short).

# CYSTITIS

Cystitis is a very common and painful infection of the lining of the bladder, usually caused by bacteria (often Escherichia coli from the bowel passing up the urethra, but sometimes by infection from the kidney. It can affect both children and adults. Symptoms are an almost constant desire to pass water, with difficulty and pain/burning sensation on doing so, an aching, cramp-like pain in the abdomen and dark, strong-looking urine which may have blood streaks in it (caused by the infection). Sexually transmitted diseases such as gonorrhoea, genital herpes and NSU, and also thrush can sometimes mimic cystitis. If you think that you are at risk go to an STD clinic where you can be treated for the disease or for cystitis rather than to your doctor.

### PREVENTION
1. Always wipe yourself from front to back to avoid transferring germs from the anus to the urethra. Especially if you suffer from cystitis regularly, you should always wash yourself with water only (use a clean face cloth kept for this purpose and bowl of water or a bidet), from front to back, after using the toilet.
2. Drink plenty. This is beneficial to general health, but cystitis sufferers should make a point of drinking about 2 litres (3 pints) of fluid a day, avoiding acidic types in favour of milk, weak tea or coffee, alkaline mineral waters and diluted fruit squashes (not juices except cranberry juice which may be beneficial). Any germs at the mouth of the urethra will be washed out before they can move up to the bladder.
3. Cystitis is sometimes known as the 'honeymoon disease', because intercourse does facilitate movement of any germs up the urethra. Avoid their presence by washing the genital area carefully with plain water both before and after intercourse (and your partner should do this too). If you have a tendency to get cystitis, you should try to drink at least 2 glasses of water before intercourse, and empty your bladder within 20 minutes of intercourse.

4. Do pass water when you feel the need to: the overfull bladder is more likely to get infected. Germs in urine have more time to reach the kidneys, blood vessel flow is restricted, slowing the arrival of infection-fighting white cells.
5. If pregnant, ensure that your bladder is properly emptied or a 'pocket' of urine can get trapped by the growing foetus. Pass water, wait five minutes and pass water again.
6. Use only water and unscented soap in the genital area: avoid talcum powder, vaginal deodorants (inadvisable anyway), bubblebaths, bath oils and milks.

### TREATMENT
Seek treatment immediately to avoid kidney damage. Your doctor will prescribe antibiotics which will cure most cases.
- Drink at least two glasses of cold water.
- Follow these with a further two glasses (approximately 300 ml (½ pint) every 20 minutes for the next 3 hours; these could have a little fruit squash (not juice) added to them, with a teaspoon of bicarbonate of soda to reduce acidity of urine, and thereby its capacity to sting.
- In addition, drink a cup of black tea or coffee every hour: their diuretic effect will speed the flushing out of germs.
- If you can, sit with a hot water bottle behind your back and another between your legs to reduce burning sensation and abdominal pain.

# CYSTS

*See also: awareness; breast examination; endometriosis; ganglions*

Cysts are abnormal sacs filled with liquid or semisolid matter. They occur in many parts of the body and arise from a variety of causes. The most common types are:

**Sebaceous cysts** Known as retention cysts, these occur where the outlet of a glandular duct is blocked. They occur after puberty, and are most common on the scalp. They can be removed for cosmetic reasons, but are never malignant.

**Ovarian cysts** These are fluid-filled sacs which can develop in the ovary. Often they disappear spontaneously, but if they become large, twisted or painful they may need investigation, treatment or removal. They are only very infrequently malignant.

**Breast cysts** Like some ovarian cysts, these are produced in response to hormonal changes. Manual examination alone cannot determine the nature of a lump. If it is suspected of being a cyst, the lump will be aspirated (fluid syringed off). If the cyst refills repeatedly it may need treatment to reduce it.

NOTE Lumps in breasts can be of various types (see **breast examination**). It is VITAL to check your breasts every month, and to go straight to your doctor if any lumps appear.

**Cycling**
See Sports

D

# DANCE

*See also: aerobics; exercise; exercises; sports*

The power of dance is built into the history of most races. Dancing has long been used as therapy in tribal communities, to induce war-like trances or to stimulate tribal feeling. Dance today, provided it is well taught, still has substantial benefits. For children, it can be an excellent way of learning good posture, getting to know the body and its movement potential. It is a route, too, to learning to express one's feelings and individuality. Because of the freedom it gives, and the relaxing inhibition-diminishing nature of dancing, it is becoming a common and useful form of therapy. Young and old enjoy dancing to various types of music: and the effects can be beneficial for problems ranging from minor emotional difficulties to lack of co-ordination and extensive physical handicap.

Dancing can provide exercise and relieve tension as well as providing plenty of fun. The success of 'aerobic-dance' recently has a lot to do with the fact that otherwise repetitive exercises and jogging are given dance rhythms and music so there is more incentive to keep going. Most forms of dance, however, are aerobic if they are vigorous enough (use your pulse rate as a guide, see **exercises**) and if you can manage 30 minutes 3-5 times a week you are likely to be increasing your fitness and reducing your stress level. Dance can be just as strenuous as any other form of exercise so it is important to warm up beforehand and cool down afterwards (see **aerobics, exercises**).

### NOTES: DANCE FOR FITNESS

- If you have any history of ill health, have any physical disabilities or, for example, suffer from high blood pressure, always check with your doctor and/or physiotherapist before starting dance classes. It is advisable, in any case, to check with your doctor before starting any new form of exercise. Use your heart rate as a guide to safe aerobic exercise, see box in **exercises** entry for instructions on how to do this.
- Build up the length of time you dance for gradually, especially if you are over 35, are unfit and have not taken exercise recently, or if you are very overweight, on a course of drugs, drink or smoke heavily, have not recently had a medical check-up or have a history of heart disease or high blood pressure, see exercise contra-indications list. Start gradually, progressively increasing the time spent dancing.
- Pregnancy and dance: it is not advisable to take up dancing or any other new form of exercise while pregnant. If you have a history of miscarriage, too, you should avoid dancing. If, however, you dance and exercise regularly, then there should be no problem with continuing gentle exercise including dance, and it is of course important to keep fit while pregnant (see **pregnancy, pre-natal beauty** and **health**).

The pulse method of controlling exercise is not as accurate when pregnant. Do not judge your exercise by previous performance, rather judge yourself by your perceived exertion. Ask your doctor and your dance tutor for advice, NEVER push yourself or continue with any movement which causes you to feel strain.

■ The unaccustomed exertion may make your muscles feel a little stiff the next day – this is quite normal especially if you have not taken much exercise recently. If, however, there is soreness or you are so stiff you can't perform the dance movements properly two days later, then you have done too much. If you suffer any unusual or unexplained pains, especially if directly related to a movement, stop dancing immediately and see your doctor about the pain as soon as you can.

■ Always warm up before dancing and cool down afterwards, keep your body warm during and after dancing and keep an eye on your pulse to ensure that you will build up fitness safely. (See **exercises** and **fitness**.)

■ The best way to learn to dance is to join a class; ensure that the instructor you choose is properly trained, that the class is small enough for individual attention, and inform your instructor of any problems you have so that you can be advised of any exercises you should go easy on or miss out on altogether.

## DANCE GUIDELINES

| DANCE TYPE | CALORIES USED PER HOUR | SUITABILITY | ADVANTAGES AND NOTES |
|---|---|---|---|
| Aerobic-dance | 620 | Not suitable for people with back or joint problems. Always wear proper aerobic-dance shoes and ensure that the classes are held in a hall with a sprung floor, are not overcrowded and taken by a qualified instructor | Combines a workout with dance movements to make it more enjoyable. If well taught, aerobic-dance should exercise every part of the body and has been shown to improve general fitness substantially |
| Belly-dancing | 230 | Gentle belly dancing is suitable for most people | Fun to do as well as being good exercise. Improves general flexibility of joints, especially hips, strengthens all abdominal or tummy muscles and lower back |
| Classical ballet | 550 | Not good for people with joint problems, especially knees and hips, not good while pregnant due to strain on joints and balancing postures. Otherwise suitable for most people as a form of exercise if begun very gently. Improves posture and co-ordination | Requires discipline. If used as a form of exercise arms, shoulders and upper back will need additional exercise. (See **arms, back, shoulders**.) Strengthens leg muscles and improves balance |
| Disco dancing | 350-650 | Suitable for everyone: simplest form, swaying to disco music, requires little skill or concentration and thus is universally approachable and beneficial | Sustained disco-dancing can provide good aerobic exercise. Gentle disco-dancing is good for maintaining mobility as you get older. In any form it is enjoyable and relaxing, good for counteracting stress and a social form of exercise |
| Contemporary dance | 550 | Contemporary dance requires good flexibility and co-ordination (although training itself should improve this) and a reasonable standard of fitness | It provides more flexibility than strength, particularly in the torso as rib-cage and hips begin to move independantly. The same goes for modern ballet which also strengthens the legs. Arms and hands get plenty of exercise and good co-ordination and sense of rhythm are promoted |
| Rock 'n' roll | 350-650 | Everyone can enjoy this, but some of the movements will be difficult for older people, anyone with joint movement restrictions. If learning rock 'n' roll, start easily, gently, do not force the swinging movements or you may damage your back or hip muscles | Gentle rock 'n' roll provides some exercise but more enjoyment. Fast, energetic rock 'n' roll requires co-ordination, strength, flexibility, good timing and plenty of practice to provide good, safe aerobic exercise |
| Square/Highland dancing | 400 | Traditionally a family occupation and suitable for all age groups. Relax into the rhythm of movements and symmetrical patterns for the best therapeutic results | Advantages and benefits are mainly in the field of relaxation, although regular highland dancing (preferably with other exercise, too) will provide exercise for heart and lungs: join a local association with weekly meetings |
| Waltz/traditional dancing | 200 | Suitable for everyone | Improves co-ordination, even concentration, good social exercise. Strengthening benefits are small: good for feet and ankles, but general enjoyment and social value high |

NOTE: These figures are VERY approximate. Energy expenditure depends both on body weight, intensity of exercise and room temperature. They show roughly how many Calories would be burned by a 140 lb (63 kg) woman dancing for one hour.

Follow a daily exercise routine (see **exercises**) and wear whatever you feel comfortable in but keep warm for maximum safety and comfort. Wear leather soled jazz shoes or a similar type for all these (except aerobic dance): rubber shoes will prevent the necessary freedom of foot movement

# DANDRUFF

*See also: hair; sebum; trichologist*

Dandruff (pityriasis capitis) is a common condition in which the scalp is covered with flakes of dead skin. It is quite normal for the scalp to be mildly flaky at times: the skin sheds dead cells in this way. Such flakiness is only dandruff when it is both severe and persistent. It results from faster than normal skin cell growth, and from too much or too little sebum being produced by the scalp's sebaceous glands. Flakiness can be precipitated by travelling and excessive central heating which can overdry the scalp. If too little, the hair becomes dryer and the skin sheds white flakes, if too much, the hair becomes oily and sheds yellow flakes. There is some evidence that it is caused by bacteria or fungal infection and that dehydration and stress exacerbate it.

### COPING WITH DANDRUFF

- First ensure that you are eating well (see **diet**). The incidence of dandruff is thought to be connected with the lack of several vitamins, particularly vitamins A and B6. Try incorporating extra quantities of foods containing these vitamins in your diet (see **vitamins**).
- Wash your hair daily or every other day with a mild shampoo formulated for frequent use, using only one wash and rinsing well with warm water. Change shampoos too, as flakiness could be an allergic reaction.
- If this is not effective, first try massaging your scalp (see **massage**) with a little olive or coconut oil a few hours before washing: much 'dandruff' is over-dry skin just like on any other part of the body. Stronger measures involve swabbing your scalp with an antiseptic solution or a weak solution of cetrimide, available in powder form. Dilute 1 teaspoon in 2 pints/1.2 litres/5 cups warm distilled water. Or try a commercial anti-dandruff shampoo containing tar, zinc pyriothine or selenium sulphide.
- Natural remedies, used internally or externally, abound. Burdock tea is a traditional herbal remedy: use 1 teaspoon of grated fresh or dried burdock root and rhizome, add 1-2 teaspoons of fresh yellow dock root and boil in 250 ml (1 cup) of water for 10-15 minutes. The resulting tea should be drunk three times a day. External remedies aim at alleviating itching. Try 60 ml (¼ cup) of nettles steeped for 10 minutes in 500 ml (2 cups) of boiling water, cooled and added to 60 ml (¼ cup) of cider vinegar, and massaged into the scalp twice a day. Alternatively try a chamomile rinse: steep 2 tablespoonfuls of dried chamomile flowerheads in 500 ml (2 cups) of boiling water for 10-15 minutes. Cool and use as final rinse after shampooing.
- If your dandruff does not clear up quickly, take medical advice. Cortisone lotions are often helpful but should not be continued for long.

# DEHYDRATION

*See also: after-sun preparations; bathing and baths; crash dieting; skin; water*

Over two-thirds of the human body is composed of water. Fluid lost through sweating, urinating and defaecating to flush out waste products has to be replaced for normal body functioning. If the amount of fluid lost is not adequately replaced, all body cells become dehydrated. Mild dehydration can result in lack of energy and constipation, but severe dehydration can cause death. Dehydration can be exacerbated by other factors: increased sweating in climatic extremes, fever/raised body temperature, physical activity, vomiting and diarrhoea, sunburn and severe burns. In such cases fluid intake needs to be stepped up to counterbalance the extra loss.

You should drink at least 750 ml-1 litre (6-8 cups) of fluid each day. A large part of this should be in the form of water or fruit juices: not all drinks replenish fluid stores usefully. Alcohol, tea and coffee are diuretics; that is, they promote fluid loss. Food, as well as drink, is a source of water. Vegetables like marrow (squash), cucumber and courgettes (zucchini) have a particularly high water content. The body normally gets approximately 1-1.5 litres (8-12 cups) of fluid from various foods each day.

Less dangerous is the superficial dehydration that can take place through the hair and skin. Climatic extremes, stress, overprocessing and salt water can all render the hair cuticle so porous that it loses water readily. To prevent this, use plenty of conditioner in such circumstances, and cover your hair or consider using a hair preparation specially designed to coat the hair when sunbathing (several sun product ranges include one). Skin reacts similarly, but needs more frequent attention. Use a slightly heavier moisturizer for its extra depth of protection from the elements, and use it on all exposed skin: not just the face and neck, but hands, feet and arms. Keep necessary moisture in but unwanted moisture out when you have a cold: constant dampness makes your nose sore. Dry your nose very thoroughly and apply a barrier cream or moisturizer frequently during the day.

# DENTAL HYGIENIST

*See also: dental procedures; dentist; teeth*

The role of the dental hygienist in the professional care of the teeth has become increasingly important now that the importance of preventive dentistry is generally accepted. In the UK the hygienist may only work under the direction of a dental surgeon who will refer the patients after examination, but in the US the hygienist may be dealt with direct. Among the jobs which the dental hygienist per-

forms are: scaling (removal of calculus, a hard calcium deposit which builds up on the teeth); polishing; teaching effective brushing and flossing techniques; advising on choice of toothbrushes and toothpastes; advising on diet and nutrition; applying fluoride solutions and applying fissure sealants. It is recommended that your oral hygiene and state of your gums are checked at least once a year.

**Dentures**
See Cosmetic
dentistry

# DENTAL PROCEDURES

*See also: cosmetic dentistry; dental hygienist; dentist; gums; orthodontist; teeth*

Preventive care and treatment in the mouth comprises several different speciality areas requiring a dental surgeon trained to carry out its procedures. The dental hygienist in the US and the UK works in conjunction with a dentist, carrying out certain preventive tasks such as scaling and polishing, as well as giving instruction to the patient on how best to care for teeth at home with correct cleaning. The dentist examines teeth and gums and takes X-rays to detect any disease or decay which needs treatment. He or she may need diagnostic aids such as X-rays to help assess the state of the teeth and supporting tissues. He or she carries out necessary repair work by preparing and filling teeth, may extract teeth if necessary and does 'cosmetic' work including the construction and fitting of crowns, bridges and dentures. The orthodontist is concerned with the treatment of crooked or irregular teeth, using fixed bands and wires or removable plates to straighten and regularize them.

# DENTIST

*See also: cosmetic dentistry; dental hygienist; orthodontist; teeth*

There are over 20,000 dentists registered in the United Kingdom, most of whom work within the National Health Service. You can obtain a list of those practising in your area at the local Post Office, Family Practitioner Committee, Citizens' Advice Bureau, or library. Under present regulations, adults are entitled to two free check-ups a year by an NHS dentist; children can have three. Any work which needs to be done is subject to standard NHS fees and the dentist is obliged to collect a charge decided by the government (though certain groups of people are exempt) or the treatment can be done at full cost if you are a private patient. NHS and private treatment cannot be mixed in the same course of treatment. In the US dental plans are available through insurance companies – some large companies provide cover for employees – check your company benefits. Dental care can be costly, but dental clinics which exist in major cities can be slightly cheaper than individual dentists.

## YOU AND YOUR DENTIST

It is important to visit your dentist for a check-up twice a year even if you feel that your teeth and gums are fine: do not wait until you succumb to toothache. It seems that people who do not have regular check-ups fail to do so because they fear the dentist, or merely forget how long it has been since their last check-up. You do not have to register permanently with a dentist, so it is possible to shop around until you find one with whom you feel happy. Remember, however, that building up a relationship with one dentist is beneficial to you both: you will gain confidence and lose your fear, and he or she will get to know you and your mouth and be able to plan treatment accordingly. Here are some points to look for when choosing a good dentist:

- Does he offer to examine your mouth carefully?
- Does he explain what needs to be done, and why and how this will be carried out? Does he discuss and formulate a treatment plan with you? Does he have time to discuss dental problems with you?
- Does he take a medical and dental history and ask about any medicines you are taking? He needs to know about certain medical conditions and drugs if he is to care for your health and safety as well as for your teeth.
- Does he believe in preventive care above all? If he finds anything wrong in your mouth a good dentist will explain why it happened and how you can avoid something similar happening in the future by good home care.
- Does he look for gum disease when you go for your check-up? He should probe gently between teeth and gums for any bleeding or redness and advise you accordingly.
- Does he give a local anaesthetic, if mutually thought to be desirable, before drilling, and wait for it to work? If not, he may leave some decay in the tooth to save you pain. He could also apply a topical anaesthetic (usually a lotion) to numb the discomfort of the local, if this causes distress.

# DEODORANTS

*See also: anti-perspirants; body odour; sweat*

Deodorants remove unpleasant body odours created by the action of bacteria in the sweat glands. They operate by destroying the bacteria and breaking down sweat chemically. They often contain antiseptics, as well as anti-bacterial agents, and aluminium, manganese or zinc salts which have the effect of slowing down sweat production in the

Alunite crystal is an effective and entirely natural alternative to chemically formulated deodorants. Use whenever you bathe or shower.

glands. Unlike anti-perspirants, their chief purpose is not to impede sweat production, but to prevent odour. Combined products are available.

### CHOOSING AND USING A DEODORANT

- Deodorants come perfumed and unperfumed, and in roll-on, cream or aerosol versions. If you are allergic to perfume on the skin, or if you want to avoid a 'clash' with your scent, use an unperfumed type.
- Don't use your deodorant straight after a bath or shower: it is much more effective on cool, dry skin, so wait until you have cooled down.

- Vaginal deodorants are unnecessary and can cause irritation and infection. Keep your genital area scrupulously clean by gently washing with unperfumed soap and water night and morning, and additionally after intercourse.
- Try using alunite crystal, a natural deodorant: moisten with water and rub under arms for a few seconds.
- Eat plenty of foods containing chlorophyll (such as green-leaved vegetables) and manganese, zinc and aluminium (see **minerals**) as these have effective deodorant properties when taken internally.

# DEPENDENCIES

*See also: alcohol; alcoholism; anorexia nervosa; bulimia; caffeine; drugs and medicines; smoking*

Dependency must be differentiated from habit or strong desire. Dependency has several distinctive characteristics which the World Health Organisation defines in the following categories:

1. An effect of tolerance to the drug used
2. Withdrawal symptoms on cessation of use
3. Withdrawal relief reverted to (using drink or drugs to avoid the withdrawal symptoms)
4. Psychological awareness of a compulsion or craving for the substance, often felt to be uncontrollable, and which may need treatment
5. Drug use becomes more and more unvaried
6. Drug taking becomes more and more important and takes precedence over other activities

The dependence may produce related damage to the sufferer and to those surrounding them. Habits lack one or more of these dependency characteristics. The borderline between the two can be difficult to draw and easy to pass over: it is thus important that the existence and dangers of dependency should be generally known. Eating disorders are increasingly regarded as addictive disorders (see **anorexia nervosa** and **bulimia nervosa**).

## PREVENTING DEPENDENCY

The ways in which dependency begins are as individual as its sufferers. They range from pure experimentation, pleasure-seeking, fear of being of left out, a response to a dare, chronic unhappiness, depression, loneliness, fear of ageing, to abuse or just prolonged use of a medication originally prescribed for sleeping or to treat depression.

Awareness is the chief preventive weapon against dependency. In the past, there was little general knowledge of the dark side of drinking, for example, or how to deal with it. Partial knowledge was a problem with cigarette smoking, too, as early campaigns against it emphasized only its social side – person reeking of cigarette smoke found unattractive by partner who doesn't smoke, for example. More recently, 'whole picture' campaigns detailing the full range of dangers resulting from smoking have increased general awareness: the overall number of smokers has decreased and smoking in public places is discouraged or even

### DEPENDENCY CHART

| TYPE | EFFECTS | WITHDRAWAL SYMPTOMS/NOTES |
|---|---|---|
| Cigarettes | Nicotine is a stimulant drug – it stimulates production of adrenaline and noradrenaline. Increases heart rate and blood pressure. Has obvious adverse effects on health. In large doses can produce convulsions, vomiting and tremor. One of most powerful poisons, with fatal dose for man as low as 60 mg. Smokers are 4-5 times as likely as non-smokers to get cancer of the lung, mouth, throat, oesophagus, pancreas and urinary tract and more likely to suffer from strokes and coronary heart disease. Smoking is the most common cause of acute bronchitis, and a powerful factor in the incidence of emphysema and pneumonia. Men who smoke 25 cigarettes a day are 20 times more likely to die from emphysema or bronchitis than non-smokers. The carbon monoxide in cigarette smoke replaces oxygen in the blood and puts the heart under strain: athletic performance is limited and the heart is weakened. Pregnant women endanger the foetus by this oxygen decrease, slowing its development and passing on the drug nicotine to it across the placenta. In 1985 a survey by the British Health Education Council of deaths from lung cancer, heart disease, bronchitis and emphysema found that up to 14 per cent were due to smoking – this figure should be tempered by the fact that all cancers which can be linked to smoking were not considered, and that all the diseases surveyed can be caused or exacerbated by a number of factors other than smoking. | Common chemical withdrawal symptoms: craving, sweating, shaking, hunger NOTES Recent experiments have demonstrated that nicotine addiction is only one aspect of the whole smoking dependency. Nicotine given intravenously had little effect on the smoking habits of tested groups: taste, oral satisfaction and other social and psychological factors play substantial roles. Effects of smoking on the lung cannot be completely reversed by giving up. After two or three years, however, the lungs begin to recover so that after 20 years likelihood of succumbing to serious lung and respiratory diseases is reduced to slightly above that for non-smokers of the same age and situation. |
| Sugar | High doses produce sudden energy surges. Produces dental decay. Various degenerative diseases are exacerbated by it: high blood pressure, coronary thrombosis, heart disease, arteriosclerosis. Virtually empty of nutritional value, yet full of Calories. | Craving for sweet and starchy foods, in severe cases fainting. |

forbidden. There is still a lack of knowledge of the insidious and damaging effects of dependency among young people, particularly with relation to drugs, and smoking has increased in the UK over the last five years among women of 14-17. This ignorance can lead young people to satisfy their curiosity by questioning others already involved in the drugs scene and possibly to become involved themselves. It seems that dependency will only decrease substantially if its existence and potentially fatal dangers are taught in stages from pre-teenage years at home and at school.

In addition to an awareness of specific problems, a more general awareness of individual social and emotional needs can help to eliminate some situations which can lead to dependency. In smoking, for example, the dependency is by no means just confined to nicotine, but to the whole act – the oral satisfaction, the smokescreen it provides against the outside world. Care shown by friends, family, social workers and others can help prevent habit becoming dependency.

Withdrawal from a dependency can involve a wide range of physical and emotional symptoms (see the chart below). When people refer to withdrawal symptoms they generally mean the symptoms of chemical or physical withdrawal, but psychological withdrawal symptoms need treating, too. Withdrawal can be undertaken in various ways, choice being determined by the dependency type and severity. Acupuncture has been tried in cases of smoking, for example, but drug abuse and severe alcoholism are usually treated in special treatment centres where two weeks of detoxification deal with the physical withdrawal symptoms, and six weeks of group or individual therapy helps build confidence and deals with psychological withdrawal. Additionally, family therapy has been found helpful: it is found that when families are involved in it, the addict has far better chances of recovery. At least a year of supportive treatment is usually needed after in-patient treatment. Less severe alcoholism can be dealt with by outpatient treatment.

A number of groups help addicts and their families. AA (Alcoholics Anonymous) is for alcoholics, Al-anon being the parallel organisation for friends and families of alcoholics. NA (Narcotics Anonymous) exists for all addicts, and there are also associated family groups. All these maintain strict confidentiality: look in your local telephone book for addresses and numbers, or ask your doctor, local community centre or health centre.

## DEPENDENCY CHART

| TYPE | EFFECTS | WITHDRAWAL SYMPTOMS/NOTES |
|---|---|---|
| Alcohol | Alcohol is a sedative drug which depresses the central nervous system rather like an anaesthetic. Over time, learned reactions such as polite behaviour, restraint of emotions are increasingly suppressed as alcohol levels increase, clumsiness becomes stupor, and if still more is drunk, death may result. Alcoholics become tolerant of increasing amounts of alcohol and find it increasingly difficult to drink moderately. Both social and physical effects of alcoholism are grave. Social effects are a general breakdown of former lifestyle: inability to maintain relationships or hold down a regular job, unreliability, introversion, depression, possibly violence. Physically alcoholism can cause a variety of serious problems ranging from severe brain damage and even dementia to the incurable cirrhosis of the liver (see **alcoholism**). Chronic gastritis is common: severe inflammation of the stomach which makes digestion difficult and causes weight loss is common. Where the diet is deficient as in chronic alcoholism there is malabsorption of essential vitamins and minerals, especially vitamins B and C. Alcohol addiction reduces general resistance to infection rendering illness and also depression (see entry) more likely. | Common chemical withdrawal symptoms: anxiety, insomnia with vivid dreams when sleep does come, sweating, restlessness, the famous 'shakes', involuntary periods of tremor, and 'DTs' (only in well-established alcoholism): a wide variety of hallucinations which can be terrifying, also insomnia and confusion. NOTES The step from habitual drinking to dependent drinking is not great: habits like drinking to cure a hangover increase alcohol tolerance and the likelihood of dependence. Recovering from alcoholism is a long process and one which benefits greatly from the assistance of 'sponsors' (friends or relatives who act like sponsors in helping with every aspect of recovery). Chemical withdrawal takes some time and most alcoholics need medical assistance: many clinics run detoxification programmes. Psychological withdrawal combined with continuing craving takes time to recover from, too. It has now been established that not all alcoholics need renounce alcohol for life: some do, but a small percentage, about 10 per cent, are able to rebuild 'normal' drinking habits although most of these are always at risk. |
| Caffeine | Caffeine causes an initial reduction in fatigue, increased mental activity and 'buzz' which can last several hours. Large doses cause high insulin release and weakness, fatigue, nervousness, anxiety, sleeplessness and lack of co-ordination. It is implicated in hypertension problems and its constricting effect on blood vessels exacerbates the action of LDL cholesterol on the vessels. It can also interfere with digestion. | Common chemical withdrawal symptoms: severe headache which can last up to 18 hours, loss of efficiency, restlessness, nervousness, anxiety. Psychological factors are less than in many dependencies, although for many people the addiction has been long-term (see also separate entry). |

## DEPENDENCY CHART

| TYPE | EFFECTS | WITHDRAWAL SYMPTOMS/NOTES |
|---|---|---|
| Drugs | **Tranquillizers** and many common sleeping drugs, e.g. mogadon: reduce inhibition, suppress emotions like fear, grief, interfere with driving skills. Dependency has a very strong psychological component since the drugs are often prescribed for emotional problems.<br><br>**Hallucinogens** e.g. LSD: produce changes in thought, mood, personality, self-awareness, intellectual functioning. The sense of individuality disappears, and the experience takes on a magical feel. True hallucinations occur with high doses, where the drug user believes what is in fact a hallucination to be reality (accidental death can occur due to people being out of touch with the reality of their actions), more common are pseudo-hallucinations where the user is aware that his experiences are separate from reality.<br><br>**Opiates** e.g. heroin: are depressants, but as the body mobilises forces it produces the 'high' of injecting, followed by marked depressant effect, affects digestion and causes constipation, relieves anxiety, reduces sexual drive. Tolerance increases quickly, and many people increase the dose of their drugs as they become addicted. The dangers of this dependency are very great: death can result from overdoses by first-time or experienced users and accidental death can occur as a result of activity while under the influence of these drugs. Infected needles can cause liver disease, jaundice, blood poisoning and can pass on AIDS; other dangers are vein damage, thrombosis and damage to circulation which can be so severe as to damage a limb irreparably.<br><br>**Amphetamines** e.g. dexedrine: make the user alert, talkative, sleepless, but excesses cause extreme reaction like anger, rage, irrational outbursts. Induces lack of appetite and thus weight loss. Heavy users can experience hallucinogenic effects and delusions which cause them fear, such as feelings of being persecuted. There is much disagreement over whether these drugs are truly addictive, but regular users seem to become dependent in some way on them and there are withdrawal symptoms in these cases.<br><br>**Barbiturates** e.g. seconal: act on the central nervous system to reduce anxiety, but larger doses produce slurred speech, drowsiness and sleep. After some time the drugs may tend to stop producing sleep, but the dependent will often continue increasing the dose, so tolerance rises. The borderline between the tolerable and fatal dose becomes very narrow. The drug has similar effects to alcohol, and the two used together can be fatal as the effects are cumulative.<br><br>**Marijuana:** does not produce chemical dependence. Many people use it and experience few problems except those associated with its illegality in many countries, although its use can lead to withdrawal from social life, apathy and inertia. A few people become psychologically dependent on the drug. Little is known of the health effects of marijuana, but they could be as dangerous as those of smoking cigarettes. Users may be more likely to progress to more dangerous drugs. | **Tranquillizers** and common sleeping drugs – fits, dizziness, trembling, loss of use of legs, panic attacks, obsessive morbid thoughts, heightened sensory thresholds, nausea, blurred vision, headache, depression: withdrawal can be difficult.<br><br>**Hallucinogenics** – no chemical dependence, but after-effects include extreme tiredness and a general feeling of being unwell.<br><br>**Opiates** – drowsiness followed by anxiety, excessive salivation and secretions (producing symptoms like sweating and runny nose), flu-like joint and muscle aches, stomach cramp, involuntary kicking and tremors, possibly diarrhoea and vomiting.<br><br>**Amphetamines** – whether chemical or psychological, users experience sleep disturbances, lethargy and depression.<br><br>**Barbiturates** – one of the most serious withdrawal syndromes with possibility of fatal consequences, thus usually undertaken gradually, using the addict's own drug or short-acting drugs like seconal or amytal. Unmonitored withdrawal begins with restlessness, anxiety and insomnia, followed by body temperature increases to as high as 105°F, muscle cramps, vomiting, diarrhoea, delirium and convulsions. In severe cases this can be followed by coma or death.<br><br>NOTES With all these, withdrawal should be gradual and supervised. The chemical withdrawal from these drugs is severe enough, but psychological withdrawal can be very serious too. Amphetamines, cocaine and caffeine can usually be stopped immediately but if large doses have been taken they should be withdrawn over three or four days in order to prevent very considerable psychological effects. For dependents, using drugs becomes an increasingly major part of the lifestyle, and in some cases obtaining drugs takes up most of their time. Not only do all the psychological factors lying behind the dependency need coping with, but a whole new life and lifestyle has to be built. 'Sponsors' who have little or no connection with the ex-dependent's former life are of enormous help. A wide range of clinics and groups run withdrawal courses for dependents where every aspect of their problems can be dealt with. |

# DEPRESSION

*See also: anxiety; diet; herbs; post-natal depression; pre-menstrual syndrome; stress; vitamins*

Depression is a mental state, the characteristics of which vary immensely according to its type and causes. Common manifestations are lethargy, a deep sense of sadness, emptiness, hopelessness, despair or inadequacy, inability to concentrate, lack of appetite, lack of sexual drive and difficulty in sleeping. In all cases there is a sense of unease with oneself and life, a feeling of not being happy, whether the cause is known or not.

### CAUSES OF DEPRESSION

Depression may occur as a reaction to a tragedy or other traumatic event: such cases, where the cause is at least partially understood, are known as *reactive depression*. Too much stress can trigger this type of depression, too, as can emotional insecurity and isolation. Depression may, however, arise from no known cause, and is then known as *endogenous*. Rarely, depression may form part of *manic-depressive psychosis* where alternating periods of deep depression, obsession and normality occur. It is recognized that some people have a genetic vulnerability towards depression.

Neurotransmitters are chemical substances which transmit mood and thought messages in the brain. They are thought to have a natural anti-depressive action and disturbance in their levels can cause depression. The two most significant are serotonin, formed from the amino acid tryptophan (vitamin B6, niacin and magnesium are needed for this chemical process too), and noradrenaline (norephinephrine), formed from tyrosine (vitamins B1, B2, B6, C, and niacin are needed for the process). They act by facilitating the production of endorphins, natural pain-killers (see entry).

A poor diet can exacerbate depression and produce fatigue, particularly one lacking in the B complex vitamins, vitamin C, zinc, iron, magnesium and complex carbohydrates. Because the extra oestrogen in the combined contraceptive pill may reduce absorption of vitamin B6, women taking that pill should have extra amounts of foods containing B6 in the diet.

- Some drugs, such as beta-blockers, anti-arthritis drugs and antihypertensives may produce depression as a side effect.
- Hormonal changes such as occur before a period, after having a baby and at the menopause can cause depression. This can sometimes be alleviated with hormone and/or vitamin treatment (see post-natal depression).
- Low blood sugar level (hypoglycaemia) may produce depression: counteract this with a protein-rich diet low in refined carbohydrates.
- Food allergies can produce depression: this is reversible as soon as the allergen is identified and removed from the diet. Results are noticeable within a day or so.

### TREATMENT

- Psychotherapy is a common treatment for depression. Here the psychotherapist helps the patient resolve conflicts from the past which may be buried deep in the subconscious.
- Aerobic exercise, according to a study carried out in Norway, has an anti-depressive action, possibly because of the way in which exercise raises the levels of noradrenaline (norephinephrine) in the brain.
- Many forms of treatment for depression are connected to the amine levels in the brain. Anti-depressant drugs can be a helpful short-term measure in cases of endogenous and sometimes of reactive depression. Their side effects can be severe, including insomnia, dizziness, impotence, fainting, sweating, dry mouth or blurred vision. Most patients for whom this treatment is prescribed can be weaned off the drug within 3-6 months. Long-term use is not usually advised because of the side effects and because it can interfere with perception and resolution of the depression's causes, making it more difficult to deal with.
- Minor tranquillizers such as diazepam (valium) are not now commonly prescribed to depression sufferers as their action does little to help the symptoms, and nothing to alleviate the cause. Indeed their sedative action in fact makes reaching it and coming to terms with it harder. There is also a danger of dependency with long-term doses, and of withdrawal symptoms on stopping the drug which may, in fact, encourage a return to the drug in order to regain its security and to alleviate the withdrawal symptoms.
- The use of electro-convulsive therapy (ECT) in severe cases appears to restore normal amine levels in the brain by the application of small electric shocks. Symptoms disappear (and short term memory may be impaired), but the illness can return.
- Various types of sensory stimulation can give the body a natural shock treatment: cold baths or showers; rousing music; concentrating on beautiful objects: all may help. Aromatherapy can help alleviate depression, the essential oils sassafras and melissa are some of those often used for this purpose, and herbal remedies can help, too. Some anti-depressive herbs are ginseng, lavender, lime blossom, rosemary and valerian, made into infusions to be drunk.
- Full spectrum light (unfiltered sunlight) is also believed to help lift depression: the light enters through the eyes and acts on the pineal gland in the brain, encouraging the production of serotonin.
- A treatment known as free amino acid therapy, using supplements of L-tryptophan which are converted to serotonin in the brain. may be successful in treating depression because they appear to adjust amine levels in the brain. There are several contra-indications to their use, and even where there are no contra-indications they have to be taken extremely care-

**Depilatories**
See Unwanted hair

fully. Supplements of free amino acids should not be taken except under medical guidance. You can, however, increase your body's natural tryptophan uptake by including plenty of complex carbohydrates (like unrefined cereals, peas, potatoes, pulses, raw fruits and vegetables) in your diet.

### COPING WITH AND AVOIDING DEPRESSION

There is no way that one can ensure avoiding depression: its causes are very varied, and in some cases it provides the body with an escape route from normal life when a shock has been almost too great to bear. However, some guidelines can help:

- Remember that a problem with mental health is an illness, not something that you can necessarily cure yourself or 'snap out of'. You may need help and should not hesitate to admit your problem and seek the appropriate help. Remember that if you are depressed your family and friends can suffer too, so get help.
- If you feel seriously or continually depressed, check that there is no physical cause: consult your doctor. Depression very commonly follows a viral illness such as 'flu.
- Eat a healthy diet, including plenty of complex carbohydrates, vitamins and minerals in it, as well as foods containing the various amino acids.
- Take plenty of exercise to keep muscles active and digestion healthy, also to help keep amine levels stable.
- Keep your life as varied as possible if you feel that depression is looming: alternate work with play: visiting art galleries, swimming, seeing a film, preferably with companions. Do not let yourself become isolated.
- As far as you can, deal with problems as they arise, discuss them with people you trust, rather than leaving them to simmer in your subconscious and cause anxiety.
- Defuse stress (see entry) wherever possible: high levels can cause problems.

# DERMABRASION

*See also: acne; black skin; blotchy skin; chemical peeling; contraception; cosmetic surgery; scars; skin; tanning*

Dermabrasion (skin peeling) treatment involves removal of the outer layers of skin by means of an electrically rotating brush which penetrates down to the inner skin layer. It is carried out under a general anaesthetic. It is normally used to treat acne scars, wrinkles and pigmentation blotches and can also remove rough and crêpey skin from the back of hands. Dermabrasion requires a great deal of skill – badly done, there could be serious skin damage – and should only be carried out by an expert medical

practitioner. Some doctors feel that it should never be used to treat active acne while others consider it a good treatment at this stage because it opens up the skin and allows drainage.

Abrasive brushes are selected according to the thickness of the skin and the depth and degree of peeling required. Specific areas of scarring can be treated effectively in isolation, although deep scars will not be removed.

After the operation, dressings must be changed frequently, and antibiotic ointments applied to prevent infection and crusting. The skin will be up to 20 per cent tighter, but will remain red and tender for a few weeks while healing: make-up can be worn during this time to camouflage the redness. Normal skin colour should resume in about three months, and skin should look fully improved by six months. After dermabrasion the skin should be completely protected from the sun for at least three months, and thereafter a strong sun block should be used, as ultra-violet rays can cause permanent pigmentation blotches. These patches can also occur if you are taking the contraceptive pill. If dermabrasion is planned, therefore, use another method of contraception for at least four weeks before the operation, and three weeks after. Like chemical peeling, the success of dermabrasion varies with each skin type and cannot be guaranteed.

# DERMATITIS

*See also: allergies; skin; tanning*

Dermatitis is inflammation of the skin, often accompanied by extreme itchiness. If left untreated the skin swells and forms tiny blisters which burst and weep. A crust then forms over the area. In chronic dermatitis the skin thickens with the outer layer flaking off as scales. With acne and psoriasis, dermatitis is one of the three most common skin problems. The word eczema is often used synonymously with dermatitis, particularly when referring to the atopic type which affects children.

### TYPES AND TREATMENTS

There are at least 8 types of dermatitis. Some of the most usual are described below:

**Contact dermatitis** Irritant and allergic: both occur as a result of skin contact with substances. Irritant contact dermatitis affects about 5 per cent of the population and is more common in women than men. Those who have to wash their hands frequently are particularly at risk as they wash away all the protective natural fats. The combination of this and touching common irritants like detergents – shampoo or washing-up liquid – can produce inflamed skin with dry, sore cracking. Allergic contact dermatitis is less common. Here substances which may have been handled for years can suddenly become allergens to the skin: itching, redness and tiny blisters which burst and weep develop. The dermatitis may spread away from contact areas, although the latter remain most affected. Only small amounts of the allergen are needed to produce further attacks. Common causes of this type of dermatitis are lanolin, nickel and chromium, hair dyes (containing PPD – paraphenylene diamine), rubber, glues and preservatives in creams.

Treatment: in irritant dermatitis there may be one or more factors to be avoided. Keep skin moisturized, but be very careful to use only pure products without irritants: your doctor will be able to prescribe some for you if proprietary beauty products are unsuitable. If allergic dermatitis is suspected, the cause of the problem may be discovered by discussion with your doctor and the use of patch tests. Incriminated substances must be avoided.

**Atopic dermatitis** The most common type, tending to run in families and develop in children between 2 and 6 months old, though it can begin later. Many children gradually grow out of it and it usually clears by puberty. Sufferers often have asthma and hay fever, too. Begins with itchy patches of dryness on face, spreading to the arms and legs.

Treatment: keep bathing to a minimum, using only the simplest soaps and generous quantities of moisturizer and oils recommended by your doctor. In more troublesome cases, cortisone cream and ointments are of benefit. Research into the role of diet in this field is under way; meanwhile breast-feeding for as long as possible is strongly advised. In some cases cow's milk, eggs and fish have been connected with worsening of atopic dermatitis.

**Seborrhoic dermatitis** Can occur in babies and adults, more common in men than women. Tends to occur in areas where sebaceous glands are concentrated: the scalp and face, groin and armpits, upper back and chest. Fine, scaly patches appear on reddened, itchy skin.

Treatment: applications of cortisone creams, possibly also containing an antibiotic, will be prescribed. In severe cases, continuous low dose antibiotics are helpful.

**Varicose dermatitis** Most common from middle adult life onwards. Most common among women as a result of thrombosis in leg veins. Sluggish blood flow produces pressure on vein walls in the lower leg, fluid and red blood cells leak out of capillaries and the skin in the area becomes dry and starved of nutrients.

Treatment: wear support tights or stockings, and exercise legs as much as possible to stimulate blood flow. Keep skin well moisturized. Cortisone creams may be necessary.

General measures in the treatment of dermatitis are described below.
- Do not overheat your house: a cool atmosphere reduces skin irritation.
- Cover exposed skin in cold, windy weather and keep your skin well moisturized to help avoid attacks.
- If you have dermatitis on your hands be extremely careful not to do anything which could irritate them: wear cotton gloves under rubber gloves for all washing jobs, using polish, deal-

ing with citrus fruits, etc. Avoid all cosmetic hand creams; use emollients and moisturizers prescribed by your doctor.
- Never use creams prescribed for one area on another or borrow cream prescribed for a friend or relative: they vary immensely in strength, as well as type. Consult your doctor.
- Moderate sun exposure generally helps eczema but getting too hot will make the skin itchy and uncomfortable.
- Ensure that your diet contains enough vitamins and minerals, especially A, B complex, E, inositol, zinc, copper and iodine: these play a vital role in keeping skin as healthy as possible, the sebaceous glands functioning normally, and help prevent the drying-out which exacerbates dermatitis.
- Stress and anxiety can help produce a dermatitis attack in those who are prone to them, or make one more severe. See separate entries for ways of alleviating these problems.
- Chamomile lotions may help in mild cases of irritant contact dermatitis, and there are a number of homoeopathic remedies.

# DERMATOLOGIST

*See also: acne; allergies; cysts; dermatitis; psoriasis; skin; tanning; warts*

The dermatologist is a medical specialist who is concerned with the diagnosis and treatment of all skin disorders. The title derives from dermis, the Greek word for skin. Conditions treated by this specialist derive from a variety of causes. These may be dietary (e.g. food allergies), hormonal (e.g. acne), environmental (e.g. irritant contact dermatitis) or skin cancers, or arise from a host of other medical problems (e.g. varicose dermatitis). Referral to a dermatologist is by your general practitioner in the UK. In the USA referral may be by your physician or you can consult a dermatologist direct.

# DIET

*See also: additives; allergies; appetite; blood pressure; cholesterol; diets; eating habits; energy; fatigue; fats; fattening diets; fibre; minerals; salt; slimming; sugar; vitamins*

The human body relies on food to build its tissues and provide the energy needed to maintain living processes such as breathing, digestion and heartbeat. The diet necessary for life comprises the following elements: proteins, fats, carbohydrates, vitamins, minerals, trace elements and water. The quality and balance of these components is very

**Dermis**
See Skin

**Diarrhoea**
See Diet

**Diaphragm**
See Contraception

D

important. Eating more or less than is necessary for normal growth and energy expenditure will result in weight gain or loss which, if excessive, can be detrimental to health. Excessive or inadequate ingestion of nutrients in one category – too much fat or not enough protein, for example – can be dangerous in the long and even short term. So good health depends on a good diet, and that means a diet which is balanced and moderate.

### THE IMPORTANCE OF A BALANCED DIET

A 'balanced' diet is one which contains both the right quantity and the right types of food. The quantity of food is important because the right amount ensures that you remain in the ideal weight range for your height and so avoid the health risks associated with being very much over or under weight. How much you need depends on your build, your sex, how active you are and your metabolic rate (how fast you burn up energy; see **metabolic rate**). The right types of food are important because the body needs a wide range of nutrients in varying amounts in order to function healthily. Avoiding foods which are rich in some or all of the nutrients the body needs and filling up on those which lack nutritive value is hazardous to health. Knowing what foods contain which nutrients, why they are needed and just how much is needed will help you plan a balanced diet.

- Carbohydrate in foods may be found in one or more of the following forms: sugars, starches and fibre.
- Starch is a good source of carbohydrate energy. Bread, potatoes, rice, pasta and cereals are all rich in starch.
- Carbohydrates are used by the body as a source of energy and can be stored as glycogen (or 'animal starch') in the liver and muscles, for later use; excesses are converted to fat and stored around body organs and under the skin.
- Table sugar (sucrose) provides energy but no nutrients and is therefore unnecessary in a healthy diet: just as much energy can be obtained from natural sugars in fruits and young vegetables.
- Fibre is only partially digested by humans so provides little energy, but it does play an important part in the emptying of the large bowel, among other vital functions. Good sources are wholemeal bread and pasta, brown rice, vegetables and fruit.
- Starch- and fibre-containing foods should account for about 60 per cent of a healthy diet.
- Proteins are the substances from which our bodies build tissue for growth and repair. Their chemical composition is of chains of amino acids. Foods such as eggs, meat, fish, milk and cheese contain all the necessary amino acids; vegetable sources contain 'incomplete' chains but in certain combinations can provide the correct balance.
- Protein should account for about 10 per cent of a healthy diet.
- Fats contain essential fatty acids which keep the body functions working. They carry the fat-soluble vitamins A, D, E and K. Fats are very concentrated Calorie sources and make food more palatable.
- Fats should account for about 30 per cent of a healthy diet: many Western diets contain up to 45 per cent fats.
- Saturated fats are mainly of animal origin: meat, milk, butter and cheese are high in saturated fats, as are cocoa and coconut oils. Saturated fats in the diet have been shown to raise blood cholesterol to dangerous levels (see **cholesterol**). Foods containing a high percentage of saturated fats should only be taken in moderation.
- Polyunsaturated fats tend to occur in the highest levels in plants: safflower, sunflower, corn and soya oils are rich sources, as well as fish. They tend to lower blood cholesterol levels and are therefore thought to be a good substitute for saturated fats.
- Monounsaturated fats, which occur in olive oil, nut oils, nuts and avocado pears, for example, appear to have still greater cholesterol-lowering properties than polyunsaturates.
- Alcohol and foods high in fat and sugar should be avoided, and at best regarded as special occasion treats, certainly not as everyday necessities. Cut down on them and fill the gap, if there is one, with starch.

### DIETARY VARIATIONS

A healthy diet should contain adequate amounts of the various categories of nutrients: protein, fat, carbohydrates, minerals, trace elements and vitamins. While no single food is absolutely necessary for health, cutting out certain groups of food from the diet or restricting the diet to a few types of food makes it more likely that some nutrients will be missing. People who become vegans should be well-informed as to how to achieve a complementary protein intake.

Certain religious groups have diets which are restricted to a greater or lesser extent. These have generally evolved over centuries and are not usually detrimental to health. Problems can arise for people on such diets when they move away from their indigenous area and find specialized foods difficult to obtain. Here care should be taken to ensure that missing nutrients are provided in another food form or by supplements: ask your doctor. Diets which are devised for rapid weight loss or to 'cleanse the system', and which are severely restricted in their food range, should not be undertaken unless approved by a dietician. Always ask your doctor's advice before going on a diet, too.

### VEGETARIANISM

Vegetarians are arguably healthier than meat-eaters. They tend to be slimmer and to have lower blood cholesterol levels. There are two classes of vegetarians – vegans and ovolactovegetarians:
**Vegans** reject all foods which are of animal origin – fish, eggs, milk, cheese and butter as well as meat. This makes it difficult to achieve an adequate intake of nutrients such as protein, calcium, iron, iodine

and in particular vitamin B12. This type of diet is likely to be unsatisfactory for children who need large quantities of calcium and protein while they are growing. Adult vegans should ensure that they make up these possible deficiencies by eating a good portion of legumes, nuts or soya each day to provide protein; large amounts of raisins, currants, dried figs, cabbage and leeks to get calcium; parsley, dried fruit and soya for iron (spinach and wholegrains contain large quantities of iron but it is not readily available to the body when eaten); iodized salt or vegetables grown near the sea for iodine; and vitamin B12 supplements commercially prepared from non-animal sources.

**Ovolactovegetarians** do not eat meat but do accept dairy produce in their diet, so are much less likely than vegans to suffer from lack of protein or calcium. They should, however, follow the guidelines for vegans on iron and iodine.

Protein-rich foods useful for inclusion in a vegetarian diet are: soya, brewer's yeast, pulses, tofu (a curd made from soya milk) and peanuts.

### DIETS REGULATED BY RELIGIOUS BELIEFS

**Jews** have strict religious and traditional laws about what foods are included in their diet and the way they are prepared and eaten. The term 'kosher' means 'clean' and refers to the way in which animals are slaughtered and cleansed before being eaten as meat. Animals with cloven feet, like pigs, must not be eaten, and only the forequarters of those animals which are permitted may be used. Fish with scales may be eaten but not lobsters, prawns or other shellfish. Meat and milk may not be served at the same meal.

**Hindus** eat no beef, as they have worshipped the cow for over 3,000 years. Some Hindus eat all meat other than beef, but many are vegetarians to greater or lesser degrees of strictness (some eating fish, eggs and milk, others only milk).

**Moslems** are not allowed pork or alcohol. They use a lot of oil and ghee (clarified butter) and spices in their cooking. The Islamic festival of Ramadan, during the ninth lunar month of the Islamic year, is a period of strict fasting from sunrise to sunset.

**Roman Catholics** were formerly forbidden to eat meat on Fridays. This is no longer required by the church but eating fish on Fridays is still practised by many traditional Catholics.

### SPECIAL DIETARY REQUIREMENTS

Although the guidelines on range and quantity of foods are sufficient for the average adult, individuals vary in their requirements. In particular, certain groups of people have special dietary needs, either because they are in the process of building or re-building their body tissues, or because their activity and/or metabolic rates produce different energy needs.

### Babies

In their first few months, babies need only milk, ideally human breast milk, though the modern formulas made for bottle-feeding are nutritionally adequate. Solid foods should not be introduced before 3 months of age: 4 months is the usual recommended age for starting solids, though some babies are satisfied by milk alone for as long as 6 months. Foods should be introduced gradually, starting with cereals and puréed fruit and vegetables, so that the baby's immature digestive system is not overloaded. Salt or sugar should not be added to foods, and ready-prepared foods containing these should be avoided. They are unnecessary, can damage the kidneys and can also cause the baby to acquire a taste for such seasonings which will be hard to shake off in later life (see also **salt** and **sugar**). In the past, fat babies were considered healthy, but it is now agreed that it is particularly important *not* to become overweight in the early years of life (see **eating habits**).

### Children

By the time a child is 1 year old he or she will

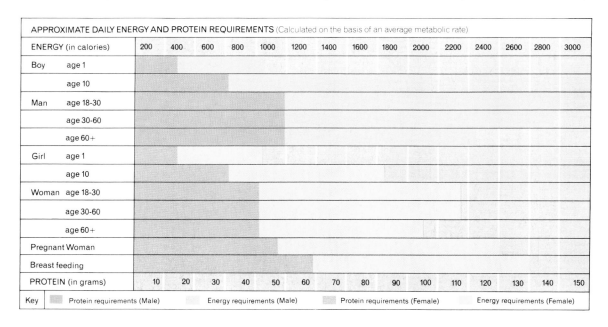

| APPROXIMATE DAILY ENERGY AND PROTEIN REQUIREMENTS (Calculated on the basis of an average metabolic rate) | | | | | | | | | | | | | | | |
|---|---|---|---|---|---|---|---|---|---|---|---|---|---|---|---|
| ENERGY (in calories) | 200 | 400 | 600 | 800 | 1000 | 1200 | 1400 | 1600 | 1800 | 2000 | 2200 | 2400 | 2600 | 2800 | 3000 |
| Boy age 1 | | | | | | | | | | | | | | | |
| age 10 | | | | | | | | | | | | | | | |
| Man age 18-30 | | | | | | | | | | | | | | | |
| age 30-60 | | | | | | | | | | | | | | | |
| age 60+ | | | | | | | | | | | | | | | |
| Girl age 1 | | | | | | | | | | | | | | | |
| age 10 | | | | | | | | | | | | | | | |
| Woman age 18-30 | | | | | | | | | | | | | | | |
| age 30-60 | | | | | | | | | | | | | | | |
| age 60+ | | | | | | | | | | | | | | | |
| Pregnant Woman | | | | | | | | | | | | | | | |
| Breast feeding | | | | | | | | | | | | | | | |
| PROTEIN (in grams) | 10 | 20 | 30 | 40 | 50 | 60 | 70 | 80 | 90 | 100 | 110 | 120 | 130 | 140 | 150 |

| Key | Protein requirements (Male) | Energy requirements (Male) | Protein requirements (Female) | Energy requirements (Female) |
|---|---|---|---|---|

| APPROXIMATE DAILY VITAMIN AND MINERAL REQUIREMENTS | | | | | | | |
|---|---|---|---|---|---|---|---|
| Sex/Age Group | Thiamin (B1) | Riboflavin (B2) | Niacin (B3) | Ascorbic (C) | Vitamin A | Calcium | Iron |
| Boy        age 1 | 0.5 | 0.6 | 7 | 20 | 300 | 600 | 7 |
| age 10 | 0.9 | 1.2 | 14 | 25 | 575 | 700 | 12 |
| Man        age 18-34 | 1.2 | 1.6 | 18 | 30 | 750 | 500 | 10 |
| age 35-64 | 1.1 | 1.6 | 18 | 30 | 750 | 500 | 10 |
| age 64 + | 1.0 | 1.6 | 18 | 30 | 750 | 500 | 10 |
| Girl        age 1 | 0.4 | 0.6 | 7 | 20 | 300 | 600 | 7 |
| age 10 | 0.8 | 1.2 | 14 | 25 | 575 | 700 | 12 |
| Woman    age 18-54 | 0.9 | 1.3 | 15 | 30 | 750 | 500 | 12 |
| age 55+ | 0.8 | 1.3 | 15 | 30 | 750 | 500 | 10 |
| Pregnant woman | 1.0 | 1.6 | 18 | 60 | 750 | 1200 | 13 |
| Breast feeding | 1.1 | 1.8 | 21 | 60 | 1200 | 1200 | 15 |
| Key | Male requirements | | | | Female requirements | | |

Other vitamins and minerals essential for a healthy diet tend to be readily available in western diets and any not listed here – see vitamins, minerals.

probably be on a good mixed diet similar to that of an adult. Milk, or other dairy products such as cheese and yoghurt, should remain an important part of the child's diet as much calcium is needed for the formation of strong bones and teeth. Vitamin D is also important for the calcification of the bones and a supplement is sometimes recommended if the child is exposed to little sunshine. The supplement is given all year round up to 2 years of age and then in the winter only to the age of 5.

Protein is essential for building body tissues. If the child does not like meat, which is often the case, care should be taken to see that he or she is getting protein combinations which will provide complementary amino acids, such as baked beans on toast or baked potatoes with cheese.

## Pregnant women
No special diet is necessary at this time and an expectant mother should certainly not 'eat for two'. Care should be taken, however, to see that the diet is varied enough to provide all the essential nutrients for herself and the foetus. Morning sickness in the first 3 or 4 months may cause problems, but avoiding fatty foods and eating frequent starchy snacks to raise blood sugar levels may help. A supplement of iron and folic acid (a B group vitamin) is often prescribed, but such supplements should only be taken when prescribed, and only supplements especially formulated for pregnant women should be used. Alcohol intake should be severely limited, preferably cut out altogether.

## Breastfeeding mothers
During lactation a woman's nutritional requirements are greater than in pregnancy. The ingredients and quality of the mother's milk depends largely on the mother's diet, so high quality protein, calcium, and iron are especially important. Altogether, approximately 500 additional Calories a day are needed (equivalent to an extra meal).

## Convalescents
People who are ill often lose their appetite, eat little food and lose weight during the period they are unwell. Once they begin to recover it is normal for the appetite to increase dramatically and the patient should be given sufficient food so that weight returns to normal. If the illness has been prolonged, muscles may be wasted. In this case, and also after injury or surgery, extra protein may be needed to rebuild body tissues. Increased metabolic rate increases the need for energy.

## The elderly
In an affluent society one of the most common nutritional problems in old people is obesity. As they become less active, the elderly need to eat less, but this makes it more important that what is eaten is nutritionally rich. A lack of variety may lead to deficiencies, particularly in vitamin C, iron and protein. Physical problems such as arthritis or lack of teeth may make preparing, handling and chewing certain nutritious foods such as oranges and potatoes difficult, leading to a reliance on refined, nutritionally poor convenience foods. Obesity is commoner, but malnutrition occurs among the elderly even in the developed countries, more often in mild forms resulting from nutrient deficiencies.

### DIETARY DANGERS
Diet is only one of the factors which influence health. Exercise, drugs like nicotine and alcohol, social and psychological factors all play their part. In theory, following a diet which has no health dangers should be simple: there is no need for special health foods – a moderate, balanced eating plan is all that is needed. In practice, many people do not eat in this sensible way and indulge in a diet which is imbalanced in favour of fat, sugar and alcohol, with too little fibre. Scientific research has implicated all of these in the incidence of diseases such as coronary heart disease, cancer and tooth decay. A high-fat, high-sugar diet combined with lack of exercise is likely to lead to excessive weight gain, then obesity, which with its related problems such as high blood pressure, diabetes and a raised blood cholesterol level increases the risk of heart disease.

Cholesterol in the blood is mainly manufactured by the body itself; only a proportion arrives via the diet. The amount of cholesterol in an average diet would not in itself raise blood cholesterol to dangerous levels. Saturated fats raise LDL (low-density lipoprotein) blood cholesterol levels (see **cholesterol**): high levels cause cholesterol deposits which harden and block arteries. Blood containing high saturated fat levels clots more readily. Polyunsaturated fats, however, have the opposite effect. There is some evidence that they, and still more so the monounsaturates, can repair damage done by saturated fats. Studies are not conclusive, however, and research continues.

Salt is found in most of the foods in a normal diet, processed and natural, so added salt is unnecessary for health, except when large amounts are lost from the body through sweating. On average we eat 10 times more salt than we need. Many middle-aged people have higher blood pressure than they should, which in turn increases the risk of heart attacks and strokes. A reduction in salt intake may produce a beneficial effect for these people, by reducing their blood pressure.

Sugar has been cited as another factor associated with heart disease, though the evidence is not as strong here as it is for fat. That sugar is harmful to teeth is indisputable. Bacteria feed on the sugar and produce acids which start the decay process. A healthy diet avoids sugar and all foods containing it: culprits are cakes, jam, fizzy drinks, canned soups and some breakfast cereals.

Fibre appears to be an important factor in preventing diseases of the large bowel such as appendicitis, cancer and diverticulitis. These diseases are rare in countries where the diet contains less fat, little sugar and more starch and fibre. Fibre may also slow the absorption of sugar and fat which may be beneficial in the management of some diseases such as diabetes and coronary heart disease.

Vitamin overdosing is a possible danger, particularly with fat-soluble vitamins such as A and D which are stored in the body, if taken in excessive amounts over long periods. Vitamin C and those of the B group are water-soluble and in general any excess is excreted without ill effects, though there may be a greater risk of kidney stones occurring in people who take massive doses of vitamin C tablets. Generally speaking, for healthy people, it is better to improve vitamin and mineral intake by dietary, rather than supplementary means.

### DIETARY PROBLEMS

**Constipation** often results from a diet low in fibre or fluid, or from generally poor eating habits. Prunes are often recommended to counteract it as they contain a substance which prompts bowel motion. Pregnant women and the elderly are particularly susceptible to constipation or it can be a side-effect of iron tablets or certain drugs. To relieve it, eat more unprocessed bran, potatoes and their skins, fresh fruits and raw vegetables, drink more water and fruit juices. However, if the problem persists, consult your doctor.

**Diarrhoea** occurs as a result of infection, defective enzyme production (lactose intolerance, for example), organic disease or a side effect of certain drugs such as antibiotics. It can also be a symptom of niacin (a B group vitamin) deficiency or part of a sunstroke reaction. Take plenty of fluid to guard against dehydration. Extra dietary potassium, sodium and chlorides may be needed to replace losses. If your diarrhoea persists without obvious cause, consult your doctor. If you are taking the pill you should use an additional form of protection (see **contraception**).

**Malnutrition** is not normally found in Western societies, except occasionally among the elderly, and among vegetarians who are not careful to account for the lack of animal protein in their diet. In some Eastern and African countries, long-term malnutrition is a common problem due to carbohydrate and particularly to overall food energy deficiency. There are 2 forms: *marasmus* results from a chronic lack of protein and carbohydrate in the diet; *kwashiorkor* results from a diet in which the carbohydrate intake may be sufficient but a simultaneous lack of protein stunts growth.

| FOOD | ENERGY (Calories) | CARBOHYDRATES | PROTEIN | FAT (total) | PERCENTAGE sat* | mus* | pus* | CHOLESTEROL (mg/100 g) | FIBRE |
|------|------|------|------|------|------|------|------|------|------|
| egg | 147 | trace | 12.3 | 10.9 | 38 | 47 | 11 | 450 (yolk 1260) | – |
| cottage cheese | 96 | 1.4 | 13.6 | 4.0 | – | – | – | 13 | – |
| olive oil | 899 | – | trace | 99.9 | 15 | 73 | 12 | – | – |
| beef (fried steak) | 246 | – | 28.6 | 14.6 | 45 | 49 | 4 | 82 | – |
| chicken (roast meat) | 148 | – | 24.8 | 5.4 | 35 | 48 | 14 | 74 light/120 dark | – |
| shrimp (boiled) | 177 | – | 23.8 | 2.4 | 22 | 29 | 43 | 200 | – |
| cucumber (flesh) | 10 | 1.8 | 0.6 | 0.1 | 42 | 3 | 55 | – | 0.4 |
| potatoes (baked, with skin) | 85 | 20.3 | 2.1 | 0.1 | 23 | 3 | 74 | – | 2.0 |
| lentils (split boiled) | 99 | 17.0 | 7.6 | 0.5 | – | – | – | – | 3.7 |
| apples (with skins) | 35 | 9.2 | 0.2 | trace | 28 | 7 | 65 | – | 1.5 |
| bananas | 79 | 19.2 | 1.1 | 0.3 | 46 | 16 | 38 | – | 3.4 |
| wholemeal bread | 216 | 41.8 | 8.8 | 2.7 | 25 | 19 | 54 | – | 8.5 |
| chocolate (plain) | 525 | 64.8 | 4.7 | 29.2 | 62 | 34 | 3 | – | – |

**WHAT ARE YOU EATING?** (g/100 g of some food components)

*sat: saturated fat    mus: monounsaturated fat    pus: polyunsaturated fat

# DIETICIAN OR NUTRITIONIST

*See also: diet; diets; fattening diets; slimming*

The dietician or nutritionist applies the science of nutrition to individuals and groups, both in good or ill health. Many medical conditions require special diets, and the dietician is able to advise both in- and out-patients on foods to avoid or include in their eating plan, taking into account foods avoided by individuals for religious, moral or traditional reasons. People likely to be referred to a dietician include the malnourished or obese, those suffering from diabetes, anorexia nervosa, various digestive disorders, kidney, liver and cardiovascular problems, new mothers and babies.

# DIETS

*See also: crash dieting; Beverly Hills diet; fattening diets; F-plan diet; Scarsdale diet*

Ten years ago the word 'dieting' was almost interchangeable with 'slimming'. Apart from those who had to adjust their diet because of diabetes or some other medical problem, losing weight was the only generally accepted reason for revised eating plans. Magazines and beauty books recommended crash diets which were guaranteed to make one lose pounds in a week or so. Others were based on small groups of foods whose supposed synergistic effect was to burn up fat, for example the banana and milk diet. Still others were just so low in Calories that fluid and lean tissue loss provided swift weight reduction, but also induced fatigue, moodiness, insomnia and possibly malnutrition.

The change which has occurred is only partly due to social factors and to the fact that there is now less emphasis on the importance of a greyhound-slender silhouette. Massive advertising campaigns have alerted the public to the dangers of smoking and drug and alcohol abuse. Research into various medical problems has begun to emphasize the preventive aspect of health. Cholesterol, salt, sugar, additives and preservatives are just some of the substances which have often been drawn to public attention as the result of research reports being published. Increased general health awareness has meant that dietary emphasis is now more on fibre, raw foods, vitamin and mineral content, for example, than just Calorie content.

Weight-reducing diets now generally have a fitness angle as well as the necessary reduction in Calorie intake. They tend to emphasize the need to rethink long-term eating habits, to re-educate the palate to like foods which are actually good for the body. Indiscriminate Calorie-counting is a thing of the past. Modern diet plans aim to promote health and fitness to keep the body young and active and to help prevent illnesses like heart disease and arteriosclerosis. Alongside a self-help attitude towards health has grown a new interest in the fields of alternative and complementary medicine, an interest which will doubtless be furthered by the British Medical Council report on these subjects which was published in autumn 1986.

# DOUCHING

*See also: body odour; personal hygiene; thrush*

Vaginal douching – using a forceful jet of water, or water with herbs, cleansers or chemicals added to it – is unnecessary and potentially very dangerous. It upsets the ecology of the vagina, removing its natural, slightly acidic mucous secretions, which fight off bacteria. Douching can in fact propel germs not only into the vagina, but also into the uterus, and substances used in the douche can set up severe inflammation and irritation. The vagina is self-cleaning, and the only help it needs is as follows:

1   Scrupulous cleanliness of the surrounding genital area is essential. This means at least daily bathing or showering using only the mildest detergents, such as unperfumed soap, especially before and after sex, during menstruation.
2   Always wipe the anal area from front to back to prevent germs reaching the urinary tract or the vagina.
3   Change tampons (or sanitary towels) every 4 hours at least (it is advisable to use sanitary towels at night), avoiding scented or deodorized types and all similar sprays or talcum powders.
4   Be vigilant regarding excessive or unpleasant discharge and/or irritation. See your doctor immediately: most minor infections can be cleared up either with a single pessary application, or with a five-day course of cream and pessaries.
5   Wear loose cotton underwear.

# DRUGS AND MEDICINES

*See also: allergies; cellulite; contraception; dependencies; depression; insomnia*

The way in which drugs alter the chemical balance of the body can be complex and profound. Although many drugs have either normally imperceptible side-effects or none at all, there are some which

**Dieting**
See Slimming;
Fattening diets

**Diuretics**
See Fluid retention

**Dreams**
See Sleep

**Drinking**
See Alcohol;
Alcoholism

**Dry hair**
See Hair

**Dry skin**
See Skin

**Drying hair**
See Hair

produce side-effects ranging from low vitamin absorption to migraine. Doctors prescribing drugs are alert both to such symptoms and to contra-indications for individuals, and in mixing drugs. There is a danger, however, in that many preparations which are capable of causing problems are available without prescription.

It is important to bear in mind the possibility of side-effects, the potential of some drugs to produce dependency (see **dependencies**) and the possibility of drug allergies.

### DRUG AND MEDICINE NOTES
- If you have any unusual symptoms, check with your doctor.
- It is of vital importance to take drugs as prescribed. Don't just assume that it will be all right to drink alcohol with your drugs, for example; check it out with your doctor.
- Don't forget to inform your doctor or pharmacist of any other drugs or medications you may be using if he has not prescribed the original drugs.
- If you are unsure about timing for taking drugs, whether to take before or after food, whether you can take your new prescribed medication with ANY other form of drug which you are taking, even cough medicine or the contraceptive pill, for example, always ask your doctor or pharmacist.
- Always finish antibiotic prescriptions to ensure that your infection has cleared.
- Never use any creams, pills, inhalers or any other products which have been prescribed for anyone else.
- Avoid all drugs and medicines while pregnant, including aspirin, cough mixtures, pain killers, preparations to treat constipation, except those prescribed to you as a pregnant woman. Avoid smoking, alcohol, too, if possible, and cut down on your caffeine intake.

### NOTES ON SOME COMMON DRUGS
**Anti-depressants** Avoid alcohol: the power of sedation increases and results can be extremely dangerous. Certain forms do not go well with the contraceptive pill so check with your doctor or gynaecologist or family planning clinic. Common side effects: constipation, dry mouth, lassitude, dizziness, rashes and itching, changes in libido.
**Penicillins** Take carefully as prescribed. Common side effects: diarrhoea, development of fungal infections such as thrush. These can interfere with the effectiveness of the contraceptive pill, so use an alternative or additional method when taking these. Allergic reaction to the drug commonly manifests itself as a rash which may consist of itchy swellings (hives or urticaria) and in severe cases swelling of throat and tongue, which can be fatal, and will be worse each time the drug is taken. In this case all penicillin drugs should be avoided, as adverse reaction tends to spread to other penicillin-type medicines too.
**Tetracylines** Take these antibiotics carefully as prescribed. You could increase your vitamin intake

with prolonged courses as the drug can reduce vitamin C absorption slightly. Do not increase calcium, iron and magnesium intake as these inhibit the drug's absorption. Avoid milk and antacid products. Common side effects: nausea, vomiting, diarrhoea – because they promote secondary development of fungus and yeast organisms in body – and thrush is also common. Can increase sensitivity to sunlight.
**Aspirin** Best known as a painkiller and for reducing fever, aspirin also has anti-inflammatory properties for rheumatism. It should not be taken for more than a few days, according to the manufacturer's instructions, without seeking a doctor's advice. When prescribed for any length of time, increase your intake of vitamin C as excretion of this is increased. Common side effects: stomach pains, vomiting, gastric bleeding, prolonged daily or almost daily use of aspirin over a number of years can cause kidney damage. Aspirin is a potential allergen: allergic reaction includes wheezing and skin rashes. Like penicillin, the allergic reaction tends to increase and the drug must be avoided. Check the labels on all combined medications as aspirin is included in a wide range of preparations. Do not take while pregnant unless your doctor indicates. Do not give to children.
**Anti-inflammatory drugs** Common side effects: gastro-intestinal irritation, headache and nausea. Suppositories which bypass digestive-caused side-effects are available for several types.
**Contraceptive pill** Discussed more fully under **contraception**, but increases likelihood of candida infections in the vagina.
**Laxatives** Used in excess, these can cause dehydration, potassium loss and deplete vitamin D.
**Antacids** There are many varieties. Some have the side-effect of constipation (those containing aluminium) and some cause diarrhoea (those containing magnesium). If you are taking lots of antacids consult your doctor.
**Sleeping pills** These can be minor tranquillizers, anti-histamines or barbiturates. Never exceed stated dose and avoid alcohol. Short courses can be helpful but effects tend to diminish: always tail off, since you may suffer withdrawal symptoms.

# DYSMENORRHOEA

*See also: contraception; endometriosis; menstruation*

Dysmenorrhoea means painful or difficult menstruation and affects between 15 and 25 per cent of women. There are two types: primary dysmenorrhoea, which occurs from the first period, and secondary dysmenorrhoea which occurs at a later stage. Primary dysmenorrhoea is particularly common among young women. The incidence is greatly reduced after the age of about 25, or after the birth of a baby.

## CAUSES OF DYSMENORRHOEA

In the past women with painful periods were treated with disdain and often thought to be making a fuss, but research has shown that the cramps and nausea which often accompany menstruation are caused by excessive uterine contractions, because the uterus has been over-stimulated by prostaglandin. The cramps in turn cause restricted blood circulation and therefore pain, as in any muscle which is working too hard. Intra-uterine devices (IUDs) (see **contraception**) can produce dysmenorrhoea as they increase menstrual bleeding and seem to stimulate prostaglandin production. One type of IUD releases progestogen which prevents this happening, Progestasat, but is not generally available.

The causes of secondary dysmenorrhoea are varied and this late onset of painful periods needs a doctor's diagnosis. The cause may be a physical abnormality, some infection or a disease such as endometriosis.

## ALLEVIATING DYSMENORRHOEA
### Primary dysmenorrhoea

- Some readily available pain relievers such as aspirin impede production of prostaglandin and prevent the pain. If pain persists, your doctor can prescribe specific anti-prostaglandin drugs.
- The contraceptive pill reduces menstrual pain as its action thins the uterine lining, thus diminishing the menstrual flow and the production of prostaglandin. The combined pill inhibits ovulation, and the progestogen-only pill often causes reduced ovulation: both help as dysmenorrhoea seems to be absent or at least diminished when ovulation does not occur.
- Increase your regular calcium intake with milk and milk products for example (see **minerals** for other sources) as this alleviates the prob-

lem. Be sure to include plenty of foods rich in B and E vitamins in your regular diet, too.
- At the onset of dysmenorrhoea, try some gentle **relaxation exercises** (see separate entry), followed by lying or sitting down with two hot water bottles, one in the small of the back, one on the stomach, and sipping a warm drink: parsley tea is an appropriate herbal remedy.
NOTE Many women find that dysmenorrhoea diminishes after childbirth.

### Secondary dysmenorrhoea

- Consult your doctor as there are several possible causes. A recently-fitted IUD may account for the pain, but be sure to check with your family planning clinic or doctor: there could be ancillary problems.

■ See EXERCISES for Caution Box page 123 before starting exercise

▲ Exercise A
1 Lie on your back on the floor, with your arms by your sides, knees drawn up and legs together, so that your feet are quite close to your buttocks.
2 Breathe in. As you breathe out, slowly lift your bottom and lower body from the floor, resting your weight on your shoulders and upper back, not your neck. Knees will go forward. Keep feet flat on the ground. Hold for a few seconds, then return gently to original position and release abdomen muscles. Repeat 6 times.

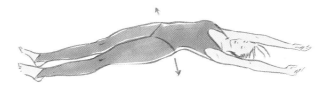

▲ Exercise B
1 Lie on your back on the floor in the same starting position as for exercise A, above.
2 Now bring your knees up to your chest, breathing out as you do so, clasping your knees with your arms to bring them up as high as possible. Hold position for a few seconds, then return to starting position, release abdomen muscles, and breathe in. Keep your back flat on floor throughout. Repeat at least 6 times.

▲ Exercise C
1 Lie on your back on the floor with your legs extended straight in front of you and slightly apart.
2 Push your hips out slightly to your right, stretch your arms above your head and elongate your whole body: you will feel the stretch in your right side. Now repeat for the other side. Repeat at least 6 times for each side, breathing easily throughout the exercise and stretching a little further each time.

# E A R S

*See also: cosmetic surgery; noise*

### CONSTRUCTION AND OPERATION OF THE EAR
The ear, which is a highly sensitive organ, has three main sections. The outer ear funnels sound waves of varying pitch (the frequency of the vibrations) and intensity (or loudness) down towards the membranous eardrum which is situated at the entrance to the middle ear. From here, the vibrations pass through progressively smaller bones, the hammer (malleus), anvil (incus) and stirrup (stapes) before reaching the snail-shaped cochlea in the inner ear. This is filled with fluid and thousands of tiny, highly sensitive fibres. Vibration of these produces an electrical impulse detailing pitch and loudness which travels along the auditory nerve to the hearing centre of the brain. Here the message is decoded and the sound is 'heard'.

### HEARING
The sense of hearing is well developed by the time a baby is born. As in any other field, the child needs sound experience in order to understand the meaning of various types. Children who lead rather soundless lives can appear backward for this reason. Hearing improves as the child matures, deteriorating as middle and old age approach.

Sound pitch or frequency is measured on the Hertz scale. One Hertz = one cycle, or vibration, per second. Humans can pick up notes as low as 20 Hertz and as high as 20,000 Hertz, while other mammals such as dogs and bats can hear sounds at much higher frequencies. Intensity or loudness of sound is measured in decibels (dB). Hearing tests involve measuring both sound pitch and intensity with an audiometer. Results are graded on a chart and any signs of deafness are clearly apparent.

### HEARING MALFUNCTION AND HEARING AIDS
Hearing malfunction is not uncommon. In the UK, 1 in 300 children need hearing aids, 1 in 100 need to sit at the front of the class and 1 in 200 need to attend schools for the deaf. 26 per cent of the middle aged have hearing problems and 60 per cent of those over 70 have significant hearing loss. Causes are various: the condition may be due to congenital defect, inflammation or obstruction within the ear interfering with the passage of sound waves, illness, or ageing. Excessive noise can also cause irreversible loss of hearing – particularly of the lower sounds.

As with any illness, the earlier the impairment is diagnosed, the greater the chance of cure or compensation. Providing the deafness is not total the use of a hearing aid can help enormously. Their chief disadvantage is their tendency to amplify all sound indiscriminately, but modern technology has improved their efficiency and appearance.

### EAR CARE
If your ears feel blocked, consult your doctor who can syringe out the wax using a jet of water directed at the eardrum to propel it out. He may suggest that you put a few drops of a pure oil like olive oil into each ear for two or three days before syringing, in order to soften the wax. What you should not do is attempt to remove wax, or to 'clean out' your ears with your fingers or an object like a cotton wool bud ('Q-tip'). Ears are very delicate indeed: ear-wax is there to capture any alien substances and prevent them reaching the inner ear. By 'cleaning' you are in fact increasing the risk of ear infection or blockage. Just wipe the outer area with a clean, moist face cloth or cotton wool pad regularly.

Do not disregard earache which does not disappear with one or two analgesics: it can be a sign of things as various as sinus blockage, dental or gum problems as well as a specific ear problem. Consult your doctor. Keep ears warm in cold weather to avoid frostbite and chilblains, and remember to include them in your suncare programme, too: ears are very exposed and can easily burn and peel painfully.

### EAR PIERCING
Correctly done, ear piercing should cause no pain or subsequent infection problems.
- Hygienic conditions are imperative. Choose a qualified beautician or go to a reputable jewellery store for ear piercing. A clean, new disposable needle should be used, your ear lobes anaesthetized before piercing, and you should be given practical advice on aftercare.
- Choose gold for the initial rings known as 'sleepers', as it is the metal least likely to carry infection, and allergy to it is rare. Choose studs rather than rings: you are less likely to catch them with a comb or hairbrush and infection can less easily be transmitted into the unhealed wound. Studs are easier to turn, a process which must be carried out daily after piercing.
- Keep ears scrupulously clean, bathing with a warm salt-water solution at the slightest hint of infection (redness, soreness or discharge). If your ears do flare up, visit your doctor.
- Don't be tempted to wear any other earrings until ears are completely healed.
- Prevent the hole closing up by wearing earrings day and night for the first three months.

The ears not only control hearing but also balance. Care for your ears by regulating noise at home and in the office, and avoid potentially damaging attempts to clean inside them, with anything other than a wet face cloth.

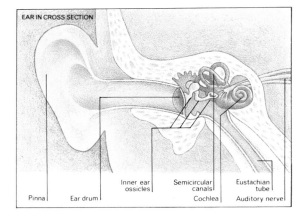

EAR IN CROSS SECTION

Pinna | Ear drum | Inner ear ossicles | Semicircular canals | Cochlea | Eustachian tube | Auditory nerve

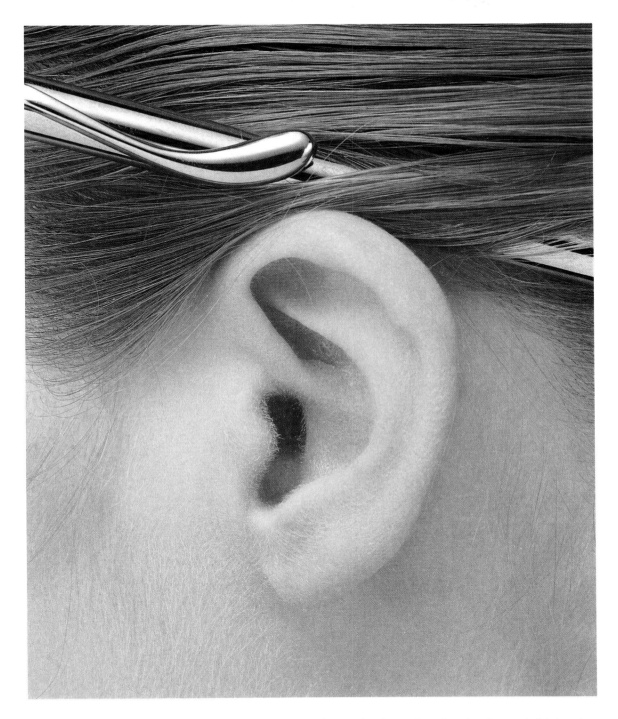

## EATING HABITS

*See also: anorexia nervosa; appetite; bingeing; bulimia nervosa; diet; fattening diets; slimming*

Eating habits are instilled into us by our parents when we are still babies and, whether good or bad, can be hard to change. Some changes can take place almost imperceptibly, however, like the volume of junk foods which most people have incorporated in their eating patterns, and the change from school or college lunches to sandwich lunches in the office, for example. Other alterations can be difficult: reducing food intake in order to lose weight, for instance, or changing over to a new, healthier diet plan.

Generally speaking most people in the developed countries eat much more than they need or is good for them, and take less exercise than the amount needed to offset this intake. Your needs are governed by your basal metabolic rate (see **metabolic rate**), age, size and level of activity. In malnutrition (and in crash dieting) your metabolic rate drops to make the most efficient use of any foodstuffs being

eaten. The ratio of lean tissue to fat tissue decreases with age and thus the elderly have a lower metabolic rate. Those requiring the most energy for their body size are athletes, people who have altered their body composition as a result of exercise to decrease fat or increase muscle mass (their metabolic rate increases), pregnant women and those who are breastfeeding, as well as children and young people who are still growing.

Eating habits can be distorted by the emotional state. Depression, happiness, sadness, fear, anxiety, falling in love: emotions like these can have dramatic effects on eating habits. Avoiding eating can actually make depression worse as low energy levels may result in fatigue and lethargy. Try to maintain your regular diet and if necessary supplement it with high-vitamin produce (see **depression**) as even short periods without some nutrients can cause deficiency. Vitamin C, for example should be taken daily. Below are some general eating habit guidelines:

■ Try to eat during the early part of the day when you are most active and needing most energy. A good breakfast and lunch will keep you feeling good all your working day. Even if you are trying to lose weight, do eat breakfast. Failure to do so may make you fatigued and listless all morning.

■ Eating a large meal in the evening is inadvisable. You may find getting to sleep difficult, and you will not be hungry at breakfast.

■ Eat regularly, including snacks between meals if you feel hungry. Provided that these are healthy snacks like fruit drinks, raw fruits and vegetables, they will not increase your weight.

■ Children's eating habits need careful supervision. Snacks between meals should be eaten well before meals to avoid depleting the appetite (children need more energy than adults).

■ The elderly may find eating little and often easiest. Sub-clinical malnutrition is not uncommon, i.e. where deficiencies exist, but are not severe enough to show symptoms.

## Eczema
See Dermatitis

## Effleurage
See Massage

## Elasticity
See Skin; Elastin and elastone

## Electrolysis
See Unwanted hair

## Elimination diet
See Allergies and allergens

## Enamel (Nail)
See Manicure

# EAU-DE-COLOGNE

*See also: scent*

Eau-de-cologne, along with eau-de-toilette and eau-de-parfum is a light and refreshing scent that can be applied frequently and liberally. All are less potent than the pure *parfum* or *extrait* (see **scent**) since their perfume content is diluted with more water than alcohol. Eau-de-parfum or parfum-de-toilette has approximately 8-15 per cent concentration of pure perfume, eau-de-toilette has 4-8 per cent, and eau-de-cologne has 2-6 per cent. Eau-de-parfum/parfum-de-toilette lasts approximately 2-5 hours, eau-de-toilette 2-4 hours and eau-de-cologne 1-2 hours. Still lighter are splash colognes and eaux fraîches which last only an hour or so.

# ELASTIN AND ELASTONE

*See also: ageing; collagen; skin; tanning*

Elastin is the protein which, with collagen, forms the major constituent of connective tissue. Its function in the skin is one of flexibility: connective tissue collagen provides tensile strength, elastin makes skin stretch and then spring back into place. Elastin steadily loses its spring with age and the thinning of skin and subcutaneous fat in middle age results in the changes seen in the skin in later life. Extensive sun exposure has a damaging effect on the elastin fibres in the dermis which results in premature wrinkling.

Elastone is the mattress of collagen and elastin fibres which develops with advancing age and becomes increasingly inflexible. Skin needs still more careful treatment now: its decreased tensile strength and stretch mean that make-up should be applied and removed ever more gently. Skin which sags once elastone has developed can only be tightened by cosmetic surgery.

# ELECTRO-DESICCATION

*See also: cysts; freckles; skin; thread veins*

Electrodesiccation is a very precise and painless form of skin treatment used for spider veins, broken blood vessels, freckles and cysts and for blemishes which often show up as the skin thins with age. It can be performed quickly by a dermatologist or cosmetic surgeon, and involves burning the blemish away by means of an electric current applied through a fine, surgical needle. A scab will form on the reddened area. This peels away after about a week exposing a new, smooth layer of skin below. Total recovery of the skin takes about 28 days.

# ENDOMETRIOSIS

*See also: dysmenorrhoea*

Endometriosis is a condition where fragments of the uterine lining, the endometrium, exist in sites outside the uterus, but within the pelvis. Each fragment forms a cyst and behaves like a miniature uterus each month, bleeding although there is no outlet for blood: the serum is absorbed. Endometriosis can be symptomless, or it can cause pain during intercourse. Many cases need no treatment, others are treated with hormones or surgery.

# ENDORPHINS AND ENKEPHALINES

*See also: aches and pains; acupuncture*

Endorphins are mainly produced by the pituitary gland and occur in the brain; enkephalines occur in the spinal fluid and brain. Both chemicals (peptides) have a natural pain-killing action similar to that of injected morphine (one of the opiates). These 'opiates' produced by the body (endogenous opiates) are the subject of much current research: they seem to be produced by a variety of physical and mental processes and their existence is thought to go some way towards explaining the successful action of placebos. Electrical stimulation of the skin or brain produces natural opiates: acupuncture is thought to activate them, too. Increased levels of the chemical serotonin, which is involved in the triggering of the sleep mechanism and in alleviating anxiety and depression (see **depression**) appear to simulate natural 'opiate' production.

# ENERGY

*See also: acupuncture; depression; diet; exercise; fatigue; minerals; reflexology; sports; vitamins*

When we talk about 'feeling energetic' we tend to mean that we are feeling lively as opposed to fatigued. Although this does convey some of the meaning energy has, scientifically speaking energy is the capacity to perform work and has nothing to do with your emotions or subjective feelings. In the body energy is needed for the growth and development of all body tissues, for muscle movement and maintenance of body tissue, and is essential to every cell constantly. The energy unit is the Calorie (see separate entry), one Calorie being the amount of heat required to raise 1 litre of water through 1°C.

### FACTORS IN ENERGY
The individual daily energy requirement is related to the basal metabolic rate (see **metabolic rate**), tempered by a variety of other factors. These are:
**Activity** The amount of work being done during the day: typing, for example, uses just over 2 Calories per minute, gardening between 5 and 7 and rowing or heavy building work from 9 to 12. Contrary to popular belief, static brainwork does not itself use extra Calories, so writing a book for example, uses only the typing Calorie requirement.
**Age** Children have a higher rate proportional to their size than adults, the elderly a lower one.
**Pregnancy and lactation** The rate is higher at these times but not enough to merit 'eating for two' (see **diet, pregnancy).**
**Body and environmental temperature** When fever causes an increase in temperature, the metabolic

rate rises by 8 per cent for every 0.5°C: the body needs more thiamine to release extra energy (some disorders such as an underactive thyroid decrease the rate). Hot weather causes a decrease in the rate, cold weather an increase.
**Food intake** When dieting, the body responds as if to malnutrition by reducing the metabolic rate.

The body's energy comes from food. Energy-producing nutrients (fats, proteins and carbohydrates) are used by the body as fats and glucose and oxidated to produce energy (and meet other physical needs as do the other constituents of food such as vitamins; see **diet**). The body adjusts the way it deals with dietary elements quite readily: in Western countries people derive about 35-45 per cent of their energy requirements from fats, but in poorer countries this may be as low as 15 per cent. Where glucose is available, this is used first. In dieting, fat is burnt for energy too, in a process called **ketosis** where the diet is low in carbohydrate (see entry). For the complete oxidation of fats, and thus further optimum energy use, some glucose is necessary. The body can lay up some energy stores: fat is stored around the organs and under the skin, while glucose is partly stored as glycogen in the liver.

121

### INCREASING ENERGY

Since energy production is one of the chief bodily concerns, the process involves most of the range of nutrients. For maximum energy, eat a balanced diet, incorporating plenty of B vitamins, especially thiamine which plays a key role in energy production. Two other particularly important elements are phosphorous, which aids in the initial metabolism of fats and starches and magnesium which is important in the conversion of blood sugar to energy.

High energy foods are wholegrains, raw wheatgerm, blackstrap molasses and brewer's yeast, all rich in B vitamins. Instant energy is obtainable from foods containing natural glucose which passes straight into the blood during digestion. Many foods contain glucose: fresh fruits, vegetables like sweet potatoes, young sweetcorn and young peas, onions, and also honey. These are thus some of the best snack choices. Added sugar is quite unnecessary: these and other foods contain various sugar types, and the body can obtain all it needs, naturally, if a balanced diet is eaten.

Table sugar contributes just empty Calories, and increases likelihood of suffering problems such as heart disease and tooth decay (see separate entry).

# EXERCISE

*See also: anxiety; awareness; energy; exercises; fitness; sports; stress*

Exercise, where all or part of the body is stimulated into movement, is essential to healthy life. Even people who are confined to bed have to be kept mobile in order to prevent problems ranging from depression to bedsores and thrombosis. Most bodily functions necessarily involve some form of movement, even eating, so it is by no means an optional extra, but a vital physical activity like digestion, growth and repair.

When we use the word 'exercise' we usually mean a systematic, progressive form of physical activity undertaken to improve general physique, well-being and fitness, rather than movement generally. Exercise of this kind can confer a wide range of benefits on the body, providing it is carried out within safe limits. Most benefits are to be gained from movement requiring dynamic, rhythmic use of large muscles for long periods of time, such as that in swimming and many other sports. Exercise can improve strength, flexibility, cardiovascular and local muscular activity, body composition and endurance. Exercise for fitness should incorporate all these, but specific instructions regarding frequency, type, duration and intensity of exercise must be followed both for safety and best results (see **exercises** for more details).

### EXERCISE BENEFITS

■ By increasing fitness, exercise can keep heart and lungs in good condition, thus giving some protection against cardiovascular disease and increasing resistance to infection.

■ Regular exercise improves circulation, reduces overall cholesterol level while increasing percentage within it of HDL cholesterol which gives some protection against cardiovascular disease (see **cholesterol**).

■ All forms of exercise, if carried out according to safety guidelines (see **fitness** and **exercise**) can increase fitness and improve health, provided that other factors such as poor diet, congenital health problems, certain physical disabilities, are not present.

■ Exercise promotes energy release from food: hence the tradition of walking off a good meal. Helps remove toxic substances from the body.

■ It can improve posture, keep joints fit for longer by maintaining the range of movement within them and preventing 'seizing up'.

■ Exercise can help alleviate many physical problems such as those of the circulation, lung disorders as well as joint and muscle problems: in such cases, exercise should be carried out under the supervision of a trained specialist.

■ Exercise aids relaxation and is thus helpful in dealing with many psychological problems. Aerobic exercise (see **aerobics**) helps alleviate stress, anxiety, tension, depression caused by stimulation of production of the hormone noradrenaline (norepinephrine) and neurotransmitters (messenger chemicals) which occur in the brain.

■ Exercise improves your self-image. Greater self-confidence leads in its turn to improved performance at work and can help to improve your sexual self-confidence, too.

# EXERCISES

*See also: abdomen; aerobics; ankles; back; breathing; dysmenorrhoea; feet; fitness; hands; muscles; neck; post-natal care; posture; pregnancy; sports; weight training; yoga*

The body needs varied exercise to maintain its joints and muscles in good working order and to maintain the efficiency and health of the whole body. The health-related components of fitness are strength, local muscular endurance, cardio-respiratory endurance, flexibility and body composition. Various types of exercise produce benefits in different spheres. Aerobic exercises help keep the heart and lungs healthy and tend to improve posture which helps prevent future structural problems, while still others concentrate on strengthening, stretching and firming muscles in specific body areas, and improving joint movement too.

Thus it is important not to get into a rigid schedule where exercises are always done in the same order or repeated the same number of times. Nor is it ideal for just one sport or form of exercise to be

## CAUTION BOX

### Contra-indications

It is always advisable to consult your doctor before undertaking any new programme or type of exercise, however fit and well you feel.

Read the list below: if any of these conditions apply to you, you MUST consult your medical adviser before starting any form of fitness training, exercise or sport. This is not to say that you will not be able to exercise at all. However, the type, duration, intensity and frequency of your exercise will need professional supervision if it is to be safe and thus beneficial.

- Overweight, clinically obese (over 30 per cent of your body weight being fat for women, 20 per cent for men), underweight
- Cardiovascular problems including hypertension, any history of heart attacks, strokes or family history of any of these
- Joint problems, pain or limited movement in joints
- Diabetes
- Epilepsy
- Any drugs or medication (except the contraceptive pill)
- Drinking or smoking heavily
- Breathless on small exertion or at rest
- Extremely inactive and in a sedentary job
- Any chronic illness
- Pain or tightness in the chest
- Pregnant
- Over 35, especially if inactive

### Heart rate monitoring – safely

Research has shown that between 60 per cent and 90 per cent of your maximum heart rate is a safe training zone for exercise. Establish your training zone by
1   Taking the figure of 220 beats per minute (the maximum rate of beating of the heart) as a maximum figure, then subtracting your age in years to find your own age-adjusted maximum heart rate.
2   Now work out 60 per cent and 90 per cent of the figure by dividing your maximum heart rate by 10, multiplying it by 6 for the 60 per cent figure, then by 9 for the 90 per cent figure. For example, if you are 20 your maximum heart rate will be 200, and your training zone between will be 120 and 180 beats per minute.

### Using your training zone

Take your resting pulse rate before starting to exercise: you will find that this figure decreases very slowly as your fitness increases. To find your true resting rate, however, you will need to take your pulse first thing in the morning before any activity as all sorts of factors such as eating and drinking coffee can come into play later. Take your pulse rate again while warming-up: you should gradually build up the intensity of this until you are just below the threshold of your training zone. Once into your main exercise, take your pulse intermittently to ensure that you remain in the section of your training zone suitable for you:
- 60-70 per cent if unfit
- 70-80 per cent when medium fit
- 80-90 per cent when fit

and take your pulse again when cooling-down, checking that you have dropped down below your training zone.

### Taking your pulse

Your pulse is on the thumb side of your inside wrist. Use the first two fingers (not your thumb) of your other hand to feel the pulse by just touching the area gently. Your most accurate results will be obtained if you take your pulse for 6 seconds (and multiply by 10 to get the minute figure) within a second of stopping exercise.

adopted. The reasons for this are partly psychological. When boredom sets in, there is a corresponding decrease in benefits:
1   Less initial stress reduction: the mind is not diverted from other considerations as it would be with a new form of exercise stimulation. This form of diversion actually produces mental relaxation.
2   Reduced physical benefits as decreased energy is put into the activity.

Very important, too, is the way in which unvarying exercise patterns can sometimes lead to a decrease in long-term joint and muscle health. Joints need their full range of exercise in order to maintain that range: repetitive stresses due to inappropriate exercise can produce a grooved pathway leading to decreased movement, drying of the joint and premature ageing, even arthritis. But remember that exercise which is too frequent or too intense for you can lead to such problems. Muscles need varied exercise too: they are arranged in pairs to pull in opposite directions and need stretching and strengthening (see **muscles**). And muscle improvements are exercise/activity specific – yet another reason to keep your exercise varied.

For safest exercising, read the warm-up notes on page 125. *DO* warm up before any exercise or sport, and cool down at the completion of your workout. Sudden bursts of exercise can be very dangerous. See the warm-ups section.

Choose exercises and sports which you enjoy: you are more likely to get maximum benefits from these since you will be keener to keep them up.

Always wear appropriate clothing: leotard and tights, or shorts and shirt, with suitable shoes, where necessary: take advice from your exercise specialist. You must wear the correct shoes for aerobic dancing, for example, to protect joints from shock.

Start your exercise regime by walking more each day. For example, get off the bus one stop early and walk to work; do not use the elevator but walk up and down stairs. Build up gradually, then start to take extra exercise for 15 minutes, 2 or 3 times a week. Build up to half an hour 3 times a week.

Listen to your body, never push yourself to the point of pain. There should not be pain in exercise, but a sense of using the body to its best potential. In aerobic exercise, don't increase the stress on heart and lungs too fast or you will damage, not benefit them. Build up the length of time of sustained exercise using the pulse method (see caution box).

E

**E**

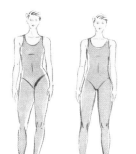
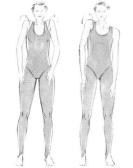
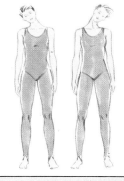

| **1 POSTURE** Ex A, See p. 207 | **2 POSTURE** Ex B, See p. 207 | **3 NECK** Ex B, See p. 197 | **4 NECK** Ex A, See p. 197 |

■ See EXERCISES for Caution box page 123 before starting exercise

**How to Evolve Your Daily Exercise Plan**
What follows is a blueprint for your first exercise scheme. The first 13 exercises provide a good basic starting point with a good warm-up and cool-down routine. You can add to this routine or adapt it at will. Then follows a further series of general exercises, incorporating strengtheners, stretchers and aerobic exercises which provide a good basic routine. Finally come two relaxation exercises (see **relaxation**, p.218).

| **5 BACK** Ex A, See p. 33 | **6 AEROBICS** Ex D, See p. 12-13 | **7 AEROBICS** Ex C, See p. 12-13 |

| **8 BACKS** Ex B, See p. 33 | **9 LEGS** Ex A, See p. 176 | **10 LEGS** Ex C, See p. 176 |

| **11 LEGS** Ex D, See p. 176 | **12 BACK** Ex D, See p. 34 | **13 LEGS** Ex B, See p. 176 |

If you begin to feel that any exercise is pushing you too far, stop. Try to exercise for very slightly longer each time until you build up to a good level. Use your pulse as a guide, but you should feel slightly breathless after your exercise session.

Any pains resulting from exercise should be investigated immediately. Pain from a damaged joint or muscle may disappear, only to raise its head again in a more serious form later if left untreated.

Avoid sitting still for more than an hour. If you are desk-bound, get up and move around each hour. Every two hours, stretch your body. Choose seating which supports your back up to the bottom of the ribcage: this will help to prevent you slumping in the chair and crumpling up the spine.

## Warm-ups and cool-downs

Warming up and cooling down effectively before and after exercise are extremely important components in effective, safe, fitness acquisition. As you will see from the heart rate monitoring system, your heart rate does increase quite substantially during exercise, as does your body temperature. In warming up, first should come rhythmical movements, then slow and gradually increasing intensity of exercise, using the existing range of movement in all joints to its fullest (not aiming to increase it at this stage). The cardiorespiratory system needs preparation if there is to be no dangerous strain; muscles contract and relax more easily when warm; all the responses to exercise stimuli occur more swiftly when warm-ups are done.

The length of time you need to spend warming up depends on your level of fitness, your age and your sport, activity or performance level. Young, active people, for example, may only need 5 minutes warming up and 5 minutes cooling down, while unfit or older people may need 10 minutes or more. Avoid high intensity bursts of activity or prolonged sessions at first, since these could be dangerous if you are not ready for them. Also, work at your own speed, follow professional advice on techniques. Never exercise when you are feeling unwell, have a temperature or a virus infection.

### ADDITIONAL EXERCISES

These additional exercises, which include strengtheners, stretchers and aerobics, provide an excellent daily routine when added to the basic plan of 13 warm ups.

| 1 THIGHS | 2 BUTTOCKS | 3 ARMS |
|---|---|---|
| Ex A, D See p. 245 | Ex B See p. 58 | Ex C See p. 26 |
| **4 ABDOMEN** | **5 BREAST** | **6 LEGS** |
| Ex A, C, D See p. 6, 8 | Ex B See p. 50 | Ex D See p. 176 |
| **7 THIGHS** | **8 BUTTOCKS** | **9 ARMS** |
| Ex B See p. 245 | Ex A See p. 58 | Ex B See p. 26 |
| **10 BACK** | **11 LEGS** | **12 BACKS** |
| Ex A, D See p. 33, 34 | Ex C See p. 176 | Ex E See p. 34 |

# EXFOLIATE

Massaging away dead skin cells, an electric face brush reveals fresher, younger skin. When exfoliating your face avoid the sensitive eye area.

*See also: acne; brushes; buffing; moisturizing; toning*

As our skin grows new cells, it casts off the old. These dead cells tend to clog the pores, causing spots and blackheads as well as making the skin's surface look dull and grey. Exfoliation is a mild form of peeling to remove these flaking cells, revealing the clearer, softer skin tissue beneath and boosting the circulation. Skin creams and moisturizers can then penetrate through to the new layer faster and more effectively. The simplest form of exfoliation is to rub the face or body gently with water and a coarse-textured sponge, but there are many special exfoliation products. Body skin benefits from exfoliation once a month or more, using a sponge, loofah, brush or commercial exfoliation product.

Facial exfoliation should take place after cleansing, and always be followed by a moisturizing cream. Products should be concentrated on the oily parts of the face, avoiding the eye area, and used with care on dry or sensitive skins. Sufferers of inflamed acne should consult their doctor before attempting exfoliation treatment, as the aim is to invigorate, not irritate the skin. Young skins should be exfoliated once a week. As the skin ages, exfoliation should become a routine skin treatment, twice a week or more even though surface skin is shed and replaced at a progressively slower rate.

E

### EXFOLIATING PRODUCTS

- Soapless 'soaps' or liquid, water-soluble cleansers can be applied with a complexion brush or a rough, facial pad such as a Buf Puf. Suitable for dry or sensitive skins.
- Abrasive creams, gels or lotions containing grains such as oatmeal act as peeling agents when massaged into the skin, and then rinsed off. Suitable for oily skins.
- Cleansing peel-off masks can also effectively remove dead surface skin as well as deep-cleanse. Suitable for all skins.
- Astringents and clarifying lotions which contain alcohol used sparingly can act as mild exfoliants. Suitable for most skins but may be too harsh for particularly sensitive skins and over-stimulating for very oily skins.

### HOW TO EXFOLIATE

1. Cleanse skin thoroughly.
2. Follow the instructions given on your chosen preparation, but don't scrub too hard as this can cause broken veins.
3. Use small, circular movements to remove from the forehead, cheeks and chin, and a vertical action to wipe the neck, nose and perimeters of the face.
4. Rinse with water if required and pat dry.
5. Moisturize face to finish, or if exfoliating your body, apply a body lotion.

## EYEBROWS

Eyebrows grow in about every six weeks and should be well-defined and tidy since they balance the face and give it character.

Straggly hairs can be plucked or snipped away and sparse areas filled in with a coloured pencil or eyebrow shadow. Some beauticians use waxing to shape eyebrows: it is difficult to get a good shape using this method, and should only be carried out by a professional. Make sure that you keep to the basic shape of the eyebrow. Use two make-up brushes as a guide to where your eyebrows should begin and end, remember that over-plucked, highly arched eyebrows can look far more unnatural than thick, straight brows.

### SHAPING EYEBROWS

1. Before plucking, cleanse the face and dab away any excess oil or dirt from the brows with cotton wool soaked in toner or antiseptic lotion.
2. With an eyebrow brush or a clean, old toothbrush, brush hairs upwards and outwards.
3. Using clean, slant-edged tweezers, start plucking from the inner corner of the eye: a magnifying mirror will help. Pluck hairs singly from the root and always from underneath the brow in the direction of hair growth. The curve should be a gradual tapering, following the line of the brow to the outer corner of the eye.

4. Brush the brows into shape, wipe with toner and then moisturize. Leave the skin to settle before applying make-up.

### COLOURING AND DEFINING EYEBROWS

Eyebrows can be defined or filled in with pencils or eyebrow shadow before applying eye make-up. Dry skins need oilier pencils, naturally moist skins need lighter, powder-based pencils.

1. First powder lightly with a translucent powder and brush into shape.
2. If you are using a pencil make sure it is very sharp and start from the inner corner of the eye using light strokes in the direction of growth to resemble hair growth (never draw a continuous straight line).
3. Blend in colour with fingertips.

Eyebrow powder should be applied in the same way using a slant-edge brush. Use a clean, dry mascara brush to brush through brows again.

### IMPROVING EYEBROWS

- Use gloss to make eyebrows shine, hair gel to set the shape.
- Encourage growth in sparse eyebrows by stroking them with warm olive oil or vaseline.
- For stronger definition on coarse-textured brows, brush and colour with a mascara wand.
- A permanently scowling expression, characterized by.knotted brows and a frown line on the forehead can be treated very effectively with cosmetic surgery to relax the muscles that hold the brows in place.

## EYELASHES

*See also: artificial lashes, mascara*

Eyelashes protect the eyes from dust particles and act as a frame for the eyes. Their natural colour and length generally benefit from emphasis of the following kinds:

- Mascara should be applied in light coats, to darken the lashes. Ensure lashes are unclogged after using mascara: comb them with a fine eyelash comb.
- Dyeing the lashes negates the need for mascara and can be very successful. This must be done professionally by a beautician. A lash tint generally lasts 4-6 weeks, as eyelashes renew themselves about every 6 weeks. This is especially good for the pale blondes' or redheads' lashes but dye brown, not black.
- Artificial lashes can look natural if carefully applied, but glues can cause irritation.
- Eyelash curlers lift short or thin lashes to give an illusion of length and thickness as well as opening up the eyes.
- A nightly application of castor oil or Vaseline gently dabbed on to the lashes can help to strengthen and condition them.

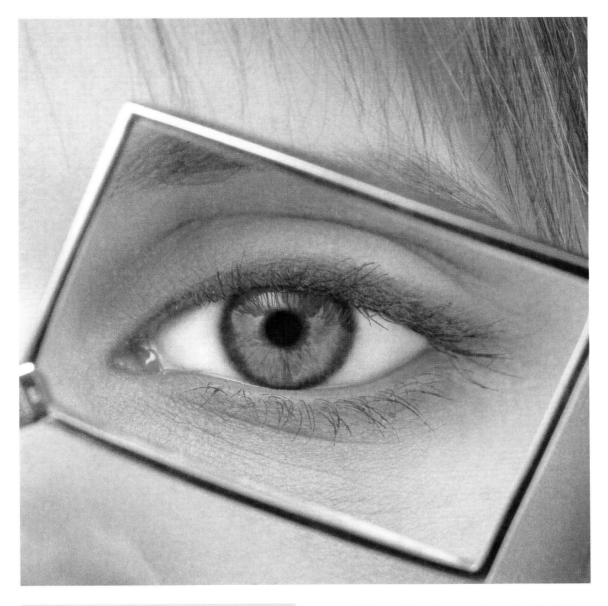

# EYES

*See also: contact lenses, eye make-up; glasses*

### STRUCTURE AND OPERATION OF THE EYE

The eye, almost a sphere, measures approximately 2.5 cm (1 inch) in diameter and works in much the same way as a basic camera. Light reflected from the viewed object strikes the transparent cornea and passes, by way of the pupil, on to the retina at the back of the eye. As it passes through the lens, which is situated just behind the pupil, the image is inverted. This reversed image is transmitted by the rod and cone cells of the retina to the optic nerve (an extension of the brain itself) and thence to the back of the brain which reverses the image and decodes it. The whole process takes place in a split second.

In newborn babies sight is not fully developed; the eye does not become completely mature until six or seven years of age. Sight then fluctuates – the amount of myopia or hyperopia gradually altering with the changes of natural ageing.

### EYE CARE

Like ears, eyes are very delicate and must be treated with care. An important factor in looking after them is getting good reading light, which should come from behind or above rather than in front. Avoid fluorescent lighting – it causes glare and light is often badly directed – if you can. The eye's own automatic care mechanisms are the eyelid which closes to keep out foreign bodies such as dust and chemicals, the pupil which contracts to exclude excessive glare and light, and the blinking action. Blinking activates the tear ducts, washing out irritants, and keeping the eye moist. Caring for your eyes by heeding simple guidelines will help prevent some of the more common problems.

- If your work involves a great deal of reading, take ten minutes' break every hour or so, to rest your eyes (and get up and move around).

Treat swollen, puffy eyes with cooling pads soaked in iced water, or chamomile teabags soaked in cold water. If eyes are continuously pink and puffy, you may be allergic to one of your eye make-up products. Establish which one is responsible by a process of elimination, and replace it with a hypo-allergenic type.

Ensure that creams and make-up do not block the tiny pores along the inner eyelid. These secrete oils which protect the eye.

Apply eye make-up very gently (see **eye make-up**). Avoid getting anything in the eye, especially fibrous, harsh mascaras, and never use sharp eye pencils. Always test the point with a clean thumb and forefinger first: it should be rounded, not sharp. Apply make-up the kindest, as well as the most efficient way: a soft brush or cotton wool bud may be gentler than a rough fingertip.

Avoid 'eye whiteners': their temporary effect camouflages red blood vessels, but can ultimately exacerbate them. If your eyes are persistently red, consult your doctor or optician: there are a variety of possible causes. If eyes are very itchy, a plain eyewash may help.

Be meticulous about eye make-up removal every evening. Powder or metallic shadow particles or mascara fibres may work their way into the eye overnight, causing irritation.

### SIGHT TESTING

Every child's eyes should be examined by the age of four years in order to obtain maximum benefit from any necessary treatment. Initial tests look for normal focussing and check that the muscles affecting the movement of the eyes are working properly. Even if no problems appear, a close check should be kept on the state of a child's eyes.

Even if glasses are not needed during childhood, teens, twenties and thirties it is important to keep having your eyes examined regularly so that the health of the eye may be monitored. Particularly vital is retesting once you reach 40-45 for any sign of eye disease such as cataract or glaucoma, as well as the presbyopia (loss of elasticity in the lens) which develops at this time of life.

In the US patients with average vision are classed as having 20/20 vision (6/6 in the UK) according to the Snellen Acuity test. The examination will also establish if any astigmatism is present and can

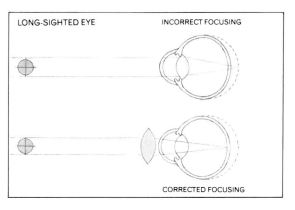

LONG-SIGHTED EYE     INCORRECT FOCUSING

CORRECTED FOCUSING

Hyperopic or long-sighted people (above) find difficulty in seeing objects close at hand clearly. This can be corrected with positively-powered or convex lenses (either glasses or contacts) to decrease the depth of focus so that images focus sharply on the retina.

Myopic or short-sighted people (below) find difficulty in seeing distant objects clearly. This can be corrected with negatively-powered or concave lenses (either glasses or contacts) to increase the depth of focus so that images focus sharply on the retina.

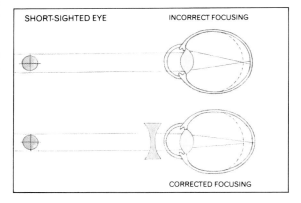

SHORT-SIGHTED EYE     INCORRECT FOCUSING

CORRECTED FOCUSING

identify any other problems such as colour blindness which may have gone unnoticed. The optometrist or optician can then determine the prescription required to relieve any visual problems and glasses or contact lenses (and sun glasses possibly) made up to the prescription.

### SIGHT DEFECTS

**Myopia (short sight)** Tends to run in families and appears, characteristically, in late puberty. It is caused either by the eyeball being too long or the lens of the eye being of stronger power than necessary. Negatively-powered lenses, in the form of glasses or contact lenses, correct myopia.

**Presbyopia** Caused by loss of elasticity in the lens, corrected by positively-powered lenses.

**Hyperopia (long sight)** Caused by a lens too weak for the length of eye, or too short an eye for the strength of lens. It makes all objects, except those far away, seem blurred. Positively-powered lenses for glasses or contact lenses, correct hyperopia.

**Astigmatism** This is caused by non-spherical curvature of the cornea or the lens, resulting in blurred vision. The condition is corrected by a special lens.

**Cataract** Caused by a gradual clouding of the lens inside the eye, which becomes worse with old age and results in increasingly blurred vision. If this

Light comes into the eye through two lenses, first the cornea, then a crystalline lens lying behind it, with the iris regulating the amount of light which enters. The beam focuses on the sensitive retina, a message is sent down the optic nerve to the brain and then an image can be 'seen'.

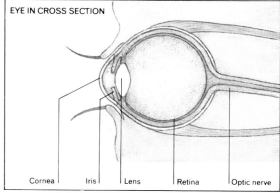

EYE IN CROSS SECTION

Cornea    Iris    Lens    Retina    Optic nerve

becomes very severe the affected lens is completely removed and glasses, contact lenses or a lens or cornea implant worn to correct the deficiency. The condition can also be caused by injury.

**Colour blindness** This is not actual blindness but an inability to distinguish between certain groups of colour. The condition is generally inherited: women are usually the carriers, men the sufferers. Colours confused include grey and purple, green and blue, red and green. The condition cannot be cured.

**Detached retina** Sometimes the retina becomes separated from a section of the eye called the choroid layer either as a result of tissue degeneration, physical injury or seepage of the gelatinous fluid that fills the eye. Provided that the condition is caught in time and is not too advanced, the retina can be surgically repaired. Modern laser techniques have aided this treatment. Left untreated, a detached retina will result in total blindness.

**Glaucoma** Can develop gradually over years and tends to run in families, so frequent checks, especially from middle age are important for early detection. There are two types: 'open angle' where the symptoms of disturbed or tunnel vision are not normally noticed until the disease is quite well advanced. This is the most common type. The second type is 'angle closure', much less common, where the symptoms of hard, red, tender eyes, loss of visual acuity and swelling of the cornea causing characteristic coloured 'haloes' seen around lights occur earlier.

**Strabismus (squint)** Usually apparent very early in children and should be attended to immediately. The causes are varied and can only be determined by an optician. In adults a squint is usually a result of some form of muscle failure, often aggravated by fatigue or caused by trauma.

### EYE DISORDERS
#### Conjunctivitis
Commonly known as 'pink eye', conjunctivitis is a broad term for the inflammation of the mucous membrane which forms the outer layer of the eye and lines the eyelid. Seek medical advice if eye continues to be red and sore. It can be caused by allergy, infection or irritation and makes the eye feel sore and gritty, and water profusely. At night the eye may become gummed up. Unless the condition is severe, it is best left alone apart from gentle bathing with warm, boiled water. In severe cases antibiotic eye drops or ointment may be prescribed.

#### Blepharitis
This is inflammation of the eyelid. It can be caused by allergy to eye make-up, an accumulation of dandruff in the eyelashes, or an infection. Wash the eyelids with warm, boiled water and switch to a hypo-allergenic brand of make-up. Seek your doctor's help if the condition persists.

#### Styes
These occur when the hair follicles at the base of the eyelashes become blocked and infected. Resist the temptation to rub or the infection may spread. If the stye is bad, an antiseptic ointment may help.

## EYE MAKE-UP

The perfectly made-up eye is a result of careful blending and building up of colour. Your natural skin tone and hair colour can act as a guideline for choosing eyeshadow colours. If you are blonde, for example, avoid extremes – darks can be too overpowering, pastels too insipid (see **blondes, brunettes, redheads, Afro hair**).

Eyeshadows need not match your eyes or clothes, in fact they often look more effective if they contrast – try greys, coppers and khakis for blue eyes; enhance brown eyes with greens, violet and gold and use yellows, apricots or blue for green eyes. Browns and greys look natural for day, but at night be bolder, intensifying colour and highlighting with iridescent or frosted shadows.

Whatever the shape of your eyes, darker, matt colours detract from bad points, while pale, shiny colours emphasize good features. Older women should choose mellow honeys, soft greys and browns for their eyes rather than bright, hard colours and also avoid pastel tones or shiny products.

### EYE COLOUR PRODUCTS
**Powder-based shadow** These are made from the same ingredients as pressed face powder. Creamy powder shadows include moisturizer to help colour stay on the eyelid. Most will last up to eight hours, the better kinds fading slowly and evenly, the worst tending to streak as they fade. Apply powder-based shadows after face powder.

**Cream-based shadows** Since these contain water and oil they are good for dry skins and blend into the skin easily. Although they last longer than powder shadows, they are messier to apply (unless in pencil form). Always apply after foundation, then set with a light film of powder to prevent creasing.

**Gels** These are transparent, glossy products suitable for offsetting a tan in summer.

### THE RIGHT EQUIPMENT
- Small soft artists' brushes make some of the best powder shadow applicators.
- Use a clean mascara wand (or a lash brush or comb) to separate lashes after applying mascara, and an eyebrow brush (or a clean, old toothbrush) to smooth eyebrows.
- Eyelash curlers will lift and lengthen lashes. See **eyelashes** for how to use them. Use before applying mascara.
- An eye primer prepares eyes for shadow, helps colour to last longer and prevents creasing of the shadow.

### EYE HIGHLIGHTERS
During daylight, your own skin tone will often naturally highlight the area beneath the brow bone, especially if the socket and eyelid have been shaded. If you want to use a highlighter, stick to light cream, beige or pinky shades – white looks too severe. For evenings, create shine with frosted shadows, whites or iridescent powders in silvers and golds.

MAKE-UP FOR YOUR EYE TYPE

### Close-set eyes
1   Apply highlighter to the inner corner of the eye, to widen the eyes.
2   Use a darker shadow blending from the centre towards the outer corner of the eye.
3   Line the outer corner with an eyeliner pencil.

### Wide apart eyes
1   To draw eyes together use a dark colour on the inner socket area.
2   Blend gradually to a lighter shade on the out-side of the eye.
3   Outline eye with dark pencil.

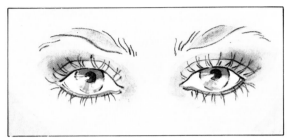

### Deep-set eyes
1   Avoid using dark colours in the socket line or highlighter on the brow bone.
2   Use pale muted shades on inner eyelids and apply darker shadow on the outer corners of both lids to balance the eye depth.
3   Use only a little mascara.

### Round eyes
1   Keep eyeshadow light in the inner corner of the eyes and use dark shades on the outer corners of the upper and lower lid. Blend upwards.
2   Avoid highlighting the centre of the upper lid.
3   Lining the inner rim of the lower lid with a dark pencil will have a narrowing effect.

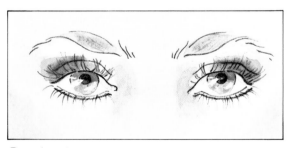

### Prominent eyes
1   Dark matt colours should be used to set back and define the eye; avoid frosted or pale shades.
2   Apply shadow from the centre to the outer corner of the upper lid.
3   Highlighting the browbone will help to even out a prominent eyelid.

### Droopy eyes
1   Avoid putting dark colours on the outer half of the eyelid, and ensure that any colour is blended upwards and outwards to lift the eye.
2   Shading in the socket line will help to draw back the eye.
3   Avoid using heavy eyeliner on the upper lid, but outline the lower lid.

### Small eyes
1   To enlarge the eye use light colours on the inner lid. Emphasize the outer corner of the eye and below the lower lashes with a darker shade, and an extra coat of mascara.
2   Use a white pencil to draw a fine line inside the rim of the lower lid.
3   Never outline the entire eye area as this will close in and narrow the eyes.

Sponge applicators are suitably gentle for the eye area and give even application for eyelid creams or powders. Use finer sponge applicators or a soft brush for darker colour on lower part of lid and under lower lashes.

Always apply eyeliner after eyeshadow, using a soft pencil (never drag at skin) or a fine brush. Paint across eyelid from the centre outwards with a steady hand.

Mascara comes last – after curling lashes – brushed from root to tip, built up in fine layers.

## EYELINERS

Depending on which you choose, eyeliners can give a thinly defined line of colour around the eye, or a soft, smudgy look that should tone with your hair and lashes. Browns and greys look natural for the day, darker colours with brilliant tones are stronger and look good for evening.

**Liquid liners** Usually water-based, last longer and give a sharp, straighter line than wax-based pencil eyeliners which create a muted look especially flattering to older faces.

**Cake liners** Blocks of powdered watercolour which are dampened and applied with a brush.

- Make sure that the eyeliner applicator does not drag the skin or let colour streak into the eye.
- Although some eyeliners are hypoallergenic, many can cause eye irritation, so test before buying.
- To keep bacteria at bay, change applicators frequently.
- Avoid lining the inside of lids where possible, and never moisten the liner with saliva.
- Pencils cause the least infection problems as their surface is constantly renewed.
- Kohl liners are thicker, softer and more waxy.

### How to line your eyes

Always line eyes after applying your eyeshadow.

1. With a steady hand and using a soft pencil or pointed brush, draw a line along the upper lid and underneath the lower lid keeping as close as possible to the base of the lashes.
2. Line only the outer half of the lid if your eyes are too close together, otherwise finish the line just before reaching the inner corner of the eye.
3. Soften the line by dampening with a brush.

## EYEBROW COLOURS

It is best, generally, to use browns or greys on eyebrows as dark colours look harsh and ageing. Remember to adapt the colour if you have coloured your hair. For a party look, dust with gold shadow or brush with bright blues or purples.

## MASCARA

Mascara adds the final frame to your eyes and finishes your eye make-up. Whether you prefer to use a cake mascara or a wand applicator (see **mascara**), always apply two light coats rather than a single heavy one, and work from roots to tip.

- Use waterproof mascara for sports or swimming activities so it won't streak or smudge.
- If you wear contact lenses or have easily irritated eyes, choose a hypoallergenic or non-flake mascara without lash-building fibres.
- Black mascara looks good if you are very dark, but can be severe if not: try browns or blues for day if your hair is blonde or brunette. By night electric blues, emerald greens and violets can be stunning and festive.
- Try matching mascara to your most predominant eyeshadow colour, or to your eye colour.

# EYE MAKE-UP REMOVER

*See also: allergies and allergens; cleansing; contact lenses; eyebrows; eyelashes; eye make-up; herbs; mascara; pH*

With today's water- and smudge-proof products it is important to remove eye make-up very thoroughly, and to prevent bacteria which may cause infection from accumulating. Ordinary skin cleansers are not suited to the delicate tissue surrounding the eye, and soap and water can irritate. Eye make-up removers are specially formulated for the purpose and come in oil, liquid and cream forms. Some are pH balanced (their acid/alkaline level similar to that of skin, see **pH**), while others contain herb and plant extracts such as cornflower or chamomile which cleanse and sooth. A water-soluble remover is best. There are also extra-gentle products for sensitive eyes. Eye make-up removers are one of the most likely causes of eye allergies. Isolate the use of each eye product to determine whether it is your remover that provokes reaction.

## CLEANSING YOUR EYES

1. Contact lenses should be removed so they are not smudged with make-up or grease.
2. With clean hands, pat on a remover over brows and eyelids, and leave to dissolve for a few minutes.
3. Wipe off gently with dampened cotton wool.

Mascara is easier to remove if a tissue is placed beneath the lashes, then the make-up remover rolled on and off with a cotton wool bud. Remove any residue with a dampened cotton wool pad or tissue to prevent fibres clinging to the lashes. Waterproof mascara requires one of the stronger oily removers.

# FACE

*See also: camouflage; cleansing; hairstyles; make-up; moisturizing; toning*

The bone structure, shape, skin type and complexion of the face are all largely inherited. Facial bone structure will not alter during adult life except through injury, surgery (including cosmetic surgery which uses implants to alter structural effect), or orthodontic treatment (see **teeth, orthodontist**). The muscles of the face give it shape as well as allowing movement. Exercise, as well as cosmetic surgery, can tighten them up. Practise facial expressions in the mirror each day. This will help keep muscles in good condition, improving the facial silhouette and blood supply to the skin, too.

Skillfully applied make-up and clever hairstyling can appear to alter face shape (see **make-up** and **hairstyles**). Make the most of your features by accentuating your good points; learn to recognize your faults so that you can play them down or disguise them. Consider having some professional make-up lessons to give you a new slant on colours, shading, emphasizing and camouflaging. Bear in mind, however, that you may be over-reacting to any feature you particularly loathe.

A meticulous cleansing, toning and moisturizing routine with products suited to your skin type will improve the complexion you were born with. Consult a good hairdresser to find fashionable and flattering styles. Avoid free haircut offers by trainees: generally speaking, the style you get is the one that suits the hairdresser's purpose, not yours.

# FACE POWDER

*See also: gels; lips; make-up; skin*

Face powder, loose or pressed, adds a final, protective film to 'set' make-up.
**Loose powder** is talc mixed with kaolin, zinc stearate, colour, scent and preservatives.
**Compressed powder** is bound together with wax or oil and comes in convenient compacts. It can be used without foundation, but tends to cake, so should be used sparingly especially on older skins.

### How to choose face powder
- If you use powder over foundation, choose a loose, translucent powder light enough to allow the colour of your foundation to show.
- Powders used without foundation should tone with your natural skin colour.
- Women with dry skins should choose a 'dewy' or moisturizing powder containing oil; non-greasy or matt powders are best for oily skins.
- Avoid heavily tinted powders. The colour they appear to be in the box can be different on your

face and may change further according to individual skin chemistry.

### How to apply powder
Powder should be used on top of cream products, but before applying powder colours. It should not be worn if you are using gel for blushing or bronzing.

With a powder puff or brush, apply over the face, generously to a young skin and lightly to dryer and older skins. Avoid powdering between the eyes, as this accentuates and deepens lines. Powder your lips between the first and second coats of lipstick to prevent the colour from bleeding. Press powder firmly into oily areas of the face (usually the central panel), and remove any excess with a wide brush.

# FACIALS

*See also: beauty salons; clay; cleansing; collagen; exfoliation; hypo-allergenic products; lasers; masks; moisturizing; mud; skin; toning*

Having a facial is a wonderful way of relaxing. Facials vary from the simplest mask applied at home – a quick alternative to the full facial (see **masks**) – to a host of more sophisticated treatments in beauty salons which may involve the use of electrical currents, aromatic oils or specialized creams or ampoules, depending on your skin's condition. Because the efficacy of facials can vary enormously according to the skill of individual practitioner, it is very difficult to give advice. It is possible, however, to indicate where specialized facials are not generally thought to have any substantial value.

Facials aim to cleanse, tone and improve the texture of the skin, sometimes to moisturize it, and to stimulate circulation within it. They cannot banish or prevent wrinkles (see separate entry) nor can they provide a facelift.

Full facials in a salon generally begin with a close examination of the skin, followed by cleansing and toning, as it is important to begin treatment with a grease-free skin. The face may then be steamed (see below) so that impurities can be brought to the surface and subsequently removed by a variety of methods including extraction and exfoliation. To increase circulation and relax the muscles the face is massaged with cream or gel before a mask appropriate to your skin type is applied. Unless you are having a specialized facial (see below) the mask is removed with damp cotton wool, and the skin toned and moisturized (see **masks**).

'Mini-facials' usually consist just of deep-cleansing, toning and application of a peeling cream or mask (see **masks**) and/or a facial scrub (see **exfoliation**). In this case make-up can be re-applied immediately afterwards, but it is usually advisable after a facial to keep the skin free of make-up for a minimum of three hours, preferably longer. Normally you should have a deep-cleansing facial once a month, but this varies according to your skin and the type of facial, too.

All skins react differently to facials. Some show instant improvement, while others may look red or shiny due to increased production of sebum. It is not unusual for an outbreak of spots to occur during the few days following a facial.

### SPECIALIZED FACIALS
### Aromatherapy facials
As essential oils are very concentrated and can irritate the skin if rubbed in directly, they must first be diluted with a 'carrier' oil such as almond or soya. Once absorbed, the oils, according to their individual properties (see **aromatherapy**) can help correct surface imbalances such as dryness or oiliness which come from **within** the body. Acne, broken capillary veins and dermatitis are some other conditions for which therapists may use facial aromatherapy.

Pure plant oils are expensive. Although oils which have been adulterated by chemicals are often cheaper, they will not have the same beneficial effect on the skin, and can often cause irritation or allergies. Women with sensitive skin should in any case have a patch test before this type of facial, to check that they are not sensitive to any of the essential oils which are to be used. Massage is the most effective method of applying the oils since it not only aids absorption but increases circulation, helping to relax and tone up the facial muscles.

Depending on your skin type, a facial aromatherapy treatment can include non-chemical surface peeling, or the application of a mask or poultice. For oily skins, steaming over hot water containing a drop or two of the oils is sometimes used.

### Steam facials
Many professional facials begin with steaming the face: steam opens the skin's pores and causes perspiration, thus releasing impurities. To steam the skin, the face is held over a bowl of boiling water for five to ten minutes if skin is oily, five minutes if skin is dry, with the head covered by a towel. Sometimes herb(s) (see separate entry) or a few drops of essential oils (see **aromatherapy**) are added to the water. These all have different properties and should be chosen according to your skin type and/or condition. After this, blackheads may be extracted, and then a mask used to close the pores.

This treatment is not suitable for those with sensitive or broken skin.

### Laser facials
This treatment claims to rejuvenate ageing skin and help heal scar tissue by directing a helium laser beam on to the facial acupuncture points and over lined and wrinkled areas. The laser is said to stimulate blood circulation, renew skin tissue and tone up sagging muscles so that skin looks and feels younger and tighter. Results do not substantiate these claims. What happens is that the laser treatment causes slight redness and swelling. The swelling, which fills out wrinkles, lasts for about 15 days after which it subsides and wrinkles reappear.

Exfoliation (see separate entry) is often part of a deep-cleansing facial. This creamy exfoliant contains bran as a natural exfoliator, clay to absorb impurities and lemon as an astringent.

**False lashes**
See Artificial lashes

**False nails**
See Artificial nails

### The Payot facial

This facial is suitable for all skin types. The technique of massage is used in conjunction with creams and, when needed, specialized electrical treatments chosen after a full consultation with the individual. Its aim is to improve the skin's condition by increasing the flow of the lymphatic system, which filters the body's tissue fluids and toxins. This is done by massage of creams in the location of the lymph nodes. Massage is concentrated on the face and neck for twenty minutes and is then extended down the back to the waist.

The facial can also incorporate different electrical treatments to help absorb and activate the creams. *High frequency* current is used for acne rather than a manual massage which could break pustules and spread infection. *Galvanic current* is milder and is good for dehydrated or mature skins. It is especially effective if used in conjunction with moisturizing ampoules which contain water-soluble substances. *Vacuum suction* helps to revitalize skin and alleviate puffiness caused by water retention.

### Liftodermie

Liftodermie is the trade mark of René Guinot Limited. It aims to soften lines and firm the skin by following a deep-cleansing treatment with a serum application. Ampoules of serum are chosen according to the needs and condition of the individual's skin. They are activated on the skin by heat: this is imparted by a plastic face mask which vibrates electrically for about eight minutes.

### 'Freezing' facial

This is a para-medical treatment which is especially helpful for those with open pores, oily skin and certain acne conditions. The face is steamed and cleansed and impurities extracted. Then a carbon dioxide paste (pressurized to form dry ice) is lightly applied to the whole face with a brush. This evaporates on contact with the skin, tightening the pores and contracting the sebaceous glands so that oil secretion is slowed down. Finally, a mask appropriate to the client's skin type is applied. This treatment needs to be conducted at regular intervals before the full benefits to the skin can be seen.

### Cathiodermie

Cathiodermie is also the trade mark of René Guinot Limited. This deep-cleansing facial must be performed by a qualified beauty therapist since it involves the operation of a galvanic/high frequency machine. The machine emits a mild electric current via small rollers which massage the face, opening the pores to release accumulated dirt, grease and impurities. Part of the treatment uses a high-frequency current which further cleanses the pores, boosts the circulation by releasing oxygen into the skin, leaving it feeling toned, smooth and moisturized. If performed regularly – most people are advised to have a monthly treatment – Cathiodermie is a particularly effective treatment for acne symptoms and can also be very successful in improving the texture and therefore the appearance of scarred or damaged skin.

### Collagen and elastin facials

These facials are used for women over the age of 35. They aim to help preserve a moist, supple, firm skin, although there is no medical evidence that collagen can be absorbed through the skin.

The skin is first cleansed, then toned and steamed. The contents of an ampoule (containing a combination of soluble collagen and elastin) are then massaged into the skin. An additional massage with oil follows, before a gel mask is applied to seal in the substances used and to firm and tone the skin. The mask is removed with damp sponges, skin is then toned and moisturized. Recommendation as to frequency of these treatments depends on the condition of the individual's skin, but two treatments a week for five weeks is common.

### Bio-peeling facial

This facial stimulates and improves the texture and tone of the skin by removing the top layers of dead cells. It is a very efficient form of exfoliation, and all skin types, apart from those prone to broken veins, will benefit from it.

The skin is cleansed and toned and a solution massaged in to help loosen and soften the dead skin. Once the solution is dry, a cream mask is applied to the face. After about fifteen minutes it is removed, bringing with it the dead skin. A solution of citric acid is massaged in through circular frictional movements with the fingertips which normalises the pH of the skin (see **pH**) and has an antiseptic (anti-bacterial) action and a thin layer of gauze placed on the face for five minutes to aid absorption. The skin is then toned and moisturized.

### Bio-cellular facial

This facial is suitable for women with sallow or dry skin and those suffering from bad circulation. It should not be performed on skins which are sensitive or those with damaged facial blood vessels.

The face is first thoroughly cleansed and toned and given a light non-chemical peel. Biocellular creams (containing collagen and vitamins) are then massaged into the face and neck. Three layers of paraffin wax are applied to the entire area – this seals in the creams. When set, the mask is peeled off and the skin is toned and moisturized.

### Collagen facials

Collagen facials are used for dry, mature skins that lack tone, since they aim to reduce excessive moisture loss – a process that accelerates with age. The use of collagen is controversial: there is no medical evidence that collagen can penetrate the skin, but many beauticians find it beneficial to clients.

The skin is cleansed, toned and a non-chemical peel is used. Then a sheet of freeze-dried collagen is moulded over the face and eyelids with damp sponges. This is allowed to penetrate for about ten minutes before being removed with a spray freshener. The skin is then moisturized with collagen cream. Therapists recommend a series of five weekly treatments in each season of the year for full benefit. A collagen skin food is recommended for use at home between treatments.

# FARADIC EXERCISE

*See also: beauty salons; exercise; health farms; muscles*

Faradic exercise is a passive form of muscle exercising designed to reduce bulge and flab. Electric impulses to muscles in flabby areas imitate those from the brain and the muscles contract and relax without physical effort. The impulses come from a battery-operated machine (which is completely safe) and reach the body through carefully placed pads. Muscles contract and relax 30 times a minute, and the strength of the contraction is variable. The sensation can range from mild tingling to irritation under each pad. Treatment sessions last 35-40 minutes and should be carried out daily for up to 4-8 weeks, although results are evident after even one or two sessions.

### For and against faradic exercise

There are few contraindications to faradic exercise. Very overweight people are advised not to put yet more strain on their muscles by adopting this: they should lose weight first and use faradic exercise to tone up relieved muscles. Most people get good results, however, with inches lost from the various leg and torso areas as muscles tone up. Used gently on the face to stimulate circulation, faradic exercise can be beneficial to skin texture. The disadvantages lie in what this form of exercise omits to do. It cannot reduce skin folds left by previous obesity, although because it tones the muscles beneath, bulging is reduced. It gives the heart and lungs no exercise; it boosts only local circulation, rather than that of the whole body; it uses very few Calories (no weight loss results from faradic exercise) and it does not aid digestion. In other words, it offers none of the mental and few of the physiological benefits of other forms of exercise. Use it as part of a slimming routine if you need to, but ensure that you take plenty of other types of exercise at the same time.

# FASTING

*See also: crash diets; diet; energy; slimming*

In the fashionable dieting scene, fasts followed swiftly on the heels of the discredited restricted-food diets popularised by starlets. Fasts, we are told, give the digestion a spring clean, easing out toxins and removing all trace of junk food.

Fasts have their uses, but their dangers and disadvantages seem to outweigh their overall value. If you do fast, you MUST drink a large quantity of fluids like water, herbal teas and diluted natural fruit juices. You should drink at least 2.3 litres (4 pints) per day and preferably more. Otherwise you will feel dizzy, enervated and headachey.

### Disadvantages of fasts

- There are several groups of people who should not undertake fasts. They are: pregnant or nursing mothers, diabetics, people with kidney or heart disorders or gastric ulcers, the underweight, elderly and anyone with a serious illness or taking medication. It is mandatory for anyone intending to undertake a fast for more than one day to consult their doctor first. Sponsored fasts have become a fashionable and perhaps apposite way of raising money for the Third World, but the above contraindications to fasting *must* be taken into account.
- Fasting is not productive in the long term as a method of losing weight even for the obese.
- The body does not need cleansing in this way. The digestive system, like the ear, for example, is designed to be self-cleaning and is highly organized.

### Plus points

- Fasting may be useful in isolating food allergies, under supervision by your doctor or dietician: foods can be re-introduced one by one.
- If you are fit and healthy and have had a bout of overeating and overdrinking, fasting for one day may make you feel more alert and lively, and give you new determination to stick to a healthy diet. It is not advisable to make fasting part of a regular dietary plan. Recent claims that regular fasts prolong life have not been substantiated: eat a balanced, healthy diet rich in vitamins, minerals and trace elements as well as proteins, carbohydrates and fats.

# FATTENING DIETS

*See also: anorexia nervosa; appetite; body image; diet; eating habits; hunger; slimming*

Putting on weight can be just as much of a problem as losing it. It can, in fact, be much worse, because friends are often unsupportive since they are more likely to suffer from the opposite problem. Being slightly underweight is healthier than being slightly overweight, but check your weight with the chart on page 252 to see whether you really are below what you should be for your height and frame.

### CAUSES OF UNDERWEIGHT

If your weight drops steadily, or if you have been ill and cannot put weight back on, consult your doctor.

- In generally healthy people one of the commonest causes is a past illness which has affected the appetite. Regaining the normal hunger/appetite/eating link takes time.
- Some people have a very high metabolic rate or are full of nervous energy which burns up Calories. These people find it almost impossible to put on weight, and need not try unless illness makes them lighter or medical opinion

# F

indicates that a gain would be beneficial.

- Digestion or absorption problems can cause weight loss and need medical investigation.
- Eating disorders caused by mental problems like depression cause weight loss, as does anorexia nervosa: these need medical advice.

## PUTTING ON WEIGHT
### Diet

Generally speaking, the dietary rules for underweight people are very similar to those of a normal, balanced diet. In a normal diet, when hunger strikes, fast energy but low-Calorie snacks are the rule. Here, appetite is more sensitive, low-Calories are irrelevant, so when the appetite appears eat high-Calorie snacks such as a nutritious fruit and nut bar, a handful of nuts or a glass of milk, rather than a piece of fruit or a fruit drink. Try to avoid eating sweets and chocolate as snacks: building good eating habits is just as important for you as for anyone else. Sugar addiction just replaces one problem with another.

Try to eat three good meals a day as well as snacks, but don't overwhelm yourself with mountains of food each time. Being strong about eating regularly will help you, for a normal or overweight person, missing a meal may be acceptable, but not for you. Read the diet entry and choose your range of nutrients in foods you really like. Include plenty of vitamins A, B6, B12, copper and zinc in your diet. Set yourself whatever dietary standards you like, but don't allow others to make you feel pressurized into eating particular foods at particular times not of your choice. Try drinking a small glass of dry wine or sherry before dinner to stimulate your appetite.

### Exercise

Sitting around worrying about being thin could make you thinner: your muscles will waste away and make you still more enervated. Take plenty of gentle exercise, but walk up stairs, don't run. If you go to a dance or exercise class or go out jogging, take a snack with you in case you feel hungry afterwards. Try to reduce your anxiety and stress levels.

## FATS

See also: carbohydrate; cholesterol; diet; energy; fattening diets; protein; slimming; vitamins

Fats play a significant role in our diet. They are highly concentrated sources of energy and carry vitamins A, D, E and K. They also perform a not unimportant function in making food more palatable. Ideally, fats should account for only about 30 per cent of the diet although they frequently form up to 45 per cent.

The chemical composition of fats and oils is identical. We tend to think of fats as being hard and of animal origin, and oils as being liquid and of vegetable origin. In general this is true, but there are exceptions like vegetable-based hard margarines.

Most of the fats in our diet are made up of triglycerides which are broken down by digestive enzymes in the intestine into glycerol and fatty acids. Many of them are essential in maintaining the health of certain body functions.

Fatty acids are made up of chains of carbon atoms, each of which has four bonds. Two of these bonds are used to attach to the carbon atoms on either side. The other two are usually attached to hydrogen atoms, but sometimes there is a free bond which then forms a double bond between two carbon atoms. If all the spare bonds are attached to hydrogen atoms, the fatty acid is described as 'saturated'; if there is one double bond between carbon atoms on the chain, the fatty acid is 'monounsaturated'; if there is more than one double bond, the fatty acid is 'polyunsaturated'.

All fats and oils contain all three types of fatty acids. Animal fats tend to have a higher proportion of saturated fats, while vegetable fats contain a higher proportion of polyunsaturated fats. Saturated fats have been shown to raise blood cholesterol levels to a dangerous point (see **cholesterol**). Polyunsaturated and in particular monounsaturated fats seem to have the reverse effect, and are even considered by some to undo the harm done by saturated fats.

## FATIGUE

See also: anxiety; depression; diet; energy; minerals; pregnancy; sleep; stress; vitamins

Like pain, fatigue is an unpleasant warning sign that all is not well. Without it a variety of physical problems could continue unchecked, with dangerous results. Fatigue can manifest itself as tiredness, listlessness and lack of energy quite distinct from healthy weariness at the end of a busy day or tough game of squash. Many people, especially women, suffer from fatigue but it should not be accepted as normal or incurable where its cause is not obvious and it continues for more than a day or so. Eating a good diet, sleeping well, exercising regularly should help prevent fatigue.

### CAUSES OF FATIGUE

Fatigue is a generalized reaction which can have one or more specific causes. Poor diet is the most common: lack of B vitamins interferes with the energy production procedure; low carbohydrate intake lowers the blood sugar level; lack of iron can cause diet-induced anaemia while lack of protein causes loss of muscle tone and poor resistance to infection. Bad eating habits can cause patches of fatigue during the day, or even long-term fatigue, and the ketosis (see separate entry) which accompanies slimming diets can cause it too. Minor ailments like tooth decay, infections like thrush or herpes are other possible culprits.

## COPING WITH FATIGUE

The way to deal with fatigue depends very much on its cause. If this cannot be established, you should consult your doctor. These are some guidelines:

- Ensure that your diet is adequate for your lifestyle and that it includes plenty of iron, vitamins C, B and E and a balanced range of other essential nutrients.
- Ensure that you take some exercise each day. Try to spend half an hour three or more times a week just exercising; your muscles will gradually increase their capacity to store glycogen and will tire less easily.
- Keep alert. Alternate your activities during the day, even at work, to provide maximum variety.
- Worrying about something may be more fatiguing than doing it. If you are busy, learn to delegate and reduce your workload to what you can cope with.
- Get plenty of sleep.
- During pregnancy, rest whenever you need to and eat as much good, nutritious food (see **diet**) as your appetite dictates.
- After a miscarriage or abortion rest for at least two days.
- Avoid stress-inducing situations: these produce fatigue and in the long term can exacerbate or even cause heart problems.
- An ancient Chinese remedy is ginseng, in either extract or tea form.

# FEET

*See also: bunions; calluses; chiropodist; corns; exercises; massage; pedicure; posture; reflexology; ringworm; skin; sweat; warts*

Our feet are designed to support and balance the body in stillness and in motion, with the weight shared between ball and heel. Each foot consists of 28 bones and numerous joints, some of which can move in more than two directions. They are bound together with ligaments and muscles which give spring and elasticity to the step. The arch of the foot, running the full length of it, takes the weight and acts as a shock-absorber for the rest of the body, while the big toe and lesser toes give added stability.

By the time adulthood is reached up to as many as 9 out of 10 people may have developed a modified pattern of walking to compensate for malfunctions of feet and legs. Badly fitting shoes are a common cause of additional problems, creating unnecessary pressure and rubbing between joints and shoe, leading to calluses and corns. A tendency to bunions may sometimes be inherited, but their condition can be exacerbated by ill-fitting, narrow shoes. It is important to fit children's shoes carefully. Unless feet are exercised on a regular basis, the muscles will slacken. Poor muscle tone causes the arches and supporting ligaments to sag.

Considering that feet travel over 70,000 miles in an average lifetime, they deserve the best care and attention that you can lavish upon them. Try to pay regular visits to a chiropodist anyway, but if any foot problems develop, see one straight away. Consult State Registered Chiropodists in the UK.

Reflexologists believe that because all the organs of the body are represented by corresponding pressure points in the foot and hand, foot massage can free energy channels which will improve the function of those organs (see **reflexology**).

## FOOT CARE

- Keeping feet clean and dry helps prevent infections to which feet are prone: viral infections such as verrucas (warts) or fungal infections such as athlete's foot (ringworm). Dry between your toes carefully after bathing, because bacteria thrive in moist, dark conditions.
- Smelly feet are caused by normal bacteria being acted upon by sweat: feet have a large number of sweat glands, and they are stimulated into extra production by nervousness, emotion, fatigue and pain. Applying surgical spirit after washing and drying helps prevent odour, as does spraying feet with a foot refresher or deodorant spray. Wear deodorizing insoles in your shoes if necessary to absorb perspiration and discourage the build-up of bacteria.
- Put clean tights and stockings on every day. Avoid wearing synthetic materials on the feet as much as you can, because they hinder natural evaporation and cooling.
- Gently smooth hard areas of skin with a large emery board to prevent calluses and have a regular pedicure.
- Trim nails regularly, using good quality nail scissors, cut straight across, never down the sides. Do not make sharp corners which can dig into the toe, causing ingrown toenails, or stab wounds on neighbouring toes. File horizontally, using an emery board or sapphire/diamond file.
- Rubbing feet with a body or hand lotion helps to soften and moisturize skin which is dry. Massage and exercise feet simply by placing a ball or foot roller beneath and gently rolling it along the foot's entire length, and by smoothing with hands in one direction from toes upwards.
- Choose shoes carefully. Ensure that they are wide enough not to restrict toe movement, and are at least 1.5 cm or ½ inch longer than the foot. They should have a well-cushioned sole and feel comfortable around the heel. Shoes should never require breaking in.
- High heels create an unnatural posture, tilting the body forward so that weight is thrown on the ball of the foot. Because they place strain on the spine they can cause backache, muscle fatigue and shortening of the muscles in the calves; since the toes are pushed forward and bunched together, they can cause corns and calluses too. By varying the heights of the heels on your shoes, you will help to exercise the calf muscles and restore the body's natural balance. The perfect heel should be no more than 2.5-3.5 cm (1-1½ inches) high. But try to go barefoot and wear flat shoes, or trainers (running shoes) or very comfortable sandals (not mules) whenever possible.
- If you have to stand a great deal, try wearing clogs with curved soles: they may help reduce fatigue, while supporting the foot's arch.
- Foot baths are soothing and relaxing. If your feet are tired or sweaty, soak them in a bowl containing a cupful of salt, sea salt or Epsom salt dissolved in a gallon of warm water. Alternatively try a little lavender oil in tepid water. Do not soak cold or wet feet in hot water. Rather sit with your feet raised horizontally until they are warmer. Never apply sudden warmth to cold feet or hands.
- Wear thermal insoles if you tend to suffer from cold feet. If you have unbroken chilblains, try gently applying a mild liniment or rheumatic pain-easing cream. Alternatively, rub them with a lanolin or boracic ointment.
- If chilblains are broken, ask your chemist for a proprietary anti-inflammatory and antiseptic cream. Do not wear hot, constricting boots or shoes once you are in a warm room or car.
- Relieve puffy ankles or weary feet by lying flat on your back with your feet raised higher than your head on a plump cushion.

# FELDENKRAIS TECHNIQUE

*See also: Alexander Technique; awareness; posture; Rolfing*

The Feldenkrais technique was evolved by Moshe Feldenkrais, a Russian-born Israeli, in the 1940s. His theory is that we utilise as little as 5 per cent of the potential which our bodies have. Awareness is his keyword: Feldenkrais instructors teach their pupils awareness of how and why they move their bodies in a certain way, the way in which movement can improve the mental state, and reflect personality. Thus the opportunity is given for habitual movements, which may not be the best possible, to be abandoned and replaced with newly aware movements.

Feldenkrais believes strongly in using the whole range of movement; thus he is against regimented exercise classes. In dealing with specific body problems, practitioners work indirectly on the problem, feeling that a more direct approach might mimic the movements which are causing pain or disability. The technique is suitable for anyone, with any problem from pain to joint disability, and practitioners treat the chronically ill as well as generally healthy.

# FIBRE

*See also: cholesterol; circulation; diet; F-plan diet; haemorrhoids; heart*

Dietary fibre is the name given to several different constituents of food which are not digested and absorbed by the body. Fibre is sometimes known as roughage or unavailable carbohydrate, though neither of these terms are strictly accurate. Dietary fibre is only found in vegetable foods where it takes the form of compounds such as cellulose and hemicellulose (which form the main support structure of plants), pectin, lignin and gum. The best sources of fibre are wholegrain cereals (especially bran, which is 44 per cent fibre), vegetables, fruit and nuts (almonds are 14 per cent fibre). See also the sample food chart under **diet**.

## THE IMPORTANCE OF DIETARY FIBRE

As fibre is not digested and absorbed by the body, it contributes neither energy nor nutrients and has not in the past been allocated an official recommended daily allowance. The average 15-20 g (½-⁵⁄₇ oz) of fibre consumed per day in a typical Western diet, however, is considered by most nutritionists to be inadequate. It is generally thought that 30 g (just over 1 oz) is the optimum figure.

The importance of fibre can be evaluated by looking at the effects of a lack of it. The most common problem associated with a low fibre consumption is constipation, since fibre plays an important role in the emptying of the large bowel. Cereal fibre in particular adds bulk to stools and increases the frequency of defaecation.

More serious diseases of the digestive system – appendicitis, diverticulitis and cancer of the colon and bowel – are also associated with low-fibre diets. They are much more common in affluent countries where there is a higher proportion of meat and refined foods (from which the fibre has been removed) in the average diet than in underdeveloped countries. It may also be the case that dietary fibre is beneficial in the management of diabetes and coronary heart disease as it impedes the absorption of sugar and fat. Increased-fibre diets are often prescribed as part of treatment for these conditions. These effects, together with the fact that fibre in a meal increases the feeling of fullness without adding Calories may also be useful in preventing and treating obesity.

The value of fibre in our diet has received much attention in recent years from press, public and scientists. A great deal of the research done on fibre has concentrated on discovering exactly how fibre functions, in order to give scientific back-up to the observations made in practice. This research has given rise to many interesting ideas about fibre function. For example, pectin (found in soft fruits) has been shown to decrease the amount of cholesterol absorbed from food and, more importantly, to lower blood cholesterol concentration, thus possibly playing a part in preventing coronary

heart disease and other conditions in which cholesterol is implicated (see **cholesterol**). Pectin and guar gum seem to reduce the rate at which glucose is absorbed across the intestinal barrier into the blood. This provides a slow-release source of blood sugar which may be useful in the treatment, and possibly also the prevention of, diabetes, particularly the form of the disease which comes on late in life.

Too much dietary fibre (over 40 g/1³⁄₇ oz a day) may produce some abdominal discomfort and may impair the body's ability to absorb certain minerals, in particular zinc and iron, and possibly vitamins B6 and B12.

# F-PLAN DIET

*See also: diet; diets; fibre; slimming*

The F-plan is a slimming diet evolved by Audrey Eyton. The theory behind the diet is that a high intake of dietary fibre (between 35 g and 50 g a day) combined with a restricted Calorie intake helps increase eating and digesting time, thus preventing the normal dieting hungar pangs when stomach acids are unoccupied. The bulk of fibre is planned to increase food satisfaction, speed weight loss and excretion of some ingested calories. Additionally, the diet plans to produce a healthy eating plan providing some defence against diseases like diverticulitis, cancer of the colon, coronary heart disease and diabetes which have been linked with low dietary fibre intake. Nutritionists agree that Western diets are generally too low in dietary fibre (see **diet, fibre**) which this diet provides. But the most important factor is a long-term healthy, nutritious eating plan which will not necessarily be the outcome of following special diets like this.

# FIFTIES

*See also: ageing; colouring hair; exfoliation; greying; menopause; minerals; osteoporosis; vitamins*

With children no longer dependent on you, this decade can be one of the most liberating and stimulating. Now is the time to embark on new hobbies, even a career that will interest you for the rest of your life. If your attitude is positive you will look and feel younger.

**Body** The menopause (see separate entry) usually occurs between 48-53. This is when the ovaries cease to produce a monthly egg and the levels of oestrogen and progesterone gradually fall. If you experience discomfort, see your doctor.

**Diet** A slowdown in activity and body functions will

decrease your energy needs to about 1,800 Calories a day. Any iron supplements you may have been taking to counteract monthly loss through menstruation should no longer be needed. Hormonal changes can affect your bones. To help ward off osteoporosis, in which the bones become brittle, take extra calcium in your diet. Good sources are dairy produce especially milk, soya beans, nuts and green vegetables. Vitamins A and D are also important: take fish liver oil capsules, especially during winter when there is little sunlight to give the body Vitamin D. An increasing vulnerability to heart disease means that you must restrict the amount of fat you eat and cut down on eggs, cheese and meats, all of which increase blood cholesterol levels.

**Skin** The menopause will take its toll on the condition of your skin. A rich moisturizer in the morning and a rich night cream will counteract the extra dryness. Regular exfoliation will ensure that skin texture remains smooth and glowing.

**Hair** Your hair colour is determined by the proportion of three pigments which are deposited in the hair shaft. As you get older less pigment is laid down and white hairs appear among still pigmented hairs, giving a grey appearance. The age at which greyness begins is determined by inherited factors. If dyeing your hair, take care to ensure that the colour complements your skin tone.

# FIRMING

*See also: exercise; exercises; faradic exercise; massage; sports*

Acquiring a firm, well-shaped body is just one part of achieving total health and fitness. It is important to work towards firming up at the same time as attending to a good diet – whether you are overweight or not – and general fitness. Exclude all fizzy drinks, sweets and cakes which are empty Calories and eat plenty of fresh fruit, vegetables and wholegrains instead. Balancing your food intake, along with a good exercise routine will help achieve fitness. Most exercise has some form of firming effect. Extra exercises evolved especially for their firming potential can help get rid of post-slimming or post-natal sag where muscles have not kept pace with weight loss. They also help counteract the effects of gravity on the body. However, while firming muscles can help to improve their condition, it can not actually remove fat.

Firm muscles are those which are being properly and regularly used. Regular exercise is the best way of achieving this (see **exercises** and **sports**). Isometric exercises (see separate entry) can be helpful too, but these must not be used by anyone with a history of heart trouble and hypertension. Combat a particularly saggy area with one or two specially designed exercises.

**Inner thighs** Lie on your back on the floor with feet slightly apart, and a large cushion between knees.

Press firmly for a slow count of 5. Repeat 3 times then do 10 quick squeezes.

**Outer thighs** Sit on floor with legs stretched out in front and arms out to sides. Roll sideways on your bottom right over the outer thigh, roll back on to the other thigh. Repeat 20 times.

**Upper arms** Sitting, make loose fists. Make punching movements backwards (with arms extended behind) and forwards. Repeat these exercises morning and evening.

# FITNESS

*See also: awareness; circulation; dance; exercise; exercises; heart; lungs; sports*

Fitness, being able to do what you want and need to do, is the attainment of good physical health, achieved by a healthy lifestyle and proper exercise of the body. Fitness of body produces a sense of contentment which can improve emotional and mental well-being, too.

There cannot be one standard for fitness: it depends on your individual make-up, and on the activities for which you want to be fit. Good, all-round fitness involves the following: flexibility in joints and muscles, strength, and aerobic fitness (in terms of the heart and lungs and the muscles surrounding the cardio-respiratory system and its local muscular endurance components). In order to be of any use in making you fit, exercise must produce sustained increases in metabolic, cardiovascular and respiratory functions, the rate at which you use up energy, your pulse rate, and your breathing pattern.

### THE IMPORTANCE OF FITNESS

Being fit is important for good general health. It also opens up your physical potential, expanding the limits within which your body works, increasing its capabilities so that you can enjoy life to the fullest both in everyday activities and in leisure pursuits. In assessing the importance of fitness it is useful to look at the effects of *un*fitness:

- Lack of suppleness, strength and stamina.
- Inactivity leads to high levels of LDL cholesterol (see **cholesterol**) in the blood: this can in turn lead to weight problems and even coronary heart disease.
- Unfitness is a major factor in obesity.
- Unfitness reduces the body's resistance to infections: fit people are more resistant to colds and 'flu, for example.

In contrast, a good level of fitness, incorporating the flexibility, strength and aerobic fitness elements, will decrease the risk of injury due to physical overloading. This can be brought on even by simple everyday activities like bending and twisting to reach objects, carrying heavy bags or running for the bus, particularly as you get older. In conjunction with a well-balanced, nutritious diet (see **diet**) and healthy lifestyle –

one that is as low as possible in harmful stress and anxiety, free from cigarettes and excess alcohol – physical fitness will also pay dividends in promoting a long, happy and disease-free life. Fitness can decrease harmful stress overall, increase the ability to sleep, to relax, play a part in reducing blood pressure, in managing osteoporosis (see entry) and diabetes mellitus, in increasing strength, improving posture, and reducing body fat percentages. Last, but by no means least, fitness and the achievement of fitness are fun and add to general enjoyment of life.

### ACHIEVING FITNESS – SAFELY

There are several important points:
1. Before embarking on any new exercise or form of activity or sport, you must check with your doctor or medical adviser that it is safe for you.
2. Use your heart rate as a safe method of supervising and increasing the intensity of your exercise, see Caution Box in **exercises**. Do not use this method if you have heart or circulation problems, are taking drugs for hypertension or thrombosis, or if you are pregnant as this test will not be an accurate barometer for you.
3. Always do warming up and cooling down exercises at either end of a session. These really are important to prepare your body for the extra stress of training, and to let it readjust to normal temperature and intensity of activity afterwards (see **exercises**).) Warm-ups and cooldowns specific to the activity should always be carried out for at least 5 minutes, if young and active, 10 minutes or more if not active and/or older, at an intensity below your training zone (see Caution Box in **exercises**).
4. Avoid high intensity bursts of activity or prolonged sessions at first: these could be dangerous if you are not ready for them. While fitness can ultimately decrease your chances of suffering a heart attack, exercising too much too soon can put you in danger.
5. Work at your own speed, follow professional advice on techniques, and vary your activities to prevent boredom.
6. Never exercise if you feel unwell or have a temperature or virus infection. Always stop exercising and seek advice if you feel a pain or uncomfortable sensation unusual for you.

If you lead a generally active lifestyle, perhaps walking or cycling to work, using stairs rather than lifts, doing a lot of gardening or disco dancing, then you are probably well on the way to being fit. If not, throwing yourself unprepared into a badly-taught aerobics class is more likely to injure you or at least put you off exercise for life. To achieve fitness your exercise should be regular (at least 20 minutes three times a week) and should build up gradually in frequency, intensity (using your heart rate as a guide, see Caution Box in **exercises**), duration and type. You should never feel really stiff or knocked out, but slightly breathless after each session, before you do your cooling down exercises.

## FLAB

*See also: cellulite; diet; exercise; exercises; faradic exercise; firming; muscles; weight*

Flab is a negative word. It is only ever used to depict an aspect of oneself or others which is disliked and regarded as unattractive. When related to physique it is used to describe a body which is floppy due to overweight or obesity, lack of exercise, excessive drinking or a combination of these.

### Prevention
The best way to prevent flab is to follow a sensible diet and exercise regime. Avoid excessive alcohol intake and cut down on processed, sugary and fatty foods. Exclude all fizzy drinks, sweets and cakes and add plenty of fresh fruits and vegetables to your diet. Always discuss radical dietary changes and new exercise regimes with your doctor.

### Cure
If you think you are flabby, read the various sports,

*Being fit helps promote good health, wards off illness and gives you extra sparkle for your everyday activities as well as sports.*

exercise and diet sections of this book. Your problem may be attributable to years of a sedentary occupation with little exercise, despite a sensible diet. You may need to start building up a regular exercise regime (check with your doctor first) and incorporate some or all of the exercises in the daily exercise plan. You may be drinking too much (alcohol is extremely fattening as well as posing other hazards). You may simply be overweight and very unfit, with consequent muscle sag. Evaluate the problem, find the cause – and take action.

## FLOSSING

**Fluoride**
See Teeth

*See also: dentist; gums; teeth*

An efficient tooth cleaning regime includes flossing as well as brushing. Dental floss is a thread of nylon filaments, either waxed or unwaxed. The unwaxed type is preferable, but waxed is easier to handle if your teeth are crowded. Take a length of about 25 cm (10 inches) and pass it between two teeth, winding the ends around your fingers. Work it up gently into the gum crevice then down to the biting surface, two or three times, pulling against the side of one tooth. Repeat, pulling against the side of the adjoining tooth. Floss can be quite difficult to manipulate safely and correctly, so ask your dentist or dental hygienist to advise you on how frequently you should floss your teeth and to show you how it should be done. If your teeth have not been professionally cleaned recently, this may need to be done before your flossing will give maximum benefit and protection from decay.

Flossing is an everyday essential for good tooth care. Floss before brushing, working between each tooth all round the mouth.

## FLUID RETENTION

*See also: blood pressure; menstruation; pregnancy*

Fluid retention is also known as water retention. The swelling itself is called oedema. Symptoms vary from puffy ankles to swollen limbs or an overall 'weight' increase which is basically water rather than fat, sometimes with uncomfortable abdominal distension. If you suffer from fluid retention you should consult your doctor as there are several possible causes. People with high blood pressure often suffer from this: movement of fluid from the body tissues to the blood vessels is impaired. They may be prescribed diuretics, which because they reduce the ability of the kidneys to reabsorb water, increase water and salt excretion and reduce blood pressure. Other conditions such as heart, kidney, liver and lung disorders may also produce fluid retention. Fluid retention is quite common in pregnancy when the increasing size and weight of the uterus puts pressure on leg veins and also due to increased progesterone levels. See your doctor: unless your blood pressure has increased he will probably prescribe frequent rests with your legs raised. This increases blood circulation and takes pressure off the veins.

### CYCLIC FLUID RETENTION
One of the most common types of fluid retention is that experienced by many women during the menstrual cycle, for up to seven days prior to a menstrual period. This can produce a temporary weight gain of up to 2 kg (5 lb) which disappears when the menstrual period ends. It is caused by the progesterone build-up in the body before menstruation.

Your doctor may prescribe mild diuretics, but these can have side-effects, such as constipation because fluid is being diverted away from the colon, reduction in potassium absorption, salt/water imbalance in the body, and you may find that you have to get up frequently in the night to urinate. If you do need to take diuretics, increase the fibre and potassium in your diet and decrease the salt. Your doctor may also prescribe hormone or vitamin treatment.

**Self-help**
- Increase your dietary intake of vitamin B6, in whole-grain cereals, dried yeast, liver and kidneys (see **vitamins**). This vitamin has been found helpful with this and other aspects of pre-menstrual syndrome (PMS) (see separate entry). Some doctors recommend supplements of vitamin B6, taken daily.
- Reduce your salt intake and increase your water intake. This helps readjust your salt/water balance.
- Take plenty of exercise. This will make you feel less bloated and miserable, and will speed up circulation and thus speed removal of excess water from body tissues.
- Increase the amount of fibre in your diet (see **fibre**) with bran, wholemeal flour and bread, jacket potatoes, unpeeled fruits, vegetables and brown rice.
- You may find eating plenty of garlic, which acts as a natural diuretic, helps.
- Evening Primrose Oil supplements of 500 mg, 3 times daily, have been found helpful for a whole range of PMS symptoms.
- Never take hormones or diuretics except on your doctor's prescription: the body's hormone balance, like it water content, is finely tuned.
- Do not be tempted to reduce your fluid intake: this could cause dehydration which can do serious damage to internal organs.

# FORTIES

*See also: body moisturizers; cholesterol; diet; elastin and elastone; greying; make-up; menopause; minerals; vitamins*

At the age of forty many people go through a period of re-evaluation – of their work, family and friends – but after a couple of years life should re-stabilize and you will find that you can look forward to the rest of the decade with a renewed sense of purpose and contentment.

**Body** Hormonal changes will contribute to the accumulation of varying amounts of fat on your hips, waist, back and stomach. These pads are actually necessary to your health, provided they do not add more than 10 lb (4 kg) to your previous weight. They are thought to be involved with maintaining the oestrogen supply which will delay symptoms of the menopause, keep bones stronger (see below), improve circulation and decrease the chance of heart disease occurring. Periods may begin to become erratic several years prior to the menopause, and it is advisable not to use the natural method of contraception at this age, or unwanted pregnancy may occur.

**Diet** Your Caloric needs will reduce from 2,000 to about 1,900. Calcium is particularly important to your diet now: it helps prevent the occurrence of osteoporosis, where bones become brittle and fragile. Milk is the richest calcium source, but as many people become sensitive to the sugar (lactose) in milk as they grow older (and because they want to reduce saturated fat intake, see below), spinach, almonds and sardines can provide you with your daily requirements. Decreasing ostrogen levels will diminish your body's ability to handle cholesterol: reduce your fat intake. Reduce your salt intake, too, especially if you have high blood pressure.

**Skin** Your age will now be showing in your skin – how drastically will depend on your genetic make-up and how much you have exposed it to the sun. Most skins become drier with age. The sebaceous glands which help skin retain its natural moisture become less active, so it is important to use a rich, greasy moisturizer. Use body lotion or moisturizer regularly now. Superfatted soaps, which contain extra fats such as mineral oil, coconut oil, butter and lanolin, are also helpful for dry skins as they leave a moisture-trapping residue on the skin. Re-evaluate your make-up: the gradual change in your skin tone over recent years will make some colours more flattering than others. Avoid shiny eyeshadows; powder types are kinder to older skin and provide plenty of colour choice. Choose softer mascara colours; black is out now unless you have black skin or very dark hair. Check that your foundation still matches your skin colour – you may well need to change it. Choose peach and pink for lip colour, both of which look wonderful against older skin, and opt for glossy finishes, even adding extra gloss on top of lip colour. Choose browny tones with care, again veer towards pinker tones. Avoid harsh, sharp reds and electric pinks, and avoid flat, matt finishes for lips.

**Hair** From the age of thirty onwards the process of cell division starts to slow up, with some cells closing down entirely and others no longer having the muscle to push through the dense elastone which forms with age. Your hair will become progressively finer. Regular cutting, washing and conditoning will help maintain its glossy appearance.

Try to keep an open mind concerning hairstyles; you will find that you need a change as your hair and skin colours alter, and as the thickness of your hair decreases. Consult your hairdresser.

# FOUNDATION

*See also: camouflage; colour choice; make-up*

An even foundation is the essential canvas on which to base your make-up. It smooths out variations in skin tones and provides protection for the skin from dust and dirt. Consistencies vary, but most foundations are water-in-oil emulsions, their oiliness determined by the skin type for which they are formulated.

**Folic acid**
See Vitamin M

**Food**
See Diet

**Fragances**
See Scent

**Fragrant waters**
See Eau-de-cologne

**Fresheners**
See Toning

**Fructose**
See Diet and Sugar

### TYPES OF FOUNDATION

**Liquids** Give a light, fine coverage. They are runnier than creams and water-in-oil types are suitable for normal and combination skins. Oil-free, medicated or matt foundations are best for greasy skins.

**Creams and mousses** Suit most skins, but give dry skins extra moisture and nourishment. They are thick with a glossy texture.

**Blocks or cakes** Are dry foundations which must be applied with a damp sponge. They are suitable for oily skins.

**Gels** Are transparent and are particularly suitable for young skins which need only the lightest cover. They are good in the summer to add gleam to a tan, and to show off freckles.

**Cream concealer sticks** Are solid, thick preparations applied before foundation to cover blemishes.

### HOW TO CHOOSE YOUR FOUNDATION

First select the right foundation for your skin type. Then match it as nearly as possible to your natural skin tone, remembering that extremely pink or brown shades are unflattering to most skins. Always test the colour on your face first, the skin on your hand or arm is not the same tone.

If you cannot match your colouring exactly, try making your own foundation using three or four different shades. With your palm acting as a palette, add equal amounts of foundation and moisturizer and a little mineral water to give sheerness. Mix throughly and apply with a damp sponge.

If you have healthy, even skin you can use a tinted moisturizer or gel (with built-in ultra-violet filter) instead of a foundation. As you get older avoid heavy cream foundation which sinks into lines, making them look deeper still. Choose sheer foundations instead and remember to adjust colour as your skin tones change.

### HOW TO APPLY FOUNDATION

1  Ensure that light is shining directly on your face; shadows cause make-up to look uneven. Try to make up in the type of light in which you will be seen, whether natural, artificial, or a combination of both, for the best results.
2  Lightly moisturize face and neck if your skin is dry or normal. If you have a combination skin, use an anti-shine product down the centre panel of the face and moisturize the rest. If very oily, apply an astringent to the face before applying foundation.
3  Apply small dots of foundation using fingertips or a damp cosmetic sponge – those with sharp rather than rounded corners are best for smoothing round the nose and chin.
4  Blend gently using outward strokes away from the centre of the face, up to the hair-line and down to the neck. Cover as much of your neck as will show. Ensure good blending around the jawline, nose and hairline.
5  Do not forget to cover lips and eyelids. This will help keep eyeshadow and lipstick in place. On older skins, keep foundation away from the eye area as it sits in and accentuates wrinkles.
6  If you want a matt look, blot face with a dry lightly powdered puff.

### USING FOUNDATION

■ **For dark rings under the eyes**, apply foundation, then a concealer stick/cream concealer a shade lighter than foundation on the area, Blend well. Apply cream concealers with a damp sponge to avoid caking.

■ **If your facial skin tone is uneven** choose your foundation using jawline colour, which is usually even, as a guide. This ensures that foundation will blend naturally into the neck.

■ **If your skin only needs partial cover** and is generally good, apply foundation to that area only, blending it in with care.

■ **If you are sunburnt**, do not try to lighten red skin with pale foundation: it doesn't work. Cool skin down thoroughly, splash repeatedly with cold water, or better still lie down with a cold, wet cloth over the face for as long as necessary. Only when skin is cool apply moisturizer (otherwise it can hold in heat) lavishly. If you must use foundation, a gel type gives the best finish and a fresh, natural effect.

■ **In hot, humid climates**, an oil-free foundation lasts longest on all skin types. Moisturize dry skins extra well night and morning.

A Nose      B Jaw      C Cheeks      D Long face

## SHADING YOUR FAULTS WITH FOUNDATIONS

It is possible to hide some minor facial flaws and improve contours with skilful use of foundation two or three shades darker than your normal foundation. Unless otherwise specified, the steps below should be taken *before* your overall foundation has been applied. Powder should be applied last, to set corrections and general foundation.

Blending is vital: you are aiming for a flattering shadow, not a solid stripe. Apply with a very light touch, or skin may end up looking dirty or bruised.

**Nose** – a nose that is wide at the base can be narrowed by drawing a triangle of darker foundation directly above the nostrils and blending into the general foundation (see illustration A – Nose). A nose that is too wide at the bridge can be narrowed by drawing a triangle of foundation on either side of the inner eyebrows. A crooked nose can be made to look straighter if the outward side of the bend is flanked with dark foundation, the inward curve side with a highlighter.

**Square jaw** – can be minimized by applying dark foundation or brushing on skin-tone blusher in an elongated triangle just above the edge of the jawline and blending into basic foundation (see illustration B – Jaw).

**Cheeks** – lift the cheekbones with two shades of foundation blended in the natural hollow below the bones. Place the darkest tone just under the bone, or lighter one below, in lines from the outer corner of the eye widening towards the ear (see illustration C – Cheeks).

**Long face** – shorten with a carefully blended line of darker foundation or skin tone blusher at the end of the chin and across the top of the forehead (see illustration D – Long face).

**Blemishes** – if you have blemishes try to apply a sheer foundation with a dry sponge for effective coverage. Then, using a concealer stick to match your foundation, stroke concealer on with a brush.

**Under-eye shadows or rings** – before applying foundation, stipple on concealer gently from a stick slightly lighter than skin tone and blend carefully at the edges. Then apply foundation to match skin tone over whole face, including this area. If you use too light a concealer you will draw attention to the under-eye area.

**Red veins** – apply a green-tinted foundation lightly over affected areas before normal foundation.

# FRECKLES

*See also: chemical peeling; dermabrasion; foundation; liver spots; make-up*

If you are born with a freckly complexion it will be with you for life (although freckles fade with age). Freckle-like marks which appear later in life are in fact liver spots. Freckles are tiny marks formed where there is an excess of melanin in the skin. They are harmless, and generally considered a very

appealing feature. They tend to deepen in colour in summer, and increase in number, too. People with freckles very often have red or blonde hair, although dark hair and freckles is not unusual.

Fair freckled skins are usually extremely susceptible to sunburn: always use a very high SPF (Sun Protection Factor) preparation in the sun, or even one with a total block (see **tanning**). Use a moisturizer with built-in ultra violet filters in the summer. Since freckly fair skins are often very dry, too, they need a good night cream even when young. Olive freckled skins tend to be less susceptible to burning; nevertheless, be careful in the sun.

What foundation you use depends very much on you and how dark your freckles are. They tend to look best when well moisturized and covered only with a tinted gel foundation or even just a tinted moisturizer. Avoid heavy foundation, even for evening. If you have blemishes, use the lightest liquid foundation available in your basic skin colour, camouflage blemishes with matching concealer stick stroked on with a brush and blended carefully at the edges.

F

G

# GANGLIONS

A ganglion is a kind of jelly-filled cyst which is quite harmless. Ganglions tend to form in the sheaths of tendons and are particularly common around the wrists. Unless they are very large or cause discomfort there is no medical need for their removal. Traditionally ganglions on the wrist were treated by hitting them with a bible! The blow broke the cyst's wall, allowing fluid to escape and be absorbed into the body tissue. This is no longer considered wise and is not carried out; ganglions do, however, often dissipate of their own accord. Where necessary they can be aspirated: that is, fluid in the cyst is removed with a syringe so that the lump disappears, or they can be surgically removed. If you develop any mysterious lumps or bumps, see your doctor immediately: a lump on the wrist is not necessarily a ganglion.

# GELATIN

*See also: collagen; drugs and medicines; nails*

Gelatin is used in many products ranging from drugs and medical preparations to foods like jellies and Jello. Because it is produced by boiling collagen-containing meat products such as tendons in water, vegetarians prefer not to use it. Gelatin has a small protein content: for this reason it has in the past been included in foods for convalescents. Now, however, food supplements – such as drinks which replace a full meal – far richer in protein are readily available. Gelatin used to be advocated for strengthening nails, too, but a good, well balanced, vitamin-rich diet with plenty of sulphur plays a far more important role.

# GELS

*See also: facials; foundation; hair; tanning*

Gels are semi-solid, jelly-like solutions based on gelatinous acrylics (in the case of light gels, e.g. for hair) or film-forming agents, which dry more quickly (in the case of heavier gels, e.g. for masks). The gel itself has no beneficial properties, but acts as a carrier for setting agents or for moisturizer. They are increasingly popular for cosmetic products as they are easy and cool to handle, and non-greasy.

**Hair gels** are used to set hair after shampooing. As the hair dries, so the gel dries and hardens, holding the hair shafts in shape until dampened again, or washed, or until the coating is brushed out.

**Sun protection gels for hair** work on the principle that water evaporates to leave a protective coating of sunscreen. These gels are often heavy, and need to be washed, rather than brushed, out.

**Sun protection gels for skin** are normally only used for low SPF (Sun Protection Factor) products (see **tanning**), for skins that tan easily. Skins that need more protection are better covered with oils or creams.

**Foundation gels** are very soft, with a high water content. The moisture is absorbed by the skin, leaving just the light foundation colour on the surface.

**Blusher gels** are thicker and give light colour.

**Massage gels** are often used during facials. Without oiling the skin, they provide a medium for massage so that blood circulation in the skin can be improved. They can also be good conductors of electricity and are used in facials such as Cathiodermie (see **facials**) where gentle electric currents are passed across the skin to stimulate excretion of impurities and good blood supply.

**Gel masks** are cooling and relaxing. They can be used after deep cleansing both to moisturize the skin and close the pores. These gels dry more quickly than other types, especially if they contain clay.

# GLASSES

*See also: contact lenses; eyes; optician; tanning*

If an eye test reveals that your vision is defective in some way, your optician may prescribe the wearing of contact lenses or glasses to correct it (see **eyes**). Glasses may prove to be more suitable for you. Tell your optician of your preference, but follow his advice, because contact lenses do not suit all eyes or all eye problems.

### CHOOSING GLASSES
#### The shape
Your optician will help you to choose the glasses which flatter your face most. Consider these points:
1. Check that glasses fit neatly over the nose without slipping and make sure they don't pinch behind the ears (some alterations can be made if you particularly like one frame but do listen to advice because certain frames are unsuitable for some prescriptions). Most important of all, check that the top of the frames are in line with your eyebrows.
2. Take the shape of your face into account.
    **Heart-shaped or wide face:** glasses with wings, shaped or decorated sides.
    **Square face:** large square or rectangular frames.
    **Round face:** angular, geometric frames slightly narrower than your cheekbones, or slim frames which are wider than the cheekbones.
    **Thin face:** deep, almost square frames or curved, even, round frames.
3. Don't be persuaded into taking any glasses which you don't feel are right for you. Glasses are expensive and need to fit in with your personal style. If you can afford to buy new glasses regularly, or have several pairs, you are free to be more outrageous in your choice. Otherwise, choose a style and colour that fits in with all your clothes, taking your hairstyle into consideration, and veer on the conservative side.
4. Frame colours are now so varied that choice can be very difficult. Some of the newest are clear crystal, plain, or with inset coloured rims, diamanté or frosting. Very popular too are solid bright colours for frames, like pillarbox red, electric blue and jade green. Softer peaches, pinks, smoke, greys and tortoiseshells abound. Choose the colour very carefully if you are going to have just one pair of all-purpose glasses.

#### The material
Lenses are made from plastic or glass. They are equally good optically. Plastic lenses are much lighter, often weighing as little as 8-9 g. The newest types have a hard coat on the lens surface to improve scratch resistance, but are still more vulnerable than glass. Glass lenses are heavier, weighing up to 25 g and can break or chip if subjected to severe blows: **never** wear glass lenses for sports activities.

### SUNGLASSES
The eye is constructed to make adjustments to changes in light. It is not damaged by sunlight in normal circumstances but can be temporarily or even permanently damaged if exposed to very strong sunlight without protection. Looking at the sun, for example, can cause retinal burns (permanent central blindness) and ski-ing without protection can produce painful but temporary 'snow blindness' from ultraviolet rays. Prolonged exposure to bright sunlight can, however, cause eyestrain and headaches through continual squinting. Squinting also increases the tiny smile lines fanning out from the outer corner of the eye, deepening the dip in the collagen and elastin below the skin's surface to produce embryonic wrinkles. Wear sunglasses for comfort in bright sun, but don't wear them in normal light: you will just cut down your vision unnecessarily which can be dangerous.

Remember to protect the skin on your eyelids even under sunglasses in strong sunlight. Although some lenses provide a degree of protection from ultraviolet and infra-red rays, light can still fall behind the sunglasses on to the eyelid and the skin at the side of the eye. Wear eye make-up containing sun filters, or apply a thin layer of a sunscreen preparation.

### HOW TO CHOOSE
Lenses and frames are available in every colour and shape. The frames you choose are a matter of taste, but lenses must be chosen very carefully. The best colours for protection are dark greys, browns and greens. For maximum protection from bright sunlight it should not be possible to see the eye through the lens (but remember that photochromic lenses cannot be judged in this way, as they darken according to the intensity of available light). Pastels give minimal protection. Graduated lenses can be practical for sports and general wear, providing a range of protection according to angle of view: choose dark grey or brown.
**For general sports wear** choose good quality plastic lenses. Polycarbonate lenses are very tough and impact resistant. Where there is high light reflection and glare polarized types are best.
**For driving** it is inadvisable to wear photochromic-lensed sunglasses, because of the danger of time-lapse (minimum 30 seconds) in lens response, for example on emerging from a dark tunnel to bright sunlight. Polarized sunglasses make dotted patterns appear on toughened windscreens. Choose good-quality glass or plastic lenses.
**For general wear** photochromic lenses are the best choice since they adjust to the given conditions.

### CARE OF GLASSES
■ Keep lenses scrupulously clean. Only polish them with a soft cloth or clean handkerchief.
■ Always keep glasses in their case when not in use, particularly if in your handbag or on your desk.
■ Always put glasses down with the lenses upwards.
■ Check side screws regularly for looseness.

**Garlic**
See Herbs

**Gingivitis**
See Gums

**Ginseng**
See Herbs

**Glucose**
See Sugar

**Glycogen**
See Carbohydrates; Energy; Fats

G

# GREYING

*See also: ageing; colouring hair; fifties; forties; hair; make-up; sixties plus*

The age at which your hair turns grey is largely decided by genetics. Severe shock can cause loss of pigment in hairs, just as it can cause reversible alopecia (hair loss). Greying, however, is not reversible: the hair grows from the follicle without the red, black, yellow and green pigments in its centre, and remains unpigmented for the three to seven years it is likely to stay on your head. Much less common in the developed countries is premature greying brought about by very poor diet.

The 'grey' hairs are in fact white, but appear a shade of grey against the still pigmented hairs. Variations in greyness are accounted for by both the proportion of white hairs to pigmented hairs, and by the original pigmented hair colour. As the process advances it produces a change in your appearance just like that of any hair colour change. In addition your skin tone changes as you grow older. Some changes in hairstyle and make-up can make the best of your new colour.

### HAIR AND HAIRSTYLE

- In the early stages of greying, hair takes on a 'highlighted' appearance. Make the most of this by gradually simplifying your style: highlights always add body and lift even to simply layered hair.
- If hair turns grey in distinct streaks, especially at the temples, discuss ways of emphasizing these with your hairdresser.
- If you have long hair and generally wear it dramatically drawn back, soften the style: grey hair can make such styles look too severe. Try a more bouffant chignon, or set your hair on large curlers and backcomb it very lightly so that the hair lifts softly from the face.
- Try to cut down on perming your hair: hair dries out with age and perming exacerbates this. Try out new styles which do not need a perm (see **curling and straightening hair**).
- Avoid fussy styles which, combined with grey hair, can be very ageing.

### CAMOUFLAGE

If you cannot face the thought of going grey visibly, you have to decide early on just how you intend to cope with this. Remember that going grey gently can be extremely attractive, and that once most of your friends are grey, your coloured hair will begin to look odd. One answer is to colour subtly, then lose colour equally subtly, having gained several grey-free years. There are two main options:

- Use subtle highlights in several tones. This way the hair looks lighter rather than greyer, with more colour variation (see **highlighting**). Alternatively, lowlight your hair with your natural colour so that you can continue to look as if you are just beginning to go grey.

- Complete colouring should begin as soon as hair begins to go grey, always with a shade lighter than your original colour to tone with fading skin colour. It is most successful when colour adjustments are made gradually, if hair has not previously been chemically or naturally coloured. If you have always coloured your

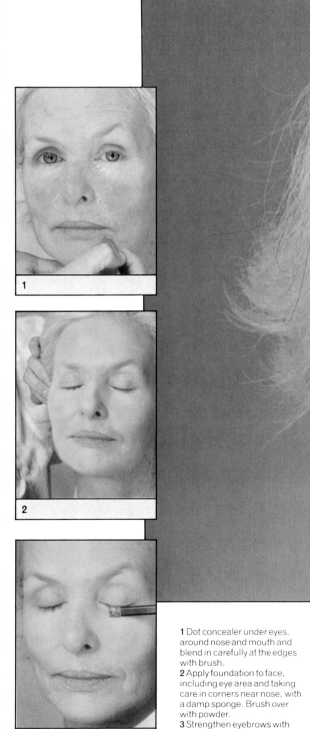

1 Dot concealer under eyes, around nose and mouth and blend in carefully at the edges with brush.
2 Apply foundation to face, including eye area and taking care in corners near nose, with a damp sponge. Brush over with powder.
3 Strengthen eyebrows with light taupe powder. Highlight lightly under eyes.

hair, there will be little noticeable difference in your appearance, except that you may have to pay more attention to the regrowth of roots and the same colour will have a slightly different result on grey hair and may need adjusting. Natural or chemical dyes may be used (see **colouring hair**).

## MAKE-UP

Unless your hair becomes grey when you are very young, your skin tone will begin to change at about the same time. The temptation is to use more make-up (and elderly people with bad sight tend to do so), but it is more flattering to use less, and less likely to draw attention to any loss of skin texture. You will

**4** Apply khaki powder from centre of lid outwards, with dark taupe on outer edge, blended upwards into a lighter shade. Dust pale pink below brow with big brush. With fine brush, paint khaki line just above lashes.

**5** Apply dark brown mascara, black on tips. Comb between applications to separate the lashes.

**6** Brush very pale blusher over temples, cheekbones, round hairline, then stronger colour on cheekbones out to temples, on jaw in front of ears, around nostrils. Moisturize lips with vitamin E oil stick, paint on pink eyeshadow powder with brush for non-crease colour.

**Gymnastics**
See Sports

almost certainly need to change the foundation colour you use, as well as the type of product, as your skin becomes progressively drier. Avoid thick cake foundations which emphasize wrinkles. Use powder very lightly, preferably a translucent type.

Choose and use blushers extra carefully now; your complexion colour should soften with the colour of your hair. Try easily manageable powder types in peach and pink rather than brown tones (see **blusher**). Softer eye colours look good with grey hair, and brown or dark grey mascaras look better than hard blue or black. Powder shadows are more flattering to the texture of older skins than shiny ones. Soft, glossy colours for lips look best. All the pinks, corals and peaches are fine, but avoid sharp reds, shocking pinks and thick, flat types of lipstick. Mauvey tones can be successful, but keep the touch light and make sure they do not clash with what you are wearing.

# GUMS

*See also: dental hygienist; dentist; diet; flossing; orthodontist; teeth*

The gums are the pink membrane and underlying tissue which cover the jawbone. Healthy gums are salmon pink in colour and feel firm. They are essential to the well-being of your teeth: after the age of sixteen more teeth are lost through gum disease than through tooth decay.

### CARE OF GUMS
Periodontal (gum) disease starts in the crevice where the gum forms a cuff around the base of the tooth, so tooth cleaning should focus on this area.
1   Use disclosing tablets or a food colouring agent like Erythrocin dye to show up areas of plaque (a sticky layer of bacteria) left after brushing your teeth. You may well find that the gum margins are the very place you have cleaned least effectively.
2   Cut down on sugary sweets and snacks to decrease the plaque that causes gum disease as well as tooth decay.
3   Calculus is hardened plaque, also known as tartar. Any that builds up should be removed regularly by a dentist who may refer you to a dental hygienist for advice or treatment.
4   Choose a dentist who includes gum evaluation as an integral part of every check-up.

### GUM DISEASE
Tell-tale signs of early periodontal disease are gums which bleed on brushing or which are soft, swollen or sore. This early stage of periodontal disease is known as gingivitis. If it is left to develop, the gum and tooth will separate. Deep pockets which trap and retain the infection caused by plaque will form, making it almost impossible to remove without help. As the disease progresses it becomes known

as periodontitis: in this stage the underlying bone which holds the tooth is attacked and destroyed. Eventually there is no support left for the tooth or teeth which become loose and have to be removed.

In the early stages of gingivitis, the problem is reversible if all the calculus is removed, and a scrupulous homecare cleaning regime embarked upon. There are also new ultrasonic methods for scaling (removing calculus from) the teeth. More advanced cases may be referred to a periodontist for specialist treatments which may include minor surgery under local anaesthetic to remove deeper pockets (gingivectomy). Once the bone is affected treatment becomes more difficult.

# GYMS AND GYM EQUIPMENT

*See also: aerobics; breasts; exercise; exercises; fitness; weight training*

The increased awareness of the importance of health and fitness has generated a multiplicity of gym equipment used not only in gyms, but also in health and fitness centres, health spas, exercise and sports centres. These establishments offer facilities which vary from just an exercise bicycle and a set of dumb bells to cavernous rooms stocked with machines designed to exercise muscles you never knew you had.

### FOR AND AGAINST THE USE OF GYMS
The benefits of regular 'work-outs' at a gym can be great and varied. Free weights provide constant resistance, machines on the cam system provide variable resistance, machines on the hydraulic system provide accommodating resistance. So your muscles (see separate entry) and joints can get varied types of exercise.

But working out in a gym will not, alone, increase your overall fitness: your cardiovascular and respiratory systems need work too, in the form of aerobic exercise (see **fitness**). You will, however, be able to focus upon and exercise problem areas, gradually building up muscle strength, flexibility and endurance. Used as part of an all-round fitness programme, your physical and mental health can only benefit, provided that you consult your doctor first (see Caution Box in **exercises**) and work under supervision, according to instruction. There has been a tendency, recently, for people with sedentary lifestyles to plunge into gym workouts without being first assessed for fitness, instruction or warm-ups and cool-downs either side of exercise. This is foolish and potentially extremely dangerous.

### CHOOSING AND USING GYM EQUIPMENT
It is important to have expert tuition and constant supervision when using a gym. Many of the

machines are designed to exercise particular muscle groups (such as the many types of the cam variety, one of which is made under the famous brand name Nautilus) and if incorrectly used can result in stress and injury. Check carefully exactly what tuition and advice you will be given, before joining a gym. Ask for a trial training session, too, as this will give you the opportunity to assess the tuition level, and also the equipment which varies considerably according to the manufacturer. If body-building rather than weight training is your aim, look for a gym with plenty of equipment so that you will not have to wait in order to continue your session in the right order. For general conditioning purposes, order of use is not as crucial.

The best way to use gym equipment is as part of your overall fitness plan. Studies have shown that regular aerobic exercise (at least three times a week, for at least 15-20 minutes) has a positive effect on improving general health, and this type of exercise should be blended with your gym work. As with any other form of exercise, you MUST warm up and cool down to start the increase of your heart rate (keeping it within your training zone in this phase) and mobilizing joints and muscles (see **exercises**). You would be wise to start mobilizing your body with some exercises at home, such as the Daily Exercise Plan (see pages 124-125). If you feel any strains or pains which are unusual for you, stop using the equipment and seek advice.

Taking your pulse rate is not a very satisfactory way of monitoring this sort of exercise. Use it to monitor your warm-ups and cool-downs, then follow professional guidance carefully and meticulously so that you increase the stress on your body gradually and safely.

## HOME GYMS

Because of the variety and complexity of many exercise machines, and the need for expert tuition and constant supervision, most are not suitable for home use. The more complex machines can be extremely expensive, but there are various less expensive options readily useable at home:

Exercise bicycles provide good aerobic exercise, but does not exercise upper body muscles. Good used as part of a warm-up.

Buy a bike which feels solid and stable, a seat adjustable so that your leg can be straight at the bottom of the stroke, for safety. Must have variable braking pressure (some have flywheels up to as much as 18 kg (39½ lb); the larger the flywheel, the smoother and more comfortable the ride so that you can increase intensity as you get fitter. Some have heart rate monitors and mileometers, too. Look for a quiet model with a book clip, so you can read while you exercise.

Rowing machines can provide excellent aerobic exercise, and also work on upper and lower body muscles. However, they are potentially harmful for people with hypertension, so check with your doctor before purchasing one of these. Look for a solid machine which is adjustable to your size, which glides easily. Some models are adjustable for sculling and for other exercises, too.

Jogging machines provide good aerobic exercise, but you will need to jog to music to avoid boredom without the stimulation of the countryside or park! Good as part of a warm-up, too. Less stressful on the body than a road, but can still shock ankles, feet, knees and lower back.

Look for a machine with a soft 'floor' to minimize shock, and with adjustable speeds to suit the intensity you need.

Free weights, benches and accessories improve local muscular endurance or strength or power in many areas depending on how used. Wrist weights can be used for small muscle groups in the arms, or if used on ankles can work on large muscle groups in the legs.

Look for traditional cast iron weights and seek good professional tuition: you should always use free weights with a partner for safety.

Rebounder trampolines, if used for jogging, can provide good aerobic exercise (check your room has a high enough ceiling!) without shock to feet and lower body. Can also be used for exercises. Look for a solidly made type which is firmly sprung so that it does not sag once you are on it.

Multi-gyms can be used similarly to larger machines in gyms, but tend to be less smooth in operation, have lighter weights and less efficient systems. Work on strength and endurance.

Try machines out carefully before buying. Test for smoothness of operation, ease of folding up if you are short of space, potential for weights. If used in association with an exercise bicycle, for example, could provide good all-round system for fitness training. Ensure that you get good tuition and read all the manufacturer's literature.

# GYNAECOLOGIST

*See also: amenorrhoea; contraception; dysmenorrhoea; endometriosis; hysterectomy; menopause; menorrhagia; menstruation; metrorrhagia; premenstrual syndrome (PMS)*

The gynaecologist is a consultant physician who specializes in the study and treatment of diseases affecting females, particularly disorders of the reproductive system. Some gynaecological problems can be dealt with by a general practitioner or at a contraception clinic. You may be referred by your physician or general practitioner to a consultant gynaecologist if you suffer from menstrual disorders such as amenorrhoea (see separate entry) or ovarian cysts, for example. Women should have a gynaecological check-up annually, involving a smear test (see entry), breast examination (see entry) and an internal examination through the vagina to check that the uterus and cervix are healthy. Gynaecologists deal with contraception, too, but qualified advice on this subject is available from several sources, among them general practitioners and doctors in Family Planning Clinics.

# HAEMORRHOIDS

*See also: diet*

Haemorrhoids, commonly called piles, are over-dilated veins in the anus both internally and at the anal opening. They are caused by excessive pressure on the veins such as occurs during pregnancy, or if you are overweight or constipated. Symptoms include bleeding, soreness, itching and local discomfort.

### PREVENTION
Ensure that your diet contains enough fibre: this helps prevent constipation which causes acute pressure when bowels open.

### TREATMENT
Although commercially available suppositories may alleviate the symptoms, you should consult your doctor. In severe cases, haemorrhoids may need to be treated by cryosurgery (freeze-removal), injections to make them contract or surgical removal. Local anaesthetic creams are often used on prescription, but these should be used with care.

# HAIR

*See also: colouring hair; curling and straightening hair; cutting hair; dermatitis; gels; hair styles; hair transplants; highlighting; massaging; mousses; pH; sebum; skin; unwanted hair*

Hair consists of keratin, a strong substance also found in animal horns. Each hair has a central cortex, a soft core or medulla in the middle, and a hard, scaly cuticle protecting the whole. The hair follicle from which it grows is also the outlet for sebum from the sebaceous gland beneath (see **skin**). This sebum oils the hair, smoothing the cuticle and giving the head of hair a healthy shine.

When hair is out of condition because you are ill or have used chemical treatments on it, the cuticle is no longer smooth. Light reflection from the hair is impaired, making it look dull and hairs tend to cling to each other rather than hang freely, making hair feel matted.

When – as is often the case, particularly with long hair – the natural sebum cannot reach the ends of the hairs, the hair needs outside help in order to maintain lustre. The unprocessed cuticle, however, is durable, able to withstand frequent use of detergent-based cleansers, adverse weather conditions and a certain amount of combing.

Beneath the surface of the skin the hair emerges from the papilla. The papilla can produce a new hair even when the previous one has been pulled out 'by the roots'. The moment that the hair leaves the follicle it is in fact dead, yet it will remain on the head for approximately 6 years. The lifespan of the hair varies from person to person.

Hair grows at a rate of approximately 14 mm (½ inch) a month, though this varies. Whatever the rate, it is metabolically fixed. Hair growth over the 100,000 to 150,000 hairs on the head is staggered so that hair loss, normally between 100 and 150 hairs a day, is usually imperceptible.

### BRUSHING AND COMBING
Brushing and combing can damage hair, especially when it has been processed in any way, and should be kept to a minimum in order to avoid damaging the hair cuticles, overstimulating the scalp and spreading any scalp problems such as seborrhoeic dermatitis (see **dermatitis**). Combing is not as damaging as brushing, because it puts less pressure on the hairs. Choose a comb with wide, rounded teeth, preferably a vulcanized rubber type. Wet hair should not be brushed or combed more than is essential as hair is most susceptible to damage at this time. Never drag at tangles, always comb out ends carefully and gently and work up towards untangling the root end of the hairs gradually. Conditioners will help, as will specially designed 'wet hair' brushes.

### DIET AND YOUR HAIR
The condition of your hair reflects how you are feeling both physically and mentally: keeping fit is as much a part of good hair care as it is important to good general health. The state of your hair is a sign of whether or not you are eating well. The following foods are particularly important for hair: those high in vitamin B, such as wholegrains, yeast extracts, eggs, liver, kidneys; vitamin D-rich items such as fish, especially herring and salmon and cod liver oil; also those high in vitamins A, such as carrots and greens, fatty fish and eggs, and C, found in fresh fruit and vegetables. Liver is the only meat which contains significant amounts of all known vitamins including vitamin C.

### HAIR TYPES
- **Oily hair** When the sebaceous glands in the scalp produce excess sebum the hair quickly becomes lank. Dark, coarse, springy hair is less likely to appear oily than fine, blonde hair which tends to lie close to the scalp anyway. Many women find that hair becomes oilier when hormone levels rise suddenly, particularly at puberty and also at ovulation and during the pre-menstrual phase of the menstrual cycle. Hormonal changes during the later part of pregnancy reduce oiliness. To keep oily hair looking clean and shining, it is necessary to shampoo frequently, but if you use a harsh formula all the time you may well get a flaky scalp condition. Always use a mild shampoo (see also **dandruff**). Frequent washing ensures a clean, unclogged scalp which might otherwise exacerbate the oily condition.
- **Dry hair** Dehydrated hair is a result of lack of sebum on the hair causing it to dry out at cellular level. Because dehydration makes the hair

less elastic, it is more susceptible to breakage and damage and will only stretch half as far as normal hair. It needs more protection than normal hair from the drying effects of sun, seawater, and stress from brushing and styling. Only shampoo once when washing, massaging scalp thoroughly, with a creamy shampoo. The cleaner the scalp, the more sebum will be able to move along the hair shaft, so don't be afraid to wash your hair as often as you want to.

**Normal hair** Healthy, silky hair without over-dry ends or over-oily roots is the easiest to care for and cope with: it withstands reasonable processing and colouring well. Wash it as frequently as you like, using a specially formulated shampoo, and condition regularly.

**Mixed condition** This hair type occurs naturally when over-production of sebum results in blockage of the hair follicle at scalp level. The hair shaft does not become oily, but the scalp is prone to flaking and possibly to dandruff problems. Oily hair with dry split ends after overprocessing can masquerade as mixed condition hair. Have your hair trimmed regularly to prevent this. When washing, treat the scalp as for oily hair, and the hair itself as for dry.

### Hair problems
**Allergies** Some people react badly to detergents in shampoos and conditioners and to colourants, tints, bleaches and perfumes, and experience scalp itching and rashes. If you tend to be sensitive to any of these test on your skin first, then on your hair. In the case of tints and colourants, patch tests should always be done (see **colouring hair**). Specially formulated cleansers as alternatives to shampoo are available from trichologists. If your facial skin is very sensitive use plenty of face cream around the

**Hairline**
See Hair transplants

**Hair pieces**
See Wigs

**Hair removal**
See Unwanted hair

edge of your hairline before washing hair to protect your skin from the detergent contained in the shampoo.

**Alopecia** (baldness) This disorder takes several forms, the most severe of which is total hair loss (see **alopecia**).

**Dandruff** It is normal for the top layer of dead cells on the scalp to be shed invisibly. Dandruff can occur either when skin cells are growing faster than normally, or when the dead cells on the surface have become clogged with dirt or sebum and failed to remove themselves naturally. A dehydrated scalp which resembles dandruff can result from dehydration while travelling. Drink masses of water to combat this. The appearance of flakiness on the scalp may be due to over-harsh detergents, may be attributed to a build-up of oil on the scalp to which dirt is attracted, or to a mild reaction to a shampoo. Whatever the case, massage the scalp well and use a small amount of a different, very mild shampoo to wash the hair. If the condition persists, consult a dermatologist or trichologist. You may be allergic to a hair product, or the itching could be a symptom of a skin condition such as psoriasis. If your scalp is very dry, massage it with a few drops of almond oil. Do consult a dermatologist or trichologist if your supposed dandruff does not clear up with these treatments, or if it has large flakes, is very itchy or makes the scalp bleed. (See also **dandruff, pH**).

**Lice** Head lice are quite common among schoolchildren and, contrary to popular belief, thrive in clean hair. Normal shampoo will not kill the eggs: buy a specially formulated shampoo at a pharmacy and follow the instructions diligently. The dead eggs must be combed out with a special fine comb.

**Trichotillomania** This is the medical name for compulsive pulling out or chewing of hair. Often a symptom of stress, it can also be a sign of sexual frustration or an attempt to gain attention. The sufferer may need counselling to help break the habit.

# HAIRDRESSERS

*See also: colouring hair; curling and straightening hair; hair; hair styles; highlighting; wigs*

Select your hairdresser very carefully: once you have had a radical (and expensive) new haircut or perm, for example, it will be with you for some time. New hair will only reappear at a rate of approximately 14 mm (½ inch) a month. Inexpert hair processing can be disastrous, leading to broken or split hair shafts or discoloration of the hair, so follow the guidelines below to help avoid disappointment.

### CHOOSING YOUR HAIRDRESSER
Full training and proficiency in all aspects of hairdressing are of course the primary considerations. Hairdressers have to serve a long apprenticeship, undertake periods of professional training and pass exams before qualifying.

Personal recommendation is often the best way to find a good hairdresser: ask a friend you trust (and whose haircut and styling always seem to suit them) for the name of their hairdresser. Magazines regularly publish lists of reputable hairdressing salons; these may help you too.

Avoid being enticed into salons with offers of free colouring, cutting or perming. There are two main dangers: one, that the choice of style will be the salon's, not yours, and it may suit neither you nor your hair; the other, that your hair will almost certainly be done by a trainee hairdresser, probably without full supervision. Results will not be reliable, and could be disastrous; in these instances one gets what one pays for.

Remember that a really good hairdresser will check the condition of your hair and scalp before starting any hairdressing process. When helping you choose a style, he or she will take into account your hairline at brow and neck, as well as the colour, texture and recent processing of your hair and will also enquire about any medication you are or have recently been using, as this will also affect the condition of your hair.

No good hairdresser will undertake to 'copy' a style from a magazine for you. He or she will want to check first that the basic look will suit you, your lifestyle and clothes, and may well suggest modifications to make the style more suitable to your hair's texture or colour, the shape of your head and your hairline, too.

# HAIR STYLES

*See also: colouring hair; curling and straightening hair; hair; hairdressers; highlighting*

A new hair style can be a tremendous morale-booster, an excellent cure for a fit of the blues and a good fashion investment. It can lift your whole appearance and update clothes you were beginning to tire of. On the whole, it is better to plan the change well in advance, especially if you are going to try out a new hairdresser (see separate entry). You can afford to bow to whim a little more safely if your hairdresser knows you well. He or she will give you a truthful opinion as to whether the style you want will suit you, and, if convinced that it will not, can suggest alternatives which will still achieve the right look. Bear in mind the aftercare problem, too. Some styles can be tiresome to care for, requiring setting on rollers and protection from rain and steam (see below).

### HAIR STYLE AND PERSONAL STYLE
To the outside world, your hair style becomes an intrinsic part of you, so be sure that your new hair style will suit you in every way. Bear in mind your personal style, fashion sense, and the type of clothes you expect to be wearing over the next 2 months or so. Your lifestyle, too, is an important

consideration. A hair style which involves frequent cutting, and needs daily curling and backcombing may be great for days spent in town, but unsuitable for windswept country life (and too time-consuming to maintain; see below). Your job may well determine your priorities: for some people high fashion is of paramount importance, for others, styling speed after washing.

### FACE SHAPE AND HAIRLINE
Almost as many rules for hair styles considered suitable for particular face shapes have been laid down as for clothes types considered suitable for particular body shapes. Magazines and 'style' books are full of rules such as those which proscribe flat shoes for short women or very short-cropped hairstyles for fat women. As with many rules, these are founded on traditional, often sensible advice. Nevertheless, to spend one's life studiously avoiding a certain look, a whole range of garments and hair styles, seems both unpleasant and unnecessary. The important thing is to be happy with your appearance: you have to look at yourself in the mirror every day and wash, condition, dry and shape your hair into the style you choose. The choice is ultimately yours, not that of any fashion arbiter or hairdresser.

Try out the style you like on yourself by pinning your hair into the closest approximation – seeing how your face looks with a fringe, for example. If you are planning a perm, try curling your hair into a similar style (or have a trial run with your hairdresser) before having the hair chemically changed. As you change your hair style you will be able to build up your own set of rules determined by your discoveries as to what suits you and what does not.

Another important consideration is your natural hairline. Particularly if you are planning a very short style, study your hairline at brow and at neck. If the neck hairline is straggly, and the hairline low on the forehead, for example, you may want to keep more length. Close-cropped styles can emphasize an attractive hairline. Look at the way the hair grows, too: often one section of hair in either hairline grows at a different angle, in a whorl, or sticks up.

Bear in mind that one day you will want to change style again and may have to wait some time for the present cut to grow out. If you like frequent style changes you would be wise to have a progression in mind when making any change. A close crop, for example, progresses well into a softly layered cut which can be chemically curled, or scrunch dried into rough curls with gel, or 'spiked' with mousse or gel to give it firmness.

### STYLE AND COLOUR
Changing your hair colour along with your style can be great fun (see **colouring hair**). If you are contemplating a permanent or semi-permanent colour change you are best advised to have colour professionally applied.

If you want a natural look, you are best advised not to change your hair colour more than a few tones. There are exceptions: if you have fair skin you have more freedom since fair-skinned people natur-

ally have hair varying from platinum blonde to black. If you are olive to black-skinned, staying on the dark side for hair looks most natural. Remember that permanent colour *is* permanent, and that if you grow your hair into a new style you will have to recolour the roots or have the whole head recoloured.

### HAIR STYLE MAINTENANCE
If you are the sort of person who really enjoys styling their hair, and can make time to do so, then you have the widest possible choice of styles. If, on the other hand, you have little time, little inclination, or are not very good with your hair, then you must take this into consideration when choosing a style.

Ask your hairdresser's advice: he or she will show you how to style your hair and will advise on the products and equipment you will need in order to do so. It is helpful to watch exactly how your hairdresser dries and shapes your hair so that you can imitate this. Many styles now involve using setting gel, lotion or mousse. These vary in strength. Lotions are the mildest, extra-strength gel or mousse the firmest (gel brushes out, mousse must be washed out). They are easy to use, on wet or dry hair, when applied to each section of hair individually as you style it. (See also **curling and straightening hair**.)

### HAIR ACCESSORIES
There are innumerable ways in which you can add detail to your hair style by using accessories,

whether plain or decorated combs, beads, pearls, ribbons, bows, grips or clips. Remember, however, that over-accessorizing your hair can have as unfortunate an effect as over-accessorizing your clothes. Be subtle in your use of decorative extras to follow and emphasize the line of your chosen hair style rather than detract from it. Choose colours and designs to match your outfit. Magazines offer new ideas regularly. Your hairdresser will advise on choosing accessories, too, and will also be able to show you how to use them in your hair, so do ask for help and watch as he or she uses them. Clips, grips and combs can be particularly hard to handle, and the hairdresser's tips will be invaluable. Take care not to damage hair.

# HAIR TRANSPLANTS

*See also: alopecia; cosmetic surgery; hair; wigs*

The technique of hair transplanting was developed in the early 1950s to treat war victims. Initially, there was much uncertainty as to whether implanted hair would 'take' or fall out. With modern methods there is a good success rate and transplanting can be used on scarred areas if the scar tissue is strong enough. Transplanting should only be carried out by a qualified cosmetic surgeon or dermatologist.

There is much dispute about the use of hair transplanting to disguise genetically induced alopecia or baldness. The surgery is often expensive, uncomfortable and sometimes does not work. Careful assessment of each patient is essential. The possibility of further hair loss which will leave the grafts exposed and give an extremely unnatural appearance (calling for yet more grafting to disguise it) is a strong consideration. This applies particularly to young men who already have extensive hair loss and are likely to lose more. Seek the independent advice of a doctor or trichologist before embarking on hair transplants.

The most common transplanting method is *punch grafting*. Carried out under local anaesthetic, tiny plugs of skin containing about 15 hair follicles are taken from the back of the head (donor site) and inserted into the balding area. About 30-100 grafts are inserted in one session although it is now possible to transplant single hairs. Several weeks later when the scalp has settled down hair starts to appear. More grafts can be added after six months and several sessions are usually required to achieve an acceptable appearance. However, there is a limit to the number of donor grafts available for hair transplanting on any one individual, and because of rejection problems grafts cannot be obtained from other people.

No hair transplant, however skilfully performed, looks completely natural. The transplanted hair always has a tufted look, but this effect can be greatly reduced by in-filling between grafts with much smaller or single hair grafting. The key to how suc-

cessful the treatment will be depends on the patient's age, hair type and the extent of baldness. Fine, blonde, straight hair, for example, gives less satisfactory results than does dark, thick, curly hair.

The male hormones, androgens, are involved in hair loss and anti-androgen drugs are used to suppress their action. Treatment for genetic hair loss with oral anti-androgen cyproterone acetate has proved beneficial in women, although this drug is at present banned in the US. Research to find an effective topical (used on the skin) anti-androgen continues with researchers confident that an effective treatment should be possible within the next few years.

### HAIR WEAVING
Hair weaving involves sewing the edges of a hairpiece to the person's own hair, as close to the scalp as possible in order to cover up a bald patch. The fitting is undertaken by a specially trained hairdresser. Woven hairpieces are secure enough for the wearer to be able to sleep, swim or shower without them coming off, as may happen with those hairpieces stuck on to the scalp with glue or double-sided tape.

As the natural hair grows, the wig loosens and restitching is required approximately every six weeks. The hairpiece is woven on a skin-coloured base and the hair used is matched to the existing hair colour, providing a very natural looking appearance. Occasional problems arise if the density of the hairpiece is greater than the original hair; other problems are hair breakage in supporting hairs and scalp problems beneath the woven section.

# HALITOSIS

*See also: dental hygienist; diet; gums; mouthwashes*

Halitosis, or bad breath, has many causes. Contrary to advertising, commercially available mouthwashes are not usually effective cures, but are only useful in short-term cases, for example, after a rich, spicy meal, where thorough teeth-cleaning and flossing would have a similar effect. Garlic is a more difficult problem: remedies for the lasting smell and taste vary from eating parsley, to sipping teas made from rosemary, peppermint or parsley.

Some halitosis results from nose, throat or lung infections; in these cases only treating the cause will bring about a cure. Bad breath as a result of smoking will not be remedied by mouthwashes, although they may provide very temporary cover: giving up smoking is the only permanent solution. Digestive problems such as constipation and diarrhoea (see **diet**), some liver diseases, hunger and the ketosis process (see separate entry) while dieting are other causes.

Periodontal disease (see **gums**) can produce severe halitosis, particularly if the disease is advanced. Guard against this by cleaning and flossing regularly, making regular visits to your dentist and/or dental hygienist, and being alert to early signs of gum disease such as bleeding, about which your dentist can best advise you.

### AVOIDING HALITOSIS

As long as the cause is not respiratory infection, which must be medically treated, halitosis can be prevented by following a healthy diet which keeps you free of digestive problems.

# HANDS

*See also: calluses; chilblains; cuticles; dermabrasion; diet; electrodesiccation; liver spots; manicure; moisturizing; moles; nails; skin; sun; tanning; witch hazel*

Our hands are on permanent show, so their softness and smoothness should be an actuality rather than an aim. Yet they are subject to constant abuse, from extremes of temperature, soaps, harsh detergents, shampoos, and quite simply, the dehydrating after-effects of exposure to water.

The hand's flexibility is derived from its structure: including the wrist it consists of 28 small bones. While the skin on the back of the hand has sebaceous and sweat glands which lubricate and soften the skin, the palm has only sweat glands. Skin on the palm tends to be drier except when heat or an emotional reaction activates the sweat glands and produces the infamous clammy hand.

Skin on the back of the hand ages and sags quickly, so should be kept extra well-moisturized. Liver spots on the backs of hands may possibly be made less obvious with a fade cream or skin lightener: they help dissolve the concentration of melanin that causes these and also uneven pigmentation and freckles.

Hands reflect your health. Swollen joints can indicate arthritis or rheumatism and although exercises can help, medical advice should be sought.

### CARING FOR YOUR HANDS

Always wear rubber gloves when doing washing up or household tasks. Apart from drying the skin, the action of soap and water on the cuticle around the nail causes it to weaken and split, allowing bacteria to enter.

Always wear a barrier cream (or a heavy hand lotion) to protect hands when washing, dry them thoroughly afterwards and finally apply moisturizer to prevent dryness and chapping.

Use tepid water and mild, unscented soap for washing hands, using a nail brush if they are very dirty. Bleach stained areas with lemon juice, and then use soap and a pumice stone. Rinse, dry and apply hand cream liberally, massaging the palms and stretching finger joints.

Wear gloves when gardening and during cold

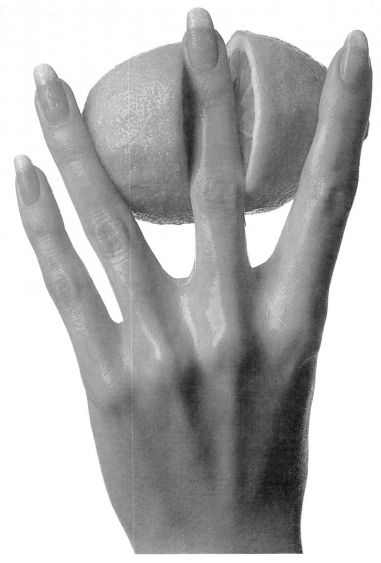

weather, to avoid chilblains. Stimulate circulation in cold hands by massaging fingers.

Use a sun filter cream every day in summer on the backs of your hands to protect them from the sun. Smooth, soft hands are spoilt by bitten, split or discoloured nails. Biting nails causes jagged and uneven growth and makes nails weak and likely to split. Eat a well balanced diet, and manicure nails regularly to keep them an equal, rounded length. If you wear polish, use oil-based removers rather than acetone-based which cause nails to dry and split.

Discourage hangnails and broken skin by a daily massage with cuticle cream, or a Vitamin E capsule (200 iu) rubbed round the nail.

### TREATMENTS
- Soak callused hands in warm olive oil.
- An application of warm paraffin wax softens and smooths hands and nails: once cool, the wax is easily peeled off.
- Smother hands with thick cream and put on cotton gloves – heat helps the skin absorb the cream.

**Headaches**
See Migraine
and headaches

# HANGOVERS

*See also: alcohol*

The symptoms of a hangover vary from dry mouth, headache and nausea to anxiety and depression which can all be traced to the effects of alcohol. Dehydration, particularly when there is diarrhoea and vomiting; an over-accumulation of acid in the blood; low blood sugar level, and irritation of the stomach may all result.

Furthermore, the action of congeners – by-products of the fermentation or distillation process – can worsen hangover symptoms. The more congeners a drink contains, the more likely you are to have a hangover: brandy has the most, then red wine, rum, sherry, whisky, beer, white wine, gin and lastly vodka.

### COPING WITH HANGOVERS
There is no scientifically proven hangover cure and no way of avoiding one except by not drinking. Hangover symptoms are actually withdrawal symptoms. Since alcohol is addictive, to turn to 'a hair of the dog' only delays sobriety, and may lead to the far greater problem of dependency.

- Coffee will not sober you up but make you wakeful and restless, dehydrate you still further, and increase the likelihood of a headache.
- Before and while drinking, line your stomach by eating foods high in fat and carbohydrate.
- Avoid high-congener drinks (see above).
- Drink as much water as you can before going to bed and again on waking.
- Do not take aspirin: it will irritate your stomach still further. Take paracetamol (acetaminophen in US).

# HAY FEVER

*See also: allergens and allergies; dermatitis*

Hay fever is one of the most well-known allergic reactions. Symptoms include wheezing, sneezing, even asthma, streaming nose and eyes. Traditionally these have been treated with anti-histamines, but large doses cause unwelcome drowsiness. Since the pollen season is long – tree pollens are in the air from January onwards, grass pollens from mid-May until September, moulds continuing on until October – such treatment is not ideal. Desensitization, a gradual build-up of resistance, to the specific pollens to which there is allergy can be successful, especially if carried out several years running. Various preventative drugs can block development of hay fever. Where decongestants and anti-histamines are not enough, cortisone sprays may be prescribed.

# HEALTH AND HEALTH CHECKS

*See also: awareness; diet; exercise; fitness*

Good health is our most precious possession, directly related to both the quality and length of our lives. All-round good health implies physical fitness, mental soundness and emotional stability. Without health, every area of our lives is sure to suffer: work, relaxation and relationships.

It often appears that some people are 'naturally' healthy while others are not. There is an element of chance in the bad health that may befall us, but the supply of nutrients before birth, and our diet during early life are also very important in forming healthy bones and tissues. Early lessons help form healthy eating and exercising habits, too. Yet good health is mainly a matter of resolution – it is within the reach of most people, male and female, young and old, though it may take time to achieve.

The most important factors which contribute to the state of our health are diet, exercise and lifestyle. All these are within our control and hence we can regulate our health to a large extent.

1 The first step to good health is to cultivate an all-round awareness of health. This involves being familiar with the principles of a nutritious diet; knowing what different types of exercise your body needs; being aware of the dangers of certain habits and behaviour patterns, particularly smoking, drinking and stress.
2 The second step to good health is to recognize to what extent and in what way these factors figure in your life. Do you stuff yourself with junk food? Do you shun walking in favour of the car? Smoke thirty cigarettes a day?
3 Do something about these harmful elements in your life, in order to make it better. It may require great resolution and willpower to change your lifestyle, but it is worth the effort.

All the different facets of healthy living are interrelated. Poor diet or a smoking habit make it harder to exercise. Lack of exercise aggravates feelings of stress which in turn encourages you to smoke or drink, so make an effort in one area and it should pay dividends in the others too.

### HEALTH CHECKS
Your health is primarily your own responsibility, but despite a healthy lifestyle, disease can strike. If you know something is wrong you will go to your doctor for his advice, but in many cases the chances of complete recovery or reversal are much greater if the problem is caught early on – *before* you become aware of the symptoms. This form of preventive health screening has been popular in the US for many years and general and specific health checks are becoming more widespread in the UK.

**General physical check-ups** give an overall picture of your health and should indicate if there are more specific problems which need further investigation. For a fit person, once every two years from the age of 35 should probably be adequate. In the US an annual physical examination including a gynaecological check up is recommended. If you are embarking on a special diet or new form of exercise a general check-up is always advisable.

**Blood pressure checks** are important because high blood pressure is a risk factor in coronary heart disease. Anyone over 35 should have a blood pressure reading every year. People of any age who are overweight, who smoke, or who take the contraceptive pill should be checked at least annually.

**Blood cholesterol checks** are also important in spotting a higher risk of coronary heart disease. Their use is controversial. The National Health Service in the UK only provides for these where there are signs of high cholesterol. Tests early on in life can pick up congenital high lipid levels which can then be treated: later tests then monitor levels. This is especially important where other risks are present, such as being overweight, a heavy smoker or taking the contraceptive pill, which increase the likelihood and dangers of high blood cholesterol levels: more frequent checks are necessary. Pre-menopausal women are less at risk than men (who should have annual checks from the age of 35), but they should still have occasional tests. In the US annual checks are recommended for all adults.

**Electrocardiogram (ECG) readings** show up certain, although by no means all, abnormalities of the heart, and in a healthy person can give a baseline pattern against which future differences can be measured and the causes investigated. They are most valuable for men over 35 (the group most at risk from cardiovascular diseases).

**Breast examinations** to check for lumps are essential for every woman from the age of puberty. Self-examination should be learned and carried out every month just after the end of the period, when any lumps will be most obvious (see **breasts, breast examination**). Clinical examination by a health care professional should be carried out yearly after the age of 35, and yearly before, too, if you are on the contraceptive pill. Mammography (low dose X-ray) as a routine screening device is normally used only for women who run a relatively high risk of breast cancer: particularly those over 50, those over 40 with a family history of breast cancer; those with a history of cancer in one breast.

**Cervical smears or 'Pap' tests** are used to detect the presence of potentially cancerous cells on the cervix. This test is one of great value since, if pre-malignant (pre-cancerous) cells are found early enough, the disease can almost always be totally cured. In the UK the NHS recommends that the test be done at least every five years from the age of first intercourse and more frequently if you have a history of sexually transmitted diseases, frequent partner change or if a repeat is recommended after the last smear. Many people feel that, due to the link between frequent partner change and the incidence of cervical cancer, the smear should be taken every year from the age of first intercourse. In the US an annual check is recommended.

**Pelvic examination** should be carried out at the same time as the cervical smear, to check for any abnormalities of the uterus, ovaries or vagina.

**Dental check-ups** of both the teeth and gums should be carried out every six months.

**Sight testing** should be carried out in a child throughout the school years. Regular testing is important, especially in later years, to detect glaucoma and cataracts. Sight tests check for long (far) or short (near) sightedness and any other problems such as a squint so that corrective glasses or contact lenses can be prescribed.

**Pre-pregnancy checks** should be carried out for immunity to rubella (German measles).

**Ante-natal check-ups** are essential for every pregnant woman. From the second to the sixth month checks should be once a month, then once a fortnight, then once a week in the last month. The mother's weight and blood pressure are checked. Urine is tested for protein and sugar. Blood will be tested to identify blood type, assess haemoglobin levels, establish immunity to German measles, for syphilis and possibly to detect some foetal abnormalities. At about 13 weeks a second blood test will be done to check for spina bifida in the foetus. Ultrasound scans may be carried out to check the baby's size, position and for certain abnormalities. An amniocentesis (drawing off a small amount of amniotic fluid for examination) may be offered if it is thought that there may be a risk of the baby suffering from Down's syndrome or spina bifida.

# HEALTH FARMS

*See also: exercise; exercises; fitness; health; massage; slimming and fattening diets; stress*

When the ultra-slender form became fashionable in the 1920s, discreet establishments in Europe and the United States began to offer slimming 'cures'. Later, specialized skin treatments, medical or paramedical treatments were incorporated. During the last ten years what health farms offer has undergone a further change. They have widened their scope to encompass every aspect of all-round well-being.

Health resorts are often equipped with a barrage of equipment such as exercise machines, swimming pools and hot tubs, and have beauty and health clinics providing every beauty treatment, and exercise and relaxation classes too. Most health farms also have hairdressing salons.

Visits to health farms are now often treated as holidays, and the benefits can last much longer than those from two weeks on a beach. The time spent away from the outside world can provide a useful pause for rethinking one's lifestyle. Of course there are a host of specialists on hand to advise you on diet, exercise, fitness, ways of coping with stress, and to suggest how you might start on a new regime.

Facilities do vary from place to place so study available information before making your choice.

**Hearing**
See Ears

# HEART

*See also: aerobics; biofeedback; blood pressure; cholesterol; circulation; diet; exercise; exercises; fibre; fitness; relaxation; stress*

### THE HEART IN ACTION

The heart, which is a muscular organ about the size of a clenched fist, weighs about 255 g (9 oz), and is situated between the lungs in the centre of the chest. It consists largely of the cardiac muscle (myocardium) surrounded by membranes. It is basically a simple pump which beats on average 70 times a minute. It consists of two halves, each subdivided into an upper part, the atrium and a lower part, the ventricle.

Deoxygenated blood arrives from the body, by way of the large venae cavae (veins) in the right atrium. From here it passes through the tricuspid valve, which shuts immediately to prevent seepage, into the right ventricle and travels through the pulmonary valve to the pulmonary artery and then on to the lungs for reoxygenation. This newly oxygenated blood then returns to the left atrium through the pulmonary veins, passes to the left ventricle through the mitral valve, and is then pumped out into the body through the aorta, the body's main artery, and then its many branches.

The contractions of the myocardium which cause the heart to pump are instigated by a series of electrical impulses. These are meticulously timed to perpetuate a regular beat and can be monitored on an Electrocardiograph machine.

### KEEPING YOUR HEART FIT

Medical research, particularly in the last two decades, has produced evidence that regular sustained exercise, good diet, and the control of stress can all lead to a lower incidence of heart disease.

### DIET

A diet that is good for the heart is balanced. Step up your consumption of fruit and vegetables and eat as many of them as possible raw. Cut down on fatty meat; substitute fish or poultry instead. Increase your daily intake of fibre and do away with white bread and flour, pastries and cakes. Eat less salt and saturated fats: season food with herbs and lemon juice, replace butter and animal fats with polyunsaturated margarine and monounsaturated or polyunsaturated oils.

### EXERCISE

Steady aerobic exercise (see **aerobics**) carried out regularly increases the heart's ability to pump blood: more is pumped through for less beats. This can actually strengthen the heart muscle, too. Oxygen reaches the tissues more quickly and waste products are removed sooner, preventing dangerous deposits from accumulating in the arteries. For most people, this can be built up steadily and gradually without danger.

Sudden violent exertion, however, may place unreasonable stress on the heart, so aim for a gradual build-up of exercise and stamina. Always consult your doctor before starting any new exercise programme and follow his advice carefully.

### RELAXATION

Stressful situations cause the hormones adrenaline and noradrenaline to be pumped into the bloodstream. They stimulate a complex chain of reactions all designed to help the body deal with the dangerous situation it is in. The heartbeat is increased and blood pressure rises as extra oxygen and newly released blood sugar is pumped to the muscles. It follows that continuing stress puts the whole system under severe strain and increases the likelihood of heart disease, arteriosclerosis, stroke and heart attack.

Relaxing will help to alleviate stress and the exhaustion, insomnia and tension which can accompany it. How you find it easiest to relax is very personal: see **relaxation** for ideas.

### DISEASE POTENTIAL

Smokers are twice as likely to die of heart disease as non-smokers: women, especially those over 30, who also take the combined contraceptive pill are at even higher risk of heart disease; excessive alcohol intake can damage the heart muscle, and overweight and obesity increase the risk of heart disease because of the increased demands they place on the whole system.

The incidence of heart disease is still lower in pre-menopausal women than in men, but it is increasing, possibly due to women leading more stressful lives, but also due to poor diet, lack of exercise and to increased smoking among women. After the menopause, the incidence for men and women of comparable age is on a par. Many doctors feel that regular health screening is particularly important to those over 40: if the reading is high, swift drug and diet action can be taken to help prevent heart disease.

The heart in cross section reveals it to be made up of cardiac muscle surrounded by membrane.

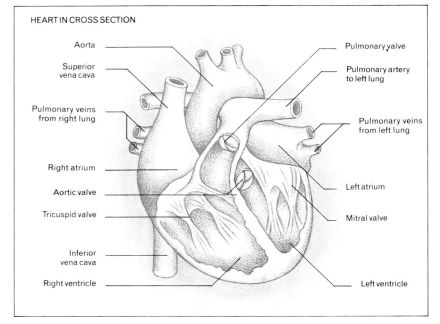

HEART IN CROSS SECTION

Aorta

Superior vena cava

Pulmonary veins from right lung

Right atrium

Aortic valve

Tricuspid valve

Inferior vena cava

Right ventricle

Pulmonary valve

Pulmonary artery to left lung

Pulmonary veins from left lung

Left atrium

Mitral valve

Left ventricle

# HENNA

*See also: colouring hair*

Henna dye comes from the plant *Lawsonia alba* which grows along the coast of North Africa and in the Middle East. To make henna, the leaves of the plant are dried, crushed into a fine powder, then mixed with water (lemon juice or vinegar is sometimes used instead). Henna comes in shades varying from red or burgundy to black or even neutral (which has no colouring properties). Moroccan henna is lightest in colour and conditioning value; Iranian is the richest and most sought after.

Non-toxic and hypo-allergenic henna is often used for its colour in natural cosmetics. Both its colouring and conditioning properties are made use of in many henna-containing shampoos and conditioners. By itself, it can be used for natural, semi-permanent hair colouring (see **colouring hair** for details), and also as a final rinse after washing to enhance natural colour and to condition.

In various cultures henna is commonly used to paint designs on the skin, especially the face, hands and feet for decoration and as part of religious ceremonies. The colour generally lasts for several weeks.

# HERBALISM

*See also: allopathy; herbs; holism*

Herbs have been used for medicinal purposes since time immemorial. Some 5000 years ago in ancient China their actions were set down in the earliest treatise on medicinal herbs. Herbs were used medicinally in ancient Egypt, Rome and Greece, in Biblical times, by North American Indians and by tribal doctors. In medieval Britain herbalists were much consulted and highly respected, but physicians using a combination of treatments gradually took over their role. One of the most famous herbals – a directory of the various herbs, their uses and properties – is that of Nicholas Culpeper, dating from the early seventeenth century.

When it became possible to extract the active ingredients from herbs to use alone, and later as synthetic drugs became common, herbalism fell into disuse, but it is now undergoing a renaissance. Modern herbalism deals with the medicinal use of herbs both externally and internally. Herbalists can treat a whole range of chronic and acute problems ranging from minor coughs and colds to major problems such as arthritis and hypertension.

Generally speaking, allopathic (see **allopathy**) doctors (practitioners of conventional medicine) in the UK and USA are sceptical of herbalism, and health standard authorities are wary too, because of the difficulties involved in testing and standardiz-

ing herbal products. However, the World Health Organization promotes it as a relevant therapy.

In modern herbalism, the emphasis is very much on preventive medicine, on treating inherent weaknesses in individuals before they become actual illnesses. Dealing with causes rather than merely alleviating the symptoms of illness is another distinctive feature.

Herbal treatment is very individual. Not only do herbalists each have different preferred herbs for the same ailment, but the most efficacious herb for the patient's problem varies, too. Some herbalists recommend fasting, or rest, or a cleansing diet when taking herbal remedies, while others permit patients to use herbal remedies at the same time as allopathic medicines are being taken unless there are contra-indications. Always check with both your doctor and your herbalist before taking herbal remedies while on a course of drugs.

Although there are many good books on herbalism and self-treatment available, you should consult a medical herbalist both for diagnosis and advice if you are thinking of using herbs in this way. And if you are on a course of treatment prescribed by your allopathic doctor, *never* stop this without discussing your feelings and plans with him or her first as you could endanger yourself.

# HERBS

*See also: aloe vera; aromatherapy; baths and bathing; herbalism; holism; infusions; jojoba*

'God of his infinite goodness and bounty hath by the medium of Plants, bestowed almost all food, clothing and medicine upon man': Thomas Johnson, Gerard's Herbal, 1636. The potential of plants, or herbs, to heal and promote health has been known and used for centuries. And this knowledge was used in the development of allopathic medicine, too. With increasing interest in the whole range of healing methods, herbalism is undergoing a renaissance. The glossary below lists some common herbs and their uses:

### Agrimony
Gargle with a decoction of common agrimony leaves and flowers to ease throat inflammation. Infuse bathwater with a handful of leaves for rheumatism, stiffness and tiredness. Herbalists use agrimony infusions for cystitis, incontinence, indigestion.

### Aniseed
Take an infusion for indigestion and for bronchitis infuse with 4 parts wine to 1 part of the infusion, 6 drops of this mixture in a wineglass of hot water to aid sleep. Helps in childhood coughs, acts as a pest repellent, aromatic oil destroys lice. Ground, it can be used in pot pourris. Ground aniseed in a facepack may help fade freckles.

### Balm
Drink an infusion for cramps, catarrh, asthma, toothache, migraine, sickness and dizziness. Promotes relaxation and sleep when used in herb pillows. Use in pot pourris for lemony scent.

### Basil
Anti-bacterial, mild laxative, its essential oil is used as inhalant to clear sinuses. Infused in bathwater helps promote sleep.

### Bergamot
Infusion can be drunk at bedtime. Infuse fresh leaves and stems in warm bathwater for tired aching limbs. Common ingredient in scent, adds orange aroma to pot pourris.

### Borage
Take an infusion as a laxative; for fever, liver and kidney problems, and as a relaxant. Use fresh leaves in facepacks for dry skin.

### Burdock
Infusion acts as a diuretic and blood purifier. Used to treat cystitis, dandruff, as a facial steam.

### Caraway
Take powdered or crushed seeds with a teaspoon of sugar in a wineglass of hot water, for colic, flatulence and upset tummy.

### Cayenne
Liniment, plasters or tincture containing cayenne (or milder form, paprika which is high in vitamin C) can be applied to the skin to increase blood flow for rheumatism, arthritis and chilblains. Gargle for toothache and sore throat.

### Chamomile
Infusion aids sleep, soothes inflammation and irritation, relieves migraine, headache, promotes relaxation, settles indigestion and wind, aids healing. Used as final hair rinse eases dandruff and enhances colour of fair hair. If used to rinse face, cleanses and keeps skin soft and supple. Used as a facial steam for acne. Lie down and put two cool damp chamomile teabags on puffy eyes or dark circles. It is soothing as an infusion for a bath.

### Chervil
Use root and leaves for flatulence. Used in cough medicines as an expectorant. Rub root on to facial blemishes to use as an astringent and antiseptic facewash.

### Coltsfoot
Used in many commercially available cough medicines as an expectorant. Fluid extract available. Contains zinc. Helps reduce redness of facial thread veins.

### Comfrey
Soothes stomach irritations, ulcers and aids in bronchitis. Contains allantoin which encourages wound-healing. Roots and leaves in poultice or ointment can be used for treating bruises, swellings and rheumatic pains. Soothing when infused in bath for irritation and rashes. Infusion of leaves can be used as a lotion for dry skin, promoting softer skin, also healing.

### Coriander
Relieves flatulence, encourages sleep.

### Dill
The leaf is a powerful diuretic. Best natural source of potassium. The root is a liver tonic and mild laxative. Used in treating skin problems.

### Dandelion
Seeds are used to make gripe water, given to babies for hiccups. Chew seeds to sweeten breath.

### Elderflower
Root infusion acts as a diuretic, also is a purgative and stimulant, used for colds and sinus catarrh. Leaves used for bruises, sprains, wounds and chilblains.

### Eucalyptus
Used as vapour bath for asthma and respiratory ailments. Oils used for burns and to prevent infection. Oil added to the bath is antiseptic. Antiseptic, deodorant, expectorant.

### Fennel
Infusion of leaves or seeds is good for tired, inflamed eyelids. Helps alleviate hunger pangs when dieting, diuretic, mild laxative, alleviates cramp and clears skin problems.

### Fumitory
Infusion acts as a tonic, laxative and diuretic. Helpful with skin problems.

### Garlic
Contains natural antibiotic: juice diluted with water can be applied to wounds, or used as an ointment/lotion. Oil can be taken in capsules. Blood thinner and purifier, can normalize blood pressure. Is a natural diuretic.

### Ginger
Used as gargle eases sore throat, stimulates circulation to alleviate cramp and chilblains. Aids digestion, relieves wind and indigestion.

## Ginseng
Anti-depressant, general tonic and performance-improver though claims for sexual performance seem unfounded.

## Golden rod
Antiseptic, diuretic, wound-healing. Use as gargle.

## Golden seal
Implicated in treating skin problems especially eczema and ringworm: promotes healing. Muscular stimulant, astringent, tonic, laxative.

## Hops
Tonic with sedative, relaxing and diuretic properties. Flowers are a natural antibiotic. Promotes sleep: stuff a pillow with dried hops, and take an infusion of hops before bed. Poultices are good for boils, swelling.

## Horseradish
Diuretic, infusion taken regularly eases blackheads and pimples. Poultice good for stiff muscles, chilblains.

## Hyssop
Infusion is good for coughs, eases catarrh. Promotes relaxation. Used in perfume manufacture. Put dried leaves in drawers and cupboards.

## Lavender
Spirits or oil can ease rheumatic and arthritic pains. Oil can ease toothache and also promote the healing of wounds. Reputed to promote hair growth if it is massaged into scalp. Infusion lifts the spirits and alleviates fatigue, stress and depression, yet can promote sleep.

## Lemon balm
Infusion is a relaxant, drunk or added to bathwater, also aids sleep, relieves depression.

## Lemon thyme
Infused in bathwater gives lemon scent. Also used in pot pourris and herb cushions. Lemon thyme cushions are a traditional headache remedy.

## Lemon verbena
Infusion acts as a mild sedative. Used as mouthwash, good for gum health. Good for pot pourris and sachets.

## Margoram
Infusion can ease headaches, used as a mouthwash sweetens breath. Oil applied to skin eases stiff joints. Eases migraine, promotes sleep.

## Marshmallow
Soothes gut irritations such as gastric ulcers and diarrhoea, also soothes coughs. Infusion used as eyewash relieves soreness.

## Mint
Infusion eases nausea, stomach ache, anxiety, insomnia and dizziness. Mint tea is refreshing in hot weather.

## Mugwort
Infusion used to bathe sprains, can be used as poultice. Used as gargle alleviates sore throats.

## Mustard
Powerful stimulant of circulation, helpful in all associated problems. Traditionally used in form of mustard plaster applied to skin. Deodorizer: rub hands or utensils with a little powdered mustard to remove smells.

## Nasturtium
Acts as an antiseptic in urinary infections.

## Nettle
Generally applicable tonic when infused, also blood purifier and skin-clearer. Juice used to stop nosebleeds.

## Oats
Nerve and uterine tonic, good for chest problems and stress. Use as facial treatment for flaky skin and other problems, tired eyes, chilblains. Oats boiled with vinegar used as a facepack is said to fade freckles and generally to improve complexion.

## Peppermint
Infusion eases nausea due to motion sickness or pregnancy. Oil is antiseptic, relieves toothache when rubbed on to gum, on to temples relieves headache. A few drops of essential oil in the bath will relieve tired muscles.

## Rose hip
Excellent source of vitamin C: syrup used for children.

## Rosemary
Spirits of rosemary or essential oil ease aches when massaged into joints. Used as hair tonic and restorer. The herb acts as a stimulant, anti-depressant and diuretic. Infuse in bathwater for migraine, drink rosemary tea for all menstrual and menopausal problems.

## Rue
Infusion can both induce sleep and act as general tonic. Crushed plants applied to lower abdomen relieve sciatica. Its bitterness keeps flies away if a bundle is hung up.

## Sage
Sage leaves can strengthen gums when rubbed in. Relaxing, soothing bath when infused, good for tension, migraine. In creams beneficial to greasy skins.

## Sorrel
Crushed stems and leaves promote healing. Infusion cleanses kidneys and blood, relieves inflamed throat.

## St Johns Wort
Strengthens nervous tissue, good for all neurological illnesses and for depression, hot flushes, promotes relaxation. In ointment used for bed sores.

## Thyme
Steam bath with essential oil of thyme helps relieve colds and stuffed-up nose, and eases sore throats if inhaled through mouth. Infusion: use as wash for skin sores and problems. Thymol, contained in the essential oil, is antiseptic. Pounded leaves with honey relieve whooping cough. Thyme and rosemary infused and used as hair rinse help prevent dandruff occurring.

## Valerian
Decoction used for insomnia, to promote relaxation. Relieves nervous tension and headache, colic. Anti-depressant. Ointment has healing properties.

## Watercress
Purifies blood: juice extracted in a blender relieves skin blemishes. Leaves on temples ease headaches.

## Witch hazel
Astringent in distilled form. Eases swelling in bruises and sprains. Used as tea or extract in treatment of haemorrhoids, diarrhoea.

# HIGHLIGHTING

*See also: colouring hair; greying; hair*

Highlighting is a process by which pigment is removed from, and in some cases new colour added to, very small groups of hairs to produce an illusion of added depth and movement. Ammonia and hydrogen peroxide are used for bleaching out some sections of hair, making them blonde, colour solutions are used for other sections to produce a still more natural look, picking up and emphasizing some of the many colours naturally in the hair.

Highlights are best for paler hair tones, from blonde to dark mouse, and also look good on hair which is going grey. Lowlights, which emphasize deeper tints, are suitable for dark or light hair.

The process of highlighting is best done professionally. Bad colour application can produce very unnatural stripy effects, and timing for colouring is very important both to achieve the desired tone and minimize damage to the hair shafts. In addition, a professional will be able to graduate the distance at which colour begins from the scalp, so that you will not have an ugly regrowth line. Highlights usually last about 4 weeks before any regrowth is visible. The roots can easily be retouched. Treat highlighted hair, which will be drier and brittler than natural hair, carefully to prevent dehydration, particularly from sun and seawater.

**Hips**
See Buttocks

Hair can be highlighted using the cap method, where small strands are drawn through holes in a rubber hat with what looks like a crochet hook, but only one colour can be used with this method. The alternative is the tinfoil method shown here, or sometimes paper/film strips are used, too.
**1** A fine hair section is laid on to a foil strip, painted almost to the roots with colouring solution, then foil is folded up carefully.
**2** Each vertical section of hair is worked down, with tiny sections being coloured, alternating several colours, and perhaps a bleach for some strands.
**3** Once the whole head is completely highlighted, a hair dryer or computerized drying machine is used to speed the colouring process – the tinfoil promotes heat, too. Hair is then rinsed, washed thoroughly and conditioned before drying.
**4** Hair is gently finger-dried for least damage to processed hair.

# HOLISM

*See also: allopathy; herbalism; herbs; homoeopathy; naturopathy*

Holism provides an approach to life, to general well-being, to illness, where the individual is very much in control and plays the fullest possible part in capitalizing on and increasing his or her potential. It has a broad span, embracing the individual's relationship to everyone and everything around them.

In terms of health, the holistic approach is that each person should play a full part in investigating the cause of any problem, in choosing the method of treatment from all those available (the whole range from homoeopathic to allopathic) and in facilitating the recovery. The opposite standpoint would be exemplified by the person who makes no attempt to understand the causes or nature of their illness, asks no questions of the practitioner consulted, grudgingly takes the treatment prescribed, and grumbles that they are not going to get better.

Dr Patrick Pietroni, a London general practitioner, set up a scheme in 1982 to incorporate holistic health care into the National Health Service in the UK. Patients suffering physical or psychological symptoms ranging from asthma and migraine headaches to insomnia and depression are asked to attend evening classes run by health centre staff in breathing, relaxation, meditation, diet and visualization (a therapy similar to autosuggestion). The early results are encouraging, although not yet statistically analysed, and show reduction in consultations and prescriptions, and a general enjoyment of the classes.

The widespread interest in health today indicates the increasing appeal of the holistic approach. Books on well-being proliferate, and there is more and more interest in ancient as well as new methods of diagnosis and treatment. In the area of childbirth holism has made an especially noticeable impact: women and their partners are encouraged to take an active part in the birth and to make choices as a result of detailed study of and advice taken from various specialists in the field.

# HOMOEOPATHY

*See also: allopathy; herbalism*

Homoeopathy is a system of medical practice formalized by Samuel Hahnemann of Leipzig in the late eighteenth century. In homoeopathy the choice of treatment is made solely by matching the patient to the range of symptoms shown by the remedy whose action, on a healthy person, most closely imitates those symptoms. This is in contrast to allopathic methods, where analysing the disease which might be causing them is the major preoc-

cupation. For homoeopaths, patients are only unwell when they actually feel ill, rather than where clinical tests show that there are the abnormalities which need treatment, as for the allopath.

Treatment is in the form of non-toxic dilutions of the chosen medicine, thought to act more strongly when diluted due to energy released by successive dilutions and shakings. The increase of symptoms for a short period which occasionally follow taking homoeopathic medicine (after which there should be improvement) is seen by practitioners as a sign that the correct diagnosis of symptoms has been made. Traditionally only one preparation is given at once, since homoeopaths believe that all symptoms which appear are part of one disease or disorder, and therefore that one preparation will cure it.

Homoeopathic doctors practise in many countries of the world, and some are also qualified as allopathic doctors. In the UK, homoeopathic medicines are readily available under the National Health Service.

# HONEY

*See also: diet; sugar*

Honey is an almost universally popular food. In addition to being a natural sweetener it has healthful, healing and beauty properties, and has also long been used to make the once commonplace alcoholic drink, mead. There are an almost infinite number of honeys which connoisseurs can distinguish between as readily as oenologists can their wine. Taste depends both on the flowers chosen by the bees and the soil and climate they grow in.

## NUTRITIONAL PROPERTIES

- Rich in natural glucose which makes it an ideal energy food, honey can immediately be used by the body, without processing. It is also rich in fructose which can swiftly be converted into glycogen in the liver. Take honey for swift energy during exercise, when you feel fatigued, or to raise blood sugar when you have a hangover.
- Honey contains small amounts of vitamin B3, iron, copper, manganese, sodium, potassium, calcium and phosphorous.
- It contains 288 Calories to each 100 g (3.5 oz).
- The preservative qualities of honey explain its use in foods in the East.

## HEALING PROPERTIES

- Honey has an antiseptic, bactericidal action. It makes a soothing and beneficial drink with hot water and lemon, or with milk in cases of throat infections, coughs and any pulmonary disorders. It is also useful in fighting some types of bacterial diarrhoea.
- Its bactericidal action combined with its capacity to absorb moisture made honey a popular treatment for some burns and open wounds for

ovaries. It seemed reasonable to prescribe drugs to replace it. Benefits of the treatment were that tissue shrinkage (atrophy) of the breasts and vagina (causing vaginal dryness), and calcium loss from the bones, which leads to shrinking and increasing brittleness of the bones after the menopause (see **osteoporosis**), were lessened.

Studies carried out in the 1970s, however, showed that oestrogen therapy increased the risk of cancer of the lining of the uterus (endometrium). Research has now shown that the addition of progestogen in the last 10 to 12 days of the cycle reduces the risk to zero. In fact, women on the combined hormone treatment have slightly more protection against cancer of the endometrium than women not on HRT. The dose of hormones given is too low to provide contraception, so alternative methods should be used where fertility is still possible.

This treatment does, however, give a withdrawal bleed similar to that experienced while taking contraceptive pills, and some women may object to this continuing. In addition some women suffer mild PMS (see **pre-menstrual syndrome**). A promising development is that of subcutaneous implants in the buttocks, abdomen or thigh which release continuous oestrogen and progestogen. They suppress menopausal symptoms without increasing the risk of cancer and produce no withdrawal bleeding.

Treatment may continue for 18 months to 2 years in the case of menopausal symptoms, but for considerably longer where there is history or danger of osteoporosis. In all cases, it should be reduced gradually rather than stopped suddenly to prevent exacerbation of symptoms. It may take the form of pills, pessaries or creams used in the vagina, or an implant. At present, women who have had cancer of the breast or womb, or a history of thrombosis or heart disease would not be prescribed HRT.

centuries. Today it is sometimes used to treat open wounds such as bedsores.
- The malic acid in honey is implicated in the alleviation of rheumatic symptoms.

### BEAUTY PROPERTIES
- Since honey is said to soften the skin, it is incorporated in many skin preparations.

# HORMONE REPLACEMENT THERAPY

*See also: ageing; hormones; hysterectomy; menopause; osteoporosis*

For some women the side effects of the menopause can be so distressing that Hormone Replacement Therapy (HRT) is suggested.

Since the 1940s it has been known that the menopause is due to lower production of oestrogen in the

# HORMONES

*See also: acne; Hormone Replacement Therapy; menopause; menstruation; pregnancy; puberty*

Hormones act in the body as chemical messengers. They are secreted by the group of glands that make up the endocrine system, absorbed into the bloodstream and carried throughout the body. They act as stimulants, influencing growth and development, metabolism, response to stress and sexual activity, and are potent even in tiny amounts. Generally speaking, the working of the endocrine glands is largely independent of the nervous system, though not entirely. The hormones they secrete do influence each other.

### FUNCTIONS OF HORMONES
While the overall balance of hormones in an individual may influence personality, particular hormones perform specialized functions. They can be grouped according to glands.

The **pituitary gland** lies in a small pocket in the skull beneath the brain. It is about the size of a pea and is attached by a stalk to the hypothalamus region of the brain. The anterior lobe of the pituitary produces: *somatotrophic or growth hormone* which is particularly concerned with the growth of the skeleton. It is secreted irregularly, mainly at night; *adrenocorticotrophic hormone* which stimulates the outer layer of the adrenal gland to produce steriods; *thyrotrophic hormone* which is necessary for the thyroid gland to function normally; *prolactin* which stimulates the production of breast milk during late pregnancy and after childbirth; *gonadotrophic hormones* which control the reproductive processes in both sexes along with the production of sex hormones: they influence the release of eggs from the ovaries at ovulation in women.

The posterior lobe produces: *antidiuretic hormone* which controls fluid balance in the blood and extracellular fluid; *Oxytocin* which stimulates smooth muscle, in particular the uterus and breast, causing milk ejection in the latter. The wide-ranging effects of the pituitary gland show why it is sometimes known as the 'conductor' of the endocrine 'orchestra'.

The **thyroid gland** is an H-shaped gland which lies in the neck. It is a smooth red organ rather like a soft liver. The thyroid produces: *thyroxine*, the body's accelerator, which stimulates metabolism and has a general effect on growth and mental development. Adequate dietary iodine is needed to manufacture the hormone; and *calcitonin* which enables calcium to be transferred from blood to bone.

The **parathyroid glands** are 4 pea-sized glands connected to the thyroid lobes. They produce: *parathormone*, which controls the body's metabolism of calcium.

The two **adrenal, or suprarenal glands** are situated above the kidneys. They are made up of an outer layer called the cortex and an inner layer called the medulla. The cortex produces hormones known as *corticosteroids*, including *cortisol* which affects the metabolism of carbohydrates and response to stress and infection, and *aldosterone* which influences the movement of sodium and potassium ions across cell membranes.

The cortex also produces hormones which stimulate the production of sex and growth hormones. The medulla is closely related to the nervous system. It produces *adrenaline* and *noradrenaline* as a reaction to emergency situations. They alter blood pressure, heartbeat rate and strength, relax the bronchial muscles and stimulate the mobilization of glycogen from the liver as fuel for the muscles.

The **pancreas** is situated in front of the kidneys and produces digestive juices as well as hormones. One of several hormones it produces is *insulin*. Insulin is produced after a meal as a response to a rise in blood-sugar levels, and promotes the storage of glycogen.

The **ovaries,** as well as forming female reproductive cells – ova, or eggs – also secrete *oestrogen* – which is responsible for growth and development of female sex organs and secondary sexual characteristics such as breast growth at puberty. Another hormone produced in the ovaries is *progesterone* which causes the growth of the uterus and the thickening of its lining (the endometrium) in preparation for menstruation (see separate entry) or pregnancy. The ovary produces *testosterone* in small quantities and this is responsible for the appearance of pubic and underarm hair.

In men, the testes, besides producing sperm, also secrete *androgens*. The most important is *testosterone* which promotes growth, development of the bones and muscles, and development of secondary sexual characteristics such as beard growth and deepening of the voice.

### HORMONE IMBALANCES AND TREATMENT

Deficiency or over-production of particular hormones can have a far-reaching effect on the body. Tumours of a gland may cause it to over-produce, while damage may cause a deficiency. Deficiencies cause a wide range of problems; insulin deficiency, for example, causes diabetes. Oestrogen and synthetic versions of progesterone called progestogens are widely used to regulate menstruation and for contraceptive protection. Hormone Replacement Therapy (see separate entry) is sometimes used in dealing with menopausal problems.

# HOT FLUSHES

*See also: Hormone Replacement Therapy; menopause*

Hot flushes (flashes) are one of the most easily recognized symptoms of the menopause. They sometimes occur during the year before the periods stop. As the hormone system moves towards the cessation of ovulation and menstruation, oestrogen levels fluctuate outside the normal menstrual pattern (see **menstruation**), and this produces surges of LH, the luteinizing hormone which stimulates progesterone production after ovulation.

These surges of LH are associated with hot flushes, which tend to start on the head and neck, spreading down to the chest. Skin temperature rises sharply; the skin reddens as blood vessels dilate to cool it; heart rate and blood pressure increase, and shaking or sweating may occur. Flushes usually last no longer than 2 minutes, but can occur several times a day, and at night, and can be distressing.

If you suffer from uncomfortable hot flushes, see your doctor or gynaecologist. He or she may prescribe Hormone Replacement Therapy (see separate entry) which can be very helpful as it rebalances the hormones which are causing the problem. The symptoms are often worse when/you are under stress. Try practising relaxation techniques and taking frequent exercise; don't 'bottle up' your problems; discuss them with your family, friends and medical advisers.

# HOT TUBS

*See also: hydrotherapy; saunas*

Hot tubs combine all the bodily benefits of warm water with relaxation and massage. Known also as whirlpools and Jacuzzis (a brand name), hot tubs are deep baths with seats for several people. The water in them is always bubbly, warm to hot, and jets of water all around the pool at different levels massage various areas of the body as you relax. Sometimes the water has added mineral salts, or carbon dioxide which makes the skin feel mildly prickly. They can be sociable and very enjoyable but bear in mind the following:

### ADVANTAGES
- Hot tubs stimulate blood circulation in the body as the water massages it.
- Hot water eases muscular and joint aches, thus encouraging joint movement.
- Soaking relaxes the body and the mind, particularly beneficial after strenuous exercise.

### DISADVANTAGES
- Hot tubs raise blood pressure, temperature and heart rate, and thus their use is inadvisable for anyone with cardiovascular problems.
- Remember that you should only spend approximately 10 minutes in a hot tub at one go for maximum benefit and minimum danger of overstressing your heart.
- Fungal infection such as ringworm (in the form of athlete's foot, for example) can readily be picked up in the warm atmosphere.
- You must shower before using a hot tub: soaps, suncreams, moisturizers and lotions can build up in the pumping system and cause damage to the machinery.

HAZARD: do not wear any jewellery while in a hot tub. It can easily be swept off by water-jets and chewed up irrevocably in the pump machinery.

# HUNGER

*See also: anorexia nervosa; appetite; bingeing; bulimia nervosa; diet; eating habits; fasting; fattening diets; slimming*

Hunger occurs when the body physically requires a top-up of food stores for energy. The sensation can be mildly uncomfortable or even quite painful. Hunger and appetite do not always coincide: they have a close, yet changeable relationship. Your appetite can demand food long before your body is actually hungry, and can continue after that hunger is satisfied. When you are ill, lack of appetite can suppress hunger. Most people tend to continue eating for a little while after hunger is assuaged, in order to fulfil the demands of appetite, too.

Hunger varies with the bodily needs of age, with

health and illness, with exercise, and changes in routine. Appetite is far more fickle: it is affected by a wide range of emotions not always connected to food, by fears and worries, pressures and stress and can to a quite considerable extent be consciously controlled.

Constructive weight control programmes deal not only with food intake, Calories and menus, but with the hunger/appetite relationship, rebuilding the 'natural' link where hunger is master. Obesity does not exist in the wild where hunger and appetite remain closely linked. It is only in the domesticated state where their relationship is broken down and reforged, that these problems exist, both for human beings and animals.

# HYDROTHERAPY

*See also: hot tubs*

Hydrotherapy is a treatment in which warm water is used to support the body and provide protection for movement of damaged joints and muscles. Exercises performed against the resistance of the water help strengthen the body without danger of further damage. The warmth of the water helps alleviate pain, too, and relaxes the muscles, both of which conspire to improve joint movement. Circulation is increased. Hydrotherapy pools are used extensively in the treatment of arthritis, bone and muscle injuries, and in the mobilization of geriatric patients. Hydrotherapy is normally supervised by physiotherapists.

Traditionally hydrotherapy was used with or without medical supervision as a treatment for a wide range of illnesses ranging from indigestion to depression. Numerous spas once offered the 'cure' in the form of immersion in cold, warm or hot mineral water baths, and associated treatments. Some of these treatments are still available, particularly at European resorts, but hydrotherapy has, generally speaking, become part of the battery of conventional medicine in the field of physiotherapy.

# HYPNOTHERAPY

*See also: dependencies; insomnia; relaxation; sleep; smoking; stress*

Hypnosis is a state somewhere between sleeping and waking, a level of consciousness similar to that of sleep-walkers, where the conscious and subconscious minds are particularly susceptible to suggestions. Events several decades past and ostensibly long forgotten can be recalled with remarkable clarity. In hypnotism the hypnotic's own will is given increased power over mind and body.

### DANGERS AND FEARS

There are few dangers in hypnotism if a qualified hypnotherapist is consulted: additionally some doctors, psychotherapists and dentists are also qualified hypnotherapists. A minority of people suffer initial abreactions such as sudden weeping as bad memories are invoked, but for the majority hypnosis is a pleasurable experience. Unless willing a patient cannot be hypnotised, nor will he or she accept suggestions which may be harmful. Thus fears that harmful suggestions given under hypnosis will have long-term effects are groundless: in such a situation the patient would probably come out of the hypnotic state and reject the suggestions.

### USES OF HYPNOTISM

Hypnotism is used in illness in two main ways:
1    Some doctors or psychologists use hypnosis almost diagnostically, to track down key events in the patient's past which may be causing current problems, so that these can be dealt with.
2    Hypnotherapy is commonly used to treat a wide range of physical and mental disorders and problems. It is commonly used in curing dependencies, phobias, bed-wetting and insomnia, to treat anxiety, tension and stress, alleviate problems like blushing, to improve performance in many areas (some athletes have used hypnotherapy for this purpose), and to increase self-confidence. The number of sessions needed varies according to the problem and the individual. Many problems do only need short treatment, followed by intermittent 'topping up'.

Before anaesthetics, hypnosis was used to eliminate the patient's awareness of pain during surgical operations. It is still sometimes used for this purpose, especially to staunch bleeding. Some dentists use hypnosis to reduce patients' fears as well as for pain-free treatment.

Since hypnotherapy makes use of your will and willpower, not only are you incapable of accepting harmful suggestions, but you will also reject those at odds with your will. Hypnotherapy will only help you to give up smoking, for example, if you really want to give up.

### THE PROCESS

Initially the hypnotherapist will ask questions to establish the nature of your problem and that hypnotherapy is an appropriate treatment for it. He or she will then explain the procedure in detail. Once a situation of trust has been established, the therapist will test your reaction to hypnosis by inducing the lightest trance, using his or her voice and words (this is the most common method although others may be used). Usually the treatment takes place (or begins) in the second session, when the patient relaxes on a couch or chair.

### SELF-HYPNOSIS

Self-hypnosis or autohypnosis is readily learnt and can be helpful in dealing with some problems, especially stress, anxiety, fear, also asthma and

## Hygiene
See Body odour; Teeth; Douching

## Hygienist
See Dental hygienist

headaches. It is also sometimes used as a relaxation method, and as a state for meditation. It MUST be taught by a qualified practitioner as there can be initial abreactions, as with all hypnosis, and should only be used on professional advice. It basically consists of following simple instructions to achieve the lightest trance, in which you can make suggestions to yourself as to how to conquer your problem, then following simple instructions to bring yourself back out of the trance again.

# HYPO-ALLERGENIC PRODUCTS

*See also: allergies; lanolin; scent; skin*

If a product is labelled hypo-allergenic it means that it is less likely to cause the user irritation. However, such products are by no means guaranteed against provoking allergic reaction in an individual. Hypo-allergenic products generally have far fewer constituents than other cosmetics, eliminating many ingredients, for example lanolin, which are well known as potential allergens or sensitizers. They are normally alcohol- and fragrance-free, contain few colouring agents and are often suitable for dry, sensitive skins which may react against harsher cosmetic products. Whether or not you have sensitive skin it is a good idea to test all products before buying. And if your skin is sensitive you may still be allergic to hypo-allergenic items. Test with a small sample, and take advice from your doctor or dermatologist.

# HYSTERECTOMY

*See also: Hormone Replacement Therapy; hot flushes (flashes); menopause*

This common operation is, in its simplest form, removal of the uterus or womb, and in a total hysterectomy the cervix or neck of the womb as well. Menstruation and the child-bearing capacity then cease, but sexual intercourse is unaffected. Sometimes a bilateral salpingo-oophorectomy is also necessary: this involves the removal of uterine tubes and ovaries, too. Again, the vagina remains intact so sexual activity is unimpaired. Removal of womb, cervix, both Fallopian tubes and ovaries, the upper part of the vagina, ligaments and lymph glands is called a Wertheim's hysterectomy, also known as pelvic clearance. This kind of extensive hysterectomy may well be carried out if the operation was for cancer, for example.

The body will function hormonally on ¼ of one ovary, but if the ovaries are completely removed, a 'surgical' menopause will be induced in women who have not yet had menopause, with its encumbrant tendency to produce irritability, hot flushes (flashes) and other symptoms (see **menopause**). Hormone Replacement Therapy (HRT) (see separate entry) is usually given in these cases, in order to replace the oestrogen and progesterone normally secreted until menopause.

### REASONS FOR HYSTERECTOMY

Whatever the reason for a hysterectomy, it should always be fully discussed with your doctor and/or gynaecologist, so that it is well understood. Recent research shows that if a woman has *full* information about the problem and operation and after effects, depression is not likely to be a problem.

Hysterectomy is performed either vaginally, or abdominally through a small incision just above the pubic hair line. It can be performed for a wide variety of reasons including fibroids, prolapsed uterus, pelvic inflammatory disease (see separate entry), cancer of the endometrium (lining of the womb), cancer of the cervix where this has spread from the cervix to the womb and other areas, cancer of the ovaries and menorrhagia (heavy, irregular bleeding).

### COPING WITH HYSTERECTOMY

Arm yourself beforehand with as much information as possible about the operation, its effects and why it has been advised for you. Examine all your fears, expectations and thoughts about it.

Ensure that you have talked over all your queries with your partner or husband properly, then with your doctor, gynaecologist, health visitor or whoever you find easiest to talk to and most helpful, and include your partner or a close friend in these discussions, too.

Ignore 'old wives' tales' which contradict informed sources of knowledge. Hysterectomy, with HRT if necessary, does not cause premature ageing, nor does it adversely affect your femininity, sexuality or sex life (hormonal changes after the removal of ovaries may reduce vaginal lubrication, which is easily dealt with by using a commercially available lubricating cream or jelly). Intercourse can normally be resumed, after a check-up, 6 weeks after the operation. Remember that there are many ways of showing affection without sexual intercourse.

Like all such operations, hysterectomy is physically stressful. Take plenty of rest immediately after the operation. Avoid lifting heavy objects and be conscientious about keeping up with all the exercises you have been advised to do.

Allow yourself to grieve over the loss of your womb. Even when you have fully agreed to the need for the operation, it is normal and natural to have an emotional reaction to this change in your body, and you will need time to accept it. Remember that within 3-6 months of having the operation many women feel better than for years previously, now that they are at last free of debilitating symptoms.

Ask your doctor, gynaecologist or health visitor to put you in touch with a hysterectomy support group which may prove helpful. Do not be afraid to ask for counselling to help you over any fears or problems.

# IMMUNIZATION

Immunization protects the body against illness and disease. It is based on the body's natural germ-fighting mechanisms in which antibodies are produced to fight germs and antitoxins produced to deal with germ-induced poisons. In inoculation (also known as vaccination), small quantities of a vaccine are injected into the body to stimulate the production of antibodies so that in future similar organisms can be fought off.

There are two types of immunization:
1  Active immunization involves injecting the patient with a small amount of a harmful substance so that it will produce antibodies to protect it should it come into contact with the real thing.
2  Passive immunization involves the infusion or injection of antibodies which were not made by the recipient, e.g. gamma globulin to protect against infectious hepatitis. This gives immunity for only a few months until the 'foreign' antibodies are destroyed.

There is now a recommended immunization programme in the UK which commences when a baby is aged about 3 months, and provides protection against whooping cough, tetanus, diphtheria, polio, German measles, measles and tuberculosis.

In the US, infants begin an immunization programme at 2 months. This includes protection from diptheria, pertussis and tetanus (DPT), polio, tuberculosis and measles, mumps and rubella (MMR). In major cities, the Board of Health operates free clinics where children and adults who present themselves as unvaccinated can receive a series of necessary immunization over a period of time.

Travel abroad may necessitate further immunization: your doctor or travel agent will recommend which jabs are advisable for which countries. Suggested and required immunization does change so check before you go; do not rely on past experience. Find out well in advance as you may need immunization from several diseases which require more than one inoculation, and need spacing out over days or weeks. Remember also that protection is not always immediate; several days may need to elapse before immunization is fully effective.
▣  Immunizations are less effective if the body has to cope with several infections simultaneously. So if you have a cold or flu it is better to wait until you are well and similarly it is better to be immunized against one thing at a time.
▣  If your immunity is reduced for some reason or if you have extensive skin disease, inform your doctor who may advise against immunization.
▣  Immunization for some diseases may make you feel mildly unwell (a low fever is common): check with your doctor so that you are not taken by surprise, but do not avoid these inoculations. Any mild symptoms you suffer are a fraction of the discomfort and even danger involved in contracting the disease itself.

# INFUSIONS

*See also: caffeine; herbalism; herbs*

An infusion is a solution resulting from one or more fresh or dried plants being steeped in water, normally boiling water. The commonest infusion in the world is tea (*Camellia sinensis*), drunk for pleasure; herbal teas, made in the same way, tend to be drunk for their medicinal properties although many, such as chamomile tea, can be delicious, too. Infusions do not have to be drunk: they can be used to add to baths, as ingredients in poultices, ointments or as scent (see **herbs**).

Although a pleasurable and very common drink, tea contains the addictive drug caffeine (see separate entry). A 250 ml (½ pint/1 cup) cup of medium-strength Indian tea contains 24-107 mg of caffeine as opposed to the 40-124 mg in similar strength coffee. China tea has less caffeine. It contains tannin and small amounts of vitamins B2 and B3.

## MAKING INFUSIONS
**Tea** Bring a kettle of water to the boil. Warm the teapot. Use a teaspoon of tea, or one teabag, per person, add an extra teaspoon or bag 'for the pot'. Pour on the water as it boils. Leave to infuse for five minutes, stir and serve.
**Herbal teas** Infused for longer than tea, usually 10-15 minutes. Commonly 1-3 teaspoons of fresh or dried herbs are used for each cup of boiling water. Depending on the herb, the leaves, flowers, root or seeds may be used. Some common herbal infusions are borage, chamomile, raspberry, tansy and peppermint (see **herbs**).

# INSOMNIA

*See also: anxiety; depression; exercise; hypnotherapy; relaxation; sleep; stress*

Insomnia hits most people at some stage in their life, and can be very distressing. It can appear as difficulty in getting to sleep, as disturbed sleep, early waking or as a combination. Insomniacs often misjudge the lengths of time for which they are wakeful, and some people can be convinced that they are suffering from insomnia when they are in fact sleeping normally. However it manifests itself, insomnia is a sign that all is not well. It may be due to a simple factor such as a lumpy bed, it may be due to anxiety, it may be due to depression: many factors can set it off. These guidelines may help you to prevent it.

## AVOIDING INSOMNIA
▣  Try to eat your last large meal no later than 2 hours before going to bed; avoid smoking.
▣  Avoid taking excessive alcohol (the effects of

**Implants**
See Cosmetic surgery

**Ingredients for cosmetics**
See Cosmetics

**Ingrowing nails**
See Nails

Iron
See Minerals

Isokinetics,
Isometrics and
Isotonics
See Muscles

IUD
See Contraception

which are sedative at first, but as you suffer withdrawal symptoms and thirst you become wakeful) and caffeine (in tea, coffee or hot chocolate) at night. Do have a hot milky drink such as Horlicks (which has been shown to aid sleep) and a snack (a biscuit, cookie or bowl of cereal) before sleep if you like.

- Examine your sleep needs carefully: they can vary from as little as 3 hours to 10 or more. Do not judge yourself by anyone else's standards.
- Late at night, avoid discussing worries, subjects about which you have extremely strong feelings, your work, and avoid reading controversial matter or thrillers. Deal with these earlier, and end the day with more soothing occupations, lighter books, reading poetry, saying prayers, meditating, relaxation techniques (see **meditation, relaxation, yoga**).
- Regular exercise is important for general health, and helps promote good sleep. Avoid strenuous exercise just before bedtime, but a gentle walk can relax you ready for bed.
- A warm bath or shower before bed is best; water that is too hot or cold will stimulate rather than relax the body.

### COPING WITH INSOMNIA
Insomnia strikes: you may well feel frightened and helpless. Firstly, remember that insomnia is a very common problem with no harmful consequences. Several studies have shown that there are no long-term dangers in insomnia, that even long tracts of lost or broken sleep can be made up in a night or two. Studies have shown that lack of sleep only affects repetitive, boring work (and even this is probably due to resentment), not other activities, so comfort yourself that you will not work any less constructively or intelligently while you are sorting out your insomnia and its causes, however strange you may feel.

If your insomnia persists for 2 weeks or more, or if you have any new physical symptoms such as aches and pains, headaches, breathlessness, or feel depressed (a common cause of insomnia) see your practitioner. You may know the cause of your insomnia if, for example, you have a particular problem at work. Otherwise try examining each area of your life, listing all the things which worry you, potential anxiety areas.

The insomnia avoidance strategies above will help you to conquer your insomnia once you have discovered its root and taken action on the discovery. In addition:
- Try to avoid 'naps' during the day; keep awake until bedtime so that you can reset your natural body clock.
- Stick to a regular bedtime as far as possible. This does not have to be early, but should be constant.
- Avoid reading, watching TV or videos in bed.
- If your doctor prescribes a short course of sleeping tablets (these can be minor tranquillizers, anti-histamines or barbiturates) you may find them helpful. Always take them as prescribed. Never increase your dosage unless on your doctor's advice and do not mix them with alcohol. However, if you take sleeping pills for any length of time you will find that their effect diminishes, and you may also find that you get side-effects such as a 'hangover' sensation. When you stop taking them you may well get withdrawal symptoms such as anxiety, increased insomnia and headaches: always cut down on these pills gradually, rather than stopping suddenly. Remember that sleeping pills will not 'cure' your insomnia, just suppress it. If the cause is transitory, they may well tide you over, but otherwise they are not the answer to dealing with the root cause of your insomnia.
- Try meditating, relaxation methods, autogenics, and self-hypnosis if it is suitable for you (see separate entries) to help you sleep.
- Have a warm bath shortly before you go to bed, with sleep-promoting plants such as basil, balm, chamomile, verbena, lime blossom, passion flower or valerian in the water in the form of infusions or oils.

# IRIDOLOGY

*See also: eyes*

Changes in the eye have long been studied for clues about a person's state of health. Records of its use date back to the Chaldean civilization.

Iridology has been in use in its current form for some 100 years. It is a painless, non-invasive diagnostic therapy which reveals disturbances and disorders in the body through the study of changes in the iris of the eye. These occur as information about such disturbances passes to the brain through the central nervous system: reflex nerve stimulation takes place in the iris in turn, producing a wide variety of changes there.

Each part of each iris (right and left are different) represents a particular body system, organ or area. Iridologists study the eyes by means of a magnifying glass and fine torch, or by taking special photographs so that they can be projected on a screen later for easy analysis. The subtlest changes are studied, in texture, brilliance, colour, density, marks, clouding, streaking, pigmented areas and pattern. The iris reveals both hereditary and present problems and can give advance warning of any system or organ malfunction. Pregnancy, being a normal condition of the body, is not shown in the eye. When an organ is removed its condition at the time of removal remains static in the iris from this time onwards.

Iridology is not used like allopathic diagnostic techniques. Its aim is to pinpoint disturbances in normal function, and disorders, but not to analyse the disease which might be causing them. Other therapists refer patients for this form of diagnosis. Iridologists do not often suggest treatment unless they are also trained therapists in another field.

# JET LAG

*See also: circadian rhythms; dehydration; insomnia*

We all know how jet lag feels: limbs like lead weights, eyelids which droop however hard you struggle to keep them open, lack of co-ordination, inability to concentrate or remember important facts, sudden mood swings. Anyone who travels to a new time-zone by plane, and thus does not have time to adjust gradually, is likely to suffer from it (particularly if your time zone changes by 4 hours or more). Travelling east seems to produce symptoms more severe than travelling west.

Jet lag has such a devastating effect because it upsets the body's delicately tuned circadian rhythm (see separate entry). It is this which rules the whole body cycle from unconscious functions like hormone secretion to ones we are aware of like excretion or hunger. It takes several weeks for the body to adjust to new light/dark, working, eating and sleeping patterns. Intermittent changes of rhythm can be accommodated by the body provided that they become stable for substantial periods. Persistent change, such as that experienced by air crews, has been shown to produce severe mental and behavioural problems: airlines supervise schedules very carefully with this in mind.

### AVOIDING JET LAG

Since air travel became common numerous theories and 'cast-iron' recipes for avoiding jet lag have been propounded. However, researchers have as yet found no way of facilitating the necessary change of body rhythm artificially.

One factor which is often ignored is that of stress. Much international air travel is for business purposes, with important meetings looming at the end of the journey. In addition, most people have some reservations or fears about flying. Extra adrenaline is thus produced, the body tensed, the mind racing, and this compounds with the general fatigue of the journey to exacerbate the problems of time change adjustment.

### GUIDELINES FOR REDUCING JET LAG

1   Reduce stress in whatever way you can. Look on the positive side of your journeying, make the best use of your captive time. Work if it will not make you feel stressed, draw, or read a book you have been meaning to get round to for ages. Relax into the soothing motion, the routine of airport and air travel, don't fight it. Practice relaxation techniques and breathing exercises.

2   Start planning your time-clock change several days before travelling. Start to go to bed an hour or two earlier or later each day several days ahead and gradually adjust your mealtimes at the same time so that your whole routine is synchronized, as normal.

3   Keep to an in-flight sleeping/eating schedule. If you are flying across the Atlantic you will by now be close to your new time scale. Advance your time another step, and adjust your meals and sleep according to this as far as possible. If doing a longer haul flight work out the best way to cope with the more radical change, in advance. Here is an example. Flying London-Sydney (24-hour flight), departing 21.00, you would do well to alter your bedtime to 21.00 in advance. Try to sleep for 3-4 hours straight after take-off, then wake and eat a meal including plenty of protein. Try to stay awake for 12 hours, then after a carbohydrate-based snack (this helps send L-Tryptophan to the brain, which in turn stimulates the sleep-inducing serotonin), sleep until arrival. You should find that you can stay awake until 20.00 or so in your new surroundings, and over the next few days you can put back your bedtime by 1-2 hours.

4   What to eat and drink. You would do well to avoid alcohol altogether. It will exacerbate the dehydration that pressurized ventilation produces. Drink lots of non-alcoholic fluids. Eat lightly according to your plan, above, avoiding rich foods which are more difficult to digest.

5   Keep your circulation active. Avoid sitting still for too long. Get up and walk around every hour or so: this will help prevent the puffy legs and ankles which result from bad lymphatic drainage. It also helps prevent thrombosis, not uncommon in people who have remained immobile during long-haul flights, and will keep joints and muscles mobile. If you cannot for any reason move around, flex your muscles, down from your head to your toes, every hour. Wear loose comfortable clothing, and avoid tight shoes, boots, socks or jeans which may restrict the blood flow in the lower legs.

6   Remember to adjust the time you take any daily medication such as the pill. Consult your doctor or gynaecologist, but you should be able to advance this gradually with your eating/sleeping advances. Do not change this suddenly as, in the case of the pill, your protection will be diminished, and in the case of other medications this could be dangerous.

7   General comfort. Moisturize your whole body well before flying, and re-moisturize your face and hands at intervals. Take a wash-bag with scent, cleansing wipes, toothbrush and toothpaste, lip moisturizer and a small towel so that you can freshen up before sleeping and on waking. Wash your hair before the journey, but if you use conditioner apply it only to the ends: the sleeplessness and inevitably increased stress of flying stimulate the male hormones (androgens) to increase sebum production, making hair oily.

8   At your destination. If you are going on holiday, don't plan anything too strenuous or demanding for the first day or so. Give your system time to adjust. Equally, after the return journey allow yourself at least a day before returning to work. If you go straight back to work it may take you much longer to recover from the jet lag.

**Jacuzzis**
See Hot tubs

**Judo**
See Martial arts

# JOJOBA

*See also: hair; herbs*

A native of Mexico and the southern US, the jojoba plant (pronounced hohoba) or *Simmondsia chinensis* is a grey-green evergreen shrub which bears small nuts containing a sought-after liquid wax widely used in industry. Cosmetically it provides a natural base for creams and ointments with little danger of hypersensitivity (allergy), and has good skin protection properties. It is widely used in hair products, too, reputed to restrict sebaceous activity and dandruff, to increase hair growth and lustre. Traditionally it is considered to have anti-inflammatory properties.

# JUNK FOOD

*See also: additives; cholesterol; diet; fats; fibre; minerals; salt; sugar; vitamins*

As junk foods have become more and more readily available, dietary research has laid ever-increasing emphasis on the dangers of eating too much of them. A meal of cola, crisps, chips and beefburgers contains unnecessary amounts of sugar, salt, saturated fats, additives and highly processed white flour, all elements which modern dietary thinking advises should be restricted. Junk foods generally contain few vitamins and minerals and are often lower in protein than desirable; in short, they are very low in food value.

The odd dose of junk food is perhaps not so very detrimental to the health of an adult whose normal diet is rich in all the necessary nutrients (see **diet**). Anything more than the odd junk snack *is* bad, and you will swiftly see the results in your skin texture and in your hair, while long-term effects could be far

**Jogging**
See Sports

**Karate**
See Martial arts

**Keloids**
See Scars

**Kelp**
See Seaweed

**Keratin**
See Hair; Nails

more serious to your general state of health.

For children, junk food is even less desirable as it can form bad dietary habits which may prove hard to break in later life. Stock up on quick, nutritious snacks for you and your children: fresh vegetables and dips, nuts, fresh and dried fruit, high fibre cereals and skimmed milk, wholegrain bread and honey (see **eating habits**). Often the craving for a 'junk' snack comes when blood sugar levels are low: have a spoonful of honey, a drink of fresh fruit juice, or a piece of fresh fruit to raise them quickly.

# KETOSIS

*See also: diet; slimming*

Ketosis is a physical condition which occurs when the body's supplies of carbohydrate are used up and energy has to be produced by burning fat instead. This may occur in severe diabetes, starvation, or a diet which restricts carbohydrate intake, particularly if it contains a relatively high level of fat as a result. People suffering from ketosis tend to have the characteristic smell of acetone on their breath. This is because acetone comes from the breakdown of acetoacetic acid, itself a result of the partial oxidation of fat in the body. Mild ketosis is not dangerous in itself although prolonged ketosis can be; acetone and acetoacetic acid (collectively known as ketone bodies) provide energy for the brain in the absence of carbohydrate stores and ketosis can readily be reversed when carbohydrates are reintroduced. However, in diabetics, severe ketosis is a measure of the seriousness of the disease and may induce coma.

# KOHL

*See also: eye make-up*

Kohl is a dark-coloured powder, traditionally made from the metallic substance antimony, that has been used for cosmetics since ancient Egyptian times. It was commonly used to line the inner and outer rim of the eyelids, darken the eyebrows or colour the eyelids. Today's kohl comes in a variety of colours, but is generally in a wax-based, pencil form which makes it smoother and less messy to apply than the old powder and rod method of application.

Using kohl can be a simple and effective way of defining the eyes, and is an alternative to using eye shadow and eyeliner. Smudge and blend the kohl carefully round the outer edges of the eye for a soft, smoky look. Kohl is inclined to look rather greasy and can easily run into the creases around the eyes. If so, it can be set by applying a little matching powder-type eye shadow on top.

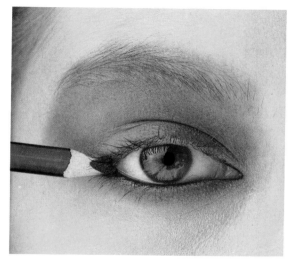

# LANOLIN

*See also: allergens and allergies; cosmetics*

Lanolin is a natural oil obtained from sheep's wool. It has excellent moisturizing and skin-protecting properties, not dissimilar to those of the sebum we ourselves produce, and was in the past widely used as a base for numerous cosmetics and soaps. Pure lanolin soap is still available. Despite its many good properties, however, it is a common allergen. It is because of this that in member countries of the European Economic Community and in the US its presence in any product must be made clear on the packaging. From being a 'product plus' factor it has become a 'product minus'. In various grades, it is still contained in some lipsticks, ointments and moisturizers. If you are allergic to lanolin, check all packaging carefully for constituents before buying.

# LASERS

*See also: eyes; facials; port wine stains*

The word laser is an acronym of Light Amplification of Stimulated Emission of Radiation. Ordinary light contains many wavelengths travelling in different directions but a laser produces a powerful beam of pure light of one colour and wavelength.

### LASER AND HEALTH
Despite the high cost of the equipment, lasers are now widely used in medicine and surgery, offering unique advantages in several fields. The Carbon Dioxide laser is a high precision, bloodless, light scalpel. In gynaecology it is used to remove pre-cancerous cells from the cervix without an anaesthetic, in most patients resulting in rapid, trouble-free healing. It may prove to be of value in micro-surgery to the Fallopian tubes for infertility and can be used to remove genital warts (see **sexually transmitted diseases**). Its value has been proved in the removal of tumours from the upper air and food passages and in the performance of delicate surgery to the brain and spinal cord.

The blue-green Argon laser beam is used to coagulate blood vessels but it will pass through clear and colourless tissues without damaging them. In the treatment of a port wine stain birthmark the beam coagulates the abnormal capillaries in the deep layer of the skin through the clear outer layer.

Using fine flexible instruments introduced through the mouth into the stomach both the Argon and infra-red Neodymium YAG lasers can be used to control bleeding from ulcers without surgery.

Several lasers are used regularly to treat disorders of the eye, and under investigation is the use of laser energy transmitted by fine glass fibres to unblock obstructed arteries.

# LEGS

*See also: exercises; muscles; thighs; unwanted hair; varicose veins*

Well exercised and cared-for legs can be the focal point of a healthy body. The leg is made up of four bones: the femur, which is the longest bone in the body, capable of supporting a vertical load of roughly 2225 lb in a young adult, the disc-shaped patella, or kneecap, the fibula, which runs down the outside of the shin, and the larger tibia, or shin bone. The knee joint, the largest joint in the body, is particularly vulnerable to injury. Strengthening the surrounding muscles through regular exercise minimizes the danger: if you plan to ski, for example, be sure to attend pre-ski classes (run by a qualified tutor) since your knees and ankles will be taking a lot of extra and probably unaccustomed stress. If you have weak knees, ask a physiotherapist what sort of exercise or activities you should or should not do, and

**Lashes**
See Eyelashes

avoid any movements which put too much strain on the joints.

## CARE OF LEGS

■ Although you can exercise the muscles in your legs with the aim of improving their shape, there is little you can do to alter the overall shape of your legs. You will discover for yourself what skirt and trouser lengths and types, hosiery colours and types flatter you most. Make your own choices; don't be browbeaten by friends who think that people with chubby legs should never wear white tights, for example: wear what *you* like yourself in, and feel comfortable in.

■ Try not to wear heels more than 2.5-3.5 cm (1-1½ inches) high for extended periods of time: they can strain the calf and the foot.

■ Always ensure that your leg muscles, like the muscles in the rest of your body, are well warmed-up before exercise (see **exercises**). Always finish off your exercise routine with cool-ing down exercises. Legs benefit from gentle shakes at the end of the cool-down, to relax them.

■ Legs are particularly susceptible to dry skin and chapping: use a moisturizing preparation or oil in the bath and moisturize generously after-wards, too. In hot, dry weather and after sun-bathing and hair removal you will need to step up your moisturizing routine.

■ Unless you have very fair hair, you will want to keep legs hair-free. Depilatory creams are easy to use on the legs, but waxing has the longest-lasting results (see **unwanted hair**).

■ Rough knees can be smoothed by gentle rub-bing with a loofah or pumice stone and soap; follow up with a rich body cream or moisturizer.

■ If your lower legs get puffy in hot weather, try putting your feet up while working, and lying with your feet higher than your head for half an hour during the day. Rhythmical movements of the lower leg and foot may help, too. If the condition persists, see your doctor.

■ See EXERCISES for Caution box page 123 before starting exercise

■ See ABDOMEN for Core Exercise box page 6 before starting exercise

**◀ Exercise A**
1 Stand tall with feet a little more than shoulder width apart, legs turned out from the hip. Breathe in and bend your knees until thighs are parallel with floor.
2 Rise, breathe out, straighten and go up on your toes. Repeat 6 times building to 36 repeats.

**▼ Exercise B**
1 Stand tall with head raised, back long and feet together. Then, with your right foot in front, lengthen your stride.
2 Breathe in keeping back straight, bend the left knee down until it just touches the floor. Do not put any weight on it. Return to starting position breathing out. Repeat 6 times for each leg building up to 24 with each leg.

**▶ Exercise C**
Stand facing wall with left leg in front of right, legs hip-width apart. Bend left knee slightly and lean forward, keeping both feet on the floor and back leg straight. Hold, then change legs. Repeat 6 times with each leg, building to 24 times each.

**▼ Exercise D**
Not suitable for anyone with a weak back. Stand with feet slightly apart, bend knees, place hands on floor and straighten legs and walk forward on your hands. Press your left heel firmly into the floor, lift your right knee and heel. Hold to count of 4, then change legs. Repeat exercise 4 times building to 24.

# LINES

*See also: camouflage; cosmetic acupuncture; elastin and elastone; skin; thread veins; wrinkles*

Many factors contribute to the formation of facial lines, including skin ageing, excessive sun exposure, genetic inheritance, tension, fatigue, concentration and diet. Expression lines result from facial muscles continually contracting in the same way, an action which increases if you habitually smoke or frown. Fine lines can be caused simply by cold weather, wind or dehydration. In the last case, central heating and air conditioning are the obvious culprits. Deep, permanent lines, however, increase with age, as the skin becomes progressively thinner and drier. The collagen and elastin fibres (see separate entries) which give skin its smoothness and elasticity become less flexible and harder as the skin ages. The eye area, with thin skin and fewer sebaceous glands, is the first to show lines. Rubbing the eyes when putting on or taking off make-up, persistently exposing eyes to the sun without sunglasses and using very heavy or oily creams make things worse and can cause sagging skin. The skin on the neck is also delicate and particularly prone to lines which can be exacerbated by bad posture or even habitually wearing tight clothes around the neck. Rubbing or continually scratching the skin thickens it and makes the lines more obvious, although these changes are reversible.

Exposure to the sun damages facial tissues irreparably, accelerating the formation of lines, causing the skin to slacken and uneven pigmentation to occur (see **sun**). Drinking alcohol dehydrates the skin and causes lines to deepen, while smoking promotes lines and deprives the skin of oxygen and the vital nutrients it needs in order to remain soft and smooth.

### ANTI-LINE TREATMENTS

Short of cosmetic surgery to remove excess skin and stretch out lined skin (which decreases the visual effect of the lines) or collagen implants (see separate entry), there is little to be done for lines. Hormone, vitamin or cell renewal creams can only temporarily soften, not banish them. Chemical peels can be carried out under the supervision of a doctor and sometimes produce a slight benefit.

It is vital to keep your skin well moisturized throughout your life, so that as much moisture is retained as possible. Dry skin encourages fine lines. Always use moisturizer. In summer use a moisturizer with a sunscreen filter, and protect your face from the sun if you want to hold lines off for as long as possible. If sunbathing, use a complete sunblock, or a very high SPF product (see **tanning**); wear sunglasses in sunny weather.

NOTE: Camouflaging lines with heavy layers of make-up and powder only emphasizes them. As you grow older apply foundation lightly, use a translucent powder and avoid powdering the eye area.

# LIP COLOUR

*See also: camouflage; colour choice; lips; make-up*

Well-chosen colour and shine, carefully applied, can enhance lips tremendously, whatever their shape. Smudged outlines, or a colour which clashes with your hair or style of dressing, can look worse than no colour at all.

**Lipstick** consists basically of oil, wax and dyes. It is generally perfumed, often flavoured and comes in a variety of forms varying from the regular tube to pots, pencils, compacts or mascara-like containers complete with wand or sponge applicators. The choice is a matter of preference, but if you want very clearly defined lips it is best to use a lip brush or pencil, at least for outlining. Moisturizing lipsticks that give added lubrication are good in extreme heat or in cold climates. Irritations and local allergic reactions are often caused by the dyes in lip colour, so if you are sensitive try out a hypo-allergenic, non-perfumed brand that does not contain indelible dye. Lips burn easily so use a lipstick with a sun screen when sunbathing or skiing, and even when walking around in sunny weather.

**Lip glosses** contain more oil than lipstick. They can be used alone for a young, natural pink look, or as a final coat over lipstick. Most are light and clear-tinted but some give almost as thick a coverage as lipstick, with a much shinier finish. Always apply gloss with a brush or wand applicator for an even distribution of colour.

### COLOUR GUIDELINES

- Lip colours look different on everyone's lips so always try them out before buying.
- Lip colour should complement your skin tone, but preferences change with fashion, the seasons, your mood and your age (see **colour choice**). Experiment with colours and finishes (matt, shiny, frosted or opaque) until you find what suits you.
- If you have dark hair with a pale complexion, rich burgundies and deep reds enliven the face.
- If you have sallow skin, avoid yellow-based lipsticks, such as oranges.
- Older skins are flattered by warm corals, roses and peaches, as bright colours can drain the face of colour.
- Good basic colours are a brownish pink lipstick or natural gloss for an understated daytime look, copper, red and bright pink for emphasis and evenings.
- If you are a redhead, it is advisable to avoid trying to match lipstick to your hair, and avoid mauves, too. Soft subtle shades are best.
- Blondes tend to look best in ruby reds, sharp pinks or tinted gloss.
- For a soft look, co-ordinate lip colour with your eye shadow and blusher.
- Try brushing the lips with a coat of silver or gold gloss for evening shimmer and shine.

**Lice**
See Hair

**Limbering up**
See Exercises

L

**Lip brushes**
See Brushes

**Lipoprotein**
See Cholesterol

### APPLYING LIPSTICK

1   Apply foundation or lip base, then powder for a smooth, dry base that will help the colour last. Medicated foundations are particularly good as they dry the lips.

2   Outline lips carefully with a lip pencil that tones with your chosen lip colour – this stops the colour from 'bleeding'. Start the line at the centre of the mouth and work outwards, ensuring that the two sides of the mouth have matching outlines.

3   Soften the line by dabbing gently with a clean finger or clean lipbrush, so that it does not stand out against lipstick.

4   Blot your mouth with a tissue and powder the edges lightly if colour has a tendency to run on you. Apply more colour to redefine the lip line if necessary.

5   Now apply colour within the line, using a lipbrush.

6   Add a coat of transparent gloss if you want a shiny look, or dust with translucent powder for a matt finish. And refrain from licking your lips, or even the best-applied lip colour will fade.

### CAMOUFLAGING YOUR LIP SHAPE

With a steady hand and clever use of lip pencils and colour, it is possible to correct faults in your lip shape. It looks more natural to do this above and below the lips rather than at the sides.

**Over-full lips** Draw a pencil line just inside your lip line and apply colour within this area alone. Avoid very light or very dark shades.

**Thin lips** Draw a pencil line just outside your natural lip line and fill in this area with a strong colour. Highlight centre with lighter shade.

**Thin bottom lip** Correct the thin lip with an outline of lip pencil just outside your natural lip line. Colour with a lighter shade within the outline.

**Thin top lip** Correct the thin lip as before and colour with a lighter shade of lip colour on your top lip. Use a darker shade on the other lip.

## LIPS

*See also: cold sores; lanolin; lip colour*

Although lips contain melanin, a pigment which helps to protect them against sunlight, they do not have any sebaceous glands so they must still be kept well lubricated, especially in very hot weather when they can become dry. Wind and extreme cold can also cause cracked lips which are susceptible to infection, and thus develop cold sores (see separate entry) or blisters. You can buy ointments to soothe and help heal cold sores from your chemist, but if the sores persist, consult your doctor. Irritations can be caused by the indelible dyes present in lipsticks and some people can develop allergies to these and other lipstick ingredients such as lanolin.

### LIP CARE

▨   Always use a lip-salve or lip-protector with a built-in sun barrier or use zinc oxide ointment when skiing or sunbathing.

▨   Wear a moisturizing lipstick in hot weather and moisturize lips before going to bed.

▨   Using a lip-base underneath your lipstick prevents the lips from absorbing colour, and the colour from smudging.

▨   When using facial scrubs or masks, always avoid covering the lip or eye area.

▨   Include the lips when having a moisturizing face massage.

# LIVER SPOTS

*See also: chemical peeling; chloasma (melasma); dermabrasion; dermatologist; herbs; lasers; skin*

Liver spots are small patches of dark pigmentation which appear in the skin and are caused by over-exposure to the sun. They are often associated with ageing, but in fact can occur at any time, on areas of the body which are regularly exposed to the sun.

The marks are not generally reversible. Avoiding sun exposure may allow some resolution but bleaching creams are of doubtful value and can irritate and, even worse, increase the degree of pigmentation. A more drastic step is that of chemical peeling (see separate entry). Again, this is not guaranteed to remove liver spots permanently, and, since it is an unpleasant process, should only be undertaken in severe cases.

# LOOFAH

*See also: cellulite; exfoliation; skin*

The loofah is the fibrous pod of the *Luffa aegyptiaca* or *L. cyclindrica* plant. It has long been used as a very simple and efficient form of exfoliation and body buffing. Softer when moistened, it can be used on the legs, arms and back with or without exfoliating cream or soap: it sloughs off dead skin cells, stimulates the local circulation and leaves the skin feeling very soft. Avoid using a loofah on broken skin. The fibrous 'felt' of the loofah can be incorporated into massage gloves, pads or massage straps which are easier to use than the pod. Always rinse your loofah thoroughly after use to remove all traces of soap or cleanser, then hang it up to dry if possible: if it is left damp it may easily become mouldy.

# LOW-CARBOHYDRATE DIETS

*See also: carbohydrates; diet; fibre; slimming; sugar*

A low-carbohydrate diet is made up mainly of protein and fat, with a very low proportion of carbohydrate in the form of starch and sugar. In practice this means more meat, poultry, fish, dairy produce and less bread, potatoes, rice, pasta and pulses.

At one time diabetics were instructed to follow a diet either very low in or entirely free from carbohydrates. Modern dietary practice, however, recommends that complex carbohydrates (starches such as potatoes and bread) are not restricted and should form 40 to 50 per cent of the daily intake and that monosaccharides such as sucrose (table sugar) are omitted.

Low-carbohydrate diets were also, until quite recently, perhaps the most popular method of losing weight. The normal practice was for potatoes to be eschewed in favour of a steak, as potatoes and all their starchy relations were considered to be particularly high in the Calories which are the enemy of the serious slimmer.

## THE PROS AND CONS OF A LOW-CARBOHYDRATE DIET
- The only real advantage of a low-carbohydrate diet is that it is one way of reducing total Calorie intake and thus encourage weight loss. However, a lot of the initial weight loss on a low-carbohydrate diet can be attributed to the elimination of body fluid normally held in by carbohydrates.
- Although it is a good idea to cut down on certain carbohydrates, such as sugar, the other forms, such as starch, are valuable foods and should account for 60 per cent of a normal, healthy diet.
- Fibre, which is considered important for health, is only found in foods high in carbohydrates (see **carbohydrates, diet**).
- Carbohydrates are protein-sparing: i.e. a diet low in carbohydrates will encourage the body to use protein foods for energy instead of leaving them to perform their valuable tissue-building and repairing functions.
- Carbohydrates are a valuable source of energy and a diet low in them is likely to cause a drop in blood sugar levels, leading to fatigue, and general irritability.

# LUNGS

*See also: aerobics; breathing; exercise; fitness*

The lungs, two large spongy lobes situated within the ribcage, are responsible for removing carbon dioxide (and some water – the lungs play a role in heat and fluid regulation in the body) from the blood and replacing it with oxygen extracted from the air. This exchange, known as gas exchange, is the chief function of the lungs. They also filter toxic materials from the circulation and act as a blood reservoir. Approximately 6 litres of air are taken into the lungs per minute when you are at rest, up to 180 in the highly-trained endurance athlete when exercising: the lung capacity of an adult male is about 5.5 litres. The function, and therefore the health, of the lungs is greatly improved by regular exercise, particularly aerobic exercise (see **aerobics, fitness**). Good breathing practices are also important in maximizing lung function (see **breathing**): you will breathe more efficiently when your fitness increases.

**Lipolysis**
See Aspiration

**Lotions**
See Body moisturizers

**Lumps**
See Acne; Breast examination; Cysts; Ganglions

**Magnesium**
See Minerals

**Malnutrition**
See Diet

# MACROBIOTIC FOODS

*See also: diet; yin and yang*

The macrobiotic diet was developed by George Ohsawa, a Japanese who suffered from tuberculosis and stomach ulcers thought incurable by Western doctors. He evolved macrobiotics from studying Eastern medicine and lived until he was in his seventies. Ohsawa believed that a perfectly balanced and therefore extremely healthy eating regime could be developed by applying to food Zen Buddhist ideas about balancing the elements of yin and yang in our lives to achieve harmony. Yin stands for the female in nature, for silence and cold; yang for the male, action and heat. In terms of food, yin is acidic, yang is alkaline (see **yin and yang**).

The regime is often, though not necessarily, a vegetarian one, based on ten progressively more limited diets, from level –3 to level 7. The perfect ratio of yin to yang is considered to be five to one. Brown rice is said to contain a perfect balance of yin and yang. Because of this it forms the basis of all macrobiotic diets; the final level is brown rice only but this extremity is dangerous and has led to malnutrition and in a few cases, death. However, the basic principles of the diet with its emphasis on grains and vegetables are very healthy indeed and can be incorporated into a well-balanced diet (see **diet**) with ease.

# MAKE-UP

*See also: applicators; artificial lashes; blusher; brushes; cleansing; colour choice; eye make-up; eye make-up remover; foundation; hypo-allergenic products; lip colour; mascara; moisturizing; pencils; toning*

Make-up can define and refine your features, enhancing the good points while minimizing the faults. It can also help protect your skin from dehydration, sunlight, dust and dirt. Good make-up should not make your face look like a painted mask. Ideally, it should allow your face to be a natural reflection of your personality, and provide a boost to your self-esteem. Whether you wear just a moisturizer with sunscreen with a light touch of eye and lip colour, or foundation, powder, blusher and the whole range is entirely a matter of personal choice. Whatever make-up look you want to achieve, colours must be selected carefully (see **cosmetics**) and applied with the correct tools.

### DISGUISE AND EMPHASIS
Unless you resort to cosmetic surgery (see separate entry), your basic facial structure cannot be changed. There is, however, a great deal you can do with subtle shading, highlighting and blending to disguise or soften features you dislike, such as a crooked nose (see **camouflage, foundation**) or small eyes (see **eye make-up**) or uneven lips (see **lip colour**). And of course you can emphasize your best features, too. Concealers and foundations can cover up dark circles under the eyes, even out skin tones, camouflage spots and veins. Use your natural colouring as a guide when choosing shades that will complement your skin and hair. The sections on Afro hair, black skin, blondes, brunettes, colour choice, oriental skin, greying and redheads give special notes on make-up colours suited to these colourings. Experiment with cosmetics – play with colour, shade and highlight until you develop a look that is yours alone.

### Make-up notes
- Make up in a light similar to that in which your make-up will be seen. For daytime use a natural source of light shining directly on to your face (a light coming from the side will cast a shadow), or a mix of natural and artificial light. For evening, make up with electric light shining directly on the face.
- Always cleanse, tone and moisturize (see separate entries) before applying your foundation, or if you are re-applying make-up for the evening. Then apply colour, stroking and blending with fingers and brushes to ensure that there are no harsh lines or streaks. Look at the step-by-step make-up shown here, and other examples in the sections on black and oriental skin types (see also **eye make-up, lip colour, foundation** and **blushers**).
- Daytime make-up tends to look best with a matt finish, set with translucent powder. In the evening, colour can be intensified and deepened, and frosted or glittery cosmetics can be used.
- Make-up for sports and summer should be light, and transparent if you are tanned. Try using natural-tinted moisturizers or gels instead of foundation. Whether you use moisturizers alone or foundations to protect and moisturize, choose products with UV filters (see **tanning**). Use waterproof mascaras and eye make-up if you will be swimming.
- In winter, light is softer and skin paler, so warm up pallid complexions with blusher rather than a darker-toned foundation. Use a richer moisturizer in dry, cold weather or in centrally heated atmospheres.
- In all extremes of climate, keep lips well moisturized and protected with a lipstick containing sunscreen and moisturizer.
- As your skin and hair gradually change colour and texture with time, your make-up will need adjusting, too (see **colour choice, greying**).
- If you have sensitive skin which is likely to react badly to certain ingredients in cosmetics, choose unperfumed or hypo-allergenic products: you may need to test several in order to find one that suits you.

1 A speedy evening look based on your daytime make-up: camouflage blemishes and brush loose powder over your skin for a matt look.
2 Highlight under eyes and around cheeks with a touch of coral powder blusher.
3 Draw a thin line of black eyeliner along edge of top lashes to enhance the eye.

Brush charcoal shadow just beneath the eyes and then dust pewter shadow below the brow.
4 Neaten the eyebrows taking out extra hairs using tweezers and lengthen slightly with fine dark brush-strokes. Smooth gold glitter shadow on lids and carefully apply false lashes to the outer corners for extra special evening glamour.

5 Moisturize lips with vitamin E oil stick, then brush on a darker lipstick than your daytime choice in the centre of your lips working out to edges, outlining lips carefully. Add a touch of gloss for added reflection. The finished look is soft, yet sophisticated: brush gold powder shadow lightly over eyebrows for more shine.

# MANICURE

*See also: artificial nails; hands; nails*

Fingernails and the surrounding cuticles need regular, careful treatment. A weekly manicure is adequate to maintain the shape of the nails, although cuticle cream should be massaged in daily to encourage growth from the base of the nail, and is especially important if the nails are brittle or dry. Always protect nails and hands with rubber gloves when washing or using harsh chemicals.

Cuticles Never push or prod the cuticle with sharp, metal instruments, never cut them (see **cuticles**).
Nails Do not attempt to grow long nails if they do not grow well naturally. Keep them all one length, and use an emery board to keep them in trim.

File in one direction, as sawing back and forth dries out the moisture in the nail. Keep the sides straight: filing too low into the corners weakens the nail. If your nails are weak or easily chipped, brush on nail hardeners which will strengthen them by wrapping the nail with a criss-cross fibrous coat. If your nails do grow long easily, keep them short and well trimmed. Soften dry nails by soaking them in warm olive oil for 20-30 minutes once a week.

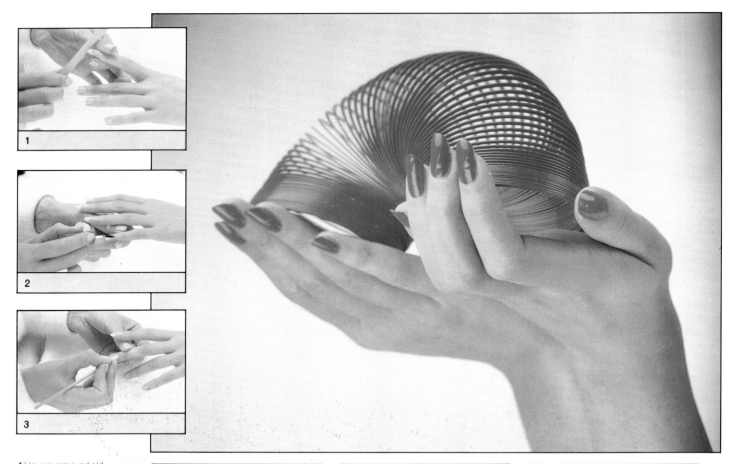

**1** Having removed old polish with oily remover on cotton wool (wind some round an orange stick to clean around cuticles), file nails with smooth side of emery board in one direction only, to prevent splitting.
**2** Dab each nail with cuticle remover and massage in with circular movements to soften them and improve circulation. Soak fingertips in tepid water containing a few drops of cuticle oil for five minutes to soften skin.
**3** Gently ease back cuticle with the tip of an orange stick wrapped in cotton wool and lift to separate from the nail.
**4** If you have not had a manicure for some time clip hangnails (spikey bits at the side of nails) gently if necessary but do not clip cuticles as this can cause infection to enter nail bed and inflammation.
**5** Massage in hand cream, then remove oiliness from nails by buffing with a piece of cotton wool. Apply base coat, then paint on two thin coats of varnish with even strokes, allowing each coat of varnish to dry thoroughly between applications.
**6** Apply top coat to prevent chipping.

Artificial nail kits are an alternative for nails in bad condition, but they can look unnatural if badly applied. The nail rebuilding treatments available at many beauty salons are sophisticated and more effective (see **artificial nails**).

### CHOOSING AND USING NAIL POLISH

Nail polishes, enamels or varnishes (all chemically similar) need not necessarily match your lips, despite the prevalence of co-ordinated ranges – try a contrast. Vibrant reds, pale ivories and pastels draw attention to nails, so unless they are in splendid shape, stick to medium-toned pinks and corals. Apricots, pinks and orangey reds enhance a tan.

For party occasions have fun painting spots, stripes and zig-zags. Choose a base colour, leave it to dry, and use a fine eyeliner brush to paint your pattern. For extra sparkle, some manicurists will set acrylic nails with 'diamonds'. Hypoallergenic varnishes should be used if your skin reacts against other types.

# MARTIAL ARTS

*See also: depression; exercise; fitness; meditation; relaxation; sports; yoga*

Although now widely thought of primarily as fighting skills, the martial arts have always been, since their development centuries ago, just as much a means of spiritual and moral growth. As well as improving striking ability, mobility, speed, timing and awareness, personal achievement and improvement are emphasized, as are other qualities like discipline, honesty and self-reliance. Some of the best known in the West are Tai-chi-ch'uan, Aikido, Judo and Karate. In many systems students are given demanding mental and physical standards to achieve both in the practice hall – the dojo – and at home. Praise when these standards are met is not customary: the aim is to an ever-improving performance on every level.

There are three main systems in the martial arts: kicking and punching, grappling, and weapons systems, one of which tends to dominate in a specific art. They originated all over the Orient and in Asia, and it is these Eastern types which have become increasingly popular in Europe and North America. In their journey to the West, many systems have changed character slightly, concentrating more on sporting or health considerations than their fighting component. The type of judo which is practised competitively, for example, excludes the fighting element which was once so important. It is a very honourable sport, in which giving way is a way to ultimate victory, and one with a strong intellectual bias using intuition and analysis.

Since many martial arts can increase aerobic fitness – improving efficiency and function of the cardio-respiratory system and local muscular endurance – and improve joint action, they are becoming more widely used for this purpose and for relaxation. All the martial arts require years of teaching to achieve a reasonable standard, and cannot be learnt from books. Contact martial arts or sports associations for recommendations as to good, trained teachers.

Apply mascara after face powder and eye colours. Curl the lashes first if you wish (see **eyelashes**). Always start with the lower lashes, brushing from the roots to the tips. First brush the top side of the lashes downwards and then brush their lower side upwards from underneath so that the lashes are uplifted and evenly coated. Repeat on upper lashes. Apply two light coats, separating the lashes in between with a clean eyelash comb. Don't be tempted to apply one heavy coat: the effect will be clogged and unnatural. Remove smudges with a cotton wool bud.

## MASCARA

*See also: cleansing; eye make-up*

There are two basic types of mascara. Cake mascara comes as a dry powder block and is applied with a damp brush. It separates the lashes very effectively, and lasts well. Wands are creamy liquid applications in a tube which are rolled on to the lashes with a circular brush, comb or rod.

Some wand mascaras contain filaments or fibres which enhance the thickness and length of the lashes. However, these can also cause irritation to the eyes so try them out before buying and be careful not to apply heavily. You should never wear this type of mascara if you have contact lenses: special flake-free types are available. Waterproof mascaras are a must for those who indulge in outdoor sports or swimming. Hypo-allergenic mascaras (see **hypo-allergenic products**) are available.

Mascara comes in basic black, brown and navy which look good for daytime wear, while bright blues, greens and purples are eye-catching for evenings: for a subtle touch use a dark mascara first, then tip lashes with colour. Vivid colours tend not to suit older women as their hair and skin grow paler: browns or greys are more flattering.

### REMOVING MASCARA
Place a tissue beneath the lower lashes, then, using a little eye make-up remover on a cotton wool bud, roll on and off both upper and lower lashes. Waterproof mascara requires an oil-based remover. Wipe the eye area with damp cotton wool afterwards.

## MASKS

Giving yourself a face mask – or having one applied professionally – not only benefits your skin, but provides you with a restful break from other activities while the mask takes effect. Masks usually contain several ingredients all combined to form a paste or solution which is applied to the whole face, excluding the eye and mouth area, and sometimes the neck, and left for a prescribed time to take effect. Some masks harden and dry on the skin and require washing off, while wax or latex (rubber)-based masks can be peeled away.

All masks will leave your skin feeling fresh and smooth: the choice of mask and the frequency of application is determined by the purpose for which it is intended and the condition of your skin. Depending on the ingredients, masks will cleanse, exfoliate, stimulate the circulation or generally refine the complexion, making it smooth and soft. The effect is, of course, temporary and masks will not remove lines, moisturize or rejuvenate the skin. Masks generally form part of a professional facial treatment, when they are specially formulated for your skin, but they are good as a quick 'facial' at home or in a salon, too.

### TYPES OF MASKS
- **Clay masks** Deep-cleanse the skin as the clay (see separate entry) and other active ingredients draw out and absorb superficial impurities. Suitable for all skins.
- **Exfoliating masks** For dull, lifeless skins. They contain abrasive, astringent ingredients – often

in the form of granules – to remove dead cells from the skin's surface and stimulate cell renewal.

**Gel masks** Liquid masks containing polymers which cause a light film to form when they dry. They are good for young skins since they act as mild exfoliants and cleanse the face lightly when sponged or rinsed away. Some contain herb or plant extracts.

**Peel-off masks** Latex rubber masks: are emulsions of latex which form a skin-like coating on the face when dry. They temporarily increase the skin's moisture content, but do not deep-cleanse. Wax masks: melted paraffin wax is smoothed on to the face and left to cool and harden before being peeled off. The wax helps soften and moisturize the skin.

**Refresher masks** These contain astringent ingredients such as camphor BP and menthol to tighten the pores, stimulate the blood flow and improve the skin's texture. From application to removal takes only about 10-15 minutes.

**Cream masks** Are mostly oil-in-water emulsions which act as temporary moisturizers to soften and dissipate lines, improve skin tone and stimulate circulation. These are suitable for all skin types, but are particularly nourishing for dry, sensitive skins as they do not set hard.

**Oil masks** Dry skins will benefit from this mask which consists of applying a cloth soaked in warm oil to the face.

**Sensitive skin masks** Often hypoallergenic, these masks are mild and should be massaged into the skin gently. They do not set hard.

**Eye masks** The eye area is VERY sensitive, so these masks, often in gel form, are mild and light and should be applied and removed extremely gently. (See **eyes** for tired eye remedies).

**Natural product masks** A great variety of foodstuffs from honey, eggs and yoghurt to cereals, vegetables and fruit can be used on their own or mixed with other ingredients according to their properties. Dry skins: melon, avocado, lettuce, carrot, egg yolk, sour cream, honey, bananas. Oily skins: beaten egg white (an excellent skin tightener), yoghurt, lemon, oatmeal, cucumber, parsley, ground almonds, yeast.

**Herb-based masks** Herbs often used in masks include: yarrow for oily skin, chamomile for cleansing, comfrey for healing and soothing infections, nettle and rosemary to stimulate circulation. An infusion of the required herb or herbs is added to a cream, gel or clay base depending on your skin type (see **herbs**).

**Sulphur masks** Sulphur is a fine, yellowish powder which some beauticians use for treating acne and oily skins. It can cause allergies, so carry out a skin test before use. Use as clay.

**Cactus jelly masks** These are used in aromatherapy treatments to cleanse and moisturize the face as well as to help the skin absorb essential oils.

### USING MASKS

1   Select the appropriate mask for your skin and purpose. If you have combination skin, you may need to use two types, one for oily areas and another for drier parts.
2   Tie your hair back from your face and cleanse the skin thoroughly (although if you are using a clay or earth-based mask these will absorb most impurities).
3   Pat your face gently with a cotton wool pad soaked in a toning lotion appropriate to your skin type.
4   Apply mask lightly, avoiding the eye and mouth areas. If including the neck, work upwards from the base, smoothing on the application evenly and right up to the edges of the face. A spatula is useful for this.
5   Lie down with cotton wool pads soaked in witch hazel on your eyes. Leave mask on for exactly the specified time.
6   Either peel or rinse mask off gently with cotton wool and tepid water according to instructions. Pat skin dry with a towel.
7   Close pores with a mild toner and moisturize thoroughly.

# MASSAGE

*See also: aches and pains; acupressure; aromatherapy; back; feet; health farms; neck and shoulders; physiotherapy; reflexology; Rolfing*

Massage, whether in the form of a foot or neck massage or of a full body massage, can bring tremendous benefits, and it is for this reason that it has been used since early times to promote health and well-being. Massage lies somewhere between touch and manipulation: therapies such as acupressure, Rolfing and of course physiotherapy use techniques closely allied to it.

### TECHNIQUES IN MASSAGE

Many different techniques can be used in massage, depending on the preference of the practitioner and the needs of the patient. Beauticians sometimes use electronic massage aids and machines like G5, which has a rubber 'brush' which vibrates at variable speed against the muscle. The Swedish massage (itself based on earlier Greek, Roman and Oriental practices) which was formulated in the early nineteenth century by Dr Peter Henrik Ling is designed to promote changes in the circulation, muscular and nervous system. It has five movements: effleurage, petrissage, tapotement, friction and vibration. Much modern massage is based on these techniques, with some later additions.

The person being massaged lies on a firm surface such as a table, preferably a special massage table, or the floor. Beds are too soft and springy. The patient lies on a towel, with areas of the body not being worked on covered with another towel for warmth. Most practitioners use a few drops of scented oil warmed (see **aromatherapy**) in the palm of the hand, to aid movement of the hands on the body; some use talcum powder.

**Effleurage** This is the lightest touch in massage, ranging from gentle to firm stroking. Used at the beginning and end of most sessions to stimulate the circulation, warm and relax muscles.

**Petrissage** A deeper kneading movement, rather like that of kneading dough, mainly used on fleshier areas. The masseur uses the tips of the fingers, or the palm of the hand, ensuring that hands remain relaxed. Use with hands on top of each other for extra pressure, or with hands working alongside each other, the left hand clockwise, the right hand anti-clockwise. Aids relaxation of tensed muscle areas, and is particularly soothing after vigorous exercise.

**Tapotement** A clapping movement carried out with hands cupped, moving alternately. Because the effect is invigorating, it is used before vigorous exercise rather than as a relaxer.

**Friction** A deep, single point muscle massage movement. Thumbs are rotated in tiny circles, moving just the deep muscles, not the skin. Used for spot treatment of problem areas after effleurage and petrissage.

**Spot pressure** Firm pressure on single points, without any other movement, often using thumbs; palms or fingers can also be used.

**Piano playing** As it sounds, rhythmical drumming with the fingers and thumbs used to release tension.

**Vibration** Light pressure on an area with fingers, associated with swift, light shaking. Excellent for promoting circulation where this is poor, and for massaging cold or numb feet or hands.

**Slapping and hacking** More advanced techniques which are best left to the professionals. Hacking is similar to slapping, but is done with the side of the hand rather than the palm. Both are used to stimulate muscles, and tend to be used either mid-session in a full body massage, or at the end if massage precedes athletics or any other vigorous activity.

### STARTING MASSAGE

If you have a grasp of the basics of physiology and a keen interest in massage you are well on the way. It is not difficult to learn, but it is much easier to acquire the range of movements with practical guidance and demonstrations: you would do well to attend one of the many day or evening classes given by qualified masseurs and masseuses.

You can massage yourself, too. Try a *scalp massage* (use no oil) if you are tired and tense: sit comfortably and shut your eyes, start with your thumbs resting just behind your ears, your fingers just touching at the bottom of your hair line at the back. Now move the fingers of each hand in circles away from each other with quite a firm touch. Work up your head to the forehead, then back along the sides. If you suffer from a dry scalp, try using a few drops of unscented oil such as olive oil rubbed into your hands, and massage a few hours before washing your hair.

Another good quick pick-up is a *foot massage*. If possible, warm your feet in a bath first, then sit yourself comfortably in a chair with the foot you are to work on resting on the other thigh. With or without oil, start with gentle effleurage, then massage the toes individually, pulling them gently, then use light spot pressure along the bottom of the foot, under the heel, arch, the ball of the foot. Now grasp the whole foot quite firmly and 'scrunch' it gently. Complete the massage with more spot pressure and then effleurage.

### POINTS TO REMEMBER

- **Avoid massage** if you are suffering from an infection, joint inflammation or swelling such as that associated with rheumatoid arthritis or hernia.
- **Take professional advice on** whether and how you should have massage if suffering from arthritis, thrombosis or oedema.
- **During pregnancy, consult** a doctor concerning body massage: foot, neck and head massage (all done while seated) could all be beneficial, however.
- **Avoid massage** on areas of skin with moles, warts and where there are varicose veins. Sensation around operation scars can be unpleasant: warn masseurs before they begin.

### EFFECTS OF MASSAGE

Massage can be relaxing or invigorating and stimulating, depending on the strokes used. Sensations range from mildly painful as knots are attacked, to a sense of relief as tension dissipates and one of soothing as your body is stroked. A full body massage can be so relaxing that you fall asleep during the 45 minutes or hour that it takes. Problems associated with tension such as stress, headaches and backache can all be helped, and the circulation is stimulated, too. When carried out in association with other treatment, massage can help repair post-operative or accidental damage to muscles and to joints (by relaxing and toning the surrounding and supporting muscles). Some doctors maintain that the physical benefits of massage last only half an hour or so, until the circulation returns to normal. But massage really can help release muscular tension: an improvement which can be maintained with help from you. And the psychological benefits of massage are enormous, in terms of relaxation, enjoyment, rest and your appreciation of your body.

# MASTECTOMY

*See also: bras; breasts; cosmetic surgery*

Mastectomy is the surgical removal of a breast, most commonly performed for cancer of the breast. The operation varies in type according to the extent of the cancer. In some cases just the tumour and surrounding breast tissue are removed in the operation known as lumpectomy or partial mastectomy; in more radical mastectomies, part of the muscles linking the upper chest muscles to the shoulder have to be removed, as well as the lymph nodes in the armpit.

Mastectomy, particularly radical mastectomy is less commonly performed than it once was due to earlier detection by women themselves and medical staff, and also much better surgery. New procedures for breast rebuilding mean that in many cases breast surgery leaves less evidence than it used to do. Rebuilding depends on many factors including how radical the operation was and the type of surgery used, the size, type and stage of development of the tumour and whether further treatment such as radiotherapy is needed. Whatever the circumstances, there must normally be a delay of a year to 18 months between the mastectomy and the rebuilding, which may take one or more operations. The consultant surgeon and a cosmetic surgeon will advise each patient according to her particular situation (see **cosmetic surgery**).

If breast rebuilding is not possible, or if there is a lapse between surgery and rebuilding, a prosthesis is provided (see **bras**).

Mastectomy is a major and daunting operation, which many women initially fear will bring a reduction in femininity and desirability, but often they find that once they are in hospital for the operation it becomes more emotionally manageable. The staff are specially trained to understand and help with all the physical and emotional problems which may arise, and there will be other patients in a similar situation with whom to share worries and problems. It is best to talk them all out as much as possible, with partner, family, and friends, too. Their support and understanding will be really helpful. Any woman facing a mastectomy should ask her surgeon all the questions on her mind, about the operations, the outlook for the future, the scars, anything that worries her. You will be surprised at how quickly you heal up and recover, and as you do so you will regain your old self-confidence in being well again and having come through a challenge with flying colours. There are support groups for mastectomy patients, which the surgeon, family doctor or local health centre will know about. Adjusting to the physical change will take some time and work, too. It is important to practise diligently any exercises which are given: the chest, shoulder and arm area will feel stiff and awkward at first. It is only natural for the body to take time to adjust to the change, and with patience that adjustment will undoubtedly be made.

# MEDITATION

*See also: awareness; insomnia; relaxation; sleep; stress; yoga*

Meditation can take many forms. At its simplest, it means pondering deeply about something. In therapeutic terms its meaning is somewhat different. It involves focusing the mind in order to reach a level of consciousness different from that normally experienced, in order to achieve emotional, spiritual and physical peace and harmony.

### THE BENEFITS OF MEDITATION
Most people can derive a wide range of mental benefits from meditating. Relaxation is one of the major reasons that many people turn to it today. The effects of stress are relieved as you sit peacefully, and realize that the world still goes on without you. As your metabolism slows down, so adrenaline and noradrenaline ebb away and your heart rate and breathing rate decrease. Regular meditation can help alleviate hypertension and depression. It can also improve self-confidence, leading to a better performance in many fields of endeavour. There are very few people for whom meditation is contraindicated, but those who suffer overwhelming anxiety, paranoia or delusions or whose testing of reality is poor may find it confusing and difficult rather than relaxing.

### VARIETIES OF MEDITATION
Meditation can be quick to learn, and can, indeed, slot easily into the routine of your life. Most types, such as Tibetan Buddhist meditation, begin with concentrating on breathing; others, transcendental meditation among them, use mantras, sounds whose stilling effects have been observed; in Zazen, counting is used to focus the mind.

There is one very simple practice, which you can do anywhere, at any time. Shut your eyes, and concentrate on your breathing. Take a deep breath, and then let it go, releasing all your worries, tensions, fears and problems as you let out the carbon dioxide which your body does not need. This will help you to relax, even in the middle of the rush hour when you are travelling to work.

In yoga, the 'corpse' position or *shavasana* involves relaxing and meditating while lying flat on one's back. There are many versions of this pleasurable and re-energizing process, and you will find it particularly restful after a busy day.

Most forms of meditation, however, are carried out in a seated position, so that the spine is straight and the pressures on it are just those of gravity, not of muscular tension. Maintaining this position – which may be very different from one's normal slouch – while remaining immobile, can both produce a great strengthening of will, and may increase self-respect and self-confidence as the urge to move is overcome. In order to focus the mind, you can begin by counting slowly from one to ten then back down to one again.

### MEDITATION NOTES
■ Many community groups provide courses in meditation, and there are a number of Buddhist and TM organizations which give classes.
■ Choose somewhere peaceful to meditate, away from distractions. With practice you may find that you can meditate anywhere, despite what is going on around you.
■ Think ahead and slot meditation sessions into your regular routine.
■ Get a special cushion or whatever you need to ensure that you are comfortable in your meditating position.

Two forms of meditation have been much talked about in recent years:

**Vizualization Therapy** overlaps to some extent with autosuggestion and autogenics. Visualization has long been used by the Tibetan Buddhists for healing in many areas. It is now used in the West to help heal disease: practitioners feel that many people who suffer diseases like cancer are those who repress their fears, stress and anxiety, and visualization is used partly to release these problems into the conscious mind. Patients are taught during deep contemplation, to make a mental picture of their disease and of the effect treatment has as it works to destroy it.

**Transcendental Meditation** (TM) is a popular technique taught by Maharishi Mahesh Yogi, which produces extensively researched benefits to the mind and body through the deep relaxation gained. TM is practised silently for 15-20 minutes twice a day while sitting comfortably with the eyes closed. During the practice the mind settles effortlessly and systematically through finer and finer levels of thinking and gains the most silent level of the mind – pure unbounded awareness. The experience is often described as one of restful alertness. At the same time the physiology settles to an equally profound level of rest, more than twice as deep as that gained during sleep.

# MELANIN

*See also: freckles; hair; liver spots; moles; skin; tanning*

Melanin is a pigment which occurs naturally in the skin, hair and also in the eyes. In the skin, it is produced in the lower epidermis (see **skin**). In sunlight, more melanin is produced by the body to protect the deeper skin layers from radiation. This is what happens when you get a tan.

Not all skins, however, can produce enough melanin to prevent burning, and in any case melanin provides no protection against the ageing effects of the sun and little against the damaging effects of ultra-violet rays (see **tanning**). Always wear sunscreens or sunblock in the sun. Freckles and moles are areas where there is a local increase in melanin production.

# MENOPAUSE

*See also: contraception; depression; fifties; forties; hormones; Hormone Replacement Therapy; hot flushes (flashes); menstruation; skin*

Menopause literally means the ending of monthly periods. It is rare for them to cease abruptly; in fact the hormonal changes which produce the menopause begin, imperceptibly, years earlier. The medical term 'climacteric' covers the whole span from when menstruation starts to decline until the final menstrual period.

The reason for the ending of the monthly menstrual flow is that the ovaries become resistant to the follicle stimulating hormone (FSH) released by the pituitary gland (see **hormones**). The egg, therefore, does not ripen and ovulation does not occur (see chart in **menstruation**). If ovulation does not occur, progesterone is not produced by the ruptured follicle, the lining of the uterus does not become rich and juicy in anticipation of pregnancy and there is, therefore no lining to shed each month.

### TIMING AND MANIFESTATION

The age at which women experience menopause can vary between 35 and 65 but tends to be around 45-54. It is rare for menstruation to cease abruptly. More commonly, the time between periods gets longer until they cease altogether, or the menstrual flow gradually lessens until you no longer have a monthly period.

Because of menstrual irregularity and uncertainty when or if you are ovulating, use some form of contraception for a year after the menopause if over 50, 2 years if under: 'unexpected' conception at this time is by no means uncommon.

The classical physical symptoms of the menopause are hot flushes (flashes) (see separate entry), night sweats and loss of lubrication in the vagina. Other symptoms include dizziness, headaches, insomnia, fatigue, digestive troubles such as flatulence, constipation or abdominal distension, breathlessness and palpitations. Emotional changes can include moodiness, tearfulness, irritability and depression. The intensity of these symptoms varies, with some women suffering only mild discomfort, while others may become severely or even suicidally depressed.

The hormone level alterations bring other changes too. Skin becomes drier and flakier as the sebaceous glands begin to shrink and produce less oil. Sometimes there is an increase in facial and body hair, caused either by a higher level of androgens (male hormones) or by an increased sensitivity to existing hormone levels. Osteoporosis – a condition in which bones become brittle and frail (see separate entry) – can result from the lower levels of oestrogen. If you have Hormone Replacement Therapy (see below and separate entry) to treat the various symptoms of menopause, it will help prevent osteoporosis, too. In any case, do increase your calcium intake and take plenty of regular, moderate exercise.

### COPING WITH THE MENOPAUSE

Attitudes to the menopause can range from ignorance to scathing disrespect and can often contribute to the loss of confidence which many women experience at this time. It is quite natural to feel uncertainty over what is happening to your body and many women experience the feeling that the end of their reproductive life signals the end of their contribution to society. In fact, the menopause can herald a new beginning where sexual relations are no longer inhibited by fear of pregnancy.

▣ Read as much as you can about the changes which your body is going through, ask your doctor about them and special menopause clinics if you have worries. The more information you have the more you will feel in control.

▣ If your symptoms are severe, see your doctor. Anti-depressants and tranquillizers are not helpful here. Hormone treatment can be immensely helpful.

▣ Discuss your feelings, whether of worry, uselessness, depression or fear, with your partner and with your children, too. If you let them know what is happening it will be easier for them to be sympathetic.

▣ Menopause often occurs at a time when your children are beginning to leave home and set up on their own. This can compound with the menopause to make you feel unnecessary to them and to your partner. Try to remember that these feelings are caused by changes in hormone levels, and that they will pass. Take up a new hobby, take on a part-time job if you do not work, or get involved in charity work.

▣ If hormonal changes have caused your vagina to become sore or dry, buy some lubricating jelly. If the problem is very severe, your doctor may advise Hormone Replacement Therapy which will help.

# MENORRHAGIA

*See also: contraception; menstruation; metrorrhagia; stress*

Menorrhagia is heavy bleeding when menstruating. This can sometimes be associated with periods which go on too long, that is, more than the normal 2 to 6 days. The condition can have several causes. Stress is a common one, also having thicker than normal endometrial tissue (womb lining) as a result of having an IUD fitted (see **contraception**). Increase the amount of iron in your diet to prevent yourself becoming anaemic from losing large amounts of blood. If menorrhagia persists or pain occurs, consult your doctor as other possible causes are hypertension, hormone imbalances and fibroids in the womb which may need treatment.

# MENSTRUATION

*See also: amenorrhoea; contraception; dysmenor-rhoea; hormones; menopause; pre-menstrual syndrome; puberty; spots*

The myths and taboos surrounding menstruation are many. In the developed countries very few cultural groups now go as far as to isolate menstruating women from society. Yet the attitude that menstruation is unclean, a 'curse' that women should cope with in silence still prevails, especially among men. Lack of knowledge in the past led to the proliferation of old wives' tales surrounding menstruation: that washing oneself or one's hair should be avoided, as should exercise, wearing thin clothing or having sex. All these are untrue, and in fact the opposite is true in most cases. Keeping the genital area clean is always important, and hormonal changes at this point in the cycle often mean that hair is particularly oily and needs more frequent washing. Exercise can help alleviate dysmenorrhoea (see separate entry); sex is just as acceptable now as at any other time, and many women find that they feel particularly sexy during menstruation.

The menarche, as the onset of menstruation is called, is one of the major physical changes that a young girl experiences. It heralds the beginning of adulthood and her ability to have children. The monthly discharge of blood is the discarding of the lining of the uterus (endometrium) which, having become thick to receive a fertilized egg, starts to shrink and gradually disintegrate if conception does not take place.

The menstrual cycle is controlled by the pituitary gland in the brain, which releases hormones to stimulate mature egg production in the ovaries. The age at which menarche occurs varies, being influenced by a variety of physical and psychological factors, but it is usually around the age of twelve. The pituitary gland releases hormones (see separate entry) which stimulate the ovaries into producing mature eggs. If not fertilized by sperm, each egg then dies and the endometrium is discarded and the cycle begins afresh.

The menstrual flow, consisting of blood, degenerated cells and a sticky fluid from the cervix, has a particular odour due to the action of bacteria in the vagina and air on the blood and any aroma is perfectly normal and nothing to do with hygiene. The length of the menstrual cycle (the time between the first day of bleeding until the first day of the next cycle) can be anything between 24 to 34 days but is usually around 29 days. The word menstruation comes from the Latin *menses*, meaning month. The duration and amount of bleeding varies. It depends on the thickness of the endometrium which can be affected by factors such as taking the contraceptive pill or having an IUD. On average, a woman can expect to menstruate for 30-35 years of her life, between 300 and 500 times.

## Menstrual problems

There are several common menstrual problems:

1 The pituitary gland in the brain releases the follicle stimulating hormone (FSH). The follicles in the ovaries develop and ripen.
2 Throughout this time oestrogen is being produced by the ovaries. This triggers the production of luteinizing hormone (LH), which triggers the release of the mature egg (ovulation) from the follicle.
3 Around ovulation there is a change in the cervical mucus, and a slight drop in the basal body temperature 24 hours prior to ovulation, followed by a rise until the end of the cycle.
4 The egg travels down the fallopian tube to the uterus: 5-7 days, egg survival is 24-48 hours, so there are usually four fertile days, two days before and two days after ovulation.
5 The ruptured follicle changes into the corpus luteum then produces progesterone, which prepares the endometrium by making it thick and juicy in readiness for the fertilized egg.
6 If fertilization does not occur, the levels of oestrogen and progesterone start to fall, the endometrium shrinks, is shed in menstruation and the cycle starts again.

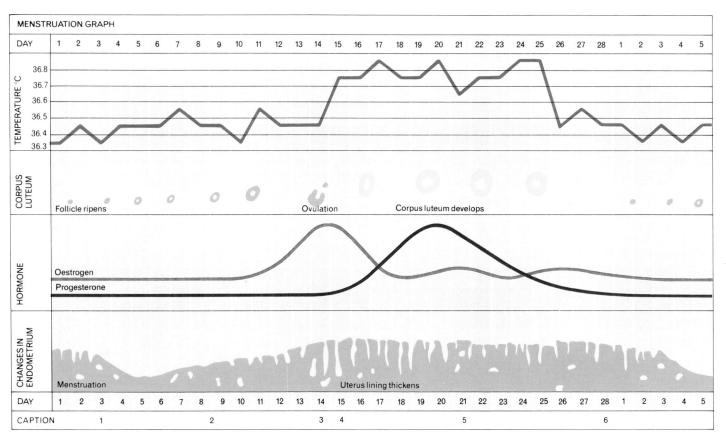

**M**

**Midwife**
See Pregnancy

**Menorrhagia** Heavy or prolonged periods
**Metrorrhagia** Irregular menstrual bleeding, spotting and breakthrough bleeding
**Dysmenorrhoea** Painful periods
**Amenorrhoea** Absence of periods
**Mittelschmerz** A pain low down in the abdomen, often to one side, which some women experience at ovulation. It occurs when the egg is rupturing the follicle, about to start the journey down the fallopian tube and lasts just a few hours. If you suffer unusual abdominal pain, consult your doctor.
**Pre-menstrual syndrome** A series of symptoms which occur before the period, including headache, nausea, bloatedness, anxiety and irritability.

All these are dealt with under their own headings elsewhere in the book.

The increased hormonal activity around menstruation also stimulates the sebaceous glands. Increasing output can result in oily skin and spots. There is little that you can do about this, but try stepping up the frequency with which you use a mild toner for these few days. Do not use *too* much or you will stimulate production still further, and remember not to touch spots or you may infect them and make them worse.

Other problems surround the use of pads or tampons to soak up the blood flow. Tampons are the most convenient method, preventing odour, giving no outward bulk, and making it easy to continue your normal exercise, including swimming. If your periods are heavy you may need to use a tampon and light, press-on towel as well for a day or two. Change tampons at least every 3-4 hours, except at night when you should insert one just before going to sleep and remove it on waking. *Never* use scented or deodorised tampons as these can cause itching, allergy and even infection. Scrupulous attention to hygiene is all that is necessary.

# METABOLIC RATE

*See also: dance; diet; exercise; fitness; ketosis; slimming; sports*

The basal metabolic rate (BMR) is the minimum amount of energy your body requires in order to maintain vital bodily processes. It is often expressed in Calories per surface area (so that it takes your size into account) of the body per day, and is measured in the fasting state at least 12 hours after a meal, when the body is lying down at rest. There is little that can be done to alter the basal metabolic rate, which is only affected by factors such as gender, age and changes in hormone levels (see **diet – Calorie requirements**). Differing basal metabolic rates help explain why it takes some people longer than others to lose weight on the same diet and exercise regime.

When diet and exercise plans refer to 'increasing your metabolic rate' they are not referring to your BMR, but to your total daily energy expenditure

a large component of which is due to physical activity. You can alter your energy balance by adjusting your food intake (i.e. if the energy Calories contained in the food you eat are greater than your total daily energy expenditure you will gain weight) or adjusting your total daily energy expenditure through physical activity (i.e. you may increase the amount, type and duration of exercise you take). In the latter case, provided your food intake remains the same or is reduced you will lose weight. Alternatively, if you reduce your physical activity without altering your food intake you will gain weight. Regular exercise can produce increased efficiency in the metabolism of energy (see **dance, exercise**).

# METRORRHAGIA

*See also: contraception; hormones; menorrhagia; menstruation*

Metrorrhagia is irregular menstrual bleeding (see **menstruation**), spotting or breakthrough bleeding between periods. Some women suffer metrorrhagia at ovulation, the time when the egg is released from the follicle. It can also happen as a result of taking the contraceptive pill, especially the progestogen-only type, or of having an IUD. All these are quite normal but if the spotting is persistent, heavy or painful you should consult a doctor, as it can in this case be a symptom of a disorder in the uterus or cervix which needs treatment.

# MIGRAINE AND HEADACHES

*See also: anxiety; diet; herbs; meditation; relaxation; stress*

Despite a great deal of research and an increase in knowledge, doctors still do not fully understand migraine, despite its being with us since at least 1200 BC. The word migraine is a corruption of the Greek word *hemicrania* meaning half skull, and is so named because it characteristically affects one side of the head. What probably causes the head pain and other symptoms is abnormal constriction of blood vessels in the brain, followed by abnormal dilation. There can be a reduction of blood flow to the brain of as much as 25 per cent. It begins with the well-known disturbance of vision which is due to the abnormal constriction of the blood vessels in the optic areas of the brain, seeing flashing lights and zig-zags; sometimes there is even temporary blindness. There may be shakiness in the legs and arms or numbness. These symptoms last for a short while, 20-30 minutes, after which nausea sets in in many cases, and then the blinding headache which is so painfully familiar to sufferers. Migraines do tend to run in families, and tend to begin well before middle age, often as early as the teens.

Some doctors now think it possible that migraines are caused by a vascular or blood disorder. There are also theories that migraine sufferers are unable to metabolize some proteins. A wide range of factors are implicated in bringing on migraine: for many people monitoring can help prevent migraine occurring or at least reduce their frequency:

- **Stress, anxiety and tension** Are very common factors indeed: see separate entries for coping with these. Insomnia and fatigue are other possible causes.
- **Hormonal fluctuation** In women. Ovulation, the days either side of the menstrual period and the early part of pregnancy are all times when sufferers seem to be more susceptible to migraine. Some women find that combined contraceptive pills are bad too, especially the now less common higher oestrogen types.
- **Certain foods, drinks and additives** Substances containing the amine tyramine, which seems to act on the vascular system, are now thought to be particularly hazardous here; matured cheese or wine, avocado and citrus fruits fall into this category. Other culprits which sufferers have highlighted are chocolate, all cheeses and dairy products including yoghurt, coffee, tea, fried foods, tinned foods, meat (especially pork), seafood, alcohol, some vegetables including onions and garlic, wheat, eggs and cola drinks. Nitrites, in preserved meats such as ham and salami, and monosodium glutamate, in Chinese dishes and canned soups and foods, are also implicated.
- **Hypertension** (see separate entry) May make migraines worse because of the extra pressure in the vessels.
- **Hunger/hypoglycaemia** Occurs when blood sugar levels are abnormally low due to insufficient carbohydrate intake. This is why some diabetics suffer migraine. Ensure that you eat properly and regularly, that means whenever your body decrees.
- **Change** Unsettling factors such as changing jobs, travelling by air which upsets your body clock, climatic alterations may be causes.
- **Noise** Can be a trigger for migraine.

### COPING WITH MIGRAINE
Study the factors above, and try to list those which could have contributed to your last attack; the combination varies for everyone. Note any early warning signs which may have occurred well before your migraine, too, such as extreme tension. Then try to cut these out, and if you suffer another attack, re-analyse and adjust your prevention scheme. Enrol your partner or family to help you, too.

Try to reduce your stress levels: take up meditation or use relaxation techniques regularly. Take plenty of exercise. Talk out your problems, do not harbour them secretly inside. Regular massages can help remove knots of tension in your muscles.

Ensure that your diet includes plenty of B complex vitamins, or take a supplement. If you have regularly suffered from migraines, ask your doctor for a prescription (see below), so that you have help at hand should you suffer an attack. Sufferers may be placed on low daily dosages of Beta blockers like Inderol or anti-depressants like Elavil which have shown to have application for migraine.

Once you feel the first signs of a migraine coming on try to meditate or practise other relaxation techniques in a darkened room. Then take any medications which you have been prescribed. The latest types of drugs are combinations of strong analgesics to kill pain and anti-emetics to prevent vomiting and feelings of nausea. If you have none, take 2 paracetamol tablets (acetaminophen in the US) or one of the Ibuprofen or Aduil tablets now available without prescription in the UK and US. Try to sleep, and use a cool damp facecloth or cool icepack on your forehead. Continue to take medication at prescribed intervals or take 2 paracetamol (acetaminophen) every four hours). Drink as much fluid as you can, just plain water or tea without milk.

When you feel well enough, take a long warm bath with an infusion of rosemary, catnip or sage (see **herbs, infusions**). Start by eating lightly, avoiding all the foods and drinks implicated in causing migraine. Another natural remedy is to take a hot footbath while keeping a cool compress on your head. You could try investigating biofeedback (see separate entry).

### HEADACHES
Headaches of other kinds too, can be extremely painful and may sometimes be related to muscular tension. This can be caused by physical factors such as eye-strain, or mental ones such as worry, stress and overwork. Cluster headaches – those which occur repeatedly over a few weeks, then disappear for months – tend to be suffered by those between 30 and 45, particularly men who drink and smoke. They always affect one side of the head, lasting for up to two hours and associated with a stuffy nose and runny eyes. The treatment is as for migraine.

Everyone has times when they are under particular stress and are prone to headaches. But leading a generally healthy life should help prevent the problem. Cutting down on alcohol and cutting out smoking reduces your likelihood of suffering cluster headaches.

Have a warm, relaxing bath (see above) to help your muscles and mind unwind. Massage your neck and shoulders gently to release tension. Take 2 paracetamol (acetaminophen) if you like, then indulge yourself in listening to music or any gentle activity which you find relaxing. If your headache persists try some sport or exercise which you enjoy or have a professional massage.

Eye or dental problems can cause severe headache, so if you suspect your headaches might be due to these, consult your optician or dentist. If your headache is severe or persists, consult your doctor, as it might be a sign of hypertension or some other problems.

**Mittelschmerz**
See Menstruation

# MINERALS

*See also: diet; hair; nails; skin; vitamins*

All the food in our diet, whether animal or vegetable, is made up of elements from the earth, sea and air. Many of these elements are essential to the metabolic functions of man. Of these, some, such as calcium, iron and sodium, play a well-understood role in the maintenance of a healthy body. Others are known to be essential to the human diet only because unwelcome side-effects occur if they are missing. In many cases these deficiencies and side-effects are only seen in animals, and the re-

sulting theory applied to humans. The chart lists all the major minerals, and those required in the largest amounts: none very large, since minerals only make up about 3 per cent of body weight. Others needed in small amounts are chlorine (normally obtained with sodium or potassium as sodium or potassium chloride), chromium, cobalt, copper, manganese, selenium, sulphur and vanadium.

The daily amounts required of each mineral element vary considerably. Those which are needed in very small quantities are sometimes referred to as 'trace' elements, although dieticians and nutritionists disagree on exactly which elements fall into this category. Suggestions that mineral deficiencies can be detected through analysis of the amounts in hair are not scientifically reliable.

## MINERAL CHART

| MINERAL | SOURCES | PROPERTIES | DEFICIENCY PROBLEMS |
|---|---|---|---|
| **Calcium** Needs presence of vitamin D in the body to be absorbed adequately. Lactose and ascorbic acid enhance absorption. | Milk, butter, cheese, tinned fish eaten with bones (eg sardines, salmon, pilchards), fortified bread, green vegetables, hard tap water. | Forms an essential part of bones and teeth. It is also necessary for blood clotting and functioning of the nervous system and muscles. | Rickets, osteomalacia, osteoporosis. Minor deficiency can produce muscle cramps. |
| **Copper** Excess can interfere with the body's absorption of zinc, and may cause irregularity in menstruation. | Liver, fish (especially shellfish), Brazil nuts, cocoa, wheatgerm, curry powder, pulses, dark green leafy vegetables, red wine. | An essential component of several enzyme systems. Necessary for the conversion of iron into a component of haemoglobin. | Occurs in newborn babies, particularly if premature, resulting in diarrhoea followed by anaemia which results in accumulation of iron in the liver. |
| **Fluorine** One part per million of water is needed to benefit teeth. | Tea, especially China tea, some drinking water, seafood. | Hardens teeth, contributing to a reduction in the incidence of dental caries (tooth decay). | Tooth decay is more prevalent in regions where there is not sufficient fluorine in the water. |
| **Iodine** Second only to iron in importance. High intake of cabbage in diet may interfere with availability to the body. | Seafood, iodised salt, kelp, vegetables grown near the sea. | Forms an essential component of two hormones in thyroid gland which have an important effect on metabolic activity and development. | Goitre (enlargement of the thyroid). Severe deficiency may lead to cretinism in children and myxoedema in adults. |
| **Iron** Needs presence of vitamin C to be assimilated properly. Women lose iron through menstruation. | Liver, red meat, egg yolk, oysters, dried apricots, raisins, molasses (in general iron from meat sources is more readily absorbed). | Stored in bone marrow, where taken up as needed to become an essential component of haemoglobin. | Hypochromic (iron-deficiency) anaemia, with initial symptoms of fatigue. Severe deficiency may lead to palpitations and dizziness. |
| **Magnesium** Is a normal component of sweat, so particularly important in diet of those visiting hot climates or taking a lot of exercise. | Present in most foods. Almond, peanuts, walnuts, sesame seeds, legumes, wholegrain cereals, cabbage, yeast extract, seafood, bananas, hard tap water. | Essential part of several enzyme systems. Plays an important role in carbohydrate metabolism, and in neuromuscular transmission. Necessary for metabolism of vitamin D and calcium. | Bodily deficiency may occur due to illness, malabsorption in chronic alcoholics, as a result of diuretics due to excessive excretion in the urine. Symptoms are depression, irritability, vertigo, convulsions, and tachycardia. |
| **Phosphorus** Excessive intake may upset mineral balance and cause a deficiency of calcium. It is a common ingredient of food additives such as baking powder, emulsifiers and preservatives. | Occurs in most foods, in particular those high in calcium, for example milk, cheese, egg yolk, whole grains, fish. | Forms an essential part of the skeleton where it is in a ratio of 1:2 with calcium. Present in other tissues of the body in ratio of 10:1 with calcium. Involved with the absorption of glucose and metabolism of glucose, fat and protein. | Dietary deficiency unknown. In rare cases, long-term use of antacids may prevent absorption giving rise to deficiency symptoms of anorexia, bone pain and demineralization of the bone. |
| **Potassium** Potassium chloride is often used as a salt substitute for those aiming to reduce their sodium intake. | Citrus fruits, apples, bananas, potatoes (especially unpeeled), dried fruit, especially prunes, molasses, pineapples, tomatoes. | Together with sodium, regulates fluid balance. Potassium is essential for normal heart function, muscle contraction and the protein synthesis. | Dietary deficiency is unlikely. Diarrhoea or repeated use of laxatives may lead to a deficiency resulting in muscular weakness, vomiting, heart attack. |
| **Sodium** Intake in Western countries is ten times greater than needed. This may be related to high blood pressure. | As salt, it occurs in many foods, particularly processed foods such as bacon, cheese, tinned meat, salami, bread and some breakfast cereals. | Together with potassium, regulates the body's fluid balance, particularly in blood plasma. | Deficiency may occur after severe diarrhoea and vomiting. Other effects may include apathy, appetite loss and muscle cramps. |
| **Zinc** Is lost in sweating. Drinking water carried in copper pipes may depress zinc levels. | Oysters, meat, egg yolk, milk, nuts, whole grains, peas and beans. | Plays an essential role in the body's enzyme systems, the development of reproductive organs, and in the release of carbon dioxide. | Deficiency results in stunted growth and delayed puberty. |

# MOISTURIZING

*See also: after-sun preparations; ageing; body moisturizers; cleansing; climate; cosmetics; creams; facials; hypo-allergenic products; skin; tanning; toning; wrinkles*

The skin is kept naturally moist by a mixture of water and oils continually secreted by the sebaceous glands (see **skin**). Some moisture loss occurs daily: the skin tends to become dry after washing or bathing, particularly in hard water areas. Evaporation increases with the ageing process and is further exacerbated by the drying effects of the wind, sun, cold, central heating and air conditioning (see **ageing, tanning**). Illness, smoking and excess alcohol intake also contribute to skin dehydration, which in turn accelerates the appearance of lines and wrinkles. Although they cannot replace lost moisture, they can help prevent the skin from losing excess moisture.

### CHOOSING YOUR MOISTURIZER
All skin types need moisturizing, but some need it more than others. There are basically two kinds of moisturizer:
**Water-in-oil** emulsions are rich, heavy creams which form a protective film of oil on the skin. They plump up the skin's surface so that lines appear reduced, and evaporate slowly. These moisturizers suit dry or ageing skins and can be used for extra protection in extreme temperatures – especially dry or cold climates – or at night (see **creams**) when the skin is more absorbent.
**Oil-in-water** creams or lotions consist of more water than oil, so are light, easily absorbed and non-greasy. They are suitable for young or oily skins, for wearing under make-up and for summer, when the skin tends to be oiler. Those that contain humectants (such as rosewater, glycerine) are good in humid conditions as they will draw moisture from the air into the skin. Avoid them in dry climates: their hygroscopic (water-attracting) action means that they will take moisture out of the skin.

### SPECIAL NOTES
If you have sensitive skin choose an unscented moisturizer; if prone to allergies choose a hypo-allergenic (see separate entry) brand. Avoid products containing known allergens such as lanolin, which is always marked on product labels.

Oily skins may not need much extra lubrication; use a non-greasy lotion. Combination skin may require the use of two products for different zones.

Tinted moisturizers can be worn as a lighter alternative to foundation (after applying regular moisturizer) or beneath foundation to even out skin tones. Green disguises a high colour or red complexion, mauve helps sallowness and apricot improves a pale skin. Choose a product with UV filters.

### USING MOISTURIZER
The skin should be moisturized in the morning and

at night, after cleansing and toning, regardless of whether or not you wear make-up. Extra moisturizing is necessary if your skin is very dry or has been exposed to sun or water. Concentrate on the neck and throat area which tends to be dry. Avoid moisturizing oily or spotty areas, and use only a small amount of cream or lotion around them.

A light, tinted moisturizer is a good alternative to normal foundation during the summer months when you want to achieve a very natural healthy effect.

# MOLES

*See also: freckles; liver spots; melanin; skin*

Moles are dark marks on the skin where there are concentrations of the pigment melanin. They may be raised or flat. They are not usually present at birth, but appear in the first or second decades. Most people have up to fifty moles. They are permanent and neither fade nor darken. Liver spots (see separate entry) can sometimes resemble moles. Normally moles are completely harmless and give no trouble at all. If they are very large indeed, your doctor may advise their removal; ask his or her advice. If they have hair growing from them, do not pluck it out with tweezers, but snip it off close to the skin. Never scratch or pick at moles. If, however, they change in size or character you should see your doctor immediately. They can, rarely, become malignant and must then be removed. People with a lot of moles and fair skin who allow themselves to become sunburned are most at risk.

**Morning sickness**
See Pregnancy

**Mouthwashes**
See Dentist;
Dentistry; Gums;
Halitosis; Teeth

# MOTION SICKNESS

*See also: biofeedback; ears; hypnotherapy*

Motion sickness can occur during any form of movement such as sailing, driving, flying and even train travel. It occurs when the delicate balance mechanisms in the ear are upset by motion, and this affects the gastro-intestinal tract. It is not known why some people's bodies are susceptible to this problem, while others adjust quite readily. Sufferers can experience quite severe nausea, sometimes vomiting, headache, giddiness and weakness, which can continue for several hours after movement has ceased, as the body adjusts.

### COPING WITH MOTION SICKNESS
There are many drugs available to alleviate this problem, formulated for children in liquid form, as tablets for adults. Two types of drugs are available: anticholinergics, whose effects last up to about 6 hours, and antihistamines, which are longer-lasting. Your choice depends on your journey length (check with the pharmacist if the type of drug is not clear on the packaging) unless you have heart disease, glaucoma or are taking anti-depressants, in which case you should avoid anticholinergics. Both have the side effect of drowsiness, and should not be taken if you have to drive or operate machinery. Do not drink any alcohol if you are taking antihistamines. Other preventive steps include minimizing movement. Move to the centre of the boat where the swell will be felt least and lie down if you can. Since fresh air also seems to help, stay outside on shipboard (and watching the horizon – a steady focus – helps) and have plenty of air in the car. If travelling by car, sit in the front seat so that you can look out through the windscreen, the perceived motion will be less than if you are looking out of the side windows. Never try to read or map-read while travelling if you suffer from motion sickness, as it will exacerbate the problem.

Biofeedback and hypnosis have both been found to be helpful in some cases. Natural remedies include chewing ginger sticks or taking ginger tea. Peppermint oil can alleviate nausea.

# MOUSSES

*See also: gels; hairdressers; hair styles; moisturizing; tanning*

Mousses are becoming increasingly popular as a way of presenting beauty products: their bulk makes them easier to handle for setting hair, moisturizing or even cleansing. Their composition is very similar to that of equivalent non-mousse products, although minor alterations are made to render them suitable for a can, and a propellant to turn them into an aerosol is added. Hair mousses act similarly to hair gels, although the resin (which is what gives the hair more body and firmness) contained in them is closer in nature to that in hair spray than that in gel. Tanning mousse is very popular, as the foaminess makes it easier to apply it evenly.

# MOXIBUSTION

*See also: acupuncture; cosmetic acupuncture*

Moxibustion is a heat treatment sometimes used in conjunction with acupuncture or auriculotherapy with the aim of increasing the effect of the needles in clearing energy channels and releasing energy. The name of the process comes from *mokusa*, Japanese for 'burning herb', and the moxa or mugwort plant *(Artemisia vulgaris)* traditionally used. The most common technique is that of attaching cones of moxa to the handles of inserted needles and setting light to them. The patient's skin is protected from ash with card circles around each needle. Alternatively a roll of lighted moxa is held close to acupuncture points until heat is felt. A variation on this treatment is using tiny electric currents to give extra stimulation to the acupuncture points.

## MUD TREATMENTS

*See also: facials; health farms; masks; massage*

Mud baths, or the application of heated mud to the body in poultice form, is a therapy used primarily to relieve arthritis and rheumatism, to rid the body of cellulite and to relieve tension. Although the precise reasons for the effectiveness of the treatment remain unclear, it is thought that the therapeutic value of mud derives from its salt, acid and mineral content. Certainly a heated mud application helps stimulate the circulation.

There are various kinds of mud treatments and types of mud used. When Parafango mud (extracted from lakes near Padua) is used, it is heated and then placed on heat-resistant paper to cool before being applied to the various areas being treated, such as hands, knees, elbows and shoulders.

For mud baths, the mud is mixed with warm water and the body immersed up to the shoulders for about ten minutes.

For home use, there are a number of beauty products available commercially, composed of organic mud, rich in vegetable and mineral extracts. These can be applied over specific areas, such as the face or bust, over the entire body, or can be used as a mud bath. They aim to cleanse, soften, exfoliate and stimulate the skin, as well as to soothe and relax the body.

## MUSCLES

*See also: aerobics; dance; exercise; exercises; sports*

A single muscle fibre is a highly specialized cell which can convert energy from chemical reactions (as in food breakdown) into mechanical energy. Each fibre is covered in connective tissue and one single muscle consists of bundles of fibres all held together by the same connective tissue. This connective fabric runs continuously throughout the muscle and joins together at the ends of the muscle to form a cord of tissue known as a tendon, or to form a sheet of tendinous tissue known as an aponeurosis. Tendons link skeletal muscles to the skeleton and allow the muscle's contractions to move the joint. The number of muscles surrounding joints depends on the functional demands upon the

joint: not only the scope of movement, but also whether the joint is load-bearing and thus requires more muscularity. There are two other types of muscle in the body: cardiac muscle, forming the heart walls, and visceral or smooth muscle, which is found in the walls of the gut and blood vessels.

Key characteristics of muscle cells are their ability to contract as a response to stimuli, their extensibility and elasticity. Their action is complex. Simply speaking, when a stimulus is received, strands within each bundle of muscle cells slide along each other to bring the ends of the muscle cell together. This occurs simultaneously in each group and a movement can result. The messages sent out from the brain to muscles are detailed even for a simple movement in one plane: one muscle has to be told to remain inactive while at the same time another springs into action and still another perhaps stabilizes the movement.

Limitations are placed on muscle movement by the range of movement of the joints, due to their differing structure and arrangement of ligaments as well as the strengths and weaknesses of the various muscles around the joint. Like joints, muscles can quite easily be damaged. Always consult your doctor before undertaking a new exercise programme and ensure that you are taught by a qualified instructor. And remember that, to be fit, muscles need to go through a wide range of movements: concentric, eccentric, isotonic and isometric, all of which they receive in everyday life.

## Natural family planning
See Contraception

## Nausea
See Migraine;
Motion Sickness;
Pregnancy

## Nautilus (T.M.)
See Gyms and
gym equipment

## Niacin
See Vitamin B3

## Nicorette chewing gum (T.M.)
See Smoking;
Dependencies

## Nicotine
See Smoking

# NAILS

*See also: artificial nails; buffing; cuticles; diet; gelatin; hands; manicure; minerals; pedicure; pregnancy*

The finger- and toenails are formed from layers of keratin – dead protein – which extend from living cells situated in the skin about 3-4 mm (⅛-¼ inch) below the visible lanula – half moon. The nail plate is sealed to the skin by the cuticle which prevents dirt and bacteria from entering the finger.

Fingernails grow faster than toenails – about 1 mm (1/16 inch) a week. It takes about five months for a completely new nail to form: growth varies with the individual, but is most rapid in youth, pregnancy and warm weather. Obviously, the nail weakens as it grows from its base, so healthy nails should be kept fairly short and curved to avoid breakage and splitting. See **manicure** and **artificial nails**.

### NAIL PROBLEMS
The appearance of your nails is partly hereditary, but illness, stress and poor diet can all affect their texture and condition. Spoon-shaped nails can be caused by anaemia (see separate entry), brittle or split nails by a vitamin or iron deficiency. They are more likely, however, to result from daily exposure to chemicals and detergents, to constant use of nail polishes, hardeners or removers which are drying and also cause discoloration.

**White spots or bands** on the nail (leukonychia), may be due to a minor trauma; another less common cause is a zinc deficiency which you can put right by taking zinc tablets or brewer's yeast or by increasing your intake of seafood and red meat.

**Horizontal ridging** on all nails can indicate a past illness or damage to the base of the nail which can slow up or stop nail growth. When growth resumes, a line can form at the half moon, but will grow out.

**Nail Inflammation** (paronychia). This is a swelling and inflammation of the skin folds surrounding the finger- or toenails. It is usually caused by a fungal or bacterial infection, and can be treated with antifungal or antibacterial ointment.

**Nail Separation** (onycholysis). An early indication of nail separation is the appearance of a white spot at the tip of the nail. It is normally caused by a fungal infection or poor blood supply which loosens the nail from its normally secure base, and can be very painful. This is commonly seen in people suffering from psoriasis (see entry).

**Nail discoloration** (onychomycosis). This is a fungal infection which most commonly affects the big toenail. The nail discolours, becomes opaque, thick, brittle and difficult to cut. To treat, the nail must be pared and filed so that an antifungal liquid can be applied to the infected surface.

**Nail clubbing** is the name given to the thickening of the tissues around the base of the finger or toenail making the nails become curved, their tips assuming a bulbous, rounded appearance.

**Ingrowing nails** are only found on the feet, occurring when the curved side edge of the nail grows into the skin, which in turn grows back over it. It can be very painful. Ingrowing toenails can be hereditary, but other causes include injuries to the toe, bad cutting (curving the corners instead of cutting straight across), or tight-fitting shoes. Seek expert advice early as they can be very painful.

**Nailbiting** is a very common sign of tension or nervousness. The habit is an extremely hard one to break, since the causes tend to be rooted in the psyche. There is no miracle cure for nailbiting. Liquids which have an unpleasant taste can be painted on to the nails to harden them and discourage biting, but the success rate is not high. Painting the nails with brightly coloured varnish can provide a constant reminder of how unattractive they look when bitten, and sometimes the thought of chewing nail varnish can be offputting. Other ruses are having a professional manicure to file and smooth the rough edges, and shame you into stopping, or bribery with the promise of some particularly sought-after gift. Nailbiters will be unable to give up the habit, however, unless they really want to do so.

# NATUROPATHY

*See also: allopathy; health farms; herbalism; holism; homoeopathy; hydrotherapy*

Naturopathy is a system of medicine, as is homoeopathy. Naturopaths believe that, given the right stimuli, the body can heal itself, and that symptoms of illness are the body's way of ridding itself of disease, and should not be suppressed.

A consultation with a naturopath will involve giving a detailed case history, but no tests such as a blood test will be done. Naturopaths use nothing which will interfere with the body, no needles or drugs. Treatment revolves around natural remedies stemming from the body itself, using methods such as acupressure, exercise for health, osteopathy, chiropractic, reflexology, psychotherapy, hydrotherapy, fasting and special diets.

Most health farms are run on naturopathic principles, although some now offer treatments such as faradic exercise of which naturopaths would not approve. Much 'modern' dietary thinking, such as the importance of fibre in the diet, has long been the practice of naturopaths and their patients.

# NECK AND SHOULDERS

*See also: exercise; exercises; massage; migraine and headaches; muscles; posture; relaxation; stress; yoga*

The neck and shoulders are very often the focal point for mental and physical tensions. Sitting or walking badly can produce knots and tightness in muscles here, as can carrying heavy weights such as suitcases (see **back, posture**). Stress and worry can make you tighten up the neck muscles, causing pain and headaches (see **stress**). Try massaging your neck using light kneading movements (see **massage**), or soaking in a hot bath infused with relaxing herbs such as chamomile, valerian and comfrey (see **herbs, infusions**). Relaxation techniques and the following exercises will help keep your neck and shoulders mobile:

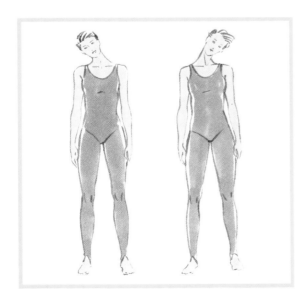

▲ **Exercise A**
**1** Stand tall with feet shoulder width apart and shoulders back and down. Ease your neck gently down to the right until you feel a slight stretch on the left side of your neck.
**2** Repeat to the left until you feel a gentle stretch on the right. Repeat 8 times working up to 24 repeats over the weeks.

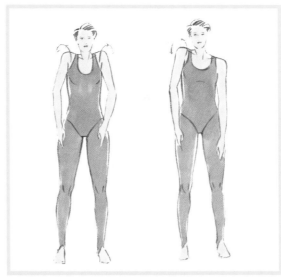

■ See EXERCISES for Caution box page 123 before starting exercise

■ See ABDOMEN for Core Exercise box page 6 before starting exercise

◄ **Exercise B**
**1** Stand tall. With a circular motion raise your right shoulder up as high as you can, then back, then down. Repeat twice, then repeat with left shoulder.
**2** Now repeat the exercise with both shoulders at once, keeping spine and neck long, 6 times.

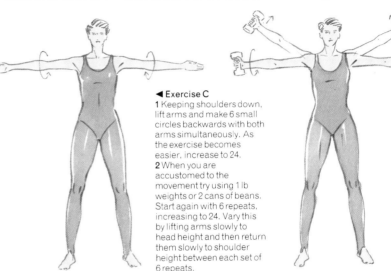

◄ **Exercise C**
**1** Keeping shoulders down, lift arms and make 6 small circles backwards with both arms simultaneously. As the exercise becomes easier, increase to 24.
**2** When you are accustomed to the movement try using 1 lb weights or 2 cans of beans. Start again with 6 repeats, increasing to 24. Vary this by lifting arms slowly to head height and then return them slowly to shoulder height between each set of 6 repeats.

# NOISE

*See also: ears; pollution*

'Noise' can often be used interchangeably with 'sound'. The word noise implies that the sound is unnecessary, excessive or unpleasant. Sound is measured in decibels. The range varies from approximately 45 decibels experienced in a quiet room to 82 decibels on the tube (subway) and up to 124 decibels from personal stereos. Persistent high or low-decibel noise – 80 decibels or over – can cause severe hearing damage and be so intrusive as to prevent sleep, thereby causing a variety of other problems. It is estimated that office personnel waste 25-30 per cent of their time fighting noise.

Although noise in itself stimulates the body, excessive noise has the opposite effect. People subjected to loud noise appear to be less responsive and aware. Others can become angry and even disturbed if subjected to persistent noise levels.

# OPTICIAN

*See also: contact lenses; eyes; glasses*

An ophthalmic optician carries out eye tests, and prescribes contact lenses, glasses and some forms of treatment for eye conditions. Tests on eyes should be carried out regularly (see **eyes**). Dispensing opticians deal with measuring and arranging for prescription glasses. Neither of these practitioners is medically qualified. The ophthalmologist, however, is a medically qualified specialist who deals with diseases of the eye, to whom you may be referred by your general practitioner or optician.

## Obstetrician
See Gynaecologist;
Pre-conceptual care;
Pregnancy;
Post-natal care

## Odour
See Body odour

## Oedema
See Fluid retention

## Oestrogen
See Hormones

## Oils
See Aromatherapy

# ORIENTAL SKIN

*See also: Afro hair; black skin; blondes; brunettes; make-up; redheads*

Oriental skin can be very pale or yellowy in colour, and tends to be sallow and even in tone. The Asian face is characteristically smooth and relatively flat, round or heart-shaped. Although the browbone is prominent, concealing dark, often almond-shaped eyes, the general bone structure is not strongly defined. Skin problems such as acne or pigmentation disorders are rare, although when spots or scars are present they are more conspicuous on such smooth, even-toned skin, and fade slowly. Orientals have little body and facial hair. They have smaller apocrine glands (see **body odour**) and as a result suffer less from sweating and body odour then Westerners.

### MAKE-UP
Make the most of your features using the make-up techniques detailed in the various sections covering the subject. Ensure that your foundation and powder are dark enough for your complexion; experiment until you find just the right tones so that, when made up, your face is not a shade lighter than your neck. Avoid yellow-based foundations which deaden the skin colouring. Enhance the eyelid with deep colouring (dark blues, mauves, kohl) blending up and outwards towards the hairline. Shading the inner socket of the eye creates the illusion of a deeper socket. Define the lower lid with a blue, black or other dark-coloured outline. Eyebrows that are sparse can be darkened a little with feathery strokes of eyebrow pencil; eyelashes, which are often short and pointed, can be curled for emphasis (before using mascara). Lips tend to be small and thin: you can make them look fuller by using strong colours – deep reds and fuchsias – and by drawing in your lip line just above the natural lip line (see **lip colour**). Blushers of soft, rosy pinks and peaches are most flattering to the rounder face.

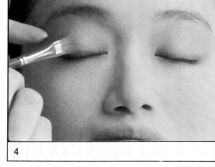

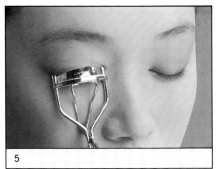

1 Apply pale, pink- or yellow-based foundation, to even and adjust skin tone, to face and neck with damp sponge.
2 After blending concealer cream under eyes, round nose, on chin with fingers to disguise blemishes and uneven skin tone, apply cream blusher from under centre eye out and up at cheekbone towards temples.
3 Brush on pale, loose powder to adjust colour, as above, and set foundation.
4 Brush ochre shadow below brow and over lids, a richer tone below lower lashes, dark, reddish brown just above top lashes as eyeliner and burned orange over whole lid.
5 Curl lashes, then apply black mascara.
6 Define eyebrows lightly with dark brown and black pencils using light, feathery strokes. Powder them to remove shine, comb through.
7 Outline lips with burned orange pencil. Fill in with matching lipstick on a lip brush working from the middle towards edges and corners.

**Orotic acid**
See Vitamin B13

**Oxygen**
See Air

# ORTHODONTIST

*See also: dentist; teeth*

An orthodontist is a dental specialist who is concerned with the correction of badly positioned teeth in order to improve facial appearance and decrease the risk of dental disease made more likely by faulty alignment or 'bite'. Orthodontic treatment can correct projecting upper or lower teeth, close gappy teeth, spread out crowded teeth and reposition rotated teeth. Treatment is usually carried out between the ages of 10 and 14 but adults can have orthodontic treatment, too, provided that teeth and gums are healthy.

The treatment may involve the extraction of one or more teeth and the wearing of a removable or fixed brace which exerts pressure on the teeth, to produce correct alignment. Newer plastic braces have removed the need for a mouthful of unsightly wires and brackets. Correction normally takes from 18 months to two or three years.

# ORTHOMOLECULAR MEDICINE

*See also: diet; minerals; naturopathy; vitamins*

Orthomolecular medicine is closely allied to megavitamin therapy as a way of treating illness. In megavitamin therapy patients are given large doses of a wide range of vitamins and minerals. In orthomolecular medicine (so named by Nobel prizewinner Linus Pauling, though he was not the first to practise it), a supplement or supplements are prescribed specifically for the condition and individual being treated.

The use of both therapies is extremely controversial for several reasons. High doses of some vitamins are potentially very dangerous. While any water-soluble vitamins (the B group and C) in excess of the body's needs are excreted in the urine, fat-soluble vitamins (A, D, E, K) are retained in the body and can be toxic. In order for this to happen, however, doses have to be between two and five times the daily recommendation, and supplements of the fat-soluble vitamins are generally poorly absorbed.

Vitamin deficiencies are uncommon in western countries but there are times when extra vitamin supplies are helpful to the body. After injury or an operation, for example, the body uses up vitamin C faster than usual to heal itself. Sufferers from premenstrual syndrome are now often prescribed vitamin B6 and some pregnant women need vitamin and mineral supplements. Treatments like these are commonly accepted, but other claims for vitamin therapy are not generally accepted by doctors.

# OSTEOPATH

*See also: Alexander Technique; backs; chiropractic; Feldenkrais; physiotherapy; posture; Rolfing*

The practice of osteopathy was established by Dr Andrew Still (1828-1917), a qualified allopathic doctor. Of central importance in osteopathy is the well-being of the spine. This is because of its vital role in supporting the whole structure of the body, linking its parts and carrying the spinal cord and also because of its connection with the muscular system. Osteopaths treat causes, not symptoms, and trace the cause of many illnesses to spinal dysfunction.

The osteopath will take your case history, observe your general level of tension and stress and the way in which you move. He or she will then examine the painful area and the entire back region in detail. X-rays and blood pressure tests may be carried out. Once the problem has been diagnosed, treatment usually takes the form of manipulation.

Osteopaths treat patients suffering from a wide range of disorders. Conditions commonly treated are all back problems, arthritis and rheumatism. Others can be alleviated, too, as the back becomes healthy again, for example breathing, asthma and blood pressure problems, sinus trouble and tension headaches.

# OSTEOPOROSIS

*See also: Hormone Replacement Therapy; hormones; menopause; minerals; vitamins*

Osteoporosis is a condition in which the bones weaken and decrease in mass. Calcium is gradually lost from the bones, making them brittle and susceptible to fracture. Joints can become painful and the vertebrae can reduce to such an extent that a permanent stoop develops. Osteoporosis is common among the elderly, and among post-menopausal women because they have less oestrogen, which plays a key part in keeping calcium in the bones (see **menopause**).

The onset of osteoporosis is to some extent part of the body's natural ageing process: in later life the body begins to excrete more calcium, and bones become more fragile. Menopausal women or those who have had their ovaries removed may be given Hormone Replacement Therapy which, among other things, slows the rate of calcium loss. Use of HRT for osteoporosis is controversial (see **Hormone Replacement Therapy**). Exercise is very important: it slows down osteoporosis and strengthens the bones. Increased calcium intake is important for everyone over 40, especially if following a high-fibre diet which itself reduces calcium absorption. It is possible that fluorine plays a role in osteoporosis prevention.

# PARAFFIN WAX

*See also: beauty salons; health farms; manicure; masks*

Paraffin wax is a white, transparent crystalline substance made by the distillation of coal, wood, tar and so on. It has particular whitening and moisturizing properties and is used by beauticians to moisturize and soften the skin – it can be used all over the body. In a paraffin wax 'bath' or body treatment, the body is coated with the warm, melted wax, then wrapped in foil and blankets and allowed to perspire for approximately quarter of an hour. Toxic wastes are drawn out through the pores, the skin is moisturized and left feeling soft and supple. The cooled, set wax is easily peeled off. The treatment gives temporary relief from muscle strain and arthritic and rheumatic pains, and also produces a temporary weight loss which lasts only until lost fluid is replaced. Treatments for the hands alone are also available as part of a manicure. The warm wax is applied after the nails have been shaped to whiten and soften the hands.

**Paba**
See Vitamins

**Pain**
See Aches and pains

**Pangamic acid**
See Vitamin B15

**Pantothenic acid**
See Vitamin B5

**Passive exercise**
See Faradic exercise

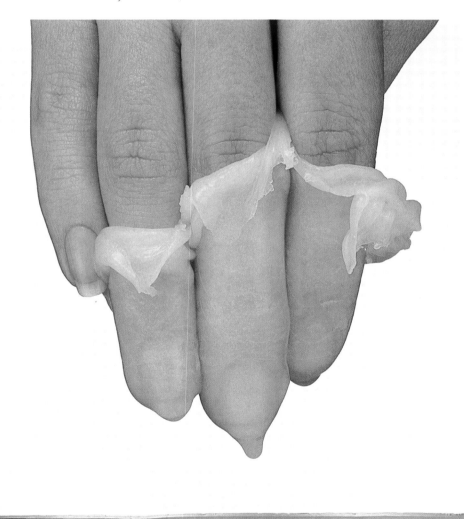

201

# PEDICURE

*See also: body moisturizers; buffing; bunions; calluses; chiropodist; corns; cuticles; feet; nails; ringworm; warts*

It is not only luxurious to have a professional pedicure, but also beneficial, particularly after a long winter of wrapping up your feet in thick tights and shoes, before the exposure of summer. It can be the only effective way of dealing with excess dead skin or calluses. Remember that fungal infections like ringworm (athlete's foot), and corns, warts (veruccas) or bunions require the treatment of a chiropodist or sometimes of a doctor.

A simple cosmetic pedicure at home takes about thirty minutes, and should be a regular beauty routine, carried out approximately every ten days, if possible.

## Equipment for step-by-step pedicure

Include: cotton wool pads, remover, pumice stone, nailfile, orange sticks, cuticle cream, transparent nail varnish, buffing pad.

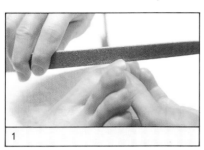

1

2

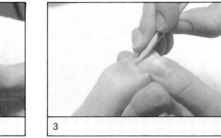

3

**1** Remove nail polish using an orange stick wrapped in cotton wool around cuticle area. Cut nails straight across to prevent ingrowth and file in one direction only.

**2** Gently rub fine pumice stone over the base and sides of feet to remove dead skin and calluses: not too vigorously over the ball of the foot or you may cause blisters and soreness.

**3** Clean beneath nail tips with cotton wool-wrapped orange stick. Massage cuticle cream into each nail, loosening cuticle with pointed end of an orange stick, easing it back with the rounded end to allow cream to penetrate to the base of nail.

**4** Moisturize and tone up feet and toes by massaging them firmly with body lotion using firm upward strokes.

**5** If necessary clip away hangnails, but do not clip cuticles.

**6** Wipe away any traces of grease from the nails. Separate toes with pads of foam, tissue or cotton wool. Apply clear base coat then two coats of colour, allowing them to dry thoroughly between applications. Paint on transparent top coat to prevent chipping. Alternatively buff in one direction only with pad and cream.

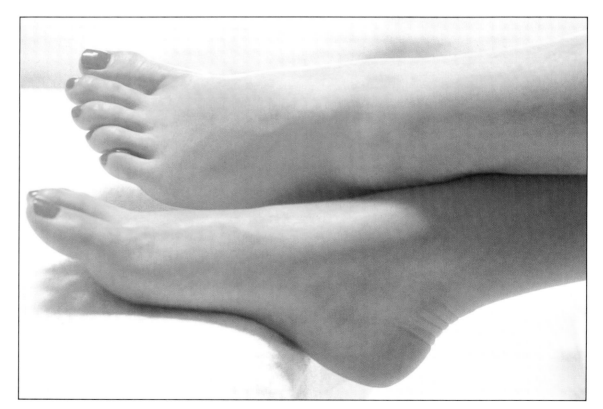

4

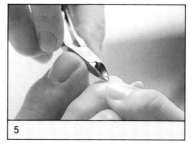

5

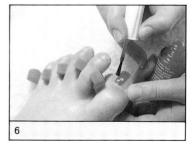

6

# PELVIC INFLAMMATORY DISEASE

*See also: contraception; dysmenorrhoea; sexually transmitted diseases*

Pelvic Inflammatory Disease (PID) can occur in any part of the womb, the fallopian tubes (where an infection is known as salpingitis), ovaries and surrounding area. It can arise for a variety of reasons: as a result of having an intra-uterine device (IUD) fitted (see **contraception**) or simply from using an IUD; after a spontaneous or induced abortion; miscarriage or birth; or as a result of infection from a sexual partner who has chlamydia or gonorrhoea (see **sexually transmitted diseases**).

The symptoms are varied. Among them are tenderness in the abdominal area, sharp or dull pain, deep pain in the vagina during examination or sexual intercourse, heavy or irregular periods, swellings in the womb. If you suspect that you have PID and suffer any of these symptoms, see your STD clinic, general practitioner, gynaecologist or family planning doctor immediately. PID carries a risk of infertility which swift treatment may be able to negate. It also increases the possibility of future ectopic pregnancies, in which the egg implants outside the uterus and must be removed. Treatment of PID may be with antibiotics such as oxytetracycline or erythromycin. Metronidazole may be prescribed and sexual partners examined too.

which need to be kept reasonably sharp in order to extend, give shape to or fill out the brows. Use an oily-textured pencil for dry skin, a powder-based pencil in light strokes if the skin is naturally moist.
**Lip pencils** Thin lip pencils can be used to give the lips a clear outline before colour or gloss is applied. They help prevent lipstick smearing and running into the lines around the mouth.
**Nail pencils** These are white pencils used to clean and colour behind the nail tips when coloured varnish is not being worn.

# PENCILS

*See also: applicators; colouring hair; cosmetics; eye make-up; kohl; lips; manicure; nails*

Make-up pencils are generally wax-based cosmetics that act as smooth applicators to outline and define lips, brows and eyes. They are available in many colours, in both matt and iridescent finishes. Before buying, test for softness and colour durability by applying colour to the back of your hand. If the colour fades or streaks after a few hours, or if the pencil pulls or scratches the skin, it is unsuitable. Crayon-style pencils respond to body heat, so will soften as they are used.

### TYPES OF PENCIL
**Eye pencils** These can outline or colour part, or all, of the eye rim or lid. Harder pencils are suitable for lining, while softer pencils can be used for colouring the lid. Make sure to blend in the colour well with your fingertips to avoid harsh lines. Kohl pencils are good for lining and shadowing.
**Eyebrow pencils** These have narrow, firm points

# PERSONAL HYGIENE

*See also: anti-perspirant; baths and bathing; body odour; deodorant; pH; thrush*

The vagina is self-cleaning. It secretes fluid which, combined with bacteria and cells being shed, produces a mild acid as a barrier to infection. It needs neither douching (except in the case of some medications prescribed for vaginal infections) nor deodorizing. Washing with an unperfumed soap or pH-balanced liquid soap and water is all that is needed. Slight discharge is quite normal, but if it smells strongly or changes in amount or colour, consult your doctor. You may have a mild yeast infection which is easily remedied with pessaries.

When menstruating, bath, shower and wash as usual. Change your tampon frequently especially during the first day of your period (see **menstruation**) to avoid unpleasant odour, which only occurs when blood comes into contact with air.

**Phosphorus**
See Minerals

**Pigmentation**
See Melanin

**Pill, The**
See Contraception

**Pimples**
See Acne

**Pink eye**
See Eyes

**Plaque**
See Teeth

**Plastic surgery**
See Cosmetic
surgery

**Polish for nails**
See Manicure; Nails

# pH

*See also: hair; skin*

Many products are now labelled 'pH-balanced'. The pH scale of 1-14 records the acidity or alkalinity of a solution. A reading of 7 is neutral; anything higher is alkaline, anything lower is acidic. A reading of 1 or 2 would denote a strong acid. pH measurements for skin and hair are rather vague, because they are normally taken in solution. Skin is slightly acid at around 6.5, due to the natural mantle of fatty acid which gives it protection. pH-balanced products for the skin aim to maintain this level, so that the skin retains its natural protection If products used are too alkaline, such as soaps which have a pH of around 8, the fatty mantle will tend to be stripped. Because of this, it is a good idea to use a balanced moisturizer which restores the natural pH after washing the skin with soap. Babies do not have the protection of the acid mantle, and special products such as 6.5 pH liquid soaps are available for them.

Hair has no fatty mantle to protect it. The 'natural' pH of hair is often referred to as its iso-electric point, which, at around 4.5, is the point at which the hair would carry no negative or positive electric charge. A properly balanced shampoo would maintain this iso-electric point, whereas an improperly formulated one may impart an electrostatic charge. Some shampoos will leave the hair with a residual negative charge. One of the most important roles which conditioners play is to add their mildly positive charge to hair so that it will finally be left with no strong charge at all. Over-dry hair, such as hair which has been processed, is hard to brush or comb, and static is created during the process: the lubricants in conditioner will help avoid this, too. Combined shampoos and conditioners have the ingredients to neutralize any electrostatic charge.

Balancing the pH of hair depends on selecting the properly formulated shampoos and conditioners for your hair.

# POLLUTION

*See also: air; air ionizers; noise*

The Royal Commission on Environmental Pollution in the UK defines pollution as follows: 'The introduction by man into the environment of substances or energy liable to cause hazards to human health, harm to living resources and ecological systems, damage to structures or amenity, or interference with legitimate uses of the environment.' The effects of pollution can either be conspicuous, such as in the case of mining waste tipped on the seashore, or invisible, as in the depletion of the ozone layer. Recent leaks from nuclear processing plants and other plants producing dangerous substances have demonstrated just how important strict safeguards governing their operation and disposal of waste are. Whether in remote country areas or cities, pollution affects us all. Awareness of its potential dangers, and the many problems surrounding dealing with it, enable us to put informed pressure on manufacturers, governments and health authorities to monitor and counter it and to keep us all informed.

### WHO IS AT RISK?
Everyone is subjected to some level of pollution. Those most at risk live in areas with high concentrations of pollution, for example those who live in large, industrial cities, or close to power, industrial or nuclear plants. Smokers are more likely than non-smokers to suffer lead or cadmium poisoning, to suffer lung cancer as a result of inhaling radon particles and generally to feel the effects of air pollution. Pollution is a vast problem, but we can do a great deal to reduce it. Careful management of all types of waste, good use of fuel, simple processes like washing fruit and vegetables carefully all cut down pollution and our chances of suffering ill-effects. Awareness, and action on larger issues is all-important, too.

# PORES

*See also: acne; beauty salons; blackheads; cleansing; skin; toning; whiteheads*

The skin contains innumerable pores which act as channels for the oil secretions produced by the sebaceous glands and which exude moisture and impurities from the sweat glands.

Both open and blocked pores are a common problem which tend to occur in coarse, oily skins, but they can be found in dry skins, too. Open pores can be hereditary: they can appear as clusters of blackheads on the cheekbones. They are generally caused, however, when the opening of the sebaceous glands becomes blocked with dead skin cells so that an excess of oil is built up, stretching the skin. This makes the pores appear noticeable and can result in the formation of blackheads and whiteheads (see **acne; blackheads; whiteheads**). Other factors that can contribute to pore problems are:

■ Smoking, excess alcohol and lack of fresh air.
■ Insufficient or irregular skin cleansing.
■ Hormonal changes, especially at puberty when oil production from the sebaceous glands is increased.
■ Heat and hot climates may both produce pore blockage.
■ Stress is an aggravating factor.

### TREATING PORE PROBLEMS

No external application, whether it is an astringent or a splash of cold water, is able to close pores permanently, although some lotions can help to dissolve the grease which is clogging the pores. Following a good skin care routine helps prevent an accumulation of oil. Cleanse, tone and moisturize the skin twice a day, and have regular deep-cleansing facials (see **facials**), which have a temporary tightening effect. Regular exfoliation (see separate entry) removes dead skin cells, keeping the oil flowing from the sebaceous glands. Never scrub too vigorously or use harsh detergent products. These can encourage sebum production, as well as hardening the surface of the skin, so that the pores remain blocked.

# PORT WINE STAINS

*See also: camouflage; lasers*

Port wine stains are birthmarks caused by a concentration of blood vessels which stain the face or other parts of the body red, or in some cases deep purple. The marks may fade to some degree with time, but generally do not disappear entirely. Camouflage make-up (see **camouflage** – corrective camouflage) is one reasonably effective method of concealing such marks.

Recently Argon laser therapy has been used to treat these disfiguring marks. The blue-green rays which they emit can only be absorbed by the red blood corpuscles. The laser beam clots the blood which causes the redness, and eventually the port wine stain is replaced by normal pink skin tissue. Deeper colours will absorb more energy from the laser, and since port wine stains tend to become redder and closer to the skin's surface with age, mature skins (over 30) tend to respond best to this treatment. It must be emphasized, however, that laser treatment is not successful in all cases – it can leave scar tissue. It is also an expensive treatment, and must only be administered by a trained medical practitioner to avoid severe scarring and damage to the skin which might otherwise occur if carried out inefficiently.

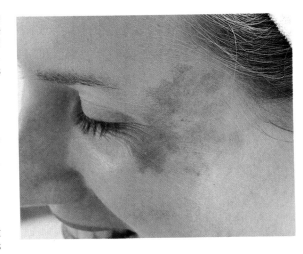

This birthmark was caused by abnormal capillaries which stain the facial area a claret colour. See **Camouflage** for ways to conceal such a mark.

# POST-NATAL BEAUTY AND HEALTH

*See also: diet; exercises; manicure; pedicure; post-natal depression; pregnancy; stretch marks*

After childbirth, the body's return to its pre-pregnant tone and shape is effected by both the involuntary action of hormones and the voluntary action of muscular activity in exercise. Your exercise plan must be gradual, to keep pace with slow hormonal readjustment. At the heart of it are simple breathing and posture exercises which will be explained by your physiotherapist or midwife and should begin on the day after the birth. A gradual retoning of the muscles of the pelvic floor and abdomen are essential. Other exercises are specifically designed to relax and restrengthen, and will also relieve strain on vulnerable backs. By your six-week post-natal (post-partum) checkup you should be able to step up your toning programme.

### BEAUTY

The routines established to cope with the demands of life with a new baby must in turn take into account the mother's own imposed routine. It is important not to neglect yourself while learning your new role.

■ Set some time aside every day to spend on yourself. Do not allow maternal duties to override usual beauty routines such as attention to nails, hair, make-up, cleansing.
■ Fatigue is probably your greatest enemy so rest as much as possible.
■ Eat wisely.
■ Although comfort is important and you will be unable to wear some of your pre-pregnancy clothes straight away, try to get out of your maternity wear as soon as you can.
■ Hair often becomes slightly thicker during pregnancy and will begin to thin during the first 5 months after the birth: this is quite normal. Good diet, with an emphasis on fresh foods,

will keep your hair healthy. Go regularly to the hairdresser, perhaps trying new styles, but do not have chemical processing, such as perming or bleaching, done at this time when the hair's reaction is unstable.

### NUTRITION

A well-balanced, high-quality diet is as important after the birth as before. Good eating habits will speed the recovery of full vitality while maintaining maximum health for mother and baby.

The immediate post-natal period is not the time to react against nine months of weight gain by attempting reduction diets. Return to your pre-pregnant weight is best achieved naturally with other body changes, aided by breastfeeding. If you are breastfeeding try to include 3 between-meal snacks. If you are still over your normal weight (see **weight**) six months after your baby's birth, tailor your diet (see **slimming**).

Constipation can be a problem, so incorporate plenty of fibre in your diet (see **fibre**) and drink plenty of water. Milk-based drinks may form a larger part of your daily intake now. They are rich in most nutritional necessities, including calcium, and provide some extra fluid and Calories needed if breastfeeding. Nutrients are passed to your baby in breast milk, so avoid a high acid intake which may upset your infant. Do not take any form of drug or medication which your doctor has not prescribed or advised you to take. Avoid smoking: remember that you are subjecting your baby to all the dangers of passive smoking if you do.

# POST-NATAL DEPRESSION

*See also: depression; post-natal beauty and health*

'Baby blues' – a day or more of feeling emotionally confused and vulnerable in the first post-natal week – probably affect 50 per cent of women. Fatigue, hormonal changes, reaction from the elation of birth and the effect of discomforts such as sore breasts, stitches and minor difficulties with the new baby may play a part.

Post-natal (post-partum) depression is another matter; it affects 10 per cent of women. It may develop from the 'blues' but more usually manifests itself after hospital discharge and within three months of the birth, although sometimes it appears later. Symptoms can include despondency, lethargy, weepiness, lack of concentration, feelings of inadequacy, tension, panic, irritability, obsessional thoughts and fears, lack of libido after several weeks of the depression and loss of appetite. Often these are associated with physical complaints such as back ache, palpitations and dizziness. There is no set pattern and no link with race, culture or social class. Ninety per cent of post-natal depressions are said to be mild, but the depression can last for

months and even from pregnancy to pregnancy if untreated. Individual risk factors are maternal age, subfertility, inadequate family support and previous history of psychiatric problems.

'Puerperal (post-partum) psychosis' is a severe form of post natal depression or schizophrenia, marked by a loss of sense of reality, which affects 1 in 500 women, usually within one month of delivery. Chances of recurrence are high.

There are probably always a number of precipitating factors in post-natal depression. Among them are unremitting fatigue, hormonal upset, adjustments to motherhood and new relationship structures, unrealized expectations of the new role, the baby and oneself, the experience of the birth itself and the consequent sense of loss which can be experienced at the end of nine months of carrying the child.

### COPING WITH POST-NATAL DEPRESSION

The first step is to recognize your predicament and try to accept it, to reassure yourself that the problem is temporary, that you will recover. Early diagnosis is important: do not suffer in silence. Try to talk to your partner, family and friends. Go to your doctor or obstetrician who will monitor your progress.

Take steps to combat physical exhaustion. Rest as much as possible – you really need it. Get someone else to feed the baby at night, and see your doctor if you have insomnia (see also **insomnia**).

Try to eat well and regularly (see **post-natal beauty and health**). Hypoglycaemia (low blood sugar) exacerbates fatigue and low morale.

Progesterone treatment is sometimes prescribed, particularly if the depression is affected by your menstrual cycle or seems to be linked to breastfeeding (it does not affect lactation). Premenstrual syndrome sufferers (see separate entry) seem to be at high risk of going on to develop post-natal depression, for which progesterone treatment is also often effective. Your doctor may well advise you to use contraceptives other than the pill while depressed (see **contraception**).

Isolation contributes to post-natal depression. The company of an undemanding companion during the illness does help and may be crucial. In the UK, your health visitor is often a useful source of help and advice and will be able to inform you of local post-natal support groups, many of which are excellent. In the UK the National Childbirth Trust, in the US and UK the La Leche League International provide support with all pregnancy and post-natal problems, including depression.

Unrealistic expectations are a major hazard. It is important to realize that motherhood involves adjustments to many new and even contradictory roles. 'Mothering' is not all instinctive: many of the requisite skills and emotional responses have to be learnt, which takes time. There are no absolutely 'right' ways of being a mother: set your own standards and take no notice of those that friends seem to expect of you.

Talking about how you feel and why is beneficial. Further psychological help in the form of counselling will help you to sort out confused ideas. Your doctor, obstetrician, health visitor or marriage guidance council can refer you for counselling.

## PREVENTION

Forewarned is forearmed: be aware of the possibility of post-natal depression and ensure that your partner and family understand this too. Emotional support from them is really practical in this situation, and physical help is important too.

Rest and peace, especially in the weeks just after the birth, help prevent post-natal depression. Try not to become so caught up in the physical and emotional demands of motherhood that you lose sight of your own needs.

Progesterone injections during and immediately after labour may forestall post-natal depression. This may be used in some situations, particularly where there is a history of post-natal depression. Anti-depressant medication in the last few months of pregnancy is not advisable.

# POSTURE

*See also: Alexander Technique; back; dance; exercises; Feldenkrais; martial arts; osteopathy; pregnancy; Rolfing; sports; yoga*

The word posture very probably conjures up images of being instructed to put your shoulders back, head up and straighten your spine. This traditional military 'correct' pose does not, in fact, offer the ideal standing position for the body. Its aim seems to be more to instil an upright moral attitude to life than ensure healthy posture. Yet it does highlight one important aspect of posture – that it really can affect your intellectual and mental state as well as your physical condition. Numerous therapies, such as the Alexander Technique, Feldenkrais, Rolfing and meditation (see separate entries) focus on the importance of good posture for mental and physical health, and posture is also emphasized in physiotherapy, osteopathy and chiropractic. A therapy developed quite recently in the US called Body Alignment, aims to correct the relationship between the various parts of the body in order to effect a wide range of benefits to general health. The therapy has much in common with the Alexander Technique and physiotherapy in particular.

Good posture means that all parts of the body are in a balanced relationship with each other. The spine is in a structurally sound, straight and elongated position so that it can take the force of gravity with least strain; the bones and ligaments keep the body erect, leaving the muscles relaxed and free. Weight distribution should be even, each foot taking equal amounts when standing, each buttock when sitting. It sounds effortless, and can become so, but very often bad habits which have become automatic have to be unlearned first.

The advantages of good posture are great. Using the body to its full potential keeps joints and mus-

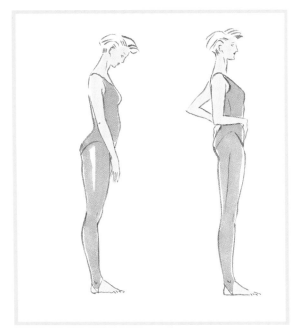

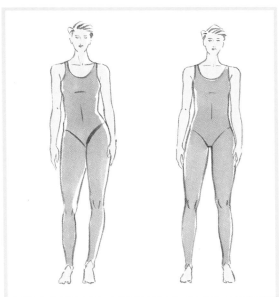

cles healthy. Avoiding unnecessary strain on them also helps prevent premature joint ageing, muscle strain and the abnormal lengthening or shortening of muscles which is an unavoidable result of years of using the joints incorrectly.

Other physiological benefits are a real sense of liberation and suppleness in the body, with increased ability to move freely, sit and stand more comfortably and more impetus to take extra exercise. Back and other joint pain, digestive and circulation problems and headaches can all be alleviated. Improved posture can help reduce stress, insomnia, anxiety and improve self-image. It can improve your body shape, too, as abdominal muscles are held in their correct supporting position.

The exercises above will help you to evaluate your own posture, and to improve it.

■ See EXERCISES for Caution box page 123 before starting exercise

■ See ABDOMEN for Core Exercise box page 6 before starting exercise

◀ **Exercise A**
1 Stand sideways on to a mirror and study your silhouette. Probably your shoulders will be hunched, your neck forward, bottom and tummy both protruding.
2 Lift your head and lengthen your spine, keeping chin in and shoulders back and down. Now tuck your bottom under by tilting your pelvis so that your pubic bone comes up closer to your ribs.

◀ **Exercise B**
1 Stand facing the mirror, with legs slightly apart. Do you stand with all your weight on one leg and your pelvis twisted? Note that this tips your shoulders too.
2 Now stand with weight evenly distributed, hips and shoulders level and weight balanced between heel and ball of each foot. Practice standing like this until it becomes second nature.

**Potassium**
See Minerals

**Powder**
See Face powder

# PRE-CONCEPTUAL CARE

*See also: anorexia nervosa; contraception; diet; pregnancy; smoking; stress; weight*

The concept of pre-natal care stems from increasing interest in 'preventive medicine', in being positively healthy rather than simply free of obvious disease. While little is known about the causes of individual congenital susceptibilities, there is growing evidence linking the health of foetus and baby to the health not only of the mother, but of both parents in the months prior to conception.

It is known that all a baby's major organs and systems are formed within 8 to 12 weeks of conception, when traditional ante-natal care is often only beginning. Women who are contemplating pregnancy are advised to undergo rubella (German

measles) antibody screening: if they have no antibodies they can be vaccinated and should then avoid pregnancy for at least three months. They are advised to achieve their recommended weight, cease smoking, stop drinking alcohol and to take other simple health precautions in preparation for the important early stages of pregnancy.

Pre-conceptual care also goes further, and looks closely at the diet of both parents at the time of conception and the way it can affect inherited conditions. An imbalance may well contribute to damaged genes. 'Foresight', based in Guildford, Surrey, is an organization which leads the promotion of pre-conceptual care in the UK. Pre-conceptual Clinics offering counselling and testing facilities for all prospective parents, not only those with a history of unsatisfactory outcome of pregnancy, are becoming more numerous. They enable couples to make a commitment to the health of their children.

# PREGNANCY

*See also: dentist; diet; hormones; post-natal beauty and health; post-natal depression; pre-conceptual care; stretch marks; teeth*

In the nine months of pregnancy, major physical adjustments are matched by emotional changes of equal intensity. Signs of pregnancy may include a missed or slight menstrual period, nausea and sickness, tender, enlarged breasts, frequent passing of urine, sudden dislike of familiar food or drink, fatigue and lassitude, feelings of faintness. If you think you may be pregnant, see your doctor for confirmation and to commence routine ante-natal care.

### PRE-NATAL TESTING

The first pre-natal test confirms pregnancy by detecting in urine the presence of the hormone chorionic gonadotrophin (see **hormones**). By the 35th day after your last menstrual period this reaches quantities measurable in the usual test available from doctors and some pharmacists, and a positive test is 99 per cent accurate. Most commercially available tests before this time are not as accurate.

During the course of ante-natal care, specific tests will include frequent checks of maternal weight gain, blood pressure and urine. The foetal heart will be tested too, with sonic aid from three months and a stethoscope from around five months. Early on the mother's blood will be tested for haemoglobin and rubella antibodies. At around four months if not earlier, women may be offered an alpha fetoprotein (AFP) blood test which can indicate foetal problems such as spina bifida. A positive AFP test will normally be followed by an amniocentesis, in which a little of the fluid surrounding the baby is drawn off, to confirm the findings of the blood test. When tested this fluid can reveal conditions like Down's Syndrome. The likelihood of these increases in proportion to maternal age, so women who have reached their mid-thirties or over may be offered a routine amniocentesis.

Ultrasound scans are increasingly available. They form a picture of the uterus, placenta (afterbirth) and foetus without the damage to cells which X-rays produce. Often undertaken at four months of pregnancy and around seven months, scanning can monitor exactly the position and growth of foetus and placenta, confirm the estimated date of birth by monitoring the size of the head of the foetus, diagnose twin pregnancy and reveal certain abnormalities, particularly of spine and head.

## MORNING SICKNESS

This is often one of the first signs of pregnancy, and one from which few women escape entirely. It may be experienced as anything from vague passing nausea to debilitating vomiting. Although commonly occurring first thing in the morning, it is not always confined to that. The causes are not fully understood, but are thought to be closely involved with the hormonal upheaval which, like the nausea and sickness, is at its height in the first three months of pregnancy. Sickness diminishes and disappears after 10-14 weeks of pregnancy, but may possibly recur in the last three months.

## COPING WITH MORNING SICKNESS

- Eat some toast or dry biscuits before getting up.
- Have small, frequent meals.
- If you really crave a certain food, don't resist: you probably need it.
- Avoid those foods (and smells) which make you feed nauseous: these are usually rich and fatty.
- Iron tablets, often prescribed for pregnant women, may increase sickness and should never be taken on an empty stomach.
- Do not take any unprescribed tablets without consulting your doctor. If you vomit repeatedly all day or nausea becomes unbearable you must tell your doctor.
- Remember that your sickness will not harm the baby and that it will almost certainly improve after three months, and that it is recognized as a sign of a stable pregnancy.

## PREGNANCY NOTES

Throughout your pregnancy ensure that all your questions and worries are answered by doctors and midwives: this is an important part of their job.

Your need for rest – around two hours extra a day – is greatest in the first and last three months. In months three to six many women experience the 'mid-trimester bloom', a feeling of vibrant wellbeing, but should continue to rest more than usual.

Look after your teeth. Because of changes in hormone levels your gums may be tender and bleed readily. See your dentist regularly. In the UK, dental care is free on the National Health Service throughout your pregnancy and until one year after the baby's birth. Make an appointment to see your dentist as soon as pregnancy is confirmed.

The extra weight you gain in pregnancy puts a strain on your feet which may lead to problems or exacerbate existing ones like corns and calluses.

■ See EXERCISES for Caution box page 123 before starting exercise

◀ Exercise A
1 Check your posture regularly in this way: hold on to a chair back with feet hip-width apart and rise up on tiptoes. Stretch your whole body upwards.
2 Now relax back into a standing position. Is your neck long, jaw relaxed, shoulders lowered? Is your spine neither arched backwards nor tipped forwards. Let arms hang loose, hands unclenched, feet taking the weight between heels and balls of feet, arches well lifted. Check and adjust.

▶ Exercise B
Pelvic tilts play an important role in mobilizing the lower back area for the extra weight it carries in pregnancy.
1 Stand with your back against a wall, feet hip-width apart, slightly away from the wall, your knees bent slightly.
2 With head, shoulders and upper back firmly against the wall, breathe in, then as you breathe out press your waist into the wall so that your bottom tilts forward, away from the wall. Repeat several times.

▼ Exercise C
Stand tall, feet hip-width apart with hands loosely on your hips. Keeping upper body as still as possible tilt your hips forwards, to the right, back and to the left making a circle with your hips. Repeat several times building up a smooth rhythm.

▼ Exercise D
Sit on a pillow with your knees bent and the soles of your feet close together. Hold on to your ankles and lengthen your back, keeping shoulders down and lifting your ribs up away from your hips. Hold for as long as possible building up to a minute if you can, breathing in and out deeply. Release and allow your body to flop and relax.

P

Do not neglect foot care. Get feet into good shape at the beginning of pregnancy. You will find it increasingly difficult to reach them by the end! In some areas of the UK chiropody is free on the NHS.

The first three months of pregnancy are the most important because it is in this period that all the baby's organs, limbs, bones and muscles are formed. During these formative weeks the foetus is most vulnerable to adverse factors such as rubella (German measles) or harmful substances like drugs reaching it from the mother via the placenta. After this, very few infections can harm the foetus, which grows and matures in the remaining months of pregnancy. Nevertheless, you *must* continue to check with your doctor before taking any drugs or medicines at all.

Cut out smoking in pregnancy. Apart from all the widely known ill effects of smoking generally, there is a positive correlation between mothers-to-be who smoke and small-for-dates babies who continue to lag behind in growth and development well into the school years. Minimize alcohol intake to a very occasional glass of wine at a party. If you can, avoid drinking altogether. There is increasing evidence that alcohol has a damaging effect on the foetus.

The growing foetus takes all the nutrients it requires from its mother – at the expense of her own needs, if necessary. Be that as it may, you do *not* need to eat for two. Eat sensibly (see **diet**). Concentrate on fresh fish, fruit and vegetables, with wholemeal bread and some dairy products. Drink plenty of water, fruit juice and herbal teas. An adequate fluid intake will combat a hormone-induced tendency to constipation. Your doctor may advise you to take vitamin and mineral supplements, particularly in the last three months.

Take advantage of the various types of ante-natal classes on offer. They help you prepare for birth and parenthood and also advise on dealing with possible problems in later pregnancy such as backache and muscle cramps.

### LOOKING GOOD IN PREGNANCY
For many women, pregnancy is a time of 'blooming' and your changing self-image can provide the catalyst for a variety of beauty innovations. The effort and reward of looking good is an important morale-booster for every woman, perhaps particularly for the unlucky few who suffer extreme morning sickness, debilitating fatigue, or difficulty in assimilating their changing role emotionally. The habit of a little extra self-indulgence is a useful one to acquire before the arrival of an all-absorbing ever-demanding baby whose dependence can cause you to neglect your own needs.

Take particular care of your skin and hair, which in the first three months may react as it usually does before a menstrual period. Later in pregnancy, temporary pigmentation changes can cause freckles to become more pronounced and superfluous facial hair more obvious and in need of bleaching.

Breast size increases in very early pregnancy and again at around 20 weeks. Wear a well-fitting bra throughout pregnancy, even at night if you feel more comfortable with it on (see **bras**).

**Preservatives**
See Additives

# PRE-MENSTRUAL SYNDROME

*See also: contraception; depression; diet; dysmenorrhoea; fluid retention; hormones; menstruation; migraine and headache; minerals; vitamins*

The phrase 'Pre-menstrual Tension' was first coined in 1931 by Robert Frank, a physician in New York. The condition is now more commonly known as the pre-menstrual syndrome (PMS), since tension is just one aspect of it. Sufferers commonly experience a varying number of a wide range of symptoms for the seven to fourteen days leading up to their menstrual period. Since PMS became more widely investigated in the late seventies and early eighties, some doctors have quoted the percentage of women affected by PMS as ranging from 10 per cent to as high as 90 per cent. It seems that while 90 per cent of women suffer some symptoms of PMS just before a period, these are usually slight and in many cases infrequent, or are reflections of other problems. Only 10-15 per cent suffer severe and possibly incapacitating PMS. Although doctors still do not fully understand the syndrome, research has fostered greater understanding of susceptibility and produced some helpful treatments.

### CAUSES
PMS is thought to be caused by the drop in the body's natural progesterone levels in the second half of the menstrual cycle. Research has shown that the drop does not differ substantially between women, and so individual susceptibility to hormone fluctuation seems to be a key factor.

Vitamin B6 has long been used in treating PMS. In a recent study, at St Thomas' Hospital in London, 61 per cent of the 65 women studied showed relief of symptoms when given Evening Primrose oil supplements. The active ingredient here is gamma linoleic acid which is involved in the production of prostaglandins and the control of insulin in the body. Prostaglandins can help alleviate many of the PMS symptoms, excluding cramp. Deficiency of vitamins A, B6 and magnesium are also implicated and involved in the control of insulin. Magnesium may be deficient in the diet if excessive amounts of calcium are eaten: too much calcium leads to poor absorption of magnesium. The female body is more sensitive to insulin during the latter half of the menstrual cycle, so it is likely that blood sugar levels are an important factor in the incidence of PMS.

### SYMPTOMS
More than 150 different symptoms have at one time or another been attributed to PMS.

**Physical symptoms** Swollen, tender breasts that feel lumpy and painful; weight gain and a bloated feeling; swollen hands, legs and feet; abdominal pain, heaviness and tenderness; backache; migraine; headache; increased sebum production affecting hair and skin, increased acne, appearance of spots; constipation; cramps.

**Emotional and psychological symptoms** Irritability; irrational anger and violence; aggressive behaviour; tension; tendency to tearfulness; depression; lack of libido.

Claims that women in the pre-menstrual phase suffer from lack of co-ordination, concentration and slow reaction, thus producing poorer quality work have been shown to be untrue in several studies on women of varying age and occupation. Public interest in PMS has made it a vulnerable scapegoat for discrimination against women.

## TREATMENT

If you suffer PMS symptoms you should see your doctor: he or she will check their causes carefully as many are common to other problems, too. The best help you can give yourself initially is to make a careful analysis of your symptoms. Note them day by day, each on a separate page so that you are not influenced by those you have noted before. Record your feelings, problems and other relevant happenings each day. Take this to the doctor with you as it will help with analysis of your problem.

If you notice only a small number of symptoms in the pre-menstrual phase, occurring in each cycle, you are likely to be suffering from PMS. More common is the case where the pre-menstrual phase highlights and exacerbates symptoms present at other stages in your cycle: these may be physical or psychological, and treatment needs to be for these, not PMS. PMS symptoms, for example, can actually be a sign of severe stress, or of grief. Some women have other problems which may falsely appear as PMS. Whatever the cause of your symptoms, self-analysis with the help of your doctor's diagnosis will set you on the road to solving the problem.

There is by no means one treatment for all cases of PMS. Effectiveness of the various types of treatment varies from woman to woman. Although combined hormone/vitamin B6 treatment has a good success rate, double-blind trials have shown B6 to be no more effective than placebos. Doctors commonly prescribe natural progesterone pills or injections, or sometimes the contraceptive pill. Vitamin B6 is often prescribed, in varying doses, often 20-40mg twice daily, but not more than 100 mg a day as this can cause insomnia and restlessness, although it is not dangerous.

Diuretics are sometimes prescribed to reduce the amount of fluid retained. Because they can deplete your potassium supply it may be necessary to supplement it. The drug spironolactone has diuretic qualities and resembles the female hormones so can have dual beneficial effect. For women who suffer severe breast pain due to high prolactin (see **hormones**) levels, the prolactin inhibitor drug bromocriptine has been given, but this needs careful monitoring, is unsuitable for people with cardiovascular problems and can cause nausea, dizziness and other side effects. Anti-depressants were frequently prescribed for PMS in the past, but are now generally only used when PMS symptoms are due to psychological causes such as severe temporary anxiety or depression. Prescribed placebo pills have been found helpful in a number of cases.

## SELF-HELP NOTES

- Try taking vitamin B6 supplements as detailed left even if not prescribed by your doctor, and vitamin B5, too.
- Try to cut down on the dairy foods in your diet, and take magnesium supplements if you still feel that you are getting excess calcium in your diet.
- Try Evening Primrose oil supplements. They have been found helpful by many women.
- Cut out caffeine (and chocolate) for the pre-menstrual phase: it increases anxiety.
- Cut down on salt and salty foods which increase fluid retention in the body.
- Include plenty of natural diuretics in your diet, such as watermelon, parsley, watercress and strawberries.
- Take plenty of exercise: it helps to alleviate depression and improves your health, sense of well-being and morale. Practise the exercises in the dysmenorrhoea section to help cramps.
- Get plenty of rest and relaxation, too, especially when symptoms are bad. Relaxation techniques and meditation may be helpful.
- Herbal remedies include rosemary, lemon balm, motherwort and St John's wort for depression and tension, vervain and dandelion leaves for fluid retention, lavender and raspberry leaves for sickness and nausea. Infuse approximately 1-3 teaspoons of the fresh or dried herb to each cup of boiling water. Make the infusion just as you would tea, and leave it to steep for five minutes before drinking (see **herbs** for other remedies).

**Processed food**
See Additives; Junk food

**Progesterone and Progestogen**
See Contraception; Hormones

# PRICKLY HEAT

*See also: drugs and medicines; skin; tanning*

Prickly heat or heat rash (miliaria) can appear as an itchy rash of small, raised red spots concentrated on the covered parts of the body. Sometimes the prickly, burning sensation is experienced without a rash. It is caused by blockage of sweat glands in the skin as a result of over-heating. Babies and obese adults are particularly susceptible, probably because of their less efficient skin cooling mechanisms. Both pale and dark skins can be affected. The most likely culprit is the photosensitivity, that is, reaction to light, of a substance which becomes an allergen when affected by sunlight. It could be a drug you are taking, such as one of the tetracyclines (types of antibiotic), a sun protection cream containing bergamot oil or other skin product.

Consult your doctor who will help analyse the cause and may prescribe anti-histamine tablets (not cream as this might cause further sensitivity). Meanwhile soothe your skin with plenty of cooling calamine creams or lotions. These contain zinc which is mildly antiseptic and astringent. Keep out of the heat.

# PROTEIN

*See also: carbohydrate; diet; diets; fat; fibre; minerals; slimming; vitamins*

Protein is an essential element in the diet. It is needed for vital body functions such as the repair of body cells and the growth of new body tissue and is used for energy, too. It makes up approximately 17 per cent of our bodies. It was once thought beneficial to eat large amounts of protein, and there are situations where a higher protein intake is advisable; for example, for children who are growing, for adults after an illness or accident to aid recovery and healing. In adulthood, however, too much protein in the diet can be detrimental, as there is an accompanying increase in the consumption of cholesterol and fat, too, in the protein-rich meats and dairy products. Furthermore, excessive protein can impair mineral and vitamin absorption. Protein should form about 10 per cent of our daily diet. The World Health Organization recommends 40g (1¼ oz) of protein daily for adults. Remember that this is 40g of protein, not of protein-containing food.

Protein contains carbon, hydrogen, oxygen and nitrogen, sometimes minerals too. It is hydrolyzed by enzymes in the body to produce amino acids. There are 22 amino acids, all of which are needed by the body. The body cannot make them, but it can convert some types to others by a process in the liver called transamination. There are 8 which cannot be produced by transamination, known as the essential amino acids, and must be included in the diet. Proteins are categorized according to their 'biological value'. Eggs have the highest biological value at 100 BV because they contain plentiful amounts of all the essential amino acids. Next come fish, meat, cheese, milk, containing the essentials in decreasing amounts, then grains, legumes, nuts and seeds which contain some, but not all of the essential amino acids.

It is quite possible to obtain protein of high biological value from purely vegetable sources, for instance a combination of rice and pulses, but it does require some knowledge of food content, though, to ensure that the combination of foods eaten together provide all the necessary amino acids.

# PSORIASIS

*See also: dermatologist; rashes; skin*

Psoriasis is a chronic skin condition which, with acne and dermatitis, is one of the most common, affecting about 1 per cent of the population. It tends to run in families – children have a one-in-three chance of getting psoriasis if a parent has it – and usually appears after puberty but can first appear at any age. Silvery-scaled red patches appear on elbows, lower back, knees and scalp but can be more extensive and so severe as to require hospital admission. It is not contagious.

The symptoms are known to be caused by accelerated cell renewal in the basal layer, with larger numbers of dead skin cells in the top layers, but what triggers this is still uncertain. The tendency to psoriasis is inherited and may be exacerbated by many factors including stress, infections such as sore throats, certain drugs and hormonal changes. Treatment will not prevent the inevitable further outbreaks.

If you have psoriasis, see your doctor, who may well refer you to a dermatologist. The effectiveness of particular types of treatment varies according to the individual and close monitoring is necessary. Dithranol is messy, can be an irritant and stains skin and clothing but can be very effective. Coal tar creams and ointments are helpful but are also rather messy. Steroid creams are the most convenient to use and are usually quite effective, but care must be taken to avoid using the very potent preparations for long periods.

Exposure to ultraviolet (UV) light can help psoriasis. In some cases UV exposure together with drug treatment to sensitize the skin to sunlight is used in a treatment known as PUVA therapy. This treatment is very effective but because of the slight risk of skin cancer it is generally only used on older patients, under strict supervision. Herbal remedies for psoriasis include thrice daily decoctions of burdock root, dandelion, figwort and yellowdock, among others (see **herbs**).

Psoriasis sufferers can join various organizations in the UK and US including the Psoriasis Association in the UK: your doctor, specialist, hospital or community centre will be able to tell you where your nearest group is. In the US, consult your local Yellow Pages for a list of Psoriasis self-help organizations nearest you.

# PUBERTY

*See also: acne; contraception; hormones; menstruation; teens*

'Puberty' comes from the Latin word *pubertas*, maturity. It is the first stage of adolescence and is the time when physical changes enable women to have children. These changes are brought about by the release of hormones controlled by the pituitary gland, which have previously been concerned mostly with physical growth. Outward signs of puberty include a sudden growth spurt, widening of the pelvic bones, development of the breasts, growth of pubic and underarm hair, a softening of the body's shape as fat tissues develop on the hips, and a gain in weight. This weight gain is thought to be the main trigger mechanism for the timing of puberty.

Probably the most important physical development of puberty, however, is the onset of menstruation. Hormones, released by the pituitary gland, are sent to the ovaries and result in the release of a mature egg (ovulation) and the shedding of the lining of the uterus or womb (menstruation). The age at which menstruation first occurs varies, being affected by living conditions, nutrition and psychological factors, but in the UK and US is usually around the age of twelve. If periods have not started by the age of sixteen, consult your doctor.

Other changes are occasioned by the increased hormonal activity at puberty.

- There is a slight expansion of the eyeball, which can result in sight changes especially hyperopia (long sight). Eyesight should be tested.
- The apocrine glands start to function, which may mean an increase in perspiration. Try out several kinds of anti-perspirants and deodorants before settling on one product.
- The sebaceous glands enlarge and make the skin and hair more oily. Blackheads, whiteheads and acne often begin to appear at this time of hormonal change (see **acne**). If acne is a problem do see your doctor who may refer you to a dermatologist. Keep skin and hair clean: cleanse and tone the skin twice a day, afterwards using moisturizer very lightly on spotty areas; hair should be washed regularly. Remember that overenthusiastic skin- and hair-cleansing will exacerbate problems by encouraging still more sebum production.
- Dietary needs change now. Extra Calories are needed to help fuel the teenage growth spurt, more calcium to help form still-growing bones, more iron – the need for which peaks with the onset of menstruation – and more Vitamin C to help the body absorb the iron.
- The physical changes of puberty go hand in hand with emotional and psychological changes. Girls often become more modest and self conscious as they grow more aware of their bodies and their sexuality, and more rebellious and aggressive as they seek to adjust to the new demands of adulthood.

# PULSES AND BEANS

*See also: carbohydrates; diet; fibre; minerals; protein; vegetables; vitamins*

Pulses, the edible seeds of leguminous plants including peas, beans and lentils, have long formed a staple part of man's diet. They are a good source of protein, a useful alternative to meat in vegetarian diets when combined to produce all the essential amino acids (see **protein**). Because they are also low in fat and cholesterol, high in fibre and generally inexpensive, they make a valuable contribution to any diet.

**Aduki beans** are small, red-brown beans with a strong flavour.

**Black-eyed beans,** like haricot, with a black spot.
**Butter beans** are large, flat, cream-coloured beans.
**Flageolet beans** are pale green with a nutty flavour.
**Chick peas** are pale brown and look and taste rather like nuts. Puréed, they make hummus.
**Haricot beans** are small, rounded, cream-coloured beans and best known as the basis of baked beans.
**Lentils** come in more than 60 varieties. Split lentils, orange in colour, disintegrate in cooking; whole lentils (Continental lentils) are green or brown and stay whole during cooking.
**Mung beans** are small, round, green beans which taste rather like peas. They can be sprouted for the bean sprouts used in Chinese cooking.
**Red kidney beans** are traditionally served with chilli. They can be poisonous if not boiled hard for at least ten minutes at the beginning of cooking.
**Split peas,** dried, halved fresh peas.
**Soya beans** are small, round and cream-coloured and have a mealy texture when cooked.

# PUMICE STONE

*See also: exfoliation; feet; pedicure; skin*

Pumice stones are pieces of light, very porous volcanic lava which have had any rough edges rounded down. They are used to remove excess dry skin on the elbows, sides of fingers, soles and heels of the feet. Always use after a warm bath when skin is pliable and rub the hard skin very gently and lightly. Don't scrub: regular light use is far better for your skin. After using pumice stone on your skin, massage in plenty of body lotion or moisturizer to make the skin feel smooth and supple.

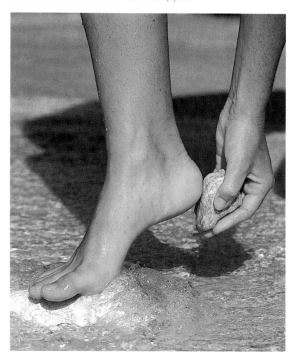

**Pulse**
See Scent

**Pulse method of exercise control**
See Exercises

**Pyridoxine**
See Vitamin B6

P

# R

## RASHES

*See also: acne; allergies and allergens; baths; dermatitis; herbs; prickly heat; psoriasis; sexually transmitted diseases; whiteheads*

A skin rash is a short-lived reaction like nettle rash or a more persistant problem requiring your doctor's advice. Commonest are acne, dermatitis, eczema or psoriasis. Some infectious diseases start with a rash, such as measles, chicken pox or rubella (German measles). Cosmetics and creams used on the skin, sun protection products, soaps, and other substances which come into contact with the skin can also cause allergic reactions in the form of a rash (see **allergies and allergens**). Some drugs and medicines taken internally can cause allergic reactions. If you are taking any and experience a sudden and severe rash, telephone your doctor immediately for advice. Otherwise check recent contact with any infectious diseases, and see your doctor quickly. Meanwhile, take a cool bath (see **herbs**) and stop using any new skin preparations.

## RAW FOOD

*See also: ageing; allergies and allergens; diet; junk food; slimming; teeth*

Many foods need cooking to make them palatable and digestible, but this inevitably destroys some of their nutrient content. A high proportion of raw, unprocessed foods in your diet will provide ample amounts of the constituents required to keep your body functioning healthily.

Heat has a variety of effects on nutrients. Some of the amino-acids in protein, particularly lysine (which is one of the eight essentials, see **protein**), are destroyed by it. Heat also makes amino acids less available for the body to use. Some vitamin A loss occurs at very high temperatures when air is present (when frying fat, for example). All the B vitamins are water-soluble and can be lost in cooking water, most are sensitive to heat. In alkaline conditions (for example, when too much salt is added), thiamine is very unstable: about 20 per cent is lost through cooking. Vitamin C is readily destroyed by heat, water, air, alkali, copper and iron, as well as by certain enzymes released when plant matter is damaged, by bruising or cutting, for example. Polyunsaturated and mono-unsaturated fats, although beneficial in their raw state, change structure when heated. Some studies have shown that a high intake of raw vegetables may lessen the risk of gastric tumours. Claims that raw food diets prolong life are not substantiated by doctors. Certain plant constituents destroyed by cooking have been shown to protect against degenerative diseases by stimulating the immune system.

## REDHEADS

*See also: Afro hair; black skin; blondes, brunettes; make-up; Oriental skin*

Red hair ranges in colour from red-gold to ginger, auburn and copper. Paler red hair tends to be fine in texture, while deeper colours tend to be coarse and grow thickly. Red hair tends to turn grey later than other colours. Redheads generally have very fair and sensitive skin. Choose skin care products with

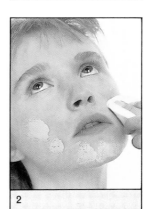

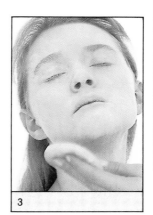

care as you may well have problems with highly perfumed products or those with a high alcohol content. This skin type is often prone to broken veins, with freckles, and burns easily due to its low melanin content (see **melanin**). It must be protected from the sun with a high protection factor sunscreen (see **tanning**), or a complete sun block, and kept well moisturized. Lashes tend to be light in colour, but can be dyed or darkened with brown mascara. Eyebrows can be darkened using light brown pencil strokes, or can be professionally dyed. Avoid over-darkening which can look too heavy with red hair.

Good eyeshadow colours for redheads are coppers, reddish-browns, greens and blues with gold, bronze and iridescent colours for night. On the face, use a tinted moisturizer rather than a heavier foundation, to let your freckles show through and add a light dusting of translucent powder for a light matt look. Avoid pinky blushers which accentuate any redness in the skin, choose tawny peaches, copper pinks, or terracottas instead.

For lips, try outlining with brown pencil and fill in with russet, peach, spicy orange or deep ginger. Use all cosmetics and scents with care as your skin, if fair, is sensitive and prone to allergy.

1 Cleanse, tone and moisturize face and neck thoroughly before beginning to apply make-up.
2 Dab on concealer stick below eyes and around nose, on any blemishes, to even out skin tone, then apply liquid foundation all over face with a damp sponge, blending in well especially around the neck area.
3 Brush on powder, then remove excess with a brush or powder puff. Comb eyebrows and dust powder off them.
4 Apply buff eyeshadow as a base all over eye area, then darker brown powder shadow near lashes. Now use moss green eye pencil near upper lashes and follow up with a matching powder to blend it.
5 Use lighter green above and below lashes and then brush on brown mascara. Comb through to prevent clogging. Then apply a layer of green mascara and comb again.
6 Brush along cheekbone with buff blusher, then add a touch of pink.
7 Outline, then paint lips with brown lipstick, blot and apply gloss for extra reflection.

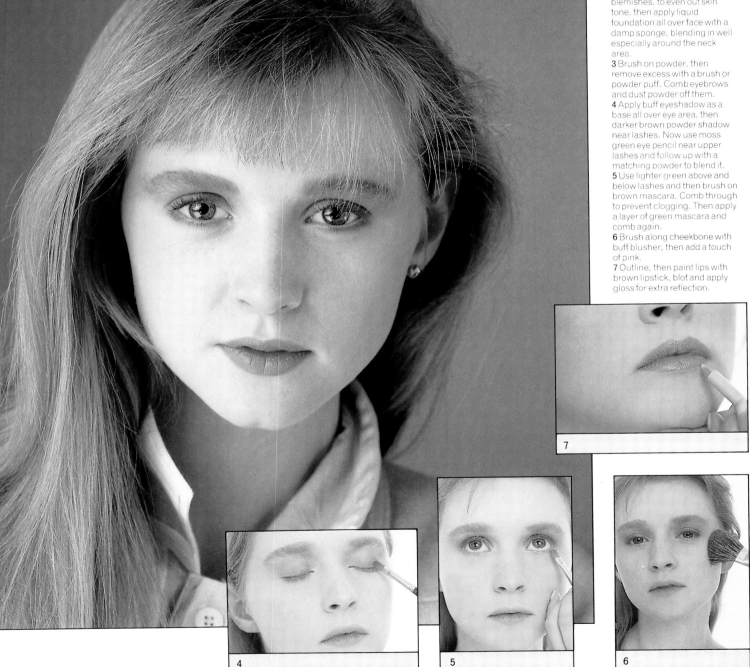

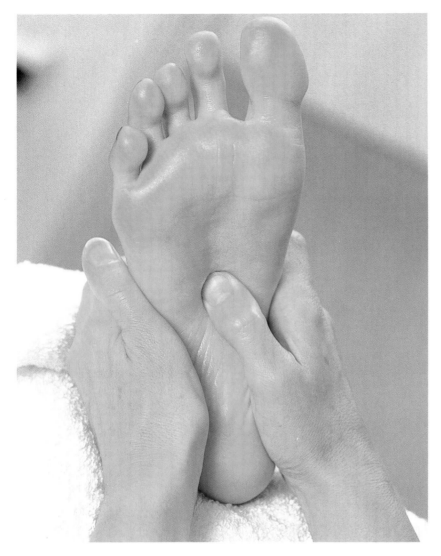

# REFLEXOLOGY

*See also: acupuncture; acupressure; iridology; relaxation; stress*

Reflexology is a very ancient form of therapy. Detailed drawings in the Tomb of the Physician in Egypt demonstrate its use as long ago as 2300 BC. It is based on the principle that there are 'reflexes' or energy channels in the feet which relate to every organ and function in the body. Reflexology may be used like iridology, for diagnosis, as well as for treatment. Problems in the body are reflected in the feet by sensitivity, sometimes described by therapists as tiny, crystalline-like lumps, in the related area of the foot. Treatment involves the use of pressure not unlike that of acupressure to free the energy channels in these areas. This may cause some minor discomfort, not pain, and leave the patient feeling deeply relaxed.

### THE TREATMENT
A case history is taken. Relaxing breathing exercises are then suggested to the patient while the feet are examined for external evidence, such as verrucas or corns, which may indicate blocking of energy channels and blood supply. Then the patient's feet are examined in detail, with the use of a firm stroking technique.

An analysis is made and sensitive spots are then treated with deep pressure therapy. The treatment lasts a varying length of time (approximately ½ hour) and several sessions are usually necessary.

### BENEFITS
Reflexology's increasing popularity at present seems to derive from its reputation for dealing with stress and tension and in promoting relaxation.

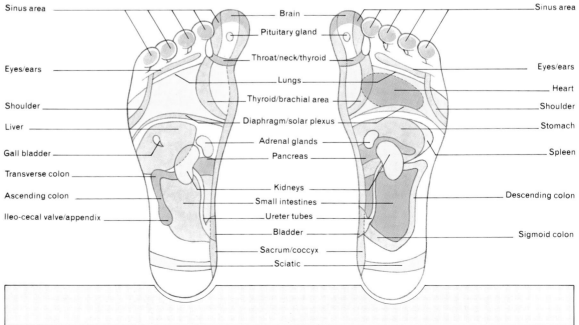

Reflexology is based on the principle that there are energy channels in the feet which relate to every organ and function in the body. Problems are reflected in the feet by sensitivity in the related area of the foot.

# RELAXATION

*See also: anxiety; autogenics; autosuggestion; biofeedback; breathing; exercise; hypnosis; massage; meditation; posture; pregnancy; post-natal health and beauty; reflexology; stress, yoga*

The ability to relax forms a vital part of a healthy lifestyle. If you cannot relax you become overtired, allowing anxiety to take hold, reducing your capacity to deal with the harmful effects of stress. You become easily aggravated; relationships suffer and you achieve less all round, especially in intellectual pursuits. Sustained over a long period, unrelieved tension and stress may lead to serious mental breakdown, as well as dramatically lowering the body's resistance to infection and disease. There are many ways to find relaxation, from listening to a favourite record to taking a warm bath after a tough day at work, meditating or exercising. The best method of relaxing varies from person to person but everybody needs regular, consistent relaxation in some form or another.

For most people, the problem lies not in recognizing that relaxation is beneficial, but in accepting that *they* need it. Next comes the hurdle of learning how to achieve it. As pressure, problems and harmful stress mount up, the need for relaxation grows stronger and increasingly difficult to achieve. Regular relaxation is, in fact, a key factor in high performance. The more pressurized your job, the more important it is to relax deeply; and even if you are not leading a stressful existence, relaxation can enrich your life. It really is worthwhile spending some time trying out various relaxation methods until you find one that you enjoy enough to practise regularly. The benefits of regular, deep relaxation will be immediately apparent.

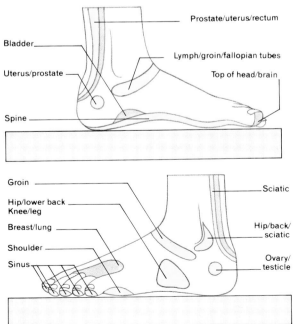

Prostate/uterus/rectum
Bladder
Uterus/prostate
Lymph/groin/fallopian tubes
Top of head/brain
Spine

Groin
Sciatic
Hip/lower back
Knee/leg
Breast/lung
Hip/back/sciatic
Shoulder
Sinus
Ovary/testicle

### RELAXATION GUIDELINES
Because of the close interaction of mind and body, relaxing one will help unwind the other too. If you are under strain, both are involved: signs of mental tension typically include the physical ones of hunched shoulders, taut neck muscles and arms crossed tightly across the torso as well as psychological symptoms.

**Learn to let go.** Accept that you really do need to relax for a period each day. Needing to relax is not a sign of weakness or inadequacy, but a bodily requirement. Practising relaxation techniques can be a sign of strength and confidence. Invest 5-15 minutes in deep relaxation each day and your work will improve greatly. The tighter your schedule, the more you need to give your mind time outside it.

**Take plenty of exercise.** While you are concentrating on a favourite sport or exercise, your mind is freed from its usual worries and occupied with more refreshing mental exercise. Exercise alleviates the muscular aches and pains resulting from stress and improves the circulation. If you are working at a desk all day, avoid back, shoulder and neck tension and pain by getting up every hour or so and doing a huge, catlike stretch and yawn, circle your shoulders back and forth and walk around. Sit on a comfortable chair that provides firm support to the lower back (see **backs**).

**Check your posture.** If posture is bad it can cause fatigue, aches and pains and reduce your overall energy (see **posture**).

**Relaxation is not synonymous with sleep.** Taking naps during the day or sleeping extra long at night may provide no relaxation at all: if your body is tense it will tend to remain so while you sleep, bringing you little gain. And some people use extra sleep as an escape from their problems. It is much more constructive to use meditation or other relaxation techniques which stimulate your mind into evaluating problem situations, not shelving them.

**Assess your breathing.** Ensure that you are involuntarily using as much of your lung area as possible. Your breathing pattern reflects your emotions, which are in turn affected by your breathing. Natural, relaxed breaths will help you to cope with any situation. Sudden, deep hyperventilation (overbreathing) is not helpful and can cause you to feel dizzy and faint, while short, shallow breaths are inadequate (see **breathing, yoga**).

**Find your own relaxation route.** There are many ways of achieving relaxation (see **aromatherapy, autogenics, autosuggestion, biofeedback, herbs, massage, meditation, reflexology, yoga**).

**Use progressive relaxation to recognize muscle tension.** Work through your body, tensing each part slightly, then consciously relaxing it. Hunch your shoulders a little, then let them relax. Frown, then let your face muscles relax again. Clench your hands, then shake them and let them flop. In tense situations reap instant benefit: tense your whole body, then breathe in and hold the breath for just a few seconds. Then breathe right out very slowly, relaxing your body from the feet up as you do so.

**Practise deep relaxation frequently.** Whenever is most convenient, though preferably before rather

Regional therapy
See Aches
and pains

**Rhythm method**
See Contraception

**Riboflavin**
See Vitamin B2

**Riding**
See Sports

**Rinses**
See Colouring hair

■ See EXERCISES
for Caution box
page 123 before
starting exercise

than after meals, practise deep relaxation. Set aside 5-15 relaxation minutes when you can be quiet, whether in the lunch hour in the office when everyone else is out or at home before breakfast. If you can, play very quiet music which will finish when your allotted time is up. If you have to set an alarm, muffle it. Try not to fall asleep. If you are very tense, practise progressive relaxation followed by deep relaxation and meditation.

### RELAXATION TECHNIQUE

1   Shut your eyes. Breathe in and on the out-breath make a slow 'hah' sound as you expel the air. Repeat twice, then breathe normally.
2   Sense the stilling of your body. Let your feet flop completely and sink into the floor. Relax your ankles, knees, let your thighs fall outwards.
3   Let your tummy rise and fall freely, relax your whole abdomen and feel your breathing ease.
4   Now let your shoulders relax and drop gently, keeping your neck straight. Concentrate on relaxing your upper back muscles, let the knots disappear as you do so.
5   Unclench your teeth, relax your cheeks, forehead, let your whole face flop and lose its expression. Feel your scalp skin loosen too.
6   Let your mind relax into the sensation of your body being at peace, unwound, and resting. Stay quietly like this, concentrating on your breathing. If your mind wanders, seek out any muscles not fully relaxed and work on them.
7   Rest in this state for your allotted time, pondering the pleasure of total relaxation, and telling yourself how peaceful and free from tension you are. Once deeply relaxed you can use meditation and visualization (see **meditation**) too.
8   Once your time is up, start to move your limbs very gradually, open your eyes and stay still briefly before getting up.

▲ Exercise A
1 Stand tall with feet hip-width apart and pelvis centred. Slowly ease your body forward, lower your head, tuck in your chin, bend your knees and roll down

until your hands reach the floor.
2 Rest in this position, breathing easily, then slowly rise up, centre your weight again and straighten knees.

▲ Exercise B
Lie on your back on the floor. Rest one hand lightly on your upper chest, the other on your abdomen so that you can feel the rhythm of your breathing.
   Now release any remaining tension by rolling your head from side to side, pressing the back of your head to the floor

and releasing, pulling your shoulders down then doing a pelvic tilt and pushing your lower back into the floor.
   Breathe in deeply, then breathe out and release completely. Relax in this way for several minutes.

## RINGWORM

*See also: feet*

Ringworm is caused by a fungus which infects the epidermis (outer layer of skin). It may occur on almost any part of the body; the groin or even the nails may become infected. Most commonly it appears as sore, itchy cracks in the skin. The commonest form of ringworm is athlete's foot *(Tinea pedis)*, which occurs between the toes. Athlete's foot was so named because it is contagious and is passed on in places such as swimming pools where warm, damp skin provides a good breeding ground. It is found among non-athletic people, but is generally less common in women than men.

### Prevention and treatment

Resist the temptation to borrow other people's shoes and be strong about not lending them yours, even if they ask. Always wash and dry feet and toes carefully, change socks and tights frequently and keep feet as dry as possible. Treat the infection with commercially available powder which has a drying and anti-fungal effect. More serious cases can be treated with anti-fungal creams and tablets; see your doctor.

## ROLFING

*See also: Alexander Technique; back; chiropractic; Feldenkrais; massage; osteopathy; posture.*

Rolfing or Structural Integration was begun by Dr Ida Rolf in the 1940s. Rolf believed that both bad postural habits and physical or emotional trauma could cause imbalance in the body and mind. The treatment is thus a method of improving integration and alignment of the whole body. When the body is held correctly, minimal strain is put on the muscles by gravity. When incorrectly held, muscles are stressed and lose elasticity. Such misuse gradually becomes habitual and involuntary.

Re-alignment takes place through intense manipulation of the connective tissues – utilizing the force of gravity, too – which encase the muscles. When manipulated, these tissues soften: the body regains energy and flexibility to re-adjust. The aim of the treatment is not, however, just to improve physical well-being and performance, but also to bring about a change in mental attitudes. Treatment often calls forth a strong emotional response from patients; some find that traumatic experiences in the past which have caused a physical imbalance are recalled. Rolfing is a therapy which requires the full co-operation and involvement of patient as well as therapist.

### The process
Treatment usually comprises a course of 10 one-hour sessions. At the beginning and end of treatment, sometimes of each session, photographs will be taken to demonstrate physical progress. With the patient lying on a couch the body is worked on systematically by the therapist using hands, fingers, knuckles, even elbows. The sensation of the deep massage can range from pleasurable to painful: the importance of complete relaxation throughout the treatment is emphasized, and helps prevent discomfort.

### Benefits
Although Rolfing can help improve posture, ease stress, headaches and tension and promote relaxation its aim is primarily to prevent such problems by promoting general physical well-being. For this reason its benefits are wide-ranging: it can help improve self-image, self-confidence and general mental and physical health.

# ROSACEA

*See also: forties; menopause; skin*

Rosacea is a condition affecting the skin on the face which usually occurs from the age of 30 onwards. It is more common among women than men and tends to appear around the time of the menopause. There are red spots and inflamed patches on the face, especially the nose and cheeks, with dilation of blood vessels. The cause is uncertain, but it appears to be linked to hormonal fluctuations in the body. Spicy, hot foods and drinks exacerbate the problem and so should be avoided by anyone experiencing these symptoms. Like acne, any form of stress or anxiety can worsen your symptoms, so practise relaxation and stress reduction (see **relaxation, stress**) to minimize their effect. You should also see your doctor or dermatologist who may prescribe medication to help reduce redness; camouflage creams will disguise it, too (see **camouflage**). Skin affected by Rosacea tends to be dry, so moisturize using a simple product.

# ROSEWATER

*See also: mouthwashes; toning; witch hazel*

Rosewater is thought to have been discovered as early as the 10th century, when rose petals and distilled water were first combined. The resulting rosewater is the basis of many creams, lotions and skin tonics, and is an excellent skin freshener on its own. In natural cosmetics it may be combined with witch hazel to make a mild toner for normal to dry skins or with glycerine to make a soothing, moisturizing cream for chapped hands. Rosewater can be used to wash the hands, as a rinse to clear hair of dry skin flakes and as a gargle to freshen the mouth. To make your own, add 30ml (1 fluid ounce) of essence of roses to 4.5l (1 gallon) of distilled water. Keep in an airtight bottle.

# ROUGE

*See also: blusher*

Rouge, the precursor of modern blusher, is a fine, dry, reddish powder originally derived from the safflower plant. Carmine is a similar red pigment produced from cochineal. Both have been used for centuries in various forms – powder, liquid or cream – to colour the lips and cheeks. Their popularity has fluctuated: in Victorian England, for example, the use of such embellishments was frowned upon, but by Edwardian times subtle use of rouge began to be acceptable. Rouge of various colours is available today. Powder rouge should be applied after foundation and powder, cream rouge after foundation but before powder. Cream rouge looks very effective in summer when the skin tends to be shiny, especially when used over a moisturizing gel.

### Rollers
See Curling and straightening hair

### Running
See Sports

**Salpingitis**
See Pelvic inflammatory disease

**Scalp**
See Alopecia; Dandruff; Hair; Trichologist; Hair transplants and weaving

**Scanning**
See Pregnancy

# SALT

*See also: diet; exfoliation; sweat; tanning*

Salt in the diet provides sodium in the form of sodium chloride, responsible for maintaining the correct osmotic pressure of the blood and tissue fluids. It is also involved in muscle activity. In temperate climates, the daily sodium requirement can be obtained from 2g (0.08oz) of salt. Salt is lost from the body through perspiration; if severe the resulting deficiency of sodium can result in a fall in blood pressure, apathy, cramps and vomiting. Many foods contain salt naturally; it is added in processing to others, particularly bread, cereals, processed meat, fish, cheese, where it acts as a preservative or makes the food more palatable.

The incidence of strokes and heart attacks is higher in countries where the amount of salt in the diet is relatively large. Since decreasing salt intake can help reduce blood pressure, it is thought to have a particularly beneficial effect for people who are susceptible to strokes and heart attacks. The World Health Organization recommends a salt intake of no more than 5g (0.2oz) a day. To achieve this, Professor Philip James of the NACNE report recommends that eliminating salt from cooking and at the table is not enough and that hard cheese, bacon and processed foods must be avoided.

Potassium chloride can be used as a salt substitute to avoid the unwelcome effects of excess sodium. Potassium also has a part to play in reducing blood pressure, so ensure that you get enough in your diet (see **minerals**).

A salt scrub helps slough off dead cells, stimulates body circulation and leaves skin soft and smooth.

# SAUNAS

*See also: health farms; relaxation; skin; sweat*

Although the Finns are usually credited with the invention of the sauna, it has been in use all over Scandinavia for centuries. The sauna is a wood-lined or wood-constructed room in which dry heat is provided by special heat-retaining stones piled on to a wood-burning – or now more commonly electric – stove. Wooden benches are provided for users to sit or lie on. The temperature is normally between 60°C (140°F) and 80°C (176°F) although it can be as low as 38°C (100°F), and the effect of the heat can be increased at will by sprinkling water on the stones. **Note:** if you have any cardiovascular problems, including hypertension, you should avoid saunas because of their stimulating effect on heart and circulation. Check with your doctor. Do not use a sauna if you feel unwell.

Saunas give the skin a thorough deep-cleanse as circulation is speeded up and waste products lost from the skin. The warmth aids muscular and general relaxation and can ease joint pain, too. Increased pulse rate and breathing mean that fresh blood supplies reach the tissues quickly, providing a sense of exhilaration and well-being similar to that experienced during and after exercise. Relaxing in a sauna before a massage improves the results. Start using a sauna for just five minutes, building up gradually if you wish.

Take off any jewellery as it may get painfully hot. To speed up the sweating process, have a shower before entering the sauna, and use the sauna naked for best results, or alternatively wrap yourself loosely in a towel.

# SCARS

*See also: acne; camouflage; chemical peeling; cosmetic surgery; dermabrasion; skin; vitamins*

Scars on the skin can result from severe acne, accidents and burns as well as surgery. They form when the damaged skin tissues fail to rebuild themselves as normal, and fibrous connective tissue is produced in the area instead. In modern surgery scars are smaller and less noticeable than in the past. Operating and stitching or other fastening techniques are improving all the time, with the help of new methods, instruments and machines. There are several types of scarring:

**Superficial scarring** The damage to the skin reaches only the epidermis (the top layers which contain dead skin cells, see **skin**). None of the live basal cells are injured. Within 28 days, therefore, the undamaged layers beneath will themselves have been pushed upwards to become the dead epidermis, and the scar will have disappeared.

**Acne scarring** This can take the form of mild, red blotchy patches on the skin or severe pitted marks all over the face and back. Both types gradually fade away. In mild cases of acne sunlight helps promote healing and reduce scarring. Despite the dangers of over-exposure to sunlight, your doctor may prescribe ultraviolet treatment (see **acne**). If the scars are deeper, dermabrasion (see separate entry) may be used, about three times, to improve texture and colour of skin.

**Deep scarring** This can occur after surgery or a serious accident. In these cases the basal layer where skin cells are formed has been damaged. Since these cells continually reproduce themselves, the scar will be perpetuated, but will fade with time. Scars should not be exposed to intense UV rays until fully healed, but sunlight can sometimes help reduce the colour difference between skin and scar. Bear in mind the dangers of too much sun (see **tanning**) and use protective cream. Dermabrasion and chemical peeling can help reduce but not remove scarring on white or pale skins (see separate entries). In cases where the scarring is

# S

disfiguring, skin grafting is sometimes used.

**Raised scars – keloids or hypertrophic cicatrices**
These occur quite commonly, caused by chemical and enzyme changes in the skin in the area and are particularly common in black skins. Normally they are left alone, but if they are a problem they are sometimes surgically removed in the hope that the new scar will be less noticeable. Some people have found Vitamin E oil or cream helpful in reducing keloids, but there is no scientific evidence for Vitamin E absorption through the skin.

Scars, like port wine stains and other skin blemishes, can often be disguised with the use of concealers. There are specially formulated products available for this purpose (see **camouflage**). The creams used are opaque and waterproof, designed to stay on the skin for longer than normal make-up. They also contain sunscreens to protect the skin.

Also remember that such blemishes are often far less conspicuous than you yourself think. Ensure that your diet contains enough vitamin C, E and zinc all of which promote healing of wounds and scars. Herbs traditionally used on the skin as poultices, or in ointments or compresses to speed healing include marigold, St John's wort and golden seal.

## SCARSDALE DIET

*See also: carbohydrates; diet; fats; fibre; minerals; protein; slimming; vitamins*

The Scarsdale Medical diet was evolved by New York heart specialist Dr H. Tarnower in the 1970s. It is a strict diet in which no substitution for the recommended foods is allowed, and some of the vegetables and fruits may be difficult to find out of season. The diet triples the average protein intake while cutting down fat and carbohydrate intake radically. All sweet, sugary foods, butter, margarine and all high-fat dairy products including full milk products are excluded. Potatoes and alcohol are also cut out. Because ketosis, which can be dangerous if it continues for any length of time, occurs when carbohydrate intake is severely cut, the diet is only followed for two weeks at a time (see **ketosis**). Weight loss is estimated at up to 9 kg (20 lb) in that two weeks. If more weight loss is desired, the diet may be recommenced after a two-week break.

The diet will undoubtedly produce weight loss. Yet it does not form the basis for a new, healthy

**1** To cover up a scar like this, start with clean, moisturized skin.
**2** Choose a specially thick covering cream available from chemists. In the UK the British Red Cross will advise and give you make-up lessons. Now begin with quite a lot of cream on the brush, working into the middle, with small dabbing movements.
**3** Continue to blend, brushing over lightly until whole scar is covered.
**4** Apply translucent powder with cotton wool, leaving to set for one or two minutes before making up in the usual way. The whole procedure takes about five minutes.

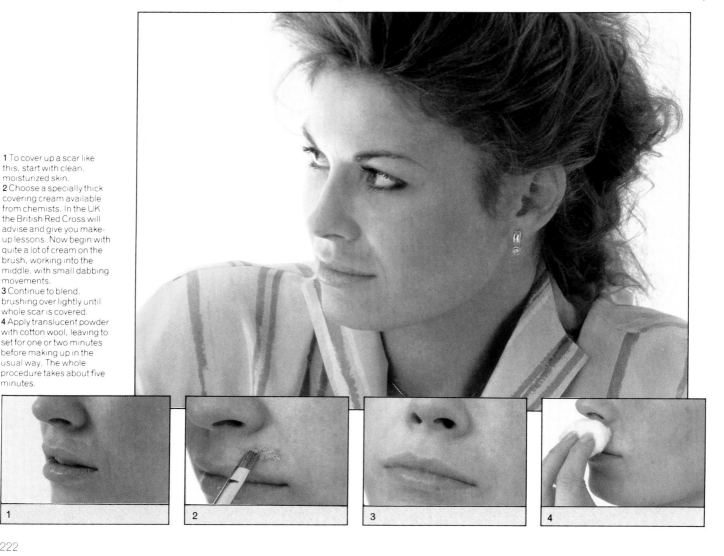

eating plan in keeping with current dietary thinking. The reduced fat intake is beneficial, but the high protein intake brings undesirably high levels of saturated fat and cholesterol with it. In addition, excessive protein intake can impair vitamin and mineral absorption (see **protein**). The low carbohydrate intake may leave you feeling fatigued, and the fibre content of the diet is lower than that generally recommended.

# SCENT

*See also: aromatherapy*

Scent is one of the most practical luxuries you can invest in. It can be evocative, nostalgic, arousing, sensual, confidence-boosting. And, depending on its ingredients, it can stimulate or relax. It can have a powerful effect on the psyche, too, and can be used therapeutically in the form of essential oils, as in aromatherapy (see separate entry). For many people, putting on scent becomes part of their morning or evening routine, essential in preparing themselves for the tasks or events ahead.

## CHOOSING SCENT
Do not expect a scent to smell the same on you as it does in the bottle or on someone else. Skin chemistry is very individual: the scent's impression will vary depending on your skin type. Scent smells sweeter and lasts longer on dark, oily skins. Various other factors, such as diet, smoking, taking medication, the environment, even your state of health can all change the impression of a perfume.

Fragrance is generally more intense in hot, humid climates, so choose a lighter scent and apply more frequently. You will need a stronger scent in dry heat: the nose's mucous membrane becomes dry and impairs the ability to smell scent effectively. Cool or showery weather 'lifts' fragrance and strengthens it, at times making it overpowering.

Always test scent on the skin, although perfume strips do give some indication of a scent's initial impact. If looking for new perfumes, seek out those with common elements to a scent you know and like: most presentation leaflets will give details of components, and perfume buyers in stores will help, too, with descriptions and information.

Smell the scent's top note in the bottle, then test on one of your pulse points (on the inside of the wrist, the crook of the arm or side of the neck) where the warmth of the skin will encourage evaporation. Smell again (not too closely as the scent will 'blind' the nose) and then leave for 1 to 2 hours so that the fragrance can develop. Smell occasionally as the scent evolves through its various 'notes'. Do not try more than two or three types of scent at the same time and space out the testing areas to avoid confusion. Apply lighter fragrances first: the nose becomes tired of heavy scents more quickly.

If you still cannot decide, take home a sample of either the pure *parfum* or eau de toilette and see whether you (and those around you) continue to like the smell after a couple of days.

Buy scent in quantities which can be used up fairly quickly. Scent, particularly pure parfum, deteriorates quickly when exposed to heat and light (the colour darkens, the texture thickens and the scent loses its top note, making it smell different on your skin). Keep bottles well-stoppered and store at room temperature away from direct sunlight. This way scent should keep for about six months and up to a year if left unopened.

## WEARING SCENT
Wear scent on the pulse points where you have tested it, between the breasts or behind the knees. Do not wear scent behind the ear as oil and sweat secretions there will destroy the fragrance. Start in the morning with a light eau de toilette and intensify with the matching parfum later in the day. Keep heavy, musky scents of the oriental and chypre type for evenings.

Make sure that you do not apply too much parfum as it can be overpowering, and remember that while your nose becomes used to scent after a time, the fragrance may still seem very strong to others.

Dabbing on a few drops of scent tends to be more wasteful than using an atomiser or aerosol which gives the most even, direct application. As scent clings to clothes, it is best not to spray them if you like to change fragrances frequently. In any case, only spray linings, as although scent evaporates, the oil that remains may cause staining and some scents have added colour.

Scent can linger for several hours, so if you want to use a different fragrance at the end of the day, have a bath or shower and change your clothes before applying the new scent. Otherwise reapply every few hours or more frequently if you are using eau de toilette or eau de cologne. Carry an atomiser in your handbag to renew scent throughout the day.

Try not to mix fragrances of any kind. Either choose other products such as bath oil, body lotion and talc in the same scent, or use unscented products (including deodorants which can smell very strong) and then apply scent. Do not try to camouflage the smell of sweat with scent – this will cause an unpleasant-smelling chemical reaction. Avoid wearing scent when sunbathing. Some of the ingredients (especially natural bergamot, commonly found in citrus fruit fragrances) react with sunlight and can cause staining on the skin, rashes or irritation, as well as accelerating the burning process.

## SCENT TYPES
Scents are generally divided up into the following families: aldehydic, chypre, floral, fougere, green, leather and oriental, each with their individual characteristics and nuances of fragrance. The strength of a particular scent depends on the extent to which the essence has been diluted. Parfum or extrait is the purest form of scent as it has the most concentrated amount of fragrance essence and lasts the longest (up to 6 hours). Scents containing a larger proportion of dilutants and the least concentration

**Sclerotherapy**
See Thread veins;
Varicose veins

**Seawater therapy**
See Thalassotherapy

**Sebaceous glands**
See Sebum; Skin

of essence are called 'eau'. These in decreasing order of strength are: eau de parfum, parfum de toilette, eau de toilette, eau de cologne, splash cologne and eau fraiche. They can be applied liberally and frequently: eau de parfum lasts a few hours, the lighter scents evaporating more quickly, so should be reapplied throughout the day.

### SCENT ELEMENTS

Scent is composed either of oils (derived from plant, flower or animal sources) or from synthetic ingredients. All these substances can be used together in the creation of a single scent – artificial formulations being in no respect inferior to natural derivatives. Fragrance is released when these highly volatile substances are dissolved in alcohol. The term 'note' is used to describe the different degrees of volatility contained in scent:

**Top note** Generally fresh and light (such as citrus, floral) and is the initial impression of scent on the nose and the skin. It can contain elements of the middle and base notes, too.

**Middle note** The heart or bouquet of a scent produced by less volatile substances (such as rose, jasmin) when the scent has dried on the skin. This note often carries the theme of the scent.

**Base note** The lingering or foundation scent provided by animal, woody resin or chemical substances which have low volatility, high fixative properties are stable and can therefore hold the fragrance and make it last.

Although almost all scents are composed of three notes (with the exception of the 'linear', noteless types such as Giorgio of Beverly Hills) there can be infinite combinations of ingredients. These can be distinguished from one another according to the proportion of ingredients as well as the order in which they are used. A good scent should develop through similar smelling notes to form one harmonious fragrance as its overall impression. Poor quality scents are often characterized by their sharply discordant fragrance phases.

# SEAWEED

*See also: diet; minerals; thalassotherapy vitamins;*

All seaweeds, including kelp – a very common variety also known as bladderwrack – contain a wide range of minerals. Foremost among these is chlorine, followed by sodium, calcium, sulphur, magnesium, potassium, phosphorus, iodine, iron, copper, zinc, manganese, and finally trace elements of others such as silver and gold. B-complex vitamins are contained, too, particularly B2 and traces of B12, which is uncommon in vegetable foods. Seaweeds are also a good source of protein. Kelp and other seaweeds can be used fresh, dried or in tablet form. Some are chopped up in salads, but more commonly they are used as seasoning and, in some cases, as setting agents.

# SEBUM

*See also: acne; hair; skin*

Sebum is the skin's natural oil. It is produced by the sebaceous glands situated below the surface of the skin (see separate entry). Ducts from these glands open into the hair follicles and sebum is thus secreted out on to the skin through the hair follicle opening. The glands only become fully active at puberty. Sebum plays an important role: it emulsifies with sweat and becomes the body's moisturizer, a thin layer of fat on the surface of the skin which helps slow the evaporation of water to keep skin supple and healthy. It is slightly acidic and antibacterial, providing extra protection from substances which might harm the skin.

Sebum moisturizes the hair shaft, too, smoothing down each hair's scaly surface to keep hair silky, healthy and lustrous. There are extra glands on the head for this purpose, and glands are more closely distributed down the central panel of the face from forehead to chin, which is why the area readily becomes oily. Sebum production varies from person to person, creating the difference between dry and oily skin and hair. It is affected by hormonal changes, and excessive sebum (and sometimes blockage of sebaceous gland ducts) is involved in problems such as acne and blackheads (see **acne, blackheads**). While cleansing is important, so is this protective acid mantle on the skin. Cleanse twice a day, no more (see **cleansing**) and preferably use pH-balanced products (see **pH**). Remember that over-astringent and medicated products designed to reduce oiliness can stimulate sebum production: because the skin is suddenly so dry, the sebaceous glands spring into action.

# SELF-HELP

*See also: awareness; health and health checks; holism; meditation; relaxation*

Self-help is as valuable in producing well-being as it is in coping with illness. In terms of everyday life, self-help depends on getting to know your whole self, the bad points as well as the good, learning to capitalize on the latter, while accepting and working with the former whenever they make themselves felt: it will not help to brush them under the carpet.

Reaching a state of self-awareness is a continuous process, and your assessment of yourself must keep pace with it. Each person finds his or her own method, whether through meditation, relaxation, counselling, prayer, self-hypnosis or whatever. In learning what motivates and affects you, a range of factors past and present which have shaped you become evident. Once you have understood what produces a given reaction, you will be better able to accept and deal with it.

Self-help means establishing your aims and working towards them, putting yourself in charge of your life. It does not mean being selfish in the sense of exploiting or hurting other people, but cultivating a healthy respect for your own needs, too.

In illness, whatever your standpoint in the holistic range of choices, you can help yourself enormously by taking a positive, yet realistic stance. Find out all you can from your doctor or other therapist treating you. Establish how best you can promote recovery: what are the best foods, exercises and activities for you. Support and care from those close to you can help enormously: share your worries and experiences with them if you can. Remember that they may feel powerless to help, and would almost certainly relish the chance to do whatever they can. If you suffer physical problems, consult a physiotherapist or occupational therapist to discuss the best ways of overcoming or dealing with them. There are numerous organizations offering support to sufferers from anything from alcoholism to migraine to cancer. Addresses and phone numbers can be obtained from your general practitioner, Citizens Advice Bureau, yellow pages, community centre, library or hospital. Take what they offer: their sympathy and advice can be enormously helpful.

# SELF-IMAGE

*See also: anorexia nervosa; body image; depression; self-help; sex and sexuality*

The way you feel about yourself helps form your lifestyle and the way you behave. This self-image is a kind of mental picture of how you see yourself, and how you think others see you. Your body image (see separate entry), is an important contributory element.

Considering how extensive a part this stored image plays in our lives, it is surprising how few of us are aware of it. We tend to accept its dictates as inalienable parts of ourself, which, of course, they are not. It is your self-image, for example, which prompts you to reject certain hairstyles as totally unsuitable for you. It is your self-image which makes you turn down an interview because the job sounds unlike you, and your self-image which makes you so certain you will catch flu when it is around because you always have before. These are examples of you as you see yourself, not necessarily you as others see you or as you could be. One of the new hairstyles might have been just right, the job too, and eating extra well and taking lots of exercise could have helped you and avoid flu. Taking control of your self-image can bring bonuses in your life, and it need not be hard to achieve.

### TAKING CONTROL
Your self-image affects your performance in every sphere of life: if you think yourself inadequate in

some way, you will be. Work to establish a contemporary, realistic and positive self-image which will help you achieve everything you want to.

Try writing down everything you feel about your abilities, character, relationships, career and aims. Then try to establish how much of this is really the way *you* feel and not how your family or partner or children feel that you should be or are. You may find self-hypnosis, meditation, yoga, autogenics and other therapies helpful in re-evaluating yourself. Avoid letting other people's assessment of you, past or present, damage your self-image. You have the potential to get to know yourself better than anyone else can. Take a long look at your achievements, gifts, abilities, and accept yourself at your own, educated value.

One area in which self-image plays a very large part is in choice of job. For most people, major decisions get made early in life when you do not know yourself well, have scarcely dipped into your potential and have to rely on the views and advice of others. Present unhappiness at work may be because you are not in the ideal field. Putting this right may mean a lot of extra work in acquiring new qualifications, or in earning money to go to college. Alternatively, it may just mean that you feel undervalued, and summoning up courage to ask for a salary and status increase may bring your job into line with your new self-image.

Look anew at your body, your sexuality, your diet, your career and lifestyle and take stock. Changes are at your disposal once you are in charge.

# SEX AND SEXUALITY

*See also: AIDS; contraception; menstruation; self-image; sexually transmitted diseases*

More books have been written on the subject of sex than on almost any other in the health field. Why? Not only because there is still a general lack of knowledge, but because nearly everyone has anxieties and inhibitions about their sexual desires and abilities which they seek to allay. Everyone just wants to find out what other people do; whether they themselves are 'normal', whether they are 'good in bed', whether they are missing out. The legacy of Victorian prudery makes it difficult for us to discuss our sexual needs and desires, likes and dislikes with each other, and prevents us from being frank with the next generation, too.

The truth is, of course, that good sex is the sex you like. There are no secrets and no magic recipes for success. Because your sexuality is an expression of many facets of your character, it is completely individual and volatile, and because it is such a profound reflection of ourselves, it is often also the focus for fears and worries. In intercourse we make ourselves very vulnerable to our partner. This pro-

**S**

found giving of oneself is yet another reason why everyone has fears about their abilities in bed at some time or another. But there are no absolutes, no such thing as being good or bad. The deciding factors in mutual enjoyment are very varied: mutual honesty and reassurance, love, caring, lack of inhibition in behaviour, learning to express your sexual likes and dislikes while appreciating those of your partner. Their relative importance varies.

Because of the relationship between our sexuality and every other area of our lives, sexual urges, inclinations and reactions are tempered by success or difficulties at work, problems in all areas of the relationship, in lifestyle and health, with children. All these tend to be reflected in bed and this can create new problems unless both partners show a great deal of understanding and patience. For example, anxiety produces diverse reactions in men and women: it often makes women take longer to come to orgasm, whereas it is likely to make men achieve it more quickly. If one partner is under extreme pressure at work, he or she may only want to make love very infrequently while the other partner happens to be feeling particularly fulfilled and is keener than ever on lovemaking. And it seems that with age, pressure of work and responsibility affects

men's sexual performance more than it does women's, diminishing the amount of energy available for sex. Sexual intuition and understanding between partners is a continual challenge.

Hugs and cuddling, stroking, touching, holding and kissing are just as much part of sex as is intercourse itself, and orgasm. What is right for you is what suits you both. Yet there will always be times when your sex life is not as relaxed and satisfying as it might be. All women experience difficulties in achieving orgasm, for example, at some time; men can have troubles with premature ejaculation – coming very quickly – among many other common worries. Usually these can be linked to difficulties elsewhere in your lives, and you will be able to sort these out together. Some of the many books on sex can be extremely helpful, too. One very common problem in post-menopausal women is vaginal dryness due to low oestrogen levels: this is easily alleviated with the use of lubricating jellies commercially available without prescription. Whatever your problems, if they persist or worry you, do not hesitate to approach your general practitioner, gynaecologist, family planning clinic or local counselling services. You will find them helpful and understanding: remember that most people suffer from sexual

problems at some point in their lives.

Sexual intercourse is not without its dangers. There is a strong link between the incidence of cervical cancer and the number of sexual partners a woman has. It seems that using a sheath or condom (see **contraception**) does cut down the risk of getting this type of cancer, and regular screening (see **health checks**) means that any pre-cancerous cells can be spotted and eliminated early on. Sexually transmitted diseases are another problem (see separate entry), and here again using a sheath does give some protection. While touching, feeling and hugging are safe with a partner who might have been exposed to AIDS, intimate kissing and sexual intercourse are risky. If you think that you may have been exposed to any sexually transmitted disease or AIDS, go to your local special clinic, or to your gynaecologist or general practitioner for examination, advice and treatment.

Wilhelm Reich, psychoanalyst, therapist and thinker, saw sexual energy as the highest, most releasing and beneficial force in life. Most of us would not disagree that enjoyable, rewarding sexual activity can enliven and enrich our whole life. It can build a self-assurance which not only benefits our moods and behaviour, promoting a sense of physical and mental well-being, but also promotes creativity and energy at work and at home.

# SEXUALLY TRANSMITTED DISEASES

*See also: AIDS; cold sores; pelvic inflammatory disease; sex and sexuality; thrush*

If you have been, or suspect that you might have been, in contact with a person infected by a sexually transmitted disease (STD), go to your nearest special clinic for testing as soon as you can, or to your gynaecologist or general practitioner. If you suffer genital soreness or itching, make an appointment to see your doctor, and meanwhile, avoid using any medication (except the Pill if you take it) until a diagnosis is made. Stop using soap in the area and wear loose-fitting underwear. Try bathing in a warm salt solution (1 teaspoon of salt to 568ml (1 pint) of water) to soothe symptoms. Since symptoms such as a burning sensation on passing urine are common to several STDs as well as to cystitis, it is always worth being checked out if there is any likelihood at all that you have been infected. Most STDs can be treated quickly and simply. The following are common STDs, symptoms and treatments:

**Gardnerella vaginalis** (anaerobic vaginosis) is not necessarily sexually transmitted; this bacterial infection of the vagina is also associated with the coil. Symptoms: watery, fishy-smelling vaginal discharge which worsens after intercourse, little or no irritation. No symptoms in male. Diagnosis: vaginal smear or culture. Treatment: metronidazole for both partners.

**Genital warts** are caused by specific types of human papilloma virus (HPV). Unlike ordinary skin warts, they are sexually transmitted. Symptoms: warty growths on genitals, appearing up to a year after exposure. No irritation unless there is another infection. Strong association with cervical cancer. Diagnosis: on appearance, sometimes on cervical smear. Treatment: may be prolonged. Podophyllin paint, or trichlorocacetic acid. Freezing (cryo-surgery) or burning can be used. Sexual intercourse should be with condom (sheath) until both partners are clear. Women should have regular smears.

**Gonorrhoea** is a sexually transmitted bacterial infection. Infection can spread to the Fallopian tubes in women causing pelvic inflammatory disease (see separate entry); in men it more rarely affects testicles. Babies born to infected mothers can develop sticky eyes (treated with drops) and young daughters can occasionally be infected from shared facecloths. Symptoms: few or none in women; urethral discharge with burning on passing urine 2-10 days after exposure in men. Diagnosis: from special smears and microbiological culture. Treatment: usually single large dose of oral penicillin.

**Genital herpes,** herpes simplex virus infection, is transmitted by genitals sexually, or by lesions on the mouth. It is similar to the virus which causes cold sores (see separate entry). It is usually only infectious when sores are present. Can be spread by mother with active sores to baby during labour. Infection has been linked with cervical cancer. Symptoms: often severe, especially in women. First attack 2-10 days after exposure, flu-like symptoms with painful genital blisters which burst to form sores, pain on passing urine. Recovery without medication may take 3 weeks. Virus then lies dormant, but in over half of cases recurs spontaneously with similar but milder symptoms. Diagnosis: definite one can only be made from virus culture of active sores. Treatment: with salt water washes, if passing urine is very painful, this can be done in a warm bath. Simple analgesics often help and acyclovir, a new drug, can be used. Infected women should have regular cervical smears and inform their obstetrician that they have had herpes.

**Non-specific urethritis** (NSU) is inflammation of the urethra. Many causes, but usually sexually transmitted, with about half the cases due to the bacterial infection chlamydia trachomatis (see also pelvic inflammatory disease PID). Symptoms: women usually notice nothing wrong, although both sexes may have mild symptoms of discharge and burning on passing urine, 1-3 weeks or more after exposure. Infection can spread to the Fallopian tubes and is the commonest cause of PID. It can also spread to the testicles. Babies born to infected mothers can develop sticky eyes and pneumonia. Diagnosis: from urethral smear or culture in male. Female tests may be normal, but both partners need treatment. Treatment: with tetracycline or erythromycin for at least 7 days.

**Pediculosis pubis (crabs)** are tiny crab-like anim-

als which live in the pubic hair, suck blood and lay minute white eggs on the hair base. Transmission is from hair to hair and is often sexually. If infected you may notice the nits or just itching up to 1 month after exposure. Treatment: with benzylbenzoate or other insecticide compounds applied to all hairy areas except scalp. Bed linen must be washed in very hot water to kill any nits.

**Syphilis** is a sexually transmitted bacterial infection now reasonably rare in industrialized countries. When it occurs, it is most common in male homosexuals. Symptoms: painless genital sore develops in either sex about 1 month after exposure. If not noticed or treated there may be a rash with general malaise. Failing to seek treatment can be very harmful in the long-term because the infection can then become dormant leading to brain and blood vessel disease many years later. Babies of untreated, affected mothers may be affected, too. Diagnosis: from the sore or blood test. Treatment: usually with penicillin injections.

**Trichomonas vaginalis** (TV or trich) is a vaginal infection due to a protozoan and is nearly always sexually transmitted. Symptoms: watery, often offensive vaginal discharge with accompanying soreness which may be severe. Men are usually carriers with no visible symptoms. Diagnosis: with vaginal swab or found on routine cervical smear. Treatment: with metronidazole taken orally for both partners.

**Urethral syndrome** is probably caused by friction during intercourse. Symptoms: as for cystitis, but no demonstrable infection in urine. Treatment: empty bladder before and after intercourse, increase fluid intake (but ensure that it is not acidic), change intercourse position. If symptoms persist the urine should be rechecked for infection.

# SIXTIES PLUS

*See also: ageing; colour choice – cosmetics; diet; greying; make-up; osteoporosis; skin*

Once you have passed 20, the dawn of every new decade can seem like rather a hurdle. And probably the sixth is toughest of all. Reaching the age of retirement should not mean retiring from life and it does not necessarily mean retiring from your job if you can help it. You will, however, have to ease your pace, which you may find hard at first. Many people find that when they do stop work, far from retiring, they are busier than ever indulging in pastimes previously precluded by lack of hours. It is a time, too, when your family group is likely to be expanding, when you are busy getting to know new relations by marriage, and babysitting for other newcomers. It can be an exciting and stimulating phase of new beginnings, provided that you forge a positive attitude and take extra care of your health.

**Body** Keep your figure in trim, your whole body healthy with regular exercise which incorporates plenty of loosening and stretching exercises and a wide range of movement to keep joints mobile. Remember to consult your doctor before embarking on any new exercise or diet regime (see **exercise** and **exercises**). Outside interests and activities play an increasingly important role in keeping you mentally and physically well when you stop work. You will find that you tend to sleep less than when you were younger: this is quite normal. If you do suffer from insomnia, avoid sleeping pills if you can (see **insomnia**). Have regular check-ups (see **health and health checks**).

**Diet** You need less food as you grow older (see **diet**) but make sure that you eat as regularly as before. Include plenty of fresh fruit and vegetables, fish, meat and poultry in your daily diet, plenty of calcium-containing products (see **minerals**) and fibre (see separate entry).

**Skin** Skin becomes drier with age, and will now need a richer, greasier moisturizer than you have used in the past, for day and night. You will need to exfoliate away dead skin cells more frequently, too. Offset the drying effects of bathing: add a glass of milk and a capful of oil to your bath and then follow by applying plenty of body lotion all over. You may experience a slight increase in facial hair due to declining levels of oestrogen: this can be bleached or permanently removed by electrolysis (see **unwanted hair**).

Skin pales with age, as does hair, so rethink your make-up. Adjust your foundation to your new skin colour (see separate entry). Avoid using heavy types and excessive powder which settles in and accentuates creases, especially in the eye area. Use softer colours for blusher, lips and eyes, avoiding black mascaras and eyeliners, frosted colour shadows and bright dramatic colours which tend to be ageing (see **make-up, colour choice – cosmetics**).

**Hair** Many people find that, having dreaded the arrival of grey hair, it actually looks very attractive and flattering to a softer skin tone. Since hair tends to become drier, avoid excessive processing: in any case, grey hair is full of natural 'highlights' and looks best in simple styles. If you cannot face going grey, you can choose from various types of colouring (see **greying**), but never dye back to your old colour: it will now be too strong for your skin.

# SKIN

*See also: acne; allergens and allergies; cellulite; chemical peeling; chloasma; cleansing; cosmetic surgery; cysts; dermabrasion; dermatitis; diet; exercise; elastin and elastone; exfoliation; facials; freckles; hypo-allergenic products; melanin; menstruation; moisturizing; moles; port wine stains; pregnancy; psoriasis; rashes; scars; sebum; stress; sweat; tanning; toning; wrinkles*

The skin is the body's protective covering and its largest organ. It provides 2.7-3.6 kg (6-8 lbs) of body weight. Skin is multi-functioning, self-renewing

and as sensitive as it is resilient. It guards our internal organs against bacteria, harmful chemicals, irritants, ultraviolet light, blows and jolts. It regulates temperature – insulating the body in cold atmospheres, cooling it by sweating when hot – and responds to temperature, pain and touch through its sensory cells. Waste matter is excreted through its pores. The natural oil, sebum (see separate entry), secreted by the sebaceous glands keeps it moist. The mixture of sebum and water is known as the acid mantle. The condition of the skin reflects emotional and physical health, tempered by the environment it functions in and the level of care given to it. Its texture, colour, natural response to sunlight and, to a great extent, rate of ageing are hereditary.

### SKIN STRUCTURE
Skin has a number of mutually dependent layers. The visible, outer layer forms the upper part of the *epidermis*, and is known as the *stratum corneum*, or horny layer. It consists of dead skin cells which are constantly being shed and replaced by upward migration of live cells from the deeper basal layer.

229

Skin renews itself completely approximately every 28 days, the process slowing down with age. The epidermis heals without scarring, but the nuclei of these cells (originally formed in the dermis) contain the vital genetic material deoxyribonucieic acid (DNA) which enables the skin to continue to reproduce itself correctly, and any damage caused to them (through burns, surgery or ultraviolet light, for example, which affects the dermis, rather than just the epidermis) will result in permanent scarring (see separate entry). As cells progress to the surface, they harden, flatten and compress to form a protective barrier which both protects the new live cells below, and at the same time is 'fed' by them.

The skin's surface is kept naturally moist and protected from bacteria by the acid mantle (see above) as well as water contact. Colour is determined by the activity of the melanocyte cells in the epidermis which produce the pigment melanin (see separate entry, and **black skin**); this level is genetically determined.

The *dermis*, the next layer, contains a mass of connective collagen and elastin fibres (see separate entries) which support the surface skin and provide its resilience and elasticity. The dermis also contains sweat and sebaceous glands, hair follicles, blood vessels, which carry all the nourishment to the skin, and nerve cells.

The deepest layer or *hypodermis* contains muscles, veins and the fat which cushions the skin. The thickness of this fatty tissue varies according to the individual's fat ratio in the body. Excessive dieting and reduction of this layer causes skin to sag, the fat reduction which occurs with age combined with the formation of elastone (see separate entry) has a similar result. Skin is thickest on areas such as the upper back, feet and hands, thinnest around the eyelids, neck and throat.

## SKIN TYPES

It is useful to categorize different skin types if only to make choosing cosmetic products easier, but it is wise not to apply the groupings too rigidly. Furthermore, your skin's requirements change frequently, because of such diverse factors as ageing, climate, pregnancy or temporary skin problems.

**Oily skin** is characterized by excessive sebum production (see separate entry) especially at puberty (see separate entry) and during the pre-menstrual phase, which makes the skin shiny. It is also prone to acne and blackheads. The oiliest area is the central panel from the forehead down to the chin, where the sebaceous glands are concentrated. The complexion may be open-pored and sallow, but it may equally well be sensitive and susceptible to allergies. Oily skin tends to develop wrinkles less readily than other types.

**Dry skin** is characterized by low level of sebum production. It is normally fair and sensitive with no open pores and a dullish appearance, feels taut after washing, and may flake and chap easily. Wrinkles and lines tend to form early especially around the mouth and eyes. Dryness is exacerbated by wind, extremes of temperature and air conditioning; it increases as the skin ages. Lack of essential fatty acids in the diet can cause dryness.

**Sensitive skin** is commonly dry and delicate, although it can be oily. It is easily irritated by extremes of temperature, some detergents, cosmetics and alcohol (used on the skin), becoming red and blotchy and sometimes forming broken veins. This skin is the most prone to allergies, marked dryness and blushing.

**Combination skin** is characterized by an oily central panel with dry cheeks. This type tends to develop with time, especially in those skins which were oily during puberty.

**Normal or balanced skin** is characterized by its smooth texture, even tone and invisible pores, with no sign of sebum or dryness. Rare, except in children. This skin tends to become drier with age.

## CARING FOR YOUR SKIN

The huge range of factors involved in caring for your skin, from eating a nutritious diet, drinking plenty of fluids, taking enough exercise, keeping the stresses and strains of life at their lowest and following a practical beauty routine are all dealt with in great detail in their individual entries. Skin problems are also individually covered. See the list at the beginning of this entry. Photosensitivity, natural or induced skin sensitivity to sun, can occur from some drugs taken internally, plant juices and cosmetics, especially those containing bergamot oil. See the tanning entry for further information.

## SKIN CANCER

Skin cancer normally originates in the epidermis. It is usually recognizable in its initial stages and if treated in time, can almost invariably be cured. More common in the elderly, it is closely linked to the cumulative effects of repeated, intemperate exposure to the sun. Most vulnerable are fair-skinned, freckled people who burn easily and seldom tan.

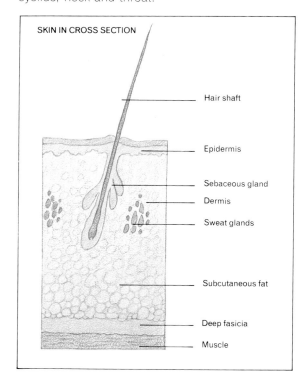

SKIN IN CROSS SECTION

Hair shaft

Epidermis

Sebaceous gland

Dermis

Sweat glands

Subcutaneous fat

Deep fascia

Muscle

The largest organ in the body, skin is multi-functioning, self-renewing and as sensitive as it is resilient.

**Solar keratoses**, scaly red patches on the skin that do not heal and are pre-malignant. They can be cured if identified and treated before they develop into basal or squamous cell carcinoma (see below).
**Basal cell carcinoma** normally affects the face, initially appearing as a small lump which enlarges, ulcerates and forms a crust. It grows locally but very rarely spreads internally. If left untreated the cancerous cells will gradually enlarge but can usually be cured with surgery or radiotherapy.
**Squamous cell carcinoma** is less common, usually appearing as an ulcer on the face or hand which refuses to heal. It may spread to other parts of the body via the circulation but the growth is usually responsive to surgery or radiotherapy.
**Malignant melanoma** is rarer still and the most dangerous form of skin cancer: if left untreated it can spread very quickly through the body. Although not always sun-related, it is more likely to occur in fair skinned individuals who burn easily and have experienced short but intense exposure to the sun. It is also more common in people who have a large number of moles. The disease can appear anywhere on the body, often arising from a mole which grows quickly, becomes irregular in shape and changes colour as it grows, often appearing speckly. It may also itch, bleed or ooze. See your doctor immediately if you develop any of these symptoms since if it is caught early enough, malignant melanoma can be cured by surgery.

# SLEEP

*See also: beds; circadian rhythms; drugs and medicines; insomnia; jet-lag; relaxation; stress*

Not all our sleeping time is spent in blissful oblivion. We spend the night alternating dreaming cycles, which occupy about 25 per cent of adult sleep time, with dreamless cycles. As you move towards sleep your body functions begin to slow down, breathing lightens. Your eyes become effectively 'blind' and your mind begins to wander as you move, unknowingly, into stage 1 sleep, sometimes accompanied by the familiar sudden 'myoclonic' jerk which results from electrical activity in the brain. This stage can occur during the day, too, in micro-sleep naps when you fall asleep with your eyes open. Through stages 2 and 3 your body slows still further, and you become more difficult to wake. At stage 4 you reach your deepest sleep and are difficult to rouse. Body processes are at their slowest, body temperature, pulse rate and breathing at their lowest. Stages 1-4 are known as synchronized sleep as brain waves become increasingly regular.

Interspersed with synchronized sleep is rapid eye movement – because eyes move around busily under the eyelids – or REM sleep. This is the busiest phase for the body and mind: breathing, pulse and

**Slimming pills**
See Slimming;
Appetite
suppressants

**Smear test**
See Health and
health checks

temperature levels all increase, and the brain activity adjusts, almost to awake levels, although muscles are virtually paralysed. Men experience erections during REM sleep because of overall arousal levels, not because they are having erotic dreams.

Knowledge of sleep cycles, their characteristics and length has come from tests where machines such as the electroencephalogram (EEG), which shows brainwave patterns, are attached to the body, and where subjects are woken at various stages of sleep. Dreaming occurs for approximately 1 in 10 sleepers in stages 3 and 4, but takes place for 8 out of 10 during REM sleep. REM dreams may be recalled on waking. Sleepwalking – unconnected to dream events – can occur during stage 4, sleeptalking in stage 2, often but not always unconnected with 'real' life. We start the night with synchronized sleep, then spend approximately 5-10 minutes in REM and continue working through the night alternating between synchronized and REM at intervals of approximately 1 to 1½ hours.

The cycle is by no means regular: before midnight, for example, we spend substantial amounts of time in the deepest stage, 4, whereas later in the night non-REM sleep is mainly in the lighter stages. The REM phases increase in length up to approximately 40 minutes, and we normally wake from one of these. It appears that REM sleep occurs at different stages of the night just before menstruation, causing a feeling of heaviness and fatigue, and that we need more REM sleep when under emotional or work pressure. Sleeping pills reduce the amount of REM sleep, while insomnia reduces both REM and stage 4 sleep.

Dreams can sometimes be recalled very clearly even some hours after waking. Although very often they seem to have little connection with daily life, they can sometimes help you to analyse the nature of unspecific anxieties plaguing you in the day, and are often used in therapy. Some people experience lucid dreams where they are aware of the divide between what they are dreaming and reality. Where such people experience recurrent nightmares, they can be taught to manipulate the dream in order to remove the horror.

During sleep the body recharges itself. Synchronized sleep seems to be the time when the body concentrates on physical processes such as cell renewal and antibody production, while during REM sleep assimilation of knowledge, events and emotional rebalancing take place. But how much sleep do we need? Individual needs vary: babies need about 18 hours (75 per cent of which is spent in REM); adults anything from 3 to 10 hours or more, irrespective of climate or number of hours of daylight. People with a high basal metabolic rate or whose energy needs have been increased by illness or pregnancy, for example, need extra sleep. Everyone's need decreases with age, however; after 30 in men, 50 in women, then again in the mid-50s and 60s, down to 5 or 6 hours in many cases. Some researchers feel that sleep may not be essential, but provides a suitable energy-saving occupation during darkness, enabling body repair to take place. Certainly we can go without sleep – or without suf-

fering ill effects – for at least 10 days, making it all up in one night of 10 hours' sleep. And various tests have shown that sleeplessness has little effect on performance. Really prolonged lack of REM sleep can, rarely, produce psychological disturbances, and bad dreams can be experienced in a process known as 'REM rebound', after, for example, using sleeping pills, as the REM sleep is made up.

Insomnia can be very distressing, although it seems to affect most people at some stage in their lives. For details on getting a good night's sleep and coping with sleeplessness, see **insomnia**.

# SLIMMING

*See also: appetite suppressants; Beverly Hills diet; body type; bulimia nervosa; diet; diets; eating habits; fattening diets; fibre; hunger; ketosis; Scarsdale diet; weight*

The desire to lose weight is widespread in affluent countries, as the ever-growing amount of literature on the subject bears witness. For many people the obsession is justified: obesity and its related problems, including high blood pressure (see separate entry), coronary heart disease and diabetes, are among the most serious and widespread diseases in the developed countries. For others – within the normal weight range for their height – (see **weight**) the motivation to be slim comes from a compulsion to conform with fashionable ideals of figure and beauty. In moderation this is harmless, but if dieting becomes obsessive and extreme it can lead to malnutrition, and to problems such as anorexia nervosa, sometimes called the 'slimmers' disease', bulimia nervosa or bingeing (see separate entries). Slimming has become the panacea, too, for a wide range of inadequacies. When excessive weight is wrongly blamed for failure at work or in love the idea is formed that losing weight will solve personal problems. It cannot. Sensible slimming, however, can be a valuable aid to health and beauty.

### THE BEST WAY TO SLIM
The pages of slimming books and magazines are filled with weight-loss schemes, ranging from fairly sane to frankly cranky. A diet which is based on a very limited selection of foods – just fruit, for example – may be fun for a day and even temporarily lose you a couple of pounds in that time. Continued it will become boring, ineffective, and dangerous.

If you seriously want to slim, you must rethink your whole approach to diet (see **eating habits**) and establish a healthy, balanced eating regime. Almost 99 per cent of diets fail ultimately, with the slimmer putting back on all the weight lost and sometimes more, because after slimming they return to the habits which made them fat in the first place. It is only worth dieting if you wholeheartedly intend to stay slim and if your usual diet made you fat to start with. This means rethinking your attitude not just for a few days, weeks or months, but for the rest of your life.

Research shows that to keep healthy slimmers and non-slimmers should cut down on sugar, saturated fat and salt and increase their fibre intake (see separate entries). Sugar is high in Calories with minimal nutrient content. Fat is also a very concentrated source of Calories and the saturated fatty acids that many fats contain are thought to contribute to coronary heart disease. Excess salt in the diet can exacerbate high blood pressure and can cause fluid retention (see separate entry), making you appear fatter than you really are. Good fibre intake is thought to help prevent heart and bowel diseases, and provides a Calorie-free feeling of fullness for the stomach.

The serious slimmer should therefore follow a diet based mainly on starch in the form of wholemeal bread, brown rice, wholewheat pasta and potatoes, fresh fruit and vegetables, with some protein and just a little fat. The food balance is that of a normal healthy diet: the amount is reduced, but not by too much. A normal intake of 2500 Calories a day could be cut by 1000 Calories to give an average weight loss of approximately 2lb (0.9kg) per week. Scientific studies have shown that anything more stringent may affect the body's reaction to food. Believing itself to be undergoing starvation, it tends to conserve energy and deposit as much fat as it can (see **crash dieting**).

### TIPS FOR SLIMMERS
- Drink plenty of liquids, especially water and fruit juices, to replace the large amount lost, particularly at the beginning of a diet.
- Encourage your partner or family to adopt healthy eating patterns as well even if they themselves are not dieting: it will benefit everyone and there will be less temptation in the food cupboard for you.
- If you do lapse, don't give up the whole idea. Sensible slimming is a long-term process and weakness one day can be balanced by extra willpower the next.
- Eat little and often to prevent hunger pangs (see **diet, eating habits**).
- There is nothing wrong with between-meal snacks as long as they are of the right kind. Raisins, low-fat yoghurts, fruit or a bowl of cereal should become your treats instead of crisps (chips) and doughnuts.
- As a general rule, eat more at the beginning of the day to give yourself more energy when you need it, that is, in waking hours, and to give yourself longer to use up the Calories.
- Avoid 'magic' diets such as meal replacements in the form of a drink or pill. You don't know what is in them, they are expensive, and they are no use to you in the long-term effort to reform your eating habits sensibly.
- Do not try to affect your body's metabolism with slimming pills, or take hormone treatments, diuretics or laxatives. If your weight problem is serious, you should seek advice from your general practitioner, nutritionist or dietician.

- While exercise plays but a small part in weight loss, it plays a large one in shaping up your new silhouette and in promoting your general health. In fact, you may discover that your problem is more lack of tone than excess weight. You may be able to stop dieting by exercising and toning programmes.

# SMOKING

*See also: dependencies*

Smoking is extremely hazardous to health. Contrary to popular belief, it is rarely a mere habit, but commonly a psychological and chemical dependency.

### THE DANGERS
In the case of coronary heart disease, strokes and thrombosis only the extent of smoking's role is disputed. It is certain that smokers are four or five times more likely to suffer from coronary heart disease and stroke and have increased chances of any deep vein or arterial thromboses. Both the number of cigarettes and longevity of smoking are significant factors in the incidence of these. Taking the combined contraceptive pill and smoking greatly increases risk.

Smokers are four or five times more likely than

S

**Sodium**
See Salt; Minerals

non-smokers to suffer from lung, throat, oesophagus and mouth cancer, also cancer of the pancreas and urinary tract. The number of cigarettes smoked daily may be of less significance in the incidence of cancer than the number of years during which smoking has taken place. Inhalers and non-inhalers seem equally at risk.

Smokers are at greatly increased risk of bronchitis, emphysema and pneumonia. Men who smoke more than 25 cigarettes a day are 25 times more likely to die from bronchitis or emphysema than non-smokers.

The carbon monoxide in cigarette smoke reduces the amount of oxygen in the blood, straining the heart – especially dangerous for sportspeople. Pregnant smokers pass toxins to the foetus, and the reduced oxygen in the blood supply arrests foetal development: their babies tend to be smaller than others. All these factors increase the likelihood of miscarriage, foetal distress or death and reduce the baby's resistance to infection in early life. It is advisable to give up smoking well before trying to become pregnant. Smoking increases the likelihood of osteoporosis (see separate entry) and can cause vitamin B deficiency.

'Passive' smoking is dangerous too; cigarette smoke does not need to be inhaled into the lungs to be dangerous, just breathed in normally. People whose partners smoke are at far greater risk than those with non-smoking partners.

### GIVING UP
As with any addiction, there is no 'cure' for smoking, just the possibility of recovery. Unless you are really committed to giving up, you will be unable to do so: the psychological dependence is even stronger than the chemical. The decision is hard, but once taken the chemical withdrawal symptoms last only two weeks or so.

Because smoking increases the metabolic rate, giving up can produce a swift drop in that rate. There follows an improved efficiency in bodily food processing, decreasing fat use for energy, and therefore a weight increase ranging from a few pounds to over 28 lb (6.4kg). Gradually reducing the number of cigarettes smoked before giving up helps to reduce weight gain: heaviest smokers gain most weight. Best of all is to take plenty of exercise which will maintain a healthy metabolic rate and help you cope with withdrawal as well. In any case, any weight gain will disappear shortly once a normal metabolic rate is established.

Drink plenty to ease chemical withdrawal symptoms and help assuage hunger pangs. Take regular exercise and eat well (see **diet**) including plenty of raw fruits and vegetables in your eating plan. Don't feel obliged to 'go it alone': try electing supporters to reinforce your willpower and help ensure permanent recovery. Various treatments and systems can help you to give up smoking. Nicorette gum helps with the initial withdrawal. Acupuncture and hypnotherapy (see separate entries) may also be helpful. Aversion therapy, where the smoker is helped to form an aversion to cigarettes or tobacco by being forced to smoke a great deal all at once, can forge a mental link between smoking and this unpleasant association, but is not common now.

# SPONGES

*See also: applicators; baths and bathing; exfoliation; foundation*

Natural sponges from the sea bed are formed from the skeletons of marine organisms and have a characteristic pattern of holes created by the ebb and flow of sea current. They are generally a sandy yellow colour. Highly porous and absorbent, they can be used for cosmetic purposes – a damp sponge is excellent for applying and blending foundation smoothly – as well as for washing and gentle exfoliation of the face and body. Slimy, soap-clogged sponges should be soaked in vinegar overnight and then rinsed thoroughly with clean water. Synthetic sponges are made from nylon or foam rubber and include eyeshadow applicators as well as general purpose bath sponges. Silk sponges are an alternative for allergy-prone skins.

# SPORTS

*See also: aerobics; dance; exercise; exercises; fitness; martial arts; muscles; posture; weight training; yoga*

You do not have to be an athlete to play and enjoy sports. Although some have special requirements (see the chart), there really is a sport – or preferably several – for everyone. A well-chosen group of activities can provide you with exercise for your whole body, aerobic fitness training and mental relaxation as well as great enjoyment. The chart below will help you evaluate and choose your sports, but DO read the caution section, pulse rate guide and warm-up/cool-down sections on pages 122-123.

## SPORTS NOTES

■ Consult your doctor before undertaking any new or stepped-up sports programme. He will advise whether it is suitable for you.

■ Always stop *immediately* if you feel any unusual discomfort or pain while playing a sport. There is no virtue in pain. It is a signal that something is wrong. Consult qualified personnel if it persists when you resume.

■ Build up your exercise gradually, especially if you are initially very unfit, using your heart rate as a safe exercise guide.

■ Always warm up before and cool down after playing any sport (see **exercises**).

The figures in the chart below are very approximate and are appropriate for a woman of roughly 140 lb or 63 kg. Calories burned depends on body weight, intensity of exercise and room temperature.

**Spa baths**
See Hot tubs

**Spas**
See Hydrotherapy; Thalassotherapy

**SPF**
See Tanning

**Spider veins**
See Thread veins

**Spine**
See Back

## SPORTS ASSESSMENT CHART

| SPORT AND REQUIREMENTS | AEROBIC EFFECT | ADVANTAGES AND SHORTCOMINGS | CALORIES BURNED (per min, av. exertion) |
|---|---|---|---|
| **Badminton** – good co-ordination; reasonable muscular endurance; competitive spirit | Moderate | **Advantages** – improves co-ordination, leg and playing arm muscle flexibility and strength<br>**Shortcomings** – competitive nature may be stressful; stereotyped actions have jarring element | 7.5 |
| **Cycling** – suits any fitness level, but needs problem-free back, knees and hips. Cycle with adjustable seat, comfortably high handlebars to avoid lower back strain | Very good | **Advantages** – improves muscular endurance and strength in lower body; easy sport to slot into most lifestyles, for example cycling to work<br>**Shortcomings** – repetitive movements, no co-ordination or general flexibility improvement | 6.5 |
| **Golf** – no particular fitness level; a good 'eye' | Poor | **Advantages** – improves co-ordination, very relaxing, good social sport<br>**Shortcomings** – does little to promote physical fitness | 4 |
| **Gymnastics** – good level of overall flexibility; general muscle strength, but not necessarily aerobic fitness | Moderate | **Advantages** – provides stretch element, improves flexibility and strength (see **muscles**)<br>**Shortcomings** – often fails to exercise both muscles in each pair thus unbalancing body | 6 |
| **Jogging** – prior build-up of joint mobility and fitness; alternate with other forms of exercise. Good, cushioned shoes essential. | Very good | **Advantages** – provides excellent aerobic fitness, relaxing joint movements<br>**Shortcomings** – possibility of joint-jarring injuries, also heart problems if not carefully self-monitored (see **exercise**). | 7 |
| **Rebounding/Trampolining** – rebounder (trampoline) and plenty of headroom. Good general health although can provide aerobic exercise for people with joint problems which prevent them from jogging or running on hard surfaces | Very good | **Advantages** – for people with joint problems (see left), or who find getting out to exercise difficult, eg when caring for young children<br>**Shortcoming** – does little for strength or flexibility | 6 |
| **Riding** – good posture (see separate entry), stirrups adjusted so that you are in perfect sitting position, skill. Hard hat | Poor | **Advantages** – improves co-ordination, strengthens posture, muscular endurance, releasing minor muscle tension in back with rocking movement and increasing back flexibility<br>**Shortcomings** – bad for severe back muscle spasm except at slow walk, bad for general flexibility | 6 at trot |
| **Rowing** – good general fitness level; determination and team spirit if not machine rowing | Very good | **Advantages** – increases overall fitness, muscular endurance and upper body strength, spinal movement<br>**Shortcomings** – inadvisable for people with disc problems, little benefit to general flexibility | 6 (more + sliding seat) |
| **Running** – absence of joint or back problems; safer with reasonable fitness level and flexible joints. Good, well-cushioned shoes | Very good | **Advantages** – improves muscular endurance, easy to fit into any part of day<br>**Shortcomings** – restricted movement and possible joint damage but less than for jogging if easy lope, rather than high steps | 11 at 7.5 mph |
| **Skiing (Cross-country)** – good all round fitness preparation, especially leg and hip muscle strength and endurance build-up: take classes. Special skis and boots. Sun goggles | Excellent | **Advantages** – improves muscular strength and endurance, cardiovascular fitness, flexibility, co-ordination, stamina and is relaxing<br>**Shortcomings** – dangerous if you start when unfit | 15-20 |

**Spots**
See Acne; Prickly
heat; Rashes;
Sexually transmitted
diseases;
Whiteheads

**Squash**
See Sports

### SPORTS ASSESSMENT CHART

| SPORT AND REQUIREMENTS | AEROBIC EFFECT | ADVANTAGES AND SHORTCOMINGS | CALORIES BURNED (per min, av. exertion) |
|---|---|---|---|
| **Skiing (Downhill)** – follow pre-ski exercise classes to build flexibility in legs, muscular strength and endurance. Sun goggles | Moderate to good | **Advantages** – improves muscular endurance, strength, co-ordination and flexibility, can be very sociable <br> **Shortcomings** – little relaxation if undertaken competitively, fear can lock joints, making injury more likely, danger of joint-jarring on ice | 15 |
| **Squash and Raquetball** – concentration, co-ordination and skill. Absence of joint problems, good general fitness | Moderate | **Advantages** – increases endurance; improves co-ordination, only moderately good for flexibility <br> **Shortcomings** – little relaxation component, can exacerbate stress if played very competitively | 8 |
| **Swimming** – almost everyone can enjoy this with little preparation. Competitive swimming requires good standard of aerobic fitness and skill training | Very good | **Advantages** – for everyone, even with joint and muscle problems, while pregnant (except breast stroke), helps build muscular strength, co-ordination, flexibility, promotes relaxation <br> **Shortcomings** – no real minus points, although swimming fails to reintroduce joints to lost movement as much as yoga does, for example | 12.5 |
| **Table tennis** – co-ordination and skill, no particular fitness level | Moderate | **Advantages** – promotes muscular endurance, stretch, variety of movement, co-ordination, no jarring; sociable <br> **Shortcomings** – does little to improve strength. | 6 |
| **Tennis** – co-ordination, reasonable level of fitness, lessons for technique. Comfortable shoes and racquet | Moderate | **Advantages** – improves co-ordination, muscular endurance and strength especially in playing arm, legs <br> **Shortcomings** – repetitive actions with limited joint movements, jarring, limited aerobic benefit especially in doubles | 7 |
| **Walking** – comfortable shoes | Good (if brisk) | **Advantages** – aids relaxation and mental problem-sorting, muscular endurance if extensive enough, flexibility if varied terrain <br> **Shortcomings** – rather restricted movement, little strength or co-ordination change | 5 (if brisk) |
| **Water skiing** – good swimming ability, nerve, reasonable level of muscle strength and endurance in arms and legs. Wet suit in cold climates | Poor | **Advantages** – improves co-ordination, muscular strength and endurance; high enjoyment and exhilaration level <br> **Shortcomings** – little benefit to flexibility, can be hard to learn, requires lessons and perseverance | 10 |
| **Windsurfing** – problem-free, strong back; do strengthening exercises for whole body; good swimming ability. Wet suit in cold climates | Moderate | **Advantages** – muscular endurance, co-ordination, relaxation; exhilarating sport <br> **Shortcomings** – can strain weak backs or knees, does little for flexibility. Danger of drifting uncontrollably | 10 |

# STEAM TREATMENTS

*See also: colds; facials; health farms; saunas; skin*

Steam treatments are an aid to relaxation, and the warmth can be particularly easing for people with joint and muscle problems. They also speed up natural exfoliation as the horny layer of skin (see separate entry) is softened to release dead cells. They increase excretion of sweat (containing toxins), cleansing the skin and opening pores: many facials incorporate steaming at the beginning. Steam inhalations can be used to treat some chest and sinus problems (see **colds, herbs**).

### USING STEAM TREATMENTS

Avoid steam treatments if you suffer from diabetes, abnormal blood pressure, thrombosis, epilepsy, bronchitis, asthma, are pregnant, have an infectious disease such as ringworm (see separate entry) or flaking skin problems such as psoriasis. Steam can help alleviate acne and blackheads. Be careful if fasting, just starting a period, or really exhausted.
**Turkish baths** start by spending three 5-minute sessions in the room, interspersed with cold showers. Finish by resting for at least 15 minutes. You may want to build up to 10 minutes for each session, but remember that your temperature and blood pressure build up and it can be dangerous to spend too long in the bath at once. Ease down with age, too, as tolerance decreases.
**Steam cabinets** are made of metal or fibreglass, designed to leave the head free, with water heaters under the seat producing steam. Use for 10-15 minutes followed by a rest of 15-20 minutes.

The benefits of massage or aromatherapy (see separate entries) are improved if given after a steam treatment. If you feel any discomfort stop your steam treatment and rest.

# STRESS

*See also: acne; acupuncture; alopecia; anxiety; aromatherapy; autogenics; autosuggestion; backs; biofeedback; biorhythms; concentration; depression; exercise; fitness; hypnosis; insomnia; jet-lag; massage; meditation; migraine and headache; premenstrual syndrome; reflexology; self-help; self-image; sports; thalassotherapy; yoga*

We cannot live without stress. It is part of our everyday existence, our thoughts and activities and one of the strongest motivating forces in our lives. At its best it can be exhilarating, creative and exciting, at worst it can precipitate serious physical and mental illness. Women appear to be more sensitive to it than men, and susceptibility and reaction vary according to personality. Stress is the body's age-old response to real or imagined danger or challenge – to a car careering towards you, or to an important job interview. When the stress is almost intolerable, as in the case of a car accident, it helps you survive and ensures that you forget a great deal of the horror, too. Specialist Professor Hans Selye called it 'the non-specific response of the body to any demand made on it'.

Stress is constructive at a level where it still improves your performance without causing any unwanted side effects. It can add to your overall well-being provided that you control its level, for example helping you to get through an arduous work project or recover from a broken love affair. But it becomes destructive when taken beyond this point. Signs to watch for are feelings of suffocating pressure after protracted stress, panic attacks, loss of memory at crucial moments, irritability with people at work, sleep and digestive problems, tiredness, forgetfulness or headaches. Stress can mimic symptoms of physical illness, too. If you still fail to learn to relax, to take rest and break up your work pattern with

**Sterilization**
See Contraception

**Stomach**
See Abdomen

**Straightening hair**
See Curling and
straightening hair

**Stretching**
See Exercises;
Posture

**Styes**
See Eyes

other activities, you move into the most dangerous phase of all. This is where prolonged arousal can cause cardiovascular problems, chronic hypertension, peptic and gastric ulcers, migraines, headaches, worsening of PMS and decrease in fertility. Common symptoms are exhaustion, insomnia, dizziness, cramps, chest and leg pains, anger, inability to cope with simplest decisions, irritation, susceptibility to disease, agoraphobia and the possibility of nervous breakdown. Unrelieved stress can cause undesirable alterations in biochemistry including hormone balance. It is clearly very important to health to endeavour to keep the stress levels in your life within control.

### STRESS AND YOU

Your reaction to stress factors, physical or mental, is entirely individual. Some people crave a large amount of stress in order to operate happily, others can bear very little. Formulate your own ways of dealing with this.

Separate out the constructive and destructive stressors in your life. Even constructive stress, such as that experienced before an examination, can be harmful in excess, but your optimum amount can increase your creativity and enjoyment of life. It is important to differentiate between the two kinds and learn where your limits for each lie.

Cut out, or at least cut down on, cigarettes, alcohol, non-medical drugs, coffee and sugar which further stimulate release of noradrenaline (norepinephrine) and stress symptoms.

Assess and adapt your destructive stressors. Remember that it is your perception and evaluation of them which gives them their stress potential. Are they work-related? Home-related? Money problems? Health problems? Do you feel over-burdened or under-stretched? Write out a list of them, then work out which factors, if any, you can jettison, and how you can reduce the harmful effects of others. Some solutions can be quite simple, such as walking or taking a train to work instead of driving. This eliminates traffic-jam anxiety and gives you mental relaxation and maybe some exercise. Other problems can call for greater attention: if you feel unfulfilled in your job, it can imbue your whole life with stress, and you may need to change your career direction. Learning to accept and adapt to change is part of coping with stress, too.

Take control: you are the one who may suffer the ill-effects of excess stress, so be firm. Learn to say no. See things in perspective, concentrate on the matter in hand. Control your time and priorities. Do not allow extra burdens of any kind which you know are too much to cope with be imposed on you. Anxiety reduces productivity, but increases the likelihood of illness. Too much stress can affect your personality and relationships, too. Reconsider your aims in life. Ensure that you are not struggling to achieve someone else's ideal of success, but your own.

Learn to relax: relaxation will help prevent the harmful physical side-effects of stress, and maintain your emotional equilibrium, too. The way you like to relax is a matter of personal choice. There are innumerable methods at your command (see **relaxation**). Practical hobbies such as painting, weaving and carving can be immensely helpful.

Eat well and exercise regularly (see **diet; exercise; exercises; sport**): both are important for good general health, especially so now when stress reduces your resistance to germs. Exercise promotes concentration and relieves anxiety, while obesity stresses the body.

Express your feelings: don't be afraid to talk about your concerns or difficulties with people you are involved with – at work, at home, in the family. It may well help to talk things over with a counsellor. If you are feeling aggravated, transfer all your nervous energy into physical activity like digging the garden. Expression will help you to cope with stress, and especially to get through the worst kinds of stress, such as death or divorce, which you may not be able to avoid. It appears that people who bottle up their problems are more likely to suffer serious stress-linked illness – possibly even cancer. And remember it works both ways: express your feelings of care and affection to friends suffering stress, too, and help to lift their burden.

Medical help: tranquillizers can help you to deal with problems such as bereavement where a few days or weeks of treatment will see you through the worst. But these can be habit-forming and should be regarded with caution (see **drugs and medicines**). Ultimately it is up to you: stress is caused by your reactions, and only you can change them. Medical herbalists recommend oats, skullcap and vervain as infusions (see separate entry and **herbs**), with valerian and passionflower to aid sleep. Add valerian, lime blossom or lavender to your bathwater; use lavender aromatherapy oil.

## STRETCH MARKS

*See also: collagen; elastin and elastone; moisturizing; pregnancy; skin*

Stretch marks first appear as fine, pink lines fading to an almost transparent whiteness, on breasts, stomach, hips and thighs. They are in fact fractures in the collagen and elastin fibres (see separate entries) which lie deep in the dermis. The skin's remarkable ability to accommodate changes in body size varies, and is genetically determined. There is an increased likelihood of marks occurring at times of rapid growth such as puberty and pregnancy. Nothing can be done to prevent stretch marks caused by pregnancy (though you should not put on more weight than is healthy), but avoiding massive weight fluctuations in non-pregnant life will make it unnecessary for your skin to stretch. Vitamin creams and moisturizers will not prevent or cure stretch marks. Ensure that your diet is high in vitamins and minerals (see separate entries) especially zinc as some studies have shown low zinc levels in stretch mark sufferers.

# SUGAR

*See also: circulation; dependencies; diet; heart; slimming; stress; teeth*

Sugar and starch are both forms of carbohydrate, which provide energy for the body. There are several different types of sugar in our diet. The monosaccharides or simple sugars include glucose and fructose, found particularly in sweet fruits. Since these can be absorbed directly into the blood without the need for digestive enzymes, they are a source of immediate energy. Disaccharides or complex sugars occur widely in the diet and include sucrose (made from sugar cane or beet) which is commonly used as table sugar and added to many processed foods. Sucrose contributes no nutrients and should ideally be excluded from a healthy diet.

Communities with a high sucrose intake show a higher incidence of obesity, coronary heart disease and diabetes. Some experiments have shown that high sucrose diets in humans raise total blood cholesterol levels and in some subjects caused the blood to clot more readily.

The harmful effect of sugar on the teeth is indisputable: it coats the teeth and is fed on by bacteria, producing acids which start the process of decay by eating into the enamel (see **teeth**). This is equally true of brown raw sugar and white refined sugar – the only difference being that raw sugar contains negligible amounts of a few nutrients.

### NON-SUGAR SWEETENERS

Alternatives to sugar for sweetening food and drink are often used by people trying to lose weight, although this prevents them from re-educating their palate (see **slimming**). Diabetics who need to avoid sugar also use them. Generally permitted 'non-Caloric' artificial sweeteners for general use include saccharin, about 300 times as sweet as sucrose, thaumatin, aspartame and acesulfam-K. Cyclamate is no longer used as it was found to be carcinogenic (cancer-causing) in large quantities. Saccharin and aspartame are also suitable for diabetics, as are the Calorie-containing hydrogenated sugars such as sorbitol, mannitol and xylitol.

# SURGERY

*See also: awareness; diet; exercise; relaxation*

It is becoming evident that physical and mental preparation for surgery should become an intrinsic part of the whole process. Research in the UK and US has shown that people who eat a healthy diet, take plenty of exercise and rest, and are not overweight, recover from surgery and leave hospital more quickly and suffer fewer complications afterwards. People who have prepared themselves psychologically for the operation, finding out everything they can about it, tend to need fewer drugs to help them afterwards.

One of the most frightening things about surgery is fear of the unknown: not only what is going to be done to you and how, but simple things like the ward or room you will be in, the people who will be caring for you. In the US, and just beginning in the UK, are schemes where adults and children can visit hospitals for a day well before their operations, and find out about the place where they are to have their operation. Whether or not this is available to you, do talk through all your worries with your general practitioner or surgeon, and ask for advice from nurses and doctors when in hospital, too, if you need it. Busy staff often forget, unless prompted, just how large the gap is between their knowledge and yours.

### GOING INTO HOSPITAL

- Find out visiting hours and transport details in advance so that you can inform friends and family who will want to come and visit you.
- Take two nighties or more, a dressing gown (robe), slippers, washkit, books, magazines and some favourite hobby such as knitting or tapestry which is easy to do in bed.
- Personal stereos, miniature TV sets and radios with earphones can all be a boon, and you could take heated rollers, tongs or a mini-hair-dryer and a travel adaptor.
- Take stamps, writing paper and envelopes, and plenty of change for public telephones (most wards have portable phones): such things are hard to get hold of when confined to bed!

# SWEAT

*See also: anti-perspirants; body odour; deodorants; exercise; pores; skin; sports*

Sweating is the body's natural temperature-regulating mechanism: as sweat evaporates from the skin's surface it has a cooling effect. It is also a means of excreting nitrogenous waste: sweat contains 1 per cent urea and sodium chloride (salt) and 99 per cent water. The amount you sweat is regulated by external and internal factors. During activities where the body temperature rises above 37.4°C (99.3°F) the three million tiny *eccrine glands* come into action. Further pressure on the system, such as sexual arousal, stress or acute fear, causes the *apocrine glands*, concentrated in the hair follicles of hands and feet, groin and armpit, to activate. The amount of salt in the body also regulates sweating: if there is too little salt in the diet, too much water will be lost and the body will dehydrate. However, most Western diets incorporate too much, not too little, salt. Sweat alone is colourless and odourless; in combination with bacteria body odour occurs (see separate entry).

Sulphur
See Minerals

Sun
See Tanning

Sunbathing
See Tanning

Sunbeds and sunlamps
See Tanning

Sunblocks and sun products
See Tanning

Sunburn
See Tanning

Sunglasses
See Glasses

Sweeteners
See Sugar

Swimming
See Sports

Syphilis
See Sexually transmitted diseases

**T'ai chi chuan**
See Martial arts

**Tannin**
See Infusions – tea

# TANNING

*See also: after-sun products; ageing; climate; glasses – sunglasses; melanin; moisturizing; moles; prickly heat; skin*

Tanning is one of the skin's methods of protecting the inner organs and tissues of the body from burning. Sunlight stimulates increased melanin production, providing pigmentary protection and brown colour. The upper layers of skin thicken to absorb the sun's energy and give further protection against damage (see **melanin**). Whether you burn easily and do not tan, or tan deeply without burning depends on your genetically determined skin melanin content. A deeply pigmented skin, therefore, needs less protection against the sun than one with a low melanin content (see chart).

It is now well established that suntanning is not, unfortunately, a harmless holiday pursuit, and that we need to rethink our attitudes to sun exposure. To a dermatologist a glowing, healthy suntan is a sign of potential skin damage.

Natural sunlight contains a mixture of ultra violet (UV) rays of which two types, UVB and UVA, affect our skin. The UVB rays cause sunburn, UVA rays do not burn but stimulate a tan. Both are damaging to the skin: you can damage your skin without burning it. Although UVA rays (the type most emitted by tanning machines and lamps, see below) are milder than UVB, and have therefore misleadingly been labelled 'safe', they also penetrate the dermis and may be responsible for damaging the collagen and elastin fibres which give the skin its strength and flexibility. In the epidermis UVA is also thought to affect the skin's inbuilt repair system which enables cells to renew themselves correctly.

The result of accumulative exposure to sunlight – and it may not show up for 10 to 20 years – is a prematurely lined, coarse and sagging skin which is in danger of developing skin cancer (see **skin**): even moderate exposure has been shown to cause degenerative signs in sensitive skin. Those most at risk from sun-related skin cancers are skin types 1 and 2 (see chart) who work outdoors, live in a sunny climate, or have sunbathed intemperately and repeatedly over the years. Getting sunburnt frequently puts you at greater risk, too. Other problems connected with overexposure to sun are development of chloasma (melasma), prickly heat (see separate entry) and photosensitivity.

Black skin has great advantages over white skin in sun exposure. As melanin is distributed more evenly and produced faster in black skin, it can absorb more UV light (30 per cent more than white skins), thus minimizing the damage to underlying cells. The thicker surface layer of skin gives more protection, and a higher concentration of sweat and sebaceous glands results in swifter skin cooling. The secretions from these glands filter the rays more efficiently. Though it is less likely, black skin can nevertheless burn if unprotected and unused to strong sunlight.

## SUNBURN

Sunburn results in blisters, peeling and pain and can damage both deep and superficial layers of skin, as well as increasing the likelihood of developing skin cancers if it occurs repeatedly.

First cool down the burn to prevent it penetrating still further into the skin. Sponge burnt areas repeatedly with either natural yoghurt, calamine, a solution of milk and water or apple cider vinegar. Or relax in a tea- or chamomile-infused bath (see **baths**) for at least 15 minutes. Burns will immediately feel less sore as their heat dissipates.

Do not apply creams to the skin until it is completely cool, because they will hold in the heat. When it is cool, apply moisturizer, preferably containing a healing substance such as aloe vera, allantoin, chamomile or honey.

In cases of really severe sunburn, especially if accompanied by sunstroke as is likely, consult your doctor. You may be prescribed anti-inflammatory drugs and analgesics which will alleviate some of the discomfort and swelling.

## SAFER TANNING

Expose your skin to the sun gradually, protected with the correct sunscreen for your skin type (see below). Even if already tanned protection is still vital: you can only stay out in the sun for twice as long as when untanned before burning starts. Remember, too, that some factors can compound the sun's effect on the skin. Snow, sand, concrete, water and reflective surfaces all reflect UV light very strongly: you can burn even under a wide-brimmed hat or parasol. Sunlight is especially powerful in high altitudes, at sea and near the Equator. Up to 50 per cent of UV rays can filter through an overcast sky. Try to sunbathe just in the early morning or late afternoon when the UVB rays are least strong. Always use a water-resistant sunscreen when swimming and reapply at regular intervals.

Avoid wearing scent or cosmetics when sunbathing – some ingredients cause a skin reaction when in contact with UV rays (see **prickly heat**). If you are taking any medications check with your doctor before sun exposure. Certain drugs, cosmetics and foods can cause a photosensitive reaction. Limit your alcohol intake.

Some skin conditions (rosacea, skin cancers) should either never be exposed to sunlight or else be protected by a total sunblock; check with your dermatologist or doctor.

High intensity sunbathing is the most damaging. Research in Australia has shown that holiday makers who cram all their sunbathing into an annual two weeks run a greater risk of developing skin cancer than farmers exposed to sun all year round. Bear in mind the implications of sunbeds, too.

## SUNTANNING PREPARATIONS

Tanning preparations protect skin from visible damage while it develops melanin and give some protection from UVA and UVB rays. No suntanning product will make skin that naturally stays pink in the sun deep bronze: your skin's reaction to sun and its tan colour are genetically determined.

T

**NPT or Natural Protection Time** is the length of time that skin can stay in the sun without burning. It varies according to skin type, its state of tan and the sun's strength.

**SPF or Sun Protection Factors** for sun products take this into account. They work on a multiplication basis: product numbers increase according to the amount of protection they contain. Using SPF8, for example, with an NPT of 20 minutes you can stay out in the sun for $8 \times 20 = 160$ minutes without burning. Sunscreens contain active ingredients such as PABA (para-amino benzoin) that filter out UVA and UVB rays, and may also contain insect repellents or moisturizers. The base can be cream, lotion, mousse, oil or gel: choose according to SPF and then skin type. Oils tend to be low SPF, creams and lotions are good for drier skins, alcohol-free products for the allergy-prone, oil-free for oily skins. Water-resistant products with UVA and UVB filters are essential for watersports and frequent swim-

ming. Total sunblocks should be used if you suffer from natural or drug-induced photosensitivity. Only those containing zinc oxide or titanium dioxide give 100 per cent protection. They should also be used on lips, which have no melanin, sensitive areas such as shoulders, collarbones, noses, and especially in conditions when reflection of the sun's rays can double their intensity, such as when ski-ing.

Beware of preparations with 'tanning accelerators': these are normally photoactive ingredients such as oil of bergamot which can speed tanning, but can cause adverse skin reactions such as rashes or patchy pigmentation because they increase the skin's sensitivity to light.

Always apply sunscreens before going into the sun: massage a generous amount well into the skin. Reapply frequently, particularly after swimming (a wet body is more vulnerable to UVA rays) or exercising when perspiration will wash it away.

### FAKE TANNING PRODUCTS

These provide a tan without any of the sun's harmful effects. The lotions or creams are basically skin dyes containing either the ingredient dihydroxyacetone (DHA) or extract of black walnut, both of which react with the skin's proteins to turn the surface layer brown. The tan fades as the skin flakes off, a process speeded by hot and Turkish baths and saunas. Although products containing walnut extract are thought to give some slight degree of sun protection, DHA products give none, and you should use sunscreens as if you were untanned when in the sun.

### SUNBEDS AND SUNLAMPS

The use of sunbeds and lamps accelerates skin ageing and increases your chance of suffering problems such as skin cancer: both UVA and UVB rays cause the same long-term damage. The most modern high-pressure lamp equipment filters out all but 0.5 per cent of the burning UVB rays, leaving UVA rays of a much higher intensity than in sunlight, which cause skin to acquire a tan very quickly. The fluorescent lamps filter out less UVB, and some types are very dangerous, producing UVB rays of 6 times the intensity of those in sunlight: avoid equipment with recommended exposure times of 10 minutes or less.

When using tanning equipment, there are precautions you must take in addition to those observed for sunbathing in general. If you fail to wear UVA goggles you can risk radiation of the eye and the possibility of cataract formation. Photosensitivity can be heightened: be particularly careful to shower off any scent, deodorants or cosmetics before using equipment. Never exceed recommended exposure times, and use only once in each 48 hours. Chloasma can become more apparent, and you are advised not to use sunbeds if you have had any problems with moles growing or changing shape or if you are pregnant.

Sunbeds prepare your skin only *very* minimally for sunlight, despite the change in skin colour. Melanin is activated so turning skin brown, but the epidermis does not thicken as it would in sun. You should treat your skin as if it were not tanned at all when sunbathing in natural light.

### SUN PROTECTION FACTOR AND YOUR SKIN

| SKIN REACTION AND TYPE | NATURAL PROTECTION TIME (NPT) in minutes | STRONG SUN: SUN PROTECTION FACTOR (SPF) | | VERY STRONG SUN: SUN PROTECTION FACTOR (SPF) | |
|---|---|---|---|---|---|
| | | Untanned | Tanned | Untanned | Tanned |
| **Ultra-sensitive,** very rarely tans, always burns badly and peels, e.g. fair skin with freckles, black or blonde hair, blue eyes. | 5 | 8 | 6 | 15 | 12 |
| **Sensitive,** burns easily and severely, minimal tanning, peels, e.g. pale skin with red or blonde hair. | 10 | 6 | 4 | 8 | 6 |
| **Moderately sensitive,** burns moderately, tans slowly but successfully, e.g. commonest Western type, any hair colour, average white skin tone. | 15 | 4 | 2 | 6 | 4 |
| **Tans easily and deeply,** burns minimally, darkens more quickly each time tanned, e.g. white or light brown skin, brown hair and dark eyes. | 20 | 2 | 1 or 2 | 4 | 2 |
| **Very rarely burns,** tans immediately and well, e.g. brown skin, dark eyes. | 30 | 2 | 1 | 2 | 1 |
| **Very rarely burns,** tans immediately and profusely, e.g. all black skin types. | 40 | 1 | 1 | 2 | 1 |

# TEENS

*See also: acne; blackheads; fifties; forties; hair; hormones; make-up; menstruation; puberty; self-image; sixties; skin; thirties; twenties*

Probably the greatest number of challenges and problems that will occur in any decade of life arise in the teens. Read the sections on puberty and menstruation for details on these changes. It is important to set good patterns for health now – so avoid drugs and smoking which can cause irrevocable damage (see **smoking** and **dependencies**), and keep alcohol intake to the low social level.

**Diet** Whatever your feelings about your body at puberty (see **self-image** and **body image**) you must eat a nutritious diet with Calories for growth and energy, approximately 2,200 a day (see **diet**). Calcium requirement is particularly high in the early teens so get plenty in your diet (see separate entry). Adequate amounts of protein are also important, and iron too once menstruation starts (see **protein** and **minerals**). Be aware of the dangers of anorexia and bulimia (see separate entries).

**Skin** The hormonal changes occurring now can cause excess sebum production, oily skin and of course acne. Although keeping your skin clean is important, do not over-cleanse: twice a day is fine. Always use moisturizer after cleansing and toning, except on very oily areas. Your skin will change after your mid-teens, often becoming drier, so be prepared to adjust to richer products. Safeguard your skin against early ageing: treat it very gently when applying and removing make-up, keep it clean, always wear sun protection products in the sun and be aware of the serious implications of sun damage (see **skin, tanning**). Have a make-up lesson from a reputable beautician to help you learn to handle all the different types of cosmetics.

**Hair** The scalp is often extra oily now because a lot of sebum is present. Wash hair as often as you need to (see **hair**), but gently and with mild shampoo. Harsh shampoos will only stimulate sebum production. Experimenting with colour and style is fun, but may be tempered at first by limits set at school and at home. Make use of spray and paint-on products which will wash out easily (see **colouring hair**).

# TEETH

*See also: cosmetic dentistry; dental hygienist; dental procedures; dentist; diet; flossing; gums; orthodontist*

A baby's first 'milk' or 'deciduous' teeth begin to form early in the mother's pregnancy. They begin to erupt through the gums when the baby is about 6 months, and by 2 years old all 20 baby teeth have usually appeared. The second set of 32 adult or

'permanent' teeth emerge at about 6 years old, gradually displacing the baby teeth. By 15, 28 teeth are normally present. The last four, known as the 'wisdom teeth' arrive at any time in early adulthood, and sometimes not at all.

Each tooth consists of a crown, the part of the tooth visible above the gum, and one or more roots. The crown is covered in enamel (the hardest substance in the body). Beneath this is dentine, extending into the roots. At the centre of the tooth is the pulp chamber, a hollow cavity containing nerve tissue, blood vessels, protective cells and materials for repair. This extends down into the root and is connected to the main nerves, arteries and veins through the tip of the root. The root itself is joined to the bone by the periodontal ligament which prevents the tooth being damaged by the force of chewing or biting.

### PREVENTIVE CARE
Cutting down on foods which are high in sugar is the first step in tooth care. Removing *plaque* through cleaning is the next line of defence. Plaque is a thin, sticky film of bacteria which clings to the teeth. On its own, plaque is harmful to the gums: it

**Tennis**
See Sports

**Tension**
See Anxiety; Stress

**Thiamine**
See Vitamin B1

Cuspid and molar teeth are shown below in cross-section. Each tooth consists of a crown and one or more roots.

can cause inflammation and lead to gum disease (see **gums**). Warning signs are red, swollen, bleeding gums: any bleeding on cleaning is unhealthy. When there is sugar in the mouth, as after eating, especially sweet foods, there is danger from plaque for teeth too. Plaque bacteria feed on the sugar, converting it to acids which eat into the protective enamel and form cavities: these deepen and then work through into the dentine which becomes infected with yet more bacteria. The next stage is for the pulp to become infected (causing toothache) and if no treatment is given the nerves and blood vessels in the pulp die and infection goes through the root to the bone, causing an abscess. This decay, or *dental caries*, can be drilled out in early stages, and the tooth filled, with amalgam in the back teeth or composite in the front teeth. If the pulp is badly infected by abscess, it may be removed and the cavity and root canals filled up in a process known as root canal treatment. Research has proved that fluoride taken into the child's body does strengthen teeth and help them resist decay. If the water supply is not fluoridated, it is recommended that children take fluoride drops. A fluoride coating can be painted on to the teeth by a dentist or hygienist. Mouthwashes and toothpastes containing fluoride can be of some help even to adults. It is essential to visit your dentist every six months.

### Cleaning
It is essential to clean your teeth at least once a day, preferably after each meal.
- Floss teeth first (see **flossing**).
- Clean using a soft nylon toothbrush and fluoride toothpaste.
- With bristles at 45 degrees to the gum, so that they can work into the gum pockets around the teeth, brush with a gentle, circular scrubbing motion, concentrating on one or two teeth at a time. Looking in a mirror work systematically around the mouth and be careful not to miss any teeth. Brush the biting surfaces.
- Rinse with water and spit out.

The whole routine should take at least 5 minutes. Use disclosing tablets to check that you are doing the job properly.

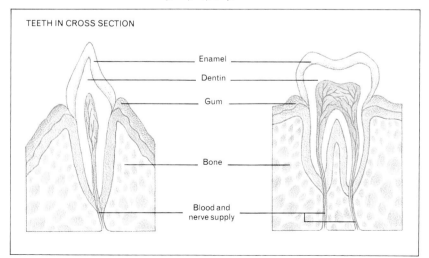

TEETH IN CROSS SECTION

Enamel · Dentin · Gum · Bone · Blood and nerve supply

# THALASSOTHERAPY

*See also: health farms; hot tubs; hydrotherapy; minerals; mud treatments; seaweed*

Thalassotherapy (from the Greek *thalassa*, meaning sea) uses seawater in a variety of ways to improve health and aims to help correct vitamin and mineral imbalances. Treatments can include drinking seawater, inhaling seawater spray, sluicing and jet-spraying the body with it, seawater massage (in which the patient is massaged in a shallow bath of water), seawater and seaweed baths, swimming and exercising in seawater pools, seawater hot tubs, a variety of mud, algae and seaweed masks, facials and body treatments. Some of these are to be found at health clinics and farms, but the whole range is available at special thalassotherapy centres where the emphasis is on providing a relaxing and rejuvenating holiday. The treatment helps alleviate stress, tension, allergies, arthritis and rheumatism, aids relaxation and improves circulation and the release of toxins through the skin. Thalassotherapy is a popular cellulite treatment (see **cellulite** and **mud treatments**).

# THIGHS

*See also: body types; cellulite; exercise; exercises; faradic exercise; massage; slimming; sports; weight*

Practically everyone goes through a phase of thinking their thighs too flabby, muscly, skinny or fat. The proportions of your thighs are genetically determined along with your whole body type (see separate entry), but they can be improved a great deal with exercise. Practise those opposite, and also the leg and daily exercises, too, for overall toning. Some sports help tone up thigh muscles: riding helps the inner muscles particularly; cycling, skiing and weight training are helpful, too (see **sports, weight training**). Faradic exercise (see separate entry) can provide temporary improvement in muscles, but should be backed up with other forms of exercise. Tone up sluggish circulation by using a loofah on your outer thighs when skin is damp after a bath or shower – it will improve skin texture too. Remember to apply body lotion to thighs after every shower or bath to keep skin supple. Watch your diet: subcutaneous fat is readily laid up on the thighs and can be hard to lose. If flab is due to cellulite, mud and other treatments may help (see **cellulite, mud treatments**). Aspiration, where fat is removed by a suction procedure carried out by a cosmetic surgeon, is a very last resort (see **cosmetic surgery**). But remember that other people are almost certain not to notice – you are probably the only person aware of their size.

### ▲ Exercise A

**1** Lie on the floor with arms stretched out at right angles to your body, feet hip-width apart and parallel. Keep lower back pressed to the floor throughout to prevent injury. Put a cushion between your knees. Press

knees together 10 times quickly, 10 times slowly.
**2** Put a small ball between your knees and repeat. Build up to 40 repeats. Add an extra step of pelvic tilting with the small ball between your knees. Repeat 6 times building to 24.

### ▲ Exercise B

**1** Start without weights on your ankles and add when you become used to the exercise. Lie on your back keeping lower back pressed to floor. With feet together bend knees up to chest.
**2** Now slowly straighten legs into vertical position. Slowly open legs out sideways and wide then close again. Repeat 4 times building to 8. Now bend legs back to chest and lower from bent position, keeping lower back pressed to floor.

### ▶ Exercise C

**1** Stand sideways on to a table with your hips facing front, shoulders down and relaxed, knees and feet forward.
**2** Lift your right hip slightly and move leg out and up slowly and steadily, keeping foot and knee facing forwards. Replace leg steadily. Repeat 20 times then turn and repeat with other leg. Build up to 40 with each leg.

■ See EXERCISES for Caution box page 123 before starting exercise

■ See ABDOMEN for Core Exercise box page 6 before starting exercise

### ◀ Exercise D

**1** Lie on your side in a straight line, with head, hips, knees and flexed feet all facing forwards. Balance yourself with your left hand on the floor and your right supporting your head.
**2** Without twisting your leg, lift gently and steadily, then bring down to touch other, but don't release. Raise it again and repeat 6 times.
**3** Now lift both legs together, keeping hips, feet and knees facing sideways. Lift high. Gradually build up to 12-18 times each.

**Throat**
See Moisturizing;
Skin

# THIRTIES

*See also: diet; exercise; fatigue; fifties; fitness; forties; sixties plus; stress; teens; twenties*

Earlier life and career choices may now no longer seem the right ones: you may find your full-time career less satisfying and want to spend more time at home with your children or they may now be growing up and you find you have more time to yourself. It is becoming increasingly common now for the thirties to be the time when women are just getting married and starting to have children.

**Body** The demands of family life and/or a career will begin to take their toll and so it is important to combine a healthy diet with regular, varied exercise. Weight problems can begin to appear, particularly among women still having children, with job and family commitments cutting into your exercise time and extra Calories easily consumed through finishing up children's food.

**Diet** The body's metabolism is slowing down. Your Calorie requirement is now reduced by 100 a day to about 1,900-2,000. This is the time to establish good eating habits (see **diet**) and it may be your last chance to eliminate bad habits known to contribute to diabetes, cancer, heart disease and hypertension. Ensure that your Calorie cutbacks do not alter your protein and essential nutrient intake which remains the same, nor deplete your stamina (see **slimming, eating habits**).

**Skin** Use richer moisturizers as skin begins to dry: use products with humectants – except when weather is very dry – for extra moisture attraction. Early signs of ageing may appear – fine lines around eyes, smile and frown lines, wrinkles – and will be more accentuated on dry skin. Your diet should include foods rich in vitamins A, E and C for healthy skin. Resist the temptation to sunbathe but if you must, wear complete sunblock or very high SPF products (see **tanning**).

**Hair** As the sebaceous glands on the scalp as well as the face slow down, both skin and hair now becomes drier. If you have always had oily hair, this will be a boon, but dry hair can be lacklustre unless it is given regular oil treatments and conditioning (see **hair**). Be prepared to adjust how often you use conditioner, and use gentle shampoos.

# THREAD VEINS

*See also: ageing; dermatologist*

Thread or broken veins are small, red or purplish marks commonly found on the face (especially round the nose and cheeks) and legs, occurring when blood vessels in the skin become dilated. They can be an hereditary problem, or appear during pregnancy when pelvic veins are under extra pressure; they may be caused by hormonal changes when taking the contraceptive pill, high blood pressure, climatic extremes or even drinking hot tea or coffee.

Spider veins or spider naevi occur only on the upper body (face, neck and chest) appearing as a small red spot from which radiates a spider-like network of tiny arteries. Unlike thread veins which contain deoxygenated blood, spider veins contain oxygenated arterial blood. They can appear for no apparent reason. Not necessarily characteristic of a particular skin type or age group, they can form as a result of underlying liver diseases, or develop with age, becoming more pronounced as the skin thins.

### TREATMENTS
Spider veins may fade after pregnancy, but they can spread and become coarser with time. Thread veins will not disappear naturally, however. Although regular or camouflage make-up (see separate entry) can superficially conceal them, both conditions can be successfully treated by the following methods:

**Sclerotherapy** involves injection of a chemical fluid into the blood vessels to close them up. Once cut off, the vein tissue is broken down and they disappear. Bruising occurs, but fades, and the face must be kept clear of cosmetics for 10 days after each session. Several treatments may be required before marks disappear completely, and there is no guarantee that new broken veins will not occur. Improvement is gradual since treatments must be spaced out, with 6-weeks between leg vein sessions, 2-3 weeks between treatments on the face.

**Electrolysis** requires a skilled operator since it involves the use of a needle and electrical current to cauterize blood vessels and stop blood flow through them. It is used for veins on the face, not the legs. The skin becomes swollen and scabs can form where the needle was inserted. Scarring will occur if these are removed. A few treatments may be necessary before improvement is noticeable.

**Lasers** are a relatively new, painless and speedy method of cauterizing broken blood vessels using a laser beam. However, treatment is expensive and must only be undertaken by a qualified dermatologist or plastic surgeon.

# THRUSH

*See also: cystitis; sexually transmitted diseases*

Thrush, otherwise known as candidiasis or vaginitis, is a common fungal infection of the vagina. The culprit is usually Candida albicans. Thrush is more common in sexually active women although it can occur in virgins. Those who are diabetic, pregnant, or having antibiotic therapy are more at risk. Symptoms for women are vulval itching and soreness with burning on passing urine, and a curdy, white, odourless discharge. Male sexual partners suffer itching and red spots on the end of the penis.

Diagnosis is made from vaginal smears and culture. Treatment is with vaginal pessaries and cream, or special tampons. If Nystatin is prescribed, use panty liners to prevent underwear discoloration and damage. To alleviate irritation, try taking salt baths (1 teaspoon salt to 568 ml (1 pint) warm water), and apply natural live yoghurt inside and at the opening of the vagina. Herbal treatment is to apply an infusion (see separate entry) of thuja twigs to the vaginal area several times a day.

# TONING

*See also: black skin; cleansing; exfoliation; facials; masks; massage; moisturizing; skin*

All toning products remove any residual grease, make-up and dead skin on the skin after cleansing. As they evaporate they temporarily improve skin texture by causing pores to close and leave the skin feeling cool and refreshed, ready for moisturizing. Products vary from those that contain alcohol to mild, alcohol-free herbal applications and flower waters.

**Astringents** are the harshest form of toners, as they contain a large amount of alcohol which tends to dehydrate the skin, sometimes causing it to flake. Astringents should only be used on oily areas, and never near the eyes.

**Fresheners** are mild toners. They are often made with herbs and contain more water than alcohol. They sometimes contain lemon juice which can help restore the skin's natural pH (see separate entry), which can be unbalanced by washing with soap, though they are also suitable for balanced skins. Non-alcoholic fresheners such as witch hazel or flower waters like orange, lavender and rosewater which can be used alone or diluted with mineral water are best for dry and sensitive skins since they are gentle and will not over-dry the skin.

**Clarifying lotions** contain less alcohol than astringents, but are more abrasive than fresheners and generally only suitable for oily skins. Some clarifying lotions are also very mild exfoliators, removing the surface layer of dead skin cells at the same time as they tone the skin.

### TONING YOUR FACE

Choose your product carefully according to your skin type. For example if your skin has dry and oily patches, use an alcohol-free product all over, or one with a low alcohol content, diluting it with water for the dry patches. Black skin with a tendency to dryness can be irritated by toners containing alcohol or resorcinol.

After cleansing or even as a light cleanser in itself, soak a cotton wool pad in toner and apply to the face, wiping gently until the pad shows no traces of make-up or grease. Then apply moisturizer (see separate entry) to the face, using care around delicate eye area.

# TRICHOLOGIST

*See also: alopecia; dandruff; dermatitis; hair; hair transplants and weaving; skin; stress*

A trichologist deals with all aspects of hair and scalp care whether your hair is healthy or suffering from some ailment. In the UK, trichologists are registered members of the Institute of Trichologists, the examining body of the profession, either as Associates (AIT) or Members (MIT), depending on how long they have been practising. The scope of their work ranges from sub-medical to cosmetic; they treat conditions like seborrhoeic dermatitis, hair loss (alopecia), damaged and broken hair and dandruff, and advise on good hair care and diet.

# TWENTIES

*See also: fifties; forties; pregnancy; sixties plus; teens; thirties*

After the emotional and physical fluctuations of your teens, the twenties are a time of increasing confidence and stability.

**Body** Physically in its prime, the body is well-equipped to deal with the extra pressures placed on it at this time. It has stopped growing and will reach its maximum muscle strength at around the age of 25-30. Nevertheless, to neglect your body now will have unwelcome repercussions later: establish a healthy diet (see separate entry) and lifestyle. If you are planning a family, get your body in shape (see **pre-conceptual care**).

**Diet** As you age your metabolic rate slows down – at a rate of 5 per cent per decade from the twenties on – and your Calorie requirement therefore decreases. Depending on body size and acitivity level, your daily Calorie intake should now be about 2,000-2,100, over a range of healthy and nutritious foods. The need for calcium diminishes when you stop growing, but with the onset of menstruation the need for iron increases. Iron deficiency can produce fatigue.

**Skin** Your skin type and its rate of ageing is genetically and sex-determined but getting into a workable skin care routine of twice-daily cleansing, toning and moisturizing, will help preserve its youthful appearance. The hormone levels are still high in the twenties and the oil and sweat glands may be even more active than in the teens, so acne and an oily skin may still be evident (see **acne**).

**Hair** The condition of the hair reflects general health. If you have a poor diet and take no exercise you will have dull, lifeless hair. Fluctuations in hormone levels, caused by the contraceptive pill or pregnancy, and any courses of drugs which you are taking can further affect the texture and condition of your hair.

**Tocopherol**
See Vitamin E

**Toothpaste**
See Teeth

**Tranquillizers**
See Drugs and medicines; Stress; Depression

**Transcendental meditation (TM)**
See Meditation

**Tweezing**
See Unwanted hair

# UNWANTED HAIR

*See also: eyebrows; hair; menopause; skin*

The amount of hair on the female body and the way it is distributed varies very much according to the individual and between different races. Hair growth is affected by hormonal changes such as at puberty, when pubic and underarm hair appears, and at the menopause, when the drop in oestrogen can cause increase in and darkening of facial hair. Some forms of drug therapy can also alter hair growth patterns. Attitudes to female body and facial hair vary enormously in different societies and from person to person. If you are troubled by excess body or facial hair growth do consult your doctor or dermatologist: hormone therapy may be able to help you. If unwanted hair is fine and downy, the following are your choices:

### CAMOUFLAGE
**Bleaching** makes facial (and in summer leg and arm hair) on fair to medium skins less noticeable. Do a patch test before using (see **colouring hair**) to

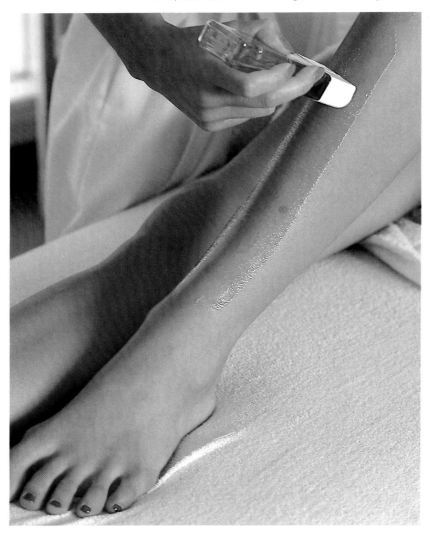

check for allergy: sensitive skins may find that products cause irritation. Always use a specially formulated facial hair product and never leave bleach on hair longer than is recommended. The effect lasts about 3-4 weeks and does not affect speed or amount of hair growth.

### TEMPORARY REMOVAL
**Abrasion** involves sandpaper-like abrasive pads or gloves rubbed gently on skin (not dampened) to remove hair: they also have the effect of exfoliating (see separate entry). This method is only suitable for legs, and not for sensitive skin. Always apply plenty of body lotion afterwards. The effect lasts 4-5 weeks and new growth does not have sharp ends.
**Depilation** creams, lotions, gels and mousses contain chemicals to dissolve hair just below the skin's surface. They can be tricky and messy to use and many products leave a lingering characteristic smell for several hours. Do a patch test before using (see **colouring hair**). The bikini line can be particularly tricky: wear your bikini bottom or similar knickers to give you the line to work to, and avoid cream getting into the vaginal area. Always use a product specifically created for the body area you are dealing with. Facial products are the mildest, but should not be used on eyebrows (use tweezing). Follow instructions carefully and never exceed recommended timings. The results should last 3-4 weeks.
**Shaving** is easy, cheap and quick. For wet shaving use a new disposable razor and shaving foam or soap and water and work in very light strokes. For electric razors, dust skin with talcum powder first. In either case work in direction of growth – this is to prevent ingrowing hairs. On legs, use moisturizer afterwards. Shaving is unsuitable for delicate areas such as the face, and for the bikini line, too, especially since regrowth can be uncomfortable, but it is fine for legs and underarms; regrowth, of raw-edge stubble, occurs in only 3-4 days but is not thicker than before.
**Tweezing or plucking** like waxing, can stimulate hair growth and should only be used on the eyebrows, definitely not on breasts or upper lip. Cleanse skin with diluted antiseptic or astringent on cotton wool. Apply warm damp cotton wool to open the pores and then pluck single hairs working along the underside of the brow (see **eyebrows**) in the direction of growth. Regrowth takes 4-5 weeks.
**Waxing** involves applying and removing it against the direction of hair growth. Hot wax is applied with a spatula when still very warm: it cools and hardens very quickly and is removed within minutes, bringing all the hairs with it. Cool wax is lukewarm when applied, and is removed with strips of fabric pressed against the waxed skin, then ripped off. Cold wax, for home use, comes ready with its own backing: briefly warm it between your hands or on a radiator, apply to skin and press firmly, then rip off. Hot and cool wax treatments are available in salons, and although you can buy home kits, it is advisable to have several professional treatments so that you can watch the technique before going it alone: otherwise you may find applying and removing wax difficult. Overheated wax can give severe burns:

use cool wax, or hot wax kits with an in-built thermostatic control. Waxing is unsuitable for very delicate areas such as the face and breasts, but can be used on legs, underarms, and the bikini line. Do not use on varicose veins, diseased skin, cuts, abrasions, warts, hairy moles, stings and hypersensitive skin. It can be quite uncomfortable, especially on the bikini line. Like tweezing, waxing can stimulate hair growth; it does not make less hair grow back. The warmer the wax, the more deeply the hair is removed: regrowth takes from 4-6 weeks.

### PERMANENT REMOVAL

**Electrolysis (diathermy)** involves passing an electric current through a fine needle inserted into the hair follicle, cauterizing the blood vessels supplying it and killing the hair, which is then removed: it can cause some discomfort. A newer method uses electrolyzed tweezers to kill the hair and remove it simultaneously: this has a lower success rate but is painless. The process takes less than a second and leaves the skin temporarily sore. It is essential that electrolysis be carried out by a trained operator to avoid infection and scarring. Very strong hairs may need 2 or 3 treatments, and a small percentage of hairs will regrow and need retreating. Even for small areas such as a lipline, removal will involve many sessions and weeks, but results are often excellent. Consult your doctor before having diathermy if you have diabetes or are having any drug therapy. It should never be used on hairy moles or warts, on the nipple if pregnant or breastfeeding, around the eyes, nostrils and ears, or where there are skin problems. Use a very mild antiseptic lotion on the area, and nothing else at all, including make-up, for 2 days after treatment.

# VARICOSE VEINS

*See also: pregnancy; thread veins*

Varicose veins are caused by defective valves in superficial veins, usually in the legs, failing to produce normal bloodflow back to the heart: they become distended, misshapen and painful. They occur mainly in people with a genetic predisposition to them, exacerbated by the following factors which put extra strain on the valves:

- Lack of fibre in the diet puts strain on the circulatory system in the lower abdomen which leads to increased blood pressure in the abdomen and, ultimately, to constipation. Blood pressure in the lower abdomen and legs rises still further with straining at stools.
- Pregnancy, which increases blood flow to the pelvic veins and slows its return to the heart.
- Lack of exercise. Especially helpful are cycling, swimming, jogging and running which all stimulate leg circulation and muscle tone.
- Increasing age.
- Being overweight.

- Past deep vein thrombosis.
- Excessive standing or motionless sitting with legs hanging down. Do not cross legs or ankles or wear any very constricting clothing, especially below the waist. Get up and move around frequently. If you have to stay standing for any length of time, rock from heel to toe, flex muscles. Rest with your legs higher than your heart whenever you can, and put a box under your desk to rest your feet on. Support tights or stockings, rolled on before you get out of bed if possible, can help stimulate blood flow back to the heart and reduce aching.

### TREATMENT

Once varicosed, veins cannot be repaired but they can be treated with sclerotherapy (see **thread veins**) so that they disappear, after which it is important to take plenty of exercise each day until bandages are removed. Alternatively the damaged veins can be removed by stripping or excision.

# VEGETABLES

*See also: diet; diets; eating habits; fibre; minerals; salt; vitamins*

We eat all parts of vegetables in our diet: fruits as in cucumber; leaves, of spinach; roots, as in parsnips; stalks, as in celery and even flowers as of cauliflowers. All are essential ingredients in a healthy diet, since they tend to be high in starch, fibre, and a great variety of vitamins and minerals, and low in protein and fat (especially saturated fat).

### PREPARING AND EATING VEGETABLES

The nutrient content of vegetables varies according to how they are grown, prepared, cooked and eaten. Vegetables grown near the sea, for example, have a higher iodine content than those grown inland. Organically grown vegetables – grown without chemical pesticides and fertilizers – are free of chemicals, but have a similar nutrient content to non-organically grown types.

Vegetables should ideally be eaten very fresh and raw. Choose a shop with fresh supplies daily and buy daily, too, as they lose nutrients (though not their fibre content) fast. If you have to store them, keep in a cool, dark place. Vegetables frozen from fresh retain nutrients better than those first refrigerated for several days.

Prepare vegetables just before you need to use them. If necessary, scrub to remove dirt, but avoid peeling: much of the nutrient value is concentrated just underneath the skin, which itself contains much of the fibre. Some vitamins are destroyed by exposure to air: chop vegetables into as large pieces as possible to reduce surface area. Shredded lettuce, chopped tomatoes and grated carrot may look prettier on the plate, but you will get more value from them if you bite into the whole vegetable.

**Ultra-violet light**
See Tanning

**UVA and UVB**
See Tanning

**Vaccination**
See Immunization

**Vegan diet**
See Diet

**Vegetable dyes**
See Colouring hair

**Venereal disease**
See Sexually transmitted diseases

**Vegetarian diet**
See Diet

**Verrucas**
See Warts

The best method of cooking vegetables is to add them to boiling water. Since many vitamins and minerals dissolve in water and heat can destroy them too, use very little water and keep the cooking time brief; save the water and add it to soups and gravies. Do not put salt in the cooking water (see **salt**). Never add bicarbonate of soda to make vegetables greener: it destroys vitamin C and thiamine. Cook in aluminium, enamel, glass or stainless steel pans: copper destroys much vitamin C and E and folic acid; iron utensils also destroy vitamin C. Steaming vegetables lightly is a good way of cooking them as is quick stir-frying. Use olive oil for delicious flavour. Cooked like this, vegetables retain their flavour and texture as well as nutrients, lessening the temptation to add salt.

# VITAMINS

*See also: aloe vera; boils; burns; colds; collagen; diet; drugs and medicines; fatigue; fattening diets; junk food; migraine; minerals; orthomolecular medicine; pre-menstrual syndrome; pregnancy; seaweed; slimming; vegetables*

Vitamins are essential nutrients for certain metabolic processes and play a vital role in normal body functioning. They are found as organic compounds in food – although a few are manufactured in the intestine – and are needed only in small quantities. They fall into two groups: fat-soluble (A, D, E and K)

## VITAMIN CHART

| VITAMIN | SOURCES | PROPERTIES | DEFICIENCY PROBLEMS |
|---|---|---|---|
| **Vitamin A** Excess may cause loss of appetite, headaches, hair loss, abdominal discomfort, fatigue, joint pain, dry itchy skin. | Occurs naturally only in animal fat: halibut and cod liver, eggs, milk, butter, cheese. Can be synthesized from carrots, tomatoes, green leafy vegetables, red palm oil, apricots. | Necessary for the manufacture of visual purple. Helps protect mucous membranes. Contributes to growth process in children. Aids in reproductive process. | Night-blindness, follicular keratosis, horny plugs in sweat glands. Reduced resistance to infection in respiratory tract. |
| **Vitamin B1 (Thiamine)** Rapidly destroyed in the presence of alkali, water-soluble. | Yeast, whole grains, milk, meat (offal in particular), green leafy vegetables. Most foods contain small amounts. | Takes part in certain metabolic reactions in the body, in particular the metabolism of carbohydrates. | Beri-beri, loss of appetite, depression, sleep disturbances, personality change, PMS. |
| **Vitamin B2 (Riboflavin)** Destroyed by light, water soluble. Not easily destroyed by heat. | Milk, eggs, liver, kidney, yeast, cheese, green leafy vegetables. | Essential for normal cell growth and development. Extra may be needed when taking exercise. | Red eyes. Cracks at corner of mouth, inflamed itchy lesions on external genitalia. |
| **Vitamin B6 (Pyridoxine)** Sometimes used to treat morning sickness and PMS. Excess impairs sensation. | Yeast, liver, wholegrain cereals, bananas. Most foods contain small amounts, produced by intestinal flora. | Especially important in metabolising the amino acids in proteins. | Deficiency rare. Breast-fed babies whose mother's intake is low may develop nervous disorders and convulsions. |
| **Vitamin B12 (Cobalamin)** One ounce enough for daily needs of entire UK population. Adversely affected by light, alkali, strong acids. | Found only in food from animal sources, in particular liver, kidney, herrings, sardines. Can be extracted from the mould *Streptomyces griseus*. | Necessary for cell division, manufacture of nerve fibre sheath. May be effective in the treatment of tiredness. | Most common in vegans. Severe deficiency may lead to pernicious anaemia, degeneration of the spinal cord, impairing movement. |
| **Niacin (Nicotinic Acid) B group** Slightly soluble in water but stable in heat, light and alkali and acids. Cereals need to be treated with alkali. | Liver, wholegrain cereals, yeast, white poultry meat, avocados, dates, coffee, fish, synthesized in the body from the amino acid tryptophan. | Vital in metabolic reactions of body, especially in energy production. Used in treatment of peripheral vascular disease, high cholesterol. | Early symptoms include loss of appetite and weight, weakness and lassitude. This may develop into pellagra with its symptoms. |
| **Pantothenic Acid B group** May reduce adverse effects of antibiotics. | Meat, whole grains, nuts, green vegetables. Found universally in foods. Also produced in gut. | Involved in several metabolic processes in the body, such as conversion of fat and sugar to energy. | Deficiency is rare. In rats it results in failure to grow and greying of the hair. |
| **Folic Acid (Folacin) B group** Adversely affected by sunlight, canning, water, oestrogen. | Dark green vegetables, liver, kidneys, yeast, egg yolk, pumpkins, wholegrain cereals. | Necessary for cell division, particularly in bone marrow to produce red blood cells. | Megaloblastic anaemia, secondary deficiency due to prolonged intake of the Pill, anti-epileptic drugs. |
| **Biotin B group** Water-soluble. Adversely affected by sulphur drugs, oestrogen, alcohol. | Kidney, liver, yeast, nuts, fruits. Produced in gut by intestinal flora. | Involved in several metabolic processes. | Effects include dry scaly skin, nausea, tiredness, muscular pain. |
| **Vitamin C (Ascorbic Acid)** Researchers disagree over role in helping cure colds (see entry) | Citrus fruits, potatoes, tomatoes, blackcurrants, strawberries, rosehips. | Plays an important role in the manufacture of collagen and helps in wound healing, resistance to infections. | Scurvy, badly constructed cartilage in growing bones. Poor quality scar tissue and breakdown of healed wounds. |
| **Vitamin D (Cholecalciferol)** May protect against cancer of colon and rectum. Overdose – diarrhoea, nausea, calcium deposits. | Cod liver oil, herring, tuna, sardines, milk, eggs, cheese, butter. Synthesized in skin by ultra-violet light. | Necessary for efficient metabolism of calcium and phosphate. Together with the parathyroid gland regulates calcium deposition in bones. | Rickets, osteomalacia, the adult equivalent of rickets, tetany and increased dental caries. |
| **Vitamin E (Tocopherol)** Fat-soluble; stored in liver, heart, muscles, blood, various glands. | Vegetable oils, peas, beans, green leafy vegetables, wheatgerm. | Prevents oxidation in the metabolism of fats. Needed for cell respiration. | Deficiency is not normally seen in humans, except occasionally in premature babies. |
| **Vitamin K** Fat-soluble. Heat-stable. Like other fat-soluble vitamins ingestion of mineral oil will impede absorption. | Green leafy vegetables, alfalfa, egg yolk, kelp, fish liver oils, cheese. Occurs in most vegetable foods. Can be synthesized in the gut. | Essential for formation of prothrombin which aids blood clotting. | Dietary deficiency rare. Secondary deficiency may occur if bile output is reduced, inhibiting the absorption, increasing tendency to bleed. |

250

and water-soluble (B group and C). Deficiency of vitamins can lead to a variety of problems and to specific diseases connected with individual vitamins such as scurvy (C deficiency) or rickets (D deficiency).

### VITAMIN SUPPLEMENTS
A healthy, balanced, mixed diet should contain sufficient quantities of all necessary vitamins. However, there are circumstances where extra vitamins are needed and it may be more convenient to take them in tablet or drop form to supplement those acquired naturally through the diet. Folic acid (part of the B complex) is often prescribed for pregnant women, and vitamin D for babies and children. Babies may be given vitamin K injections at birth to prevent haemorrhaging. After long illnesses or major operations, supplements are often given to aid recovery (B complex and C after surgery, with the addition of A in the case of severe burns). Vitamin B6 is sometimes found helpful in dealing with premenstrual syndrome and migraine (see separate entries). A new water-soluble treatment for the fat-soluble vitamins, called Aquacelle, will mean that they can be 3·4 times more readily absorbed by those who need supplements, such as cystic fibrosis and multiple sclerosis sufferers.

Except in cases where there is a specific requirement, most doctors feel that large doses of vitamins, sometimes advocated for good general health, are not helpful to the body – which has finite requirements – and can actually be dangerous. Although excesses of water-soluble vitamins can be excreted, excesses of fat-soluble vitamins cannot. They build up in fatty tissue and can be toxic (see chart and **orthomolecular medicine**).

# WARTS

*See also: feet; skin*

Warts (medically known as verrucas) are caused by a virus. In children and young people they can occur on the face, hands, elbows, knees, tending to be confined to the hands in adults. Plantar warts, those which occur on the soles of the feet, can become very painful as the pressure they are subjected to cause a thick callus to grow over them. These are common: although generally only mildly contagious, the virus is especially easily passed on in the warm, wet conditions around swimming pools and in sports areas, for example. Warts have a limited lifespan: once the body has produced the necessary antibodies they disappear, which can take months or years, and may possibly explain the success of traditional 'cures'.

### TREATMENT
If they are very large or unsightly a dermatologist can remove them using diathermy – where the tiny veins supplying the area are cauterized (see also **unwanted hair**); cryosurgery – where warts are frozen off; applications of chemicals to burn out the wart, or by excision. Genital warts are sexually transmitted (see **sexually transmitted diseases**) and these can be removed at special clinics. There is always a slight chance that the wart may reappear after removal. Medical herbalists recommend both eating garlic and rubbing it into warts, and drinking poke root infusion (see **infusions**). *Never* pick at or cut warts: you can spread the virus. If worried, consult your doctor or dermatologist.

**Waist**
See Abdomen

**Water**
See Dehydration; Diet; Jetlag; Slimming; Thalassotherapy

**Water retention**
See Fluid retention

**Waxing**
See Unwanted hair

# VITILIGO

*See also: camouflage; melanin; skin*

Vitiligo (leucoderma) is a disorder in which patches of skin lose their melanin pigment and turn pale. They can occur at any time and anywhere on the face and body, starting as small round spots which increase in size. The cause is uncertain, although it has been known to occur with Addison's disease, pernicious anaemia and cancer of the stomach, and may also be linked to stress or shock. There may also be a genetic element. On fair skins, camouflage make-up (see separate entry) may be very helpful, but on darker skins the problem is even more distressingly evident and difficult to cover. Where skin has completely lost its pigment, there is no treatment, except possibly skin grafting in very severe cases. Where some pigment remains, PUVA therapy (see **psoriasis**) may help, but this can just darken the surround skin, leaving the paler sections mottled. Avoid sunbathing which will burn pale areas, darken others. Always wear a complete sunscreen product in sunlight (see **tanning**).

# WEIGHT

*See also: anorexia nervosa; appetite; bingeing; body image; body type; bulimia; Calorie counting; crash dieting; diet; diets; eating habits; fattening diets; fluid retention; hunger; metabolic rate; slimming*

It is important to keep within a medically desirable weight scale for your height (see graph). Obesity and overweight decrease your life expectancy and increase the chance of your suffering general deterioration in every part of the body, with problems such as arthritis and coronary heart disease. It is quite natural for your weight to fluctuate, for example before a period, during stressful patches of life or illness. A change of up to about 4.5 kg (10 lbs) can be quite normal provided that the drop or increase is not too sudden or extreme, or for no obvious reason, in which cases you should seek medical advice. When pregnant, of course, your weight increases far more (see separate entry). Body mass and food requirement reduce with age: the basal

metabolic rate drops by about 1 per cent a decade and lean muscle in the body is 40 per cent less at 70 than as a young adult. Fat content, however, increases.

So many of our feelings about our weight and bodily appearance are conditioned by the views of the fashion world, and those of our friends and lovers, but keep it in proportion and try not to be unduly influenced by them. If your body weight is good health-wise (check with graph), and you feel happy with yourself, is it really worth a lifetime's slavery to worries about your figure just to please them? Worrying about weight tends to make you alter your eating habits (see separate entry) in just the wrong way, forming a pattern in which you diet crazily, then eat as much of everything unhealthy as you can. The reactions of hunger and appetite (see separate entries) can become distorted, even sometimes developing into serious problems such as bingeing, anorexia nervosa or bulimia.

Provided that you do not have any special problems such as hormone imbalances, the secret of weight maintenance is boringly obvious. Eat a balanced diet (see separate entry), reducing or increasing quantities of food as necessary, gradually rather than suddenly (see **crash dieting, slimming, fattening diets**). Take plenty of varied exercise to keep your whole body in trim and healthy and step up exercise when you feel that you have been overeating, inactive, or are a little overweight.

**Weight Control**
See Slimming;
Fattening diets

**Wine stain marks**
See Port wine stains;
Camouflage

This graph gives you an indication of the range within which your weight should fall for your height. Remember, though, that your body type (see separate entry) and size of frame affect this, too, so if large-framed you will be towards the top of the range, for example. Weigh yourself once a week, naked, using reliable scales on a hard surface. And take a long, hard look at your naked self in the mirror: ribs which are very evident, or alternatively the presence of large fat pads rather than dents just below each hip speak for themselves and are the most obvious weight guide.

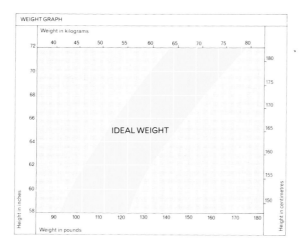

The training can involve just the use of free or hand weights such as a dumbbells (short rods with weights at each end, secured with collars) and barbells (longer rods with weights at each end secured with collars). It can also involve machines such as multigyms and Nautilus whose operation is more complicated. Best is a blend of the various options, where muscles can be conditioned through their full range, at a pace to suit the individual.

Disadvantages are that tuition and supervision are essential, at least for beginners. Gym and tuition fees can be expensive, too, and you may well want to buy your own equipment later. There are certain people for whom weight training is likely to be unsuitable: those with hypertension, heart disease, diabetes, joint or muscle problems, who are pregnant, obese, suffer dizzy or fainting fits, epileptic fits or smoke or drink heavily. Consult your doctor before undertaking weight training, and inform your trainer of past or present health problems.

## WHITEHEADS

*See also: acne; blackheads; dermatologist; pores; rashes; sebum; skin*

Whiteheads, or closed comedones, are hardened plugs of sebum which have become trapped just beneath the skin's surface. They commonly occur at times of hormonal fluctuation, such as before a period, when sebum production increases, and in acne (see separate entries). Such changes step up the skin cell renewal, too, so there tend to be extra surface dead skin cells (see **skin**) blocking pores. To prevent whiteheads forming, exfoliate (see separate entry) regularly to keep pores free, cleanse carefully – but not more than usual which can increase sebum production – and avoid touching or squeezing spots which can cause infection. Steaming the skin can help open pores and loosen plugs of sebum (see **facials** and **steam treatments**) and exfoliation or cleansing will then remove them.

## WEIGHT TRAINING

*See also: aerobics; body image; exercise; exercises; fitness; muscles*

The recent increase in the popularity of weight training is doubtless a reflection of the many benefits to be gained from a well-constructed weight training programme. It provides all the essential fitness elements: increased strength, stamina, endurance, flexibility and mobility. And weight training can improve your overall silhouette, reduce fat and decrease stress. It is non-competitive and quite distinct from weight lifting or body building.

## WIGS AND HAIRPIECES

*See also: alopecia; hair; hairstyles; hair transplants and weaving*

Wigs and hairpieces can be worn to disguise full or partial baldness (alopecia), or as fashion accessories. Those to disguise baldness are usually made of human hair and made to measure – a trichologist or hairdresser will recommend a wigmaker From a plastic template of your head a net or plastic base is made. Fine silk, which lets the scalp show through, gives the most natural-looking parting and hairline. Up to 150,000 hairs in 2 or 3 shades and varying thicknesses are knotted into it, designed to copy your natural hair colour and direction of growth. Choose hairpieces with lightweight bases to avoid scalp over-heating or itchiness. They can be attached to the scalp with double-sided tape or to surrounding hair with clips. Natural hair wigs and hairpieces will need styling by your hairdresser. In the UK if your doctor considers that a wig is essential to you for psychological reasons, it can be obtained on the National Health Service. Fashion wigs and hairpieces are machine-made, usually in acrylic fibres. When trying on wigs and hairpieces, do not set too far forward, and incorporate part of your own hairline into the new 'hairline' if you can.

All wigs and hairpieces should be cleaned regularly. Follow instructions supplied with off-the-peg wigs, for others, your wigmaker will give advice. Hand-knotted wigs or hairpieces, unlike others, should not be washed as this may rot the base or dislodge hairs: swab with dry cleaning fluid on cotton wool. Real hair items can be styled and set as normal. Only use blow-driers, tongs or heated rollers on synthetic hair if instructions permit it.

# WITCH HAZEL

*See also: acne; bruising; eyes; hair; herbs; skin; toning*

Witch hazel is an extract of leaves and bark of the tree *Hammamelis virginiana*. A soothing liquid, it is astringent and can be used alone to dry out spots and reduce surface sebum on all skin, including the scalp. Witch hazel combined with rosewater makes a good toner: for normal skin use 1 part witch hazel: 2 parts rosewater; for oily skin use equal amounts of each. It can also be used to sooth bruises and sprains. Herbalists recommend it as an infusion to ease diarrhoea and haemorrhoids. Refresh puffy eyes with refrigerated, witch hazel-soaked pads.

# WRINKLES

*See also: ageing; chemical peeling; collagen; cosmetic surgery; dermabrasion; elastin and elastone; facials; lines; moisturizing; sebum; skin; tanning*

Wrinkles occur as the skin becomes less flexible: collagen and elastin fibres develop a web of elastone (see separate entries). With age, the production of natural oil from the sebaceous glands decreases. Both the skin and the subcutaneous fat layer beneath it get thinner: these conspire to make the skin drier, more delicate and less taut. This wrinkling process is genetically determined: its speed and extent vary from person to person.

There are a number of factors which increase susceptibility to wrinkles. Chief among them are: exposure to UVA and UVB rays (see **tanning**) which damage skin; extremes of climate and heat, especially wind; dramatic weight changes; smoking (see separate entry) and excessive alcohol consumption (see separate entry). Wear sunscreen-containing moisturizers or cosmetics in sunlight, all year-round if necessary. Keep water in the skin by moisturizing regularly (see **moisturizing, body lotions**), using richer products as you grow older. Use humectants for extra help unless you live in a very dry climate. Moisturizing facials (see separate entry) are beneficial. Treat your skin very gently when cleansing and using make-up especially around the eyes and the throat: in both areas skin has fewer sebaceous glands to keep it moist. Take plenty of exercise, which stimulates the circulation so that nutrients can reach skin cells, and eat well.

There is no medically accepted evidence that vitamins in skin creams can penetrate into the deep, live layers of skin and those containing oestrogen are potentially dangerous: this can be absorbed and very temporarily plumps out wrinkles, but also gets into the bloodstream and can upset delicate body hormone balances. Laser treatments (see **facials**) for wrinkles have not been found effective. Dermabrasion, chemical peeling (see separate entries) and face lifting (see **cosmetic surgery**) can all diminish or remove existing wrinkles, but do nothing to prevent others forming.

Although it is not possible to banish wrinkles completely, it is possible to hold them at bay with a sensible attitude to the sun and a good beauty routine.

**Worry**
See Anxiety

Y
Z

# YIN AND YANG

*See also: macrobiotic foods*

According to ancient Chinese traditions, yin and yang are the two complementary extremes and opposing forces in life: movement between them and their interaction produces life energy. Yin corresponds to elements that are positive, male, hot, light, acid and active; yang to negative, female, cool, dark, alkaline, passive characteristics. Yang foods tend to grow in winter, yin in summer. Because it is considered important to produce an overall balance of yin and yang in life, *cool* yin personalities avoid yang foods, and yang personalities yin foods. Most foods are predominantly of one type, but some, like pork and rice, are balanced, which explains their great popularity in Chinese cooking. Typical yang foods are turkey, chicken, hot spices, salt, carrots and cereal grains; yin foods include cucumber, water melon, sugar and citrus fruits.

# YOGA

*See also: breathing; exercise; exercises; insomnia; posture; pregnancy; relaxation; stress*

Yoga is both a technique and a philosophy, an ancient system which was first formalized in the 2nd century BC by Patanjali, the yogi and teacher. The teachings of yoga lay stress on the inseparable link between body, mind and spirit, and the importance to health of maintaining a balance between them and the various levels of mental activity. Its aim is to allow the yogi's natural health and personal attributes to come to the fore, untrammelled by obstructions to the energy of mind or body, in order to improve the individual's all-round well-being.

Although there are many finely tuned facets to yoga, the three most commonly emphasized in the West are the asanas, pranayama and relaxation.

**Asanas** are the many possible postures adopted during yoga practice. They are taught gradually, each one perfected before the next is learnt. Every asana has specific physical, spiritual and emotional benefits. The positions are adopted slowly, with control, accompanied by an in-breath. They should be comfortable as well as firm, and are held for up to several minutes, while breathing deeply and slowly, and released on an out-breath. Where they are uncomfortable at first, breathing through the discomfort while concentrating on the aspect of the asana at which you are aiming helps produce self-improvement.

**Pranayama** is yogic deep breathing which can be of several types, ujjayi, viloma and nadi sodhana being the three main ones. It is important to remember that the only one which you should practice is the quiet, slow, deep breathing ujjayi, and that you should not feel any strain. Pranayama should be practised in a comfortable sitting position. Padmasana, lotus position, is ideal because the spine can stay extended and the body relaxed for long periods. However, for Westerners, this classic seated position is difficult to do and it is better to choose a simple one. Even sitting on a chair will do, as long as the spine stays straight and the body relaxed.

**Relaxation** is an intrinsic part of yoga. 10-15 minutes rest and stillness at the end of your yoga practice refreshes you physically and mentally as you learn to release accumulated tensions. It is not always easy to lie comfortably flat on your back if you have a specific spinal problem. Sometimes it is better to keep the knees bent up so that the back of your waist flattens, even resting your lower legs on a sofa or other suitable soft surface. Try supporting the upper spine, neck and head with a cushion if your chest is a 'caved-in' shape.

Many benefits have been credited to yoga. It improves the body's flexibility enormously and safely: some physiotherapists recommend it as the safest way of achieving versatile joint movement, even where joints have been damaged, if carried out under trained supervision. It promotes relaxation, alleviating stress, tension, migraine, headaches, fatigue and nervousness, and some premenstrual symptoms, can help reduce blood pressure, some cases of asthma, and helps improve body image, self-confidence and self-knowledge. If you have any physical problems, consult your doctor or physiotherapist before starting yoga, and learn yoga with a teacher, rather than a book. Pregnant women can continue with some yoga postures, but it is not advisable to start at this time.

**Zinc**
See Minerals

# ACKNOWLEDGEMENTS

TEXT
**Contributors:** Caroline Bradbeer; Georgina Butter; Bridget Cumming-Bruce; Lucy Dickens; Annie Mercer; Susannah Moss; Julia Sherbrooke; Madeleine Youlten.

**Consultants:** John Atkins, Member of the Institute of Trichologists; Mr D Basra FRCS; Toni Belfield, Family Planning Association; Dr Caroline Bradbeer MB BS MRCP (UK); British Holistic Medicine Association; British Homoeopathic Association; British Laser Association; Dr Ac Cecil Chen FBAcA; Mr M Clarke FBDO, First Sight; Complections London School of Make-up; Dr Charles Darley; Dr P Dally FRCP FRCPsych DPM; Brian Davidson; Anne Gillanders, International Institute of Reflexology; Dr Michael Gossop PhD; Sister Belinda Harper SRN; David Hoffman BSc (Hons) MNIMH; Institute of Herbalism; Institute of Iridology; Dr Martha Jacob MB BS; Michael Joseph, London Institute for Clinical Hypnotherapy; Nigel Karne; Arlene Kelman AA CCDP; Sarah Key; Dr Pat Last, Director of Womens Screening, BUPA; Professor Barry Lewis, MD PhD FRCPath FRCP; Dr Keith Lupprian; Tony Lycholat; Martial Arts Commission; Graham Mason; Mary McKeown of Romans, Dawes Road; Migraine Trust; National Childbirth Trust; Noise Abatement Society; John D Pullen MChS SRCh; Hugh Rushton BA (Bio Chemist), Director Clinical Research, Philip Kingsley Trichological Clinic; Danièle Ryman; Mr W G Selley FDS; Stress Foundation; Maxine Tobias; Dr P J Tyrer MD MRCP FRCPsych; Mr Mike Wilkinson, Royal Commission on Environmental Pollution; Winston at Splinters.

**Background information:** Lindsay Nicholson, also British Medical Association; British Red Cross; Champneys; Dave Clubley, Boots the Chemist, Consumer Product Development; Sally Coker; Common Cold Research Centre, Salisbury; Katherine Corbett; Essannelle; Fliff, make-up artist; The Fragrance Studio; Nancy McConkey; Rene Guinot; Helena Harnick Clinic; Harrods Perfumery; London Institute of Beauty Culture; Payot Salon; Piz Buin; Joan Price's Face Place; The Sanctuary; Selfridges Perfumery; Slendertone; Sothys Paris; Sports Advisory Council; Super Nail.

PHOTOGRAPHY
**Special photography** (Octopus): Carrie Branovan 1, 2, 3, 4, 5; Simon de Courcy-Wheeler 25, 56, 74, 88; Sandra Lousada 14-15, 40-45, 54-55, 131, 148-149, 174, 175, 181, 182, 193, 198-199, 208, 214-215, 254.

**Other photography** (Condé-Nast): David Bailey 35, 49, 76, 137, 157, 166, 245; Eric Boman 32; Alex Chatelain 37, 47, 91, 203; Patrick Demarchelier 98-99, 145; Robert Erdmann 6-7; German VOGUE/John Stember 231; Marc Hispard 22; Kim Knott 155; Brigitte Lacombe 221; Paul Lange 16, 21, 59, 73, 96, 103, 121, 125, 132, 143, 168, 183-186, 195, 213, 220, 234-243, 248, 253; Sandra Lousada 61, 153, 164, 194, 202, 204, 205, 216, 219, 222; Butch Martin 66; Michel Momy 27; Malcolm Pasley 70; Denis Piel 226; Sudhir Pithwa 233; Rico Puhlmann 29, 146, 196; Tessa Traeger 111, 161; Albert Watson 63, 67, 68, 119, 127, 133, 178, 201, 229; Bruce Weber 141.

**Co-ordination of VOGUE photographic material:** Elaine Shaw.

**Make-up for special photography:** Ariane; William Falkner; Frances Hathaway; Ruth Sheldon.
**Make-up for photography page 70:** Mark Easton at Michaeljohn.

**Hair for special photography:** Denise; Stephen; Carol Hemmings; Gianni Lonnro at Vincent Lonnro Perming Salon; Perrine.

**Hair for photography page 70:** Hair colour – Richard Burns. Hair – Steven Carey at Michaeljohn.
**Photographic styling for page 25, 56, 74, 78:** Liz Bauwens.

The publishers would like to thank the following companies for lending merchandise for photography: Stephen Glass Face Facts; Complections; Maitlands Chemists; Boots the Chemist; Floris; Molton Brown; Conran; Bourjois; Prescriptives.

Special thanks to the following for allowing themselves to be photographed: Maxine Tobias, Kim Ashfield, Christine Elliot (Knox), Brigette Buchanan (Danby), Jennifer Hocking, Carol Higgs, Wendy Charles, Mia Babalio.

ILLUSTRATIONS
**Exercise illustrations:** Rosalyn Kennedy 6, 8, 10, 12-13, 19, 22-23, 26, 33, 34-35, 50-51, 52, 58, 117, 123, 124, 176, 197, 207, 209, 218, 245. Some of the exercise drawings and their captions are based on the *Vogue Exercise Book* by Deborah Hutton.

**Beauty illustrations:** Lynne Riding 93, 130, 142, 144, 178.

**Medical illustrations:** Russell Barnett 30, 118, 128, 160, 216-217, 230, 244.

**Chart illustrations:** Cooper West 39, 81, 112, 113, 189, 252.

**Line artwork:** Technical Art Services.

**Page 81:** Contraception chart courtesy of Family Planning Association.
**Page 112:** Energy and protein chart based on World Health Organization Report, 1985.
**Page 113:** Vitamin and mineral chart based on UK Health and Social Security Report 15.
**Page 116:** Food components chart based on McCanne and Widdowson's *The Composition of Foods* published by HMSO.
**Page 216:** Illustration copyright of the International Institute of Reflexology reproduced with permission.
**Page 252:** Weight graph based on BUPA statistics with their permission.

**Editor:** Marilyn Inglis
**Art Editor/Design:** Lisa Tai
**Designer:** Clare Clements
**Production Controller:** Maryann Rogers